A New Philosophy of Discourse

A New Philosophy of Discourse

Language Unbound

Joshua Kates

BLOOMSBURY ACADEMIC
LONDON • NEW YORK • OXFORD • NEW DELHI • SYDNEY

BLOOMSBURY ACADEMIC
Bloomsbury Publishing Plc
50 Bedford Square, London, WC1B 3DP, UK
1385 Broadway, New York, NY 10018, USA
29 Earlsfort Terrace, Dublin 2, Ireland

BLOOMSBURY, BLOOMSBURY ACADEMIC and the Diana logo are trademarks of
Bloomsbury Publishing Plc

First published in Great Britain 2021
This paperback edition published in 2022

Copyright © Joshua Kates, 2021

Joshua Kates has asserted his right under the Copyright, Designs and
Patents Act, 1988, to be identified as Author of this work.

For legal purposes the Acknowledgments on p. viii constitute an extension
of this copyright page.

Cover design by Charlotte Daniels
Cover image © CurvaBezier / Getty Images

All rights reserved. No part of this publication may be reproduced or transmitted
in any form or by any means, electronic or mechanical, including photocopying,
recording, or any information storage or retrieval system, without prior
permission in writing from the publishers.

Bloomsbury Publishing Plc does not have any control over, or responsibility for, any third-
party websites referred to or in this book. All internet addresses given in this book were
correct at the time of going to press. The author and publisher regret any inconvenience
caused if addresses have changed or sites have ceased to exist, but can accept no
responsibility for any such changes.

A catalogue record for this book is available from the British Library.

Library of Congress Cataloging-in-Publication Data
Names: Kates, Joshua, author.
Title: A new philosophy of discourse: language unbound / Joshua Kates.
Description: London; New York: Bloomsbury Academic, 2020. |
Includes bibliographical references and index.
Identifiers: LCCN 2020029941 | ISBN 9781350163621 (hb) | ISBN 9781350186958
(paperback) | ISBN 9781350163638 (epdf) | ISBN 9781350163645 (ebook)
Subjects: LCSH: Discourse analysis–Philosophy.
Classification: LCC P302 .K385 2020 | DDC 401/.41–dc23
LC record available at https://lccn.loc.gov/2020029941

ISBN: HB: 978-1-3501-6362-1
PB: 978-1-3501-8695-8
ePDF: 9781-3501-6363-8
eBook: 9781-3501-6364-5

Typeset by Deanta Global Publishing Services, Chennai, India

To find out more about our authors and books visit www.bloomsbury.com and
sign up for our newsletters.

Contents

Acknowledgments	viii
Abbreviations	ix
Preface	x

Part One Discourse and Literary Studies

1	Discourse in Contemporary Literary Studies (Limit Cases and Spectra)	3
	1.1 Discourse and Literary Form	7
	1.2 The Textual and the Imaginary (Derek Attridge, Mary Poovey, and Charles Altieri)	10
2	Discourse as Literary Innovation (Charles Bernstein)	27
3	From Persons to Words: "I am Stanley Cavell"	38
	3.1 Persons	43
	3.2 Words	53
	3.3 UnBecoming	64
4	Nothing Is Metaphor	73
	4.1 Metaphor and Time	73
	4.2 Interlude on Words	81
	4.3 Discourse and Time: "Free Balloons"	86
	4.4 Traditionality	94
5	Yet It's Personal: The Politics of Personhood (Martha Nussbaum, Cora Diamond, and Stanley Elkin)	103
	5.1 The Spirit of Realism	105
	5.2 Collectivity in Elkin	113
	5.3 From Collectivity to Politics	115
	5.4 Discourse and the Political	119

Part Two Discourse and Text

6	Can the Text Be "Saved" in Discourse? (The Early Walter Michaels)	
	Introduction: Questions?	133
	6.1 Discourse and Representation	135

		6.2 Losing Belief and Saving the Text	140
		6.3 Text and Time	146
7	Why Language Can't Help (Discourse in *Truth and Method*)		152
		7.1 Language as Discourse and Tradition	154
		7.2 "Word/World" and "Word/Word" Holism	159
		7.3 Discourse Alone: World versus Worldview (*Weltansicht*)	163
8	Discourse (The Early Martin Heidegger)		170
		8.1 Interpreting Discourse (*Rede*) in BT	172
		8.2 *Sinn* and *Bedeutung* in BT	180
		8.3 Assertions, Presence-at-hand, and Truth: Heidegger's Neither/Nor	196
9	Discourse and Text (Davidson and Heidegger)		208
		9.1 Perceptions and Statements in Husserl, McDowell, Gadamer, Davidson, and Heidegger	208
		9.2 Truth Semantics in Davidson	214
		9.3 Externalist Texts	220

Selected Bibliography   227

Index   233

μὴ εἰκῇ περὶ τῶν μεγίστων συμβαλλώμεθα

Let us not at random (by way of likelihoods or likenesses) make contributions concerning the greatest subject matters.

Heraclitus

Acknowledgments

Thanks to the members of my session "Words, Words, Words," at the 2016 meeting of the ACLA for the feedback on my discussion of metaphor, a version of which can now be found in Chapter 4; to Walter Sterling and Michael Grenke for inviting me to deliver a draft of some of the material of Chapter 5 at a St. John's College Friday night lecture in 2017; and to Laura Stark for inviting me to participate in Writing as Historical Practice: A History & Theory Workshop at Vanderbilt in 2017, where I presented a version of my discussion of Gadamer now found in Chapter 7. I also owe debts of gratitude to Henry Staten, for years of provocative correspondence, as well as for recommending Bloomsbury Academic to me; to Burt Hopkins for much good talk and friendship, and, especially, for his reading of Chapter 8 and the encouragement his response provided when it was needed; to Johannes Türk, a dear colleague, for his reading and response to a version of Chapter 5; to Stephen Mulhall for so generously reading and commenting on a version of Chapter 3, when I reached out to him by email; to Bernie Rhie for his many readings of the ever evolving Part One of the present work, and much other intellectual provocation. And, finally, the greatest gratitude for, and to, the alpha and omega: Jen Fleissner and Zeke Fleissner-Kates.

Abbreviations

AP Stanley Cavell, "The Aesthetic Problems of Modern Philosophy," in *Must We Mean What We Say?: A Book of Essays* (Cambridge: Cambridge University Press, 2002; orig. 1969), 44–96.

AT 1 Steven Knapp and Walter Benn Michaels, "Against Theory," in *Against Theory: Literary Studies and the New Pragmatism*, ed. W. J. T. Mitchell (Chicago: University of Chicago Press, 1985), 11–30.

AT 2 Steven Knapp and Walter Benn Michaels, "Against Theory 2: Hermeneutics and Deconstruction," *Critical Inquiry* 14, no. 1 (Autumn 1987): 49–68.

AT.2$_1$ *Against Theory 2: Sentence Meaning, Hermeneutics: Protocol of the Fifty-second Colloquy, 8 December 1985* (Berkeley, CA: Center for Hermeneutics Studies on Hellenistic and Modern Culture, 1986).

BT Martin Heidegger, *Being and Time*, trans. John Macquarrie and Edward S. Robinson (New York: Harper and Row, 1962).

CD Charles Bernstein, *Content's Dream: Essays 1975–1984* (Los Angeles: Sun and Moon Press, 1986).

CR Stanley Cavell, *The Claim of Reason* (Oxford: Oxford University Press, 1999; orig. 1979).

EAP Stanley Cavell, "Existential and Analytic Philosophy," *Daedalus* 93 (Summer 1964): 946–74.

GCE Mary Poovey, *Genres of the Credit Economy* (Chicago: Chicago UP, 2008).

IQO Stanley Cavell, *In Quest of the Ordinary: Lines of Skepticism and Romanticism* (Chicago: University of Chicago Press, 1994).

PI Ludwig Wittgenstein, *Philosophical Investigations*, trans. G. E. M. Anscombe (Oxford: Basil Blackwell, 1986).

RI Charles Altieri, *Reckoning with the Imagination: Wittgenstein and the Aesthetics of Literary Experience* (Ithaca: Cornell UP, 2015).

SL Derek Attridge, *The Singularity of Literature* (London: Routledge, 2004).

TLP Ludwig Wittgenstein, *Tractatus Logico-Philosophicus* (London: Kegan Paul, 1922).

TM Hans-Georg Gadamer, *Truth and Method*, 2nd revised ed., trans. Joel Weinsheimer and Donald G. Marshall (London: Continuum, 2004).

Preface

1. Theory's Redux?

A New Philosophy of Discourse: Language Unbound ventures beyond the traditional confines of philosophy. While undoubtedly offering a new—and old—view of discourse (the combination accords with how all understanding on the present account works), *A New Philosophy* engages not only with analytic and continental philosophy but also with literary criticism and literature. The latter two instances, while something more than occasions, offer special conditions for testing the view of discourse presented here, part of the reason I focus on them.

The current project might well, then, appear to be a version of "theory," albeit its mixing of genres is found in many of the philosophers it treats (such as Stanley Cavell, Martin Heidegger, and Hans-Georg Gadamer). This very possibility, the existence of the entire matrix known as theory, correspondingly, already arguably underscores a certain hesitation in respect to what philosophy is or could be today. Theory as a disciplinary or intellectual labor resonates with the transformation of philosophy visible in the authors just named, as well as elsewhere. These thinkers already depart from more traditional philosophy's self-understanding and locate their inquiries in an explicitly hermeneutic register; they pursue their concerns predominantly through interpretation. *A New Philosophy of Discourse* similarly proceeds; it joins with this somewhat new or alternative mode of philosophizing oriented by reading, in contrast to templates based wholly on reason and argument. *A New Philosophy*, accordingly, embraces a novel *interpretation* of philosophy, even as it also offers a new philosophical interpretation of discourse as such.

Is *A New Philosophy*, then, theory? Ultimately, both yes and no. One reason for not simply proclaiming it so is that theory's existence has itself always been tenuous. What came to be called theory, in retrospect, was but a loose confluence of at least three distinct endeavors (and probably more): (a) philosophical developments in France, largely spurred by Husserlian and Heideggerean phenomenology (in the work of Paul Ricoeur, Emmanuel Levinas, the early Jacques Derrida, the early François Lyotard, and the early Michel Foucault); (b) inquiries that situated themselves at least in part in empirical disciplines such as linguistics, anthropology, history, psychoanalysis, or social theory (in France, but also in the Soviet Union, Eastern Europe, etc.); and (c) long-standing inquiries into the methodology of literary studies, begun in Britain in the 1920s that reached ascendancy in the United States in the postwar years.[1]

---

[1] Though I am of course well aware of Critical (Social) Theory, this was largely absent from the development of what came to be called "high theory," apart from the work of a young Samuel Weber, and of course Walter Benjamin's writings.

This trefoil begat an inherently open-ended genre of writing that became branded as "theory." The latter broached theoretical, general, or "abstract" questions concerning literature's treatment, while often including readings of individual literary works. Eventually, readings of literary criticism and philosophy, as well as social, cultural, and political theory, came to be performed, sometimes in tandem with literature, sometimes not. Still later, other artifacts—notably films, but also advertisements, TV shows, popular music, and so on—entered the mix.

The present work thus mimes theory's compositional practice, and in part adopts its focus on literature and literary instances, without being wholly identifiable with theory as such. Indeed *A New Philosophy of Discourse*, in accord with its subtitle *Language Unbound*, may finally prove too profligate, too wide-ranging, even for seasoned theorists. The present work legitimates something like theory's heterogeneous style of writing, apart from theory's past, on its own terms, while pursuing it differently. *A New Philosophy* envisions all interpretation and understanding as taking place in events of *discourse*, or what I sometimes call talk! I employ the neologism "talk!" and use it in addition to "discourse," otherwise its synonym, since "discourse" commonly is associated with the project of extending the purportedly rule-bound character of language to writing and speech, as in "discourse theory" or John Searle's version of speech-acts. In the present case, however, discourse, or talk!, is intended to affirm a tendency opposed to those projects: these terms here flag the *untethering* of discourse from language's supposed regulative determinations and ultimately of language from itself. Hence my subtitle: *Language Unbound*.

Owing to language's demotion, I further maintain that discourse or talk! so understood rules out any *constituting* differences between literature, literary criticism, the sciences, philosophy, or everyday discussion, as supposedly stemming from their "discursive rules," their "logical grammar," their purported transcendental conditions, or any other fixed frameworks. To be sure, as envisioned here, any given instance of discourse or talk!, which may include a scientific treatise, a novel, or a shopping list, stands within a sequence of previous such productions, participating in what is called a historicity or traditionality bearing expectations as to how it operates and the uses to which it may be put. Shopping lists, for example, tend to have different uses, and thus to lead different lives, than, say, the periodic table. Nevertheless, since no instance of discourse on the present construal is regulated by rules or differentiated by fixed structures, nothing assures the generic operation of any single one of its occurrences. Intermediate cases can and do arise, as, for example, "shopping lists of the stars," where shopping lists, just like the periodic table, are copied and retained. *A New Philosophy*'s own presentation, then, similarly, moves among a variety of genres, recognizing their differing employments, while combining them in pursuit of its own thinking and aims—in this way miming theory's own practice, while dispensing with many of theory's most long-standing themes and suppositions.

Because of its distance from regulative rules and structures, as well as from formative, constitutive, or even normative conditions, the present approach is indeed not to be identified with what usually is known as "discourse theory": that of Foucault, Jacques Lacan, Emile Benveniste, Roman Jakobson, or even Mikhail Bakhtin. *A New Philosophy*'s subtitle, *Language Unbound*, indeed emphasizes that my notion of discourse, or talk!, excludes any role for *language* and its avatars. Signs, signifiers, words, and so on—none of these, on the present view, prescribe to talk!, including written talk!, what can be said, meant, or shown, on any occasion. Discourse here could thus be glossed simply and entirely as language in *use*, were it not that this formulation embarrassingly suggests that language stands prior to use—just the conception that discourse as here framed upends.[2]

At first glance, the embrace of discourse apart from language may well appear counterintuitive. The bulk of this volume, accordingly, strives to show that what we do when we write, speak, and think, can and should be understood in the foregoing fashion. To accomplish this goal, *A New Philosophy of Discourse* takes conventional literary instances (novels and poetry) as exemplary, as well as cases found in the other humanities, what could be called literature more broadly understood, including any sort of novel, extended linguistic performance: Tacitus' *Annals*, the Lincoln/Douglass' debates, and so on. Extended novel discourses, especially literary ones and their critical treatments, stand in the foreground, first, because, initially, the functioning of such "texts" seems impossible to understand on my terms. Without the aid of languages, codes, and so forth, how are these discourses, many of them written, legible? Second, these same literary instances are privileged, because, perhaps paradoxically, on the present account, they are where discourse's actual operation most readily *appears*. All such extended performances, including written ones, explicitly exhibit how prior acquaintance with other previous, similarly singular instances of discourse backstop any instance of communicative understanding. Literature is thus privileged here, since it reveals the essentially hermeneutic conditions under which all use operates.

Traditionally, of course, both literature's legibility and its fictitious or imaginary character have indeed been conceived as deriving from *language*, usually from language's capacity to supply meaningful signs independent of, and prior to, use. Literature, it is believed, can present fictions—imaginary persons, places, and occurrences—thanks to drawing on a storehouse of already meaningful signs, capable of standing apart from worlded contexts. Similarly, that such inscribed imaginings can be read across various ages and times is deemed possible only thanks to the contribution of a stand-alone language presumed relatively stable and common.[3]

Language-based construals of literature's imaginariness and textuality fall by the wayside in the present treatment, however. This is arguably all to the good, moreover, insofar as such accounts were never able to fully explain how literary texts manage to gear into aspects of the world and to treat joint matters of concern. Language-oriented frameworks tamp down literature's ability to describe and comment on situations, as well as mount critiques and other sorts of interventions, a capacity that extends far

---

[2] As will be further discussed, the claim is not so much that no languages exist but rather that the optics of language, words, grammar, and so on not only do not account for but also indeed obscure what happens when understanding, expression, and interpretation take place, in which, as such, they play no role.

[3] This account is of course at once commonplace and "potted." I am aware of the various exfoliations of it, such as those that appeal to possible worlds, as found in Thomas Pavel or Lubomír Doležel, or in that reader-response theory ultimately descending from Roman Ingarden, or accounts of imagining that give language at best a secondary role, as offered by Kendall Walton. Some of these will be discussed in what follows.

beyond traditional realism, as will become clear. To this degree, *A New Philosophy of Discourse* opens a path toward a somewhat more contemporary treatment of literature, as today such referential possibilities stand in the forefront of much literary criticism. By viewing all talk!, all discourse, as engaged with worldly subjects, while deeming impossible stand-alone meanings and signs, neither a text's legibility nor its imaginariness here answer to language or its presumed constituents (words, signifiers, etc.).

To arrive at discourse so understood, *A New Philosophy*, along with the thinkers named earlier, and a variety of literature and literary criticism, passes through work in analytic philosophy, where related views of discourse or talk! are found. Whatever its other limitations, since the 1980s, analytic philosophy is the sole site where fundamentally new views of language and discourse have appeared. The present work thus joins many other recent ones in working across the so-called analytic-continental divide.[4] Donald Davidson's thinking, in particular, plays a prominent role in *A New Philosophy of Discourse*'s last chapter, as he and H. P. Grice were some of the strongest proponents of discourse's autonomy. Nevertheless, the present study also takes its distance from Davidson's, and the analytic tradition's more general holding, albeit to various degrees, that third-person declarative sentences—statements, or assertions— are the main concern of any reflection on discourse. A central achievement of *A New Philosophy* in fact consists in contesting the priority that this and pretty much all philosophy gives to making claims, in a fashion that also renders questionable the privilege of the spoken often found in philosophy's examples.[5]

As noted, *A New Philosophy* aligns with some developments in contemporary criticism, insofar as it insists that all discourse is about something. Discourse's relation to current literary studies is explored at length in Chapter 1 of the present work. There it is suggested that many of these initiatives presently embrace what Tony Bennett has called a "flat ontology," by which he intends criticism's and theory's deflation or abandonment of structuring moments and frameworks.[6] At the same time, while so proceeding, much contemporary criticism, I argue, also simultaneously *recurs* to language, to literary form, and/or to a distinct realm of values (over against facts) to identify literature's specificity and its importance, in order to establish what is sometimes called literature's "literariness."[7] One key throughline of *A New Philosophy*

---

[4] Along with such preeminent thinkers as Robert Pippin, Charles Taylor, Hubert L. Dreyfus, and, of course, Richard Rorty, including many of their students, this trend is notable in many younger European scholars, such as Jocelyn Benoist and Ruth Sonderegger. In the North American context, many Heidegger scholars also work in this fashion, some of whom will be discussed later.

[5] Neither Grice, obviously, nor Davidson more subtly, wholly restricts their analyses' purview to the making of factual (or other sorts of) claims. Yet the capacity to make assertions arguably remains the touchstone for the work they do accomplish and it organizes their understanding of other sorts of speech, those involving what are sometimes called "attitudes."

[6] Tony Bennett, "Sociology, Aesthetics, Expertise," *New Literary History*, 41 no. 2 (Spring 2010): 253–76; 254.

[7] Such "retrenchment," if it may be so called, in the present instance, does not necessarily disqualify, to be clear, the actual interpretations undertaken by these practitioners and what they possibly show concerning their given texts and themes. Nor, similarly, does the contestation of earlier common reference points, such as language itself, simply cancel out the possible achievements of contemporary theory and philosophy's forebears (poststructuralists, postcolonialists, and others)

of Discourse, accordingly, shows that what transpires in much contemporary criticism on a theoretical plane ultimately cannot succeed: namely, the combining of talk! or discourse with notions still emanating from, or standing in for, language.

On this account, two thinkers serve as anchoring points of the present study. Each of them takes talk! or discourse seriously and its conception very far, while also appealing to language, in part rethinking it on discourse- or talk!-based terms. The projects of Stanley Cavell and of Hans-Georg Gadamer each in their own way forge highly original notions of discourse, while simultaneously conceiving language and words anew. The centrality of these figures in part flows from their attempt to navigate and chart both reference points, both discourse and language, or the word at once.[8]

Influenced by Wittgenstein, and reading him in a fashion at the time unprecedented, Cavell indeed stripped away much of the philosophical and linguistic apparatus that shapes our view of language. Moreover, owing to the primacy Cavell gives to discourse in all its forms, he burst through the boundaries of his own discipline (philosophy), pursuing thinking on the sites of literature, film, and *belle lettristic* essay, as well as philosophy, thus inventing a style of composition effectively emulated here.

In turn, the present work's envisioning of interpretation in part recurs to a model Gadamer supplies, which the latter deems broadly applicable within the humanities, as does *A New Philosophy*. The present study concludes that textual interpretation consists in an interplay of question and answer, quite close to that Gadamer depicts, as might be expected for a work that embraces a notion it designates "talk!"

Nevertheless, despite their insights and breakthroughs without which the present inquiry could not be, I argue that Cavell's and Gadamer's novel appeals to language, especially words, prevents discourse's conception in their work from being fully realized; their recourse to the word hampers understanding the operation of discourse's expressions, of what texts say (in Cavell), and of its relation to its subject matters (in Gadamer). Neither discourse's drawing on the world for its own articulation nor those aspects of the world that appear in it can be mapped in terms of words, the present account contends—not words' purported "mirroring power" (Gadamer) nor their "primary uses" standing over against "secondary" ones (Cavell). Language's and words' ultimately enigmatic "pre-happening," their standing in advance of discourse, as affirmed by Cavell and by Gadamer, albeit differently, finally obscures discourse's own happening and what happens with it: it makes discourse less of an event and less bound to temporality than in its modeling here.

The present account's rejection of any structuration, even that offered by the word, brings its stance closer to some of the aforementioned innovations in literary studies (post-critique and surface reading), and distances it from many of its precursors

---

who may *both* have more fully embraced *and* more explicitly contested these linguistic frameworks. From the present point of view, any single actual interpretation of a work or works ultimately must be reckoned on its own terms through a specific engagement with the texts and issues in question in it.

[8] I am aware that this way of looking at Cavell does not do justice to the scope of his thought. In the extensive discussion of his work found in Chapter 3, I attempt to partially remedy this lacuna. Similarly, to Gadamer, who, here, receives a more targeted treatment, is owed important aspects of my own account of interpretation, as is made clear throughout the present study.

in poststructuralism and related developments. At the same time, unlike the still prevalent view in literary studies, literature, and literary criticism, as conceived here, since *about something*, also aim to offer insights, questions, and thus some, perhaps unprecedented style of *truth*, in respect to their chosen subject matters. Because the present conception removes discourse from all structures and rules, its articulations and understanding require articulating, and thus referring to, something not talk![9] Accordingly, literature, too, when viewed as discourse, bandies with versions of insight and persuasion, questioning and *truth* in respect to what it is about.

Literary criticism and literature indeed achieve their own articulations (their speaking and saying) in part thanks to what is being talked about—though what such subject matters look like in the context of what are normally called fictions may deviate greatly from their presumed appearance in assertions, or for that matter reveries, legal documents, or commands. Literature, too, however, to this extent, brings issues of aptness and insight in respect to its concerns into play, albeit such matters, not themselves fixed (as is true here of all discourse), may assume unexpected forms and span a panoply of contents, from aesthetic innovation to the setting out of complex social, human, or other sorts of problems, to an exploration of avowed or disavowed feelings and what they entail, to name but these.[10]

How literary discourse in particular, along with all discourse more generally, gears into its subjects, is sketched in the second part of *A New Philosophy*, ultimately thanks to a negotiation between Davidson's work, which cuts all ties to language as usually conceived, and Heidegger's practical viewpoint, set out in the opening sections of *Being and Time*, where Heidegger himself explicitly gives priority to discourse (*Rede*) over words and language (*Sprache*). Heidegger shows how discourse and what it is about emerge through each other on any given occasion, without any mutually encompassing, preexisting substantive structures or forms; discourse and its references instead being buttressed by an intrinsic temporality or historicity.[11]

---

[9] To some ears, especially younger ones, this suggestion may sound like a version of what Quentin Meillassoux deems correlationism. Since correlationism in Meillassoux answers to two different templates, one baleful and one not, there is no simple response to this criticism. Nothing said here, for example, implies believing that dinosaurs did not really exist, though grasping that they did exist 450,000,000 years ago is something that the dinosaurs themselves could not do, and seems to require discourse or talk! This does not ultimately appear to be a claim that Meillassoux denies; he just prefers the discourse found in mathematized scientific discourses, which for some reason he associates with the nontotalizable and radically contingent real that he believes he finds in Cantor's transfinites. See my forthcoming "The Silence of the Concepts (in *After Finitude* and Gottlob Frege)" for further discussion.

[10] On feelings, see Sianne Ngai's *Ugly Feelings* (Cambridge, MA: Harvard University Press, 2005.) How Ngai herself conceives of the relation of feeling to talk! or discourse becomes apparent in her forthcoming treatment of the gimmick, *Theory of the Gimmick: Aesthetic Judgment and Capitalist Form*, at times through an appeal to Cavell's work.

[11] Heidegger, of course, brings forward matrices that set out the operation of *Dasein* and its understanding, but these are both ultimately holistic and formalized (rather than consisting of forms), as is further discussed. To the degree, mine is a treatment that focuses on this phase of Heidegger's work and cuts its ties to much else, it can be considered a sort of "left" reading of Heidegger, specifically of *Being and Time*, perhaps resonating with the one that Herbert Marcuse envisioned at the time of *Sein und Zeit*'s appearance.

Owing to this combination of Davidson and Heidegger, which ultimately accounts for the status of the text in discourse, *A New Philosophy*, finally, stands apart from perhaps the two most decisive, and decisively opposed, developments animating current philosophy and literary studies: the radical recovery of personhood, in Cavell, Ordinary Language Philosophy (OLP), and in the focus on normativity in contemporary analytic philosophy and phenomenology more broadly, on the one hand, and that surprising return to metaphysics or speculation, focused on things, networks, and other sorts of nonhuman agents, found in much current continental thinking, on the other hand.[12] *A New Philosophy of Discourse* does not, to be clear, simply subtract persons from the event of understanding, to replace them with more impersonal instances, such as a network or self-withdrawing objects. At the same time, since discourse's operation recurs to settings that persons themselves do not master, ones ultimately embedded in unknown and indeed unknowable contexts, neither does the present work differentiate persons from all other beings and credit them as final instances.[13]

Indeed, *A New Philosophy of Discourse* neither endorses confidence in our being masters of our discourse nor posits some radical excessive beyond, to which a different sort of faith is somehow to be assigned. It refrains from doing so, since both gestures, by the present lights, turn out to be irrelevant to the situations in which we actually find ourselves, and in which we talk, think, speak, act, and write. As will become clearer, things, subject matters, and their understanding are always underway together, already in the course of being negotiated, such that no purchase can or needs be gotten on any privileged instance, either to affirm persons' understandings or to deny them root and branch in the name of an unheard of future—of the Other, of the intrinsically inconceivable—one that we, like good Nietzscheans, must create. Neither philosophy's nor anti-philosophy's credences by the present lights ultimately are to the point.

Much of *literature*, of course, already works this same terrain; literature's privilege, to the extent it has one, arguably resides in its *complexity*, in its ability to articulate aspects of things, persons, and instances of discourse together, in concrete bundlings of its own invention. Literary criticism proceeds in a parallel fashion, both because its subject is literature and because its own discourse, as an explicit interpretation of another discourse, possesses this added register. The genuinely urgent problems and questions thus do not lie in ranging any of these moments against some or all of the others— embracing things, persons, talk! or what is—but instead in investigating some actual matter of concern by way of joining these various strands together in configurations

---

[12] For normativity, see among many others, of course, Christine Korsgaard and Robert Brandom. For metaphysics, Deleuze and Latour, again, among multitudes.

[13] Much of the recent ferment in continental work clearly continues poststructuralism's (Derrida's and Foucault's) rejection of anthropocentrism, a tendency shared by thing theory, Deleuzean affects and multitudes, Latourean and other networks, as well as posthumanism, media theory, and animal studies, to name just these. On the other side, OLP and some recent analytic philosophy affirms persons and thus the human without much heeding the former tendency. Chapter 5 of *A New Philosophy*, devoted to Stanley Elkin's fictions, attempts to navigate across these alternatives without coming to rest in either. (For the status of the human in Cavell and OLP and its relation to poststructuralism, see Richard Eldridge and Bernie Rhie, "Introduction," *Stanley Cavell and Literary Studies: Consequences of Skepticism* [London: Continuum, 2011], 1–13.)

each time new that also retrieve and relate to existing ones. Concrete problems and their multiple reference points may be navigated through fictions, through interpretations of texts and artworks, in order to clarify problems or questions, but also to proffer remedies and new directions for their possible resolution. Not just literature, criticism, and the other humanities do this work, but also performances—of music, dance, and theatre—investigations into the cosmos, into history, and other modes of expression, since no swath of discourse ultimately occupies an autonomous space of its own. Accordingly, on the present view, in the wake of the collapse of language and other structures, what literary studies now must do, is what in effect has always remained for it to undertake: namely, to listen and to talk!

2. *A New Philosophy of Discourse*'s Organization and Chapters

Accounts of a work's organization and the chapters it contains are by and large a convention insisted on by editors to entice potential readers, chary of the whole, to consult at least parts of the volume in hand. Though doubtless this would be a desirable outcome in the present instance, *A New Philosophy of Discourse*, perhaps more than most, requires an introductory account of its organization. The rationale for the capaciousness of its composition, and for its proceeding, as it does, largely through interpretations (of existing texts, corpuses, and traditions), is ventured in the body of my text; nevertheless, the contours of that account should be indicated.

Interpretation, when understood as discourse, along with unfolding its text or speech-act, always simultaneously entails an inquiry into what is being talked about— the issue at hand, the problem in question, the corner of the world dug up. Accordingly, interpretation, of texts such as Cavell's writings or those of the late twentieth-century novelist, Stanley Elkin's, *do not here replace* a concern for the subject matters treated: namely, the status of discourse, of literature, of persons, of collectivity, of texts, of metaphor, as well as the semantics of language, the referential character of all discourse, and so on. Interpretation of another's text and first-hand investigation of these topics in all these instances prove coequal and equiprimordial.

On this account, however, what follows may appear to, and to some extent genuinely does, trace an idiosyncratic path, since the sequence of texts treated answers to the problems whose illumination is being sought, and the actual series of such discussions is largely guided by the insights afforded by the writings in questions. More simply put, *A New Philosophy of Discourse* is formatted according to the thinking done in it. Nevertheless, the historicity of the texts it treats is not ignored, in fact the opposite. Since, as set out further later, traditional*ity* or historic*ity* differ from a constituted tradition or history (a canon), multiple sequences of texts can be assembled with an eye to a given problem, and those texts discussed here thus have connections to one another as well as a relation to my own problems. One-time traditions here are convened with an eye to problems (concerning discourse, literature, and texts) of current and possibly future concern.

A New Philosophy divides into two parts. Part One, "Discourse and Literary Studies," is geared to a literary audience as well as a philosophical one. In it, I situate discourse within a variety of ongoing literary critical initiatives and I introduce what discourse or talk! *is* and show how it operates by examining its relation to such well-known reference points as figural language and the realist novel. Part Two, "Discourse and Text," details how discourse accounts for the textual (or literary in a broad sense), for contact with the real (reference in a broad, nonstandard sense), and unpacks the status of that showing or insight or truth (again, in a nonstandard and broad sense) that is inseparable from all discourses' operation, including literature's.

Part One: Discourse and Literary Studies

Chapter 1: *Discourse in Contemporary Literary Studies* (Limit Cases and Spectra)

Chapter 1 engages with a set of bellwether literary critics in order to measure the inroads already made by discourse as here conceived into recent literary studies. A spectrum or range of positions is set out, a practice that *A New Philosophy of Discourse* often employs. The relation of these initiatives to some of the most prominent movements on today's literary scene—surface reading, the new sociology of literature, the new materialism, and the postcritical turn—is canvassed with respect to the status of both language and history in them, all the approaches in question showing some signs, I suggest, of a turn to discourse or talk! Three recent critical undertakings are then reviewed—those of Derek Attridge, Mary Poovey, and Charles Altieri. (Discussion of a fourth, embodied by Cavell, is postponed until Chapter 3.) These authors, I argue, display an increasing reliance on discourse: Attridge foregrounds the event; Poovey favors historically inflected notions of use; and Altieri draws on Wittgenstein's later writings for parsing the critic's task. Each author, however, simultaneously limits talk!'s operation—in practice, and when reflecting on literary studies' purpose. Attridge falls back on words and their arrangements to explain his singular events of literature; Poovey on self-reflexive, albeit historicized, literary forms; and Altieri on a transcendentally inflected notion of value. After displaying how each conception draws back from a full embrace of discourse, the present work concludes that the conception of literature as discourse that these initiatives intimate must be pursued to the end. To do so, *A New Philosophy of Discourse* sketches its distance from every structural identification of literature and from all "literariness." So proceeding, the question arises, however, of how, under the present project's aegis, literature and literary interpretation are possible, assuming that they are so at all.

Chapter 2: *Discourse as Literary Innovation* (Charles Bernstein)

Whether discourse or talk! is even compatible with literature's writing and study thus must be provisionally addressed. To do so, Chapter 2, "Discourse as Literary Innovation," takes as a test case the so-called L=A=N=G=U=A=G=E poetry of Charles Bernstein. If *language* cannot be found even in L=A=N=G=U=A=G=E poetry, if Bernstein's own poems are best understood as talk!, literature's compatibility with discourse must be granted, given Bernstein's work's self-declared experiments with its own *medium*. To be clear, Bernstein himself already possesses a nuanced and rich take on these issues, doubtless in part owing to his once having been a student of Cavell's. Chapter 2, nevertheless, shows how his own writings, and those of other self-declared experimentalists, such as Gertrude Stein or Tristan Tzara, do not make use of any autonomous formal entities (such as signifiers, words, or literary forms) but innovate ways of *using* language, or talking, in the course of pursuing concrete problems and questions (such as the status of chance or the standing of poetry in contemporary society). Accordingly, although literature structurally does not fundamentally differ from any other discourses, all at bottom operating in the same fashion, what literature, even at its most experimental, actually does, and what literary critics do when reading it, may still be grasped on discourse's terms.

Chapter 3: *From Persons to Words: "I am Stanley Cavell"*

Stanley Cavell's body of work today, often under the rubric of OLP, rightfully provides a source of inspiration for a wide range of endeavors in literary studies and the humanities. Cavellean OLP combines a distancing from all fixed structures and forms (thus incorporating discourse) with a renewed engagement with what in texts matters to human beings. Chapter 3 begins by registering the seeds of these breakthroughs in Cavell's early writings on aesthetics and aesthetic judgment, and in his confrontation with some New Critics, including Cleanth Brooks. At the same time, *A New Philosophy* shows that Cavell accompanies his breakthrough with a reworking of the word, evident in his early essays, but promulgated especially in his *The Claim of Reason*. Cavell's re-envisioning of words in terms of their "projections" undergirds his thematization and practice of interpretation, it is next argued here. From Cavell's framing of words, more specifically, a distinction falls out between a word's primary uses (to which such projection pertains, able to be anticipated in appropriate contexts by a "master of the language"), and "secondary," inherently unchartable senses and uses. This distinction, however, almost by definition, leaves no room for grasping what a genuinely *novel* stretch of writing or discourse *says* on its own terms. Literary instances (as well as other extended discourses, such as essays or philosophical treatises) are all inherently secondary uses. Interpretation thus for Cavell treats and pretty much only can treat what he calls a text's "genius": understood as the organizations of its *words*—an organization deemed broadly "purposive," yet eluding any concrete purposes—as opposed to larger units of discourse. Though in practice not all of Cavell's commentaries operate in this way, and though doubtless his interpretations have inspired others that do not so function, his novel perspective on words is nevertheless central to his early reflections on interpretation, and often orient his own readings.

Chapter 4: *Nothing Is Metaphor*

Word's and meaning's status, for Cavell and other thinkers, is intimately bound up with metaphor's construal; for Cavell himself metaphors furnish the sole instance in which words possess neither a primary nor a secondary sense. "Nothing Is Metaphor" initially situates Cavell's treatment of metaphor within a wider range of glosses on this figure—the New Critical one as presented by the philosopher Max Black, and Davidson's—ultimately in order to identify what Cavell's characterization of metaphor omits: temporality and the role it plays in construing not only metaphors and other figures but also all discourse or talk! Though for Cavell no understanding is ever complete, a given expression's actual being in time effectively makes no contribution to its expression and comprehension in primary instances of talk! Similarly, for Cavell, metaphors can be recognized wholly on the basis of their words—their words in these cases issuing not in false, but in "wildly false" (or "wildly true") statements. On the present account, however, metaphor's operation is never *qualitatively* different from any other instance of discourse. Every expression, when it appears, must each time be reckoned anew with respect to the tacit sequence of past uses in which it arises and the subject matter it articulates. The frequency of the appearance of individual words found in an expression, their likelihood or unlikelihood, accordingly, has no bearing on what that expression says, its ability to speak and to operate as talk! After explaining why words' putatively independent workings also make no contribution to synonymy or catachresis, I turn to the erstwhile New Critic, Brooks, to further unpack talk!'s temporality. Brooks' view of literary interpretation makes time fundamental; all literature's speaking, for him, is inherently metaphoric or ironic, by which he means that any stretch of literature's saying is necessarily inflected, or "warped," by a context provided by other instances of discourse. Brooks' approach, once his view of nonliterary statements has been set aside, thus can begin to display how any stretch of discourse arrives at what it expresses owing to its appearing within a tacit sequence of related uses, thanks to participating in an implicit traditionality or historicity. Finally, I provisionally explicate these last notions, traditionality and historicity, by turning to an interlocutor and predecessor of Brooks himself, the early T. S. Eliot. I exemplify my work's immersion in traditionality at this moment, by at once extending and contesting Eliot's own earlier treatment of tradition.

Chapter 5: *Yet It's Personal: The Politics of Personhood* (Martha Nussbaum, Cora Diamond, and Stanley Elkin)

Having arrived at a template of discourse's operation, Chapter 5 returns to literary ground to explore the question of the status of *collectivity* in discourse. The collective is key to any conception of the political, yet it poses a problem for all radically discourse-based approaches, since *individuals* in discourse play decisive roles. This is perhaps especially true of OLP; hence, before turning to the stories of Stanley Elkin, a still under-appreciated late-twentieth-century American fiction writer, I begin by examining an early interchange between the philosophers Martha Nussbaum and Cora Diamond (one of OLP's preeminent voices). Of considerable power within a philosophical context, their realist treatments of Henry James' novels, within the horizons of contemporary literary studies, raise questions, however, precisely when it comes to the status of the collective. James shares with many of his characters, as well as his readers, such inherently collective determinations as social class or race, while Diamond's and Nussbaum's treatment of literature as a replacement for philosophical ethics, in turn, implies that James' characters also answer to the collective notion of the human or humanity. None of the aforementioned predeterminations, however, are fully reflected on as such by Nussbaum or Diamond, arguably. Elkin's stories' plots, however, consciously foreground, even as they confuse such collective identifications, specifically those of the human, the social, the racial (in one instance), and the natural (one story has its well-born protagonist consummate his forestalled marriage with a young ovulating bear). Each determination is both confused with, and distinguished from, the others, such that the identity of any one of them on its own terms cannot be maintained. By putting such identities into motion, Elkin's stories, I suggest, gesture toward a radically conceived collective instance that at once informs, yet has already escaped from, all discourse. An otherwise unidentified collectivity implicit in discourse's backgrounding makes its force felt in these tales, the ongoing conflict around which ultimately proves to be neither natural nor social nor human but political. An always, already withdrawn collectivity informs all discourse, Elkin indicates, the intrinsic nonphenomenality of which results in a clash among its various avatars, thereby establishing the political in its specificity.

Part Two: Discourse and Text

Chapter 6: *Can the Text Be "Saved" in Discourse?* (The Early Walter Michaels)

Part One has outlined the basic parameters of discourse, foregrounded its consequences for interpretation in literary studies, and has offered instances of it at work in literature and literary interpretation. Nevertheless, some of discourse's or talk!'s major theoretical and philosophical ripple effects have not yet been worked through. *A New Philosophy of Discourse* substitutes for all verbal and linguistic scaffolding a being-in-time and traditionality of concrete expressions, themselves understood as events. The intelligibility of any stretch of talk!, in addition, however, is owed to what is being talked *about*, discourse's expressive capacity here keyed to reference rather than to sense. How, then, do talk!'s subject matters enter talk!, and how can what a discourse says be retrieved over time, especially in those literary instances presently of primary concern? To flesh out these questions, *A New Philosophy of Discourse* turns to what is arguably the first appearance of a discourse conceived as wholly stand-alone in literary studies: Walter Michaels' and Steven Knapp's *Against Theory*.[14] Knapp and Michaels, in their essays and responses, depart from all formalism and every dependence on

---

[14] Prior to Knapp and Michaels, Richard Ohmann and perhaps especially Mary Louise Pratt had already taken the conception of discourse in literary studies quite far. Though approaching these questions in a rather different fashion—Pratt mainly contests Russian formalism—the present study has been inspired by her findings, which also break down barriers between literary discourse and other types of expression (See Pratt, *Toward a Speech Act Theory of Literary Discourse* [Bloomington: Indiana University Press. 1977].)

pre-constituted language, famously suggesting that if something isn't discourse (in the present sense), "it isn't language either." Once arriving at discourse, Michaels and Knapp, however, immediately retreat from it, I contend; they tether discourse to an otherwise empty notion of authorial intentionality and view literary signs, mysteriously laden with such intentions, as engaged in a labor of "representation." On the present account, however, literature's expressions are directly related to their worlded subject matters, never mere representations. Similarly, their immediate legibility, like that of all discourse, recurs not to an indwelling intentionality, but to prior encounters with other stretches of talk! The obstacle that Michaels and Knapp seek to avoid, however, by invoking intention and representation remains a genuine one for the present perspective. Since interpretation depends on what is other than discourse, yet in literary instances a shared world is by no means self-evidently at hand, how literature's subject matter *can* be sufficiently common to author and reader so as to yield a text for interpreters to read and study is a problem for discourse and demands investigation.

Chapter 7: *Why Language Can't Help* (Discourse in *Truth and Method*)

Chapter 7, "Why Language Can't Help (Discourse in *Truth and Method*)," turns to Hans-Georg Gadamer's masterwork to begin to explore how texts understood as discourse operate. Gadamer frames interpretation as a dialogue of question and answer, wherein a text's and its interpreter's standpoints undergo a so-called fusion of horizons. Gadamer in this way starts to clear up how literary and other subject matters may be shared; as Gadamer insists, the failure to be talking about the same thing eventually makes itself felt in such encounters. Nevertheless, though Gadamer was never the sort of conventionalist or formalist that Knapp and Michaels claim Gadamer was in *Against Theory II*, his own complex, discourse-based reworking of language, and especially his framing of its "mirroring word," ultimately impede grasping how its subjects enter into literary and other discourse, I maintain. Gadamer insists that aspects of the world may remain *unsaid*, but are never *unsayable*; for him, all languages and their mirroring words, similarly, can be known in advance to be intertranslatable. Yet no position exists in his own thought whence such guarantees may issue. Locating discourse's relation to the world at the level of language, even so originally conceived, accordingly, entails that discourses' subject matters remain a step removed from their actual givenness to understanding, despite Gadamer's own intentions. Just as Cavell's appeal to words' projections eclipses the foreignness of the other's text, so Gadamer's affirmation of language's mirroring word ultimately conceals the text's genuine engagement with what is other than text, and, with that, to discourse's own tenuous, because radically eventful, legibility.

Chapter 8: *Discourse* (The Early Heidegger)

The final chapters of *A New Philosophy of Discourse* thus investigate the capacity of discourse's subject matters to show themselves, especially in literary and other texts.

The text's ability to appear as intrinsically foreign to its recipient's perspective here is also unpacked. Accordingly, I end *A New Philosophy of Discourse* by surveying both literature's legibility, owed to its subject matter, and its inventiveness (its foreign perspective), first through an examination of some early writings by Heidegger, and then thanks to a single thread in Davidson's complex thought. In the early chapters of Heidegger's *Being and Time*, *Rede* (talk!) is said to precede *Sprache* (language); Heidegger, moreover, gives an account of how worlded subject matters appear in it, or in any instance of discourse. Worldly things' disclosure stems from a radical *practical* holism, where things and subject matters have *always already* been concretely intertwined with discourse in totalities of significance and their corresponding assignments. Thanks to these tacit wholes and to the contexts and practices that accompany them, all variety of things may disclose themselves, initially in terms of what Heidegger now famously calls the "hermeneutic as." This practically oriented interweaving of discourse and things permits variations, however, resulting in different, even seemingly mutually opposed, styles of talking, all of which still manage to talk about *something*—each accessing the world and the real in its own way. *Being and Times*' first part traces one such variation: from that discourse (*Rede*) found in the ready-at-hand to the perceptual reports expressed in statements. This trajectory is not privileged, however, as Heidegger's contemporaneous lectures on logic and truth make plain. Multiple variations of discourse, accordingly, are possible, with all discourse, including literary discourse, having the capacity to draw on the world and on subject matters that show themselves in their own right, albeit in relatively distinct fashions.

Chapter 9: *Discourse and Text* (Heidegger and Davidson)

After explaining how reference in the widest conceivable and varying fashion accrues to all discourse, *A New Philosophy of Discourse* turns to Davidson's writings to complete this account, while sketching how a text's expressions may appear as specific to that text and distinct from the interpreter's own viewpoint. Davidson's treatment of what in analytic circles is called externalism gives purchase on this question, once Davidson's narrower, theoretical holism has been modified by Heidegger's practical one. Externalism insists that the relation of a term or word to its subject matter as found in utterances in use depends on a specifically "external" factor, such as the atomic weight of an element or expert knowledge on trees, neither of which may be known to speakers themselves. In Davidson's case, the speaker or author themselves supply such an externalist instance. Their prior encounters with discourse and things, and their previous causal history with discourse and its subjects, link the speaker's or author's expressions to their references and thus make available what they say, *including in literature and in other written instances*. This last is possible, since the externalist linkage of author or speaker to their subject matter, for Davidson himself, only surfaces as an explicit issue *for their interpreters*, their readers, and their auditors. Such prior history, with its references, ineluctably appears within *a different horizon* than the speakers' own, implicitly shaped by that different history belonging to their discourse's recipients. Accordingly, Davidson's scheme preserves both the foreignness *of the interpreted* and the perspective *of the one interpreting*. Davidson's discourse-based externalism, accordingly, lets literary expressions retain their novelty and inventiveness, their difference from their readers, while emerging, along with their subject matters, within the interpreter's world, thus preserving their legibility. Texts in literary studies remain tethered to the things they and their interpreters talk about, while being capable of conveying understandings and imaginings of its own.

In literature and literary interpretation, then, *A New Philosophy of Discourse* concludes, all that can be found is discourse, while no discourse, including literary discourse, ever makes its way without something other than itself, some aspect of the world and of the real. Texts in the humanities at the same time express something different from the reader's preconceptions, while also undergoing an understanding repetition in which difference plays a role—texts, like all discourse, being events. Indeed both results follow from discourse's and text's status as events that take place apart from language, words, and all other formal, regulative, and/or constitutive frameworks, buttressed only by their own being-in-time and the worldly subject matters they concern. Thus what remains for literary studies and the humanities to do is indeed what they have always already begun to undertake: to question, to read, to understand, and to talk!

Part One

Discourse and Literary Studies

1

Discourse in Contemporary Literary Studies (Limit Cases and Spectra)

Let a few extremes be set out, positions that permit delineating a broad spectrum of stances toward language and history in contemporary literary studies. Their preliminary foregrounding is not meant to capture all projects in contemporary literary work, nor even necessarily its most prominent ones. These initial orienting standpoints have been chosen for their radicality in respect to the themes selected and for their ability to give some contours to specific corners of literary critical endeavor.

To establish this grid, I employ proper names and even snippets of authored texts, but no commentary is intended, not in this first phase. Nor is what I will eventually be offering a critique—so don't worry, Bruno Latour, Sharon Marcus, Stephen Best, Rita Felski, Heather Love, and fellow travelers.[1] Rather, I am attempting to pose and eventually follow out a question of interest to me and I hope to others, one that concerns some of the fundamentals of our discipline, but does not aim to culminate in a foundation or even a methodology. This question and its ramifications, it seems to me, can clarify many practices currently in place in literary studies, otherwise leaving them largely intact and not roiling their multiplicity. At the same time, this exercise also points to possible new variations for literary critical and humanistic work, some of which the present text instantiates. The *self-understanding* of literary studies thus here undergoes scrutiny and perhaps transformation; yet the modeling of that field exposed in such reflection is a far lighter, less immediately consequential sort of being than the many different approaches, strategies, and concerns that practitioners usually simultaneously employ and exhibit in their daily work. The primary import of the present study thus remains the working through of questions that by now have long accompanied literary critical work (and the humanities far longer) that some, including myself, find compelling on their own terms.

The positions from which I will begin are these: the "historical description" (in part descending from Ian Hunter) of Mary Poovey's recent work, which also overlaps with the work of John Guillory and thus still more broadly can stand in for what is sometimes called the new sociology of literature, including that of Mark McGurl,

---

[1] I am of course referring to what is now called "post-critique" largely in the wake of Latour's essay, "Why Has Critique Run Out of Steam?" (*Critical Inquiry* 30, no. 2 [Winter 2004]: 225–48) and that "surface reading," initiated by Stephen Best and Sharon Marcus ("Surface Reading: An Introduction," *Representations* 108, no. 1 [Fall 2009]: 1–21).

Heather Love, and others.[2] Secondly, literary work descending from, and also found in the singular writings of Stanley Cavell, which today is sometimes referred to by the acronym OLP, but which also includes such thinkers, significant in their own right, as Cora Diamond and Alice Crary, as well as some critics taking the so-called ethical turn.[3] Thirdly, work on, and a view of, literature, to some eyes residual, as it may appear to fly the banner of deconstruction, such as is found in a swath of revivals, transformations, and prolongations, in particular Derek Attridge's recent writings on what he calls the singularity of literature, as well as the latest offerings of Rei Terada, Andrzej Warminski, and the late Werner Hamacher, a movement with affiliations wide and deep, and which would also include (or at least abut) one wing of what was recently called the New Formalism (which sometimes combines this perspective on language with the social-political concerns of Karl Marx, Theodor Adorno, or Louis Althusser, as in Ellen Rooney's recent work).[4] Lastly, a different set of endeavors also adjacent to Wittgenstein, often involving modern and contemporary literary work, as found in Charles Altieri's and also of course Marjorie Perloff's extensive publications, but including what almost might be called a Berkeley school, as in the important work of Dan Blanton, Kent Puckett, and Joshua Gang, which deploy a similar canon—an approach that shades over into that of Walter Michaels and some of his students (Michael's own work with Steven Knapp being discussed extensively in Part Two), such as Oren Izenberg, as well as the ever-growing number of literary scholars independently drawing on the analytic philosophical tradition, and not necessarily exclusively Wittgenstein at all, such as Michael LeMahieu.

Arrayed thus, these choices are, I hope, striking. They are meant to identify initiatives that are at once important, living, but also in some respects, outliers, and by this means plant signposts for literary studies as a discipline pertaining to two broad topics: language and history.

After all, no positions *could* stand at a greater distance from one another, it seems to me, than those proffered by "Poovey" and those represented by "Cavell" (both taken synecdochically, hence the quotes) when it comes to history. Though both camps avow modernity as a working category, "Cavell" looks to literature, language, and philosophy to address a set of problems given weight in their own right, without further regard for their historical specification. These problems—very roughly the status of persons, of embodiment, of moral and aesthetic evaluation, of intimacy—hover between philosophy and literature (as will be further explored); they answer to history, however, only in the manner just described, namely, as an *initiating occasion*. "Poovey," in turn, approaches not only the resources "Cavell" employs (close reading and the realist novel) but also the concerns addressed therein, through a self-consciously *distancing*

---

[2] For the "new sociology of literature," see James F. English "Everywhere and Nowhere: The Sociology of Literature after 'the Sociology of Literature,'" *New Literary History* 41, no. 2 (Spring 2010): v–xxiii. Poovey, Guillory, and Hunter, with the relevant citations, are all discussed later.

[3] *Wittgenstein and the Moral Life: Essays in Honor of Cora Diamond*, ed. Alice Crary (Cambridge, MA: MIT Press, 2007) is a good place to start for an introduction to the more philosophical strains of OLP. For the literary ones, see, among others: *Stanley Cavell and Literary Studies*, edited Eldridge and Rhie.

[4] For the New Formalism, see Marjorie Levinson, "What Is New Formalism?," *PMLA* 122, no. 2 (March 2007): 558–69.

historicist lens, at once more finely grained in respect to period and more extensive in historical breadth, that finds its own focal point in a series of concrete social and economic transformations. "Diagnosing," or aiming to, the very space of inquiry occupied by "Cavell," "Poovey" gives to history the last word (or, as we shall see, almost), while for "Cavell" it offers merely the first.

The register of language, today less often spoken of in any case, nevertheless finds a similarly stark opposition when "Altieri's" and "Attridge's" approaches (including Hamacher, Warminski, Terada, and others) are juxtaposed. Altieri himself has explicitly criticized the linguistic premises and standpoints associated with the "Attridge" camp for the last twenty years, while plumping for the findings of Wittgenstein and that of analytic philosophy more broadly. The long-standing split between analytic and continental philosophy subtends, then, the difference between the two endeavors, with the result that for Altieri, as in analytic philosophy more generally, language and literature share reference points manifest in other areas of life and talk![5] For "Attridge" and his fellow travelers by contrast, literature opens uniquely on to language, insofar as both literature and language trail a singular otherness or alterity in their wake, the omission of which leads to their misprision. Literature, for these critics, hands over the being-language of language. "Attridge," accordingly, affirms that literature is the transient site of an irreducible and radical excess that criticism must work to tease out. That very possibility "Altieri" denies, while finding literature directed to concerns pertaining to everyday life.

Roughly, then, we have the following grid, giving us the corresponding reference points, otherwise still to be sketched.

Affirms	*Minimally*	*Maximally*
History:	Cavell	Poovey
Language:	Altieri	Attridge

This initial set of coordinates is loose, cobbled together for the present purposes; on other occasions I am happy to relinquish it, and even in the present context it is finally provisional. Nor, to be clear, is it in any way meant to exhaust the innovativeness, force, and contents of those positions so far noted or the ones that I am about to discuss. At the same time, the chart performs the work for which it has been crafted: it provides an overview of some of the large-scale registers operative within our discipline.

---

[5] As will become clearer, Altieri also subscribes to a certain exceptionalism when it comes to literary expression, though this does not redound to any of its formal properties. Toril Moi, in an article prior to her recent study, *Revolution of the Ordinary*, has commented on the great barrier she confronts when speaking of Wittgenstein to those educated in the poststructuralist idiom ("They Practice Their Trades in Different Worlds: Concepts in Poststructuralism and Ordinary Language Philosophy," *New Literary History* 40, no. 4 [Autumn 2009]: 801–24). I believe this is ultimately owed not to differences in outlook, but to the two very different construals of logic that underpin each tradition, a difference that arguably informs the analytic/continental divide itself. For a provisional charting of these waters, see my "Literary Theory's Language's," chapter four of my *Fielding Derrida*. As already noted, this difference is quite rapidly being overcome in many quarters on the continent. Scholars in Germany and France, Norway, and Denmark, as well as some in the United States and other English-speaking countries, while working on phenomenology and other continental endeavors, are all also often conversant with recent developments in analytic philosophy.

Thus, as to history, in the broadest possible terms, it has indeed functioned along a spectrum from evanescent occasion (even the New Critics acknowledged it to be such) to final instance, with "Poovey's" version arguably providing a relatively pure version of the latter. "Poovey" ceases to trade on all pre-given forms of social or cultural wholes, on structural totalities or logics, and of course eschews any sort of messianic vector. Hence, all versions of cultural studies, as well as endeavors that blend larger-scale structures into their historical negotiations (such as the Benjaminian quasi-Messianic) fall somewhere between "Poovey" and "Cavell." They all recognize something other than a rigorously ascetic and determinative history, Cavell giving us the maximal possible quotient of such an "other" and the minimum of history, with Poovey offering the opposite mix.

In turn, Attridge and company embody a belief, still widely held in literary studies in other guises, in what could be called the exceptionality of literature (and thus language and the text). Other accounts doubtless do not conceive of this exceptionality in the absolute terms found in "Attridge" and his peers. Still, for many, literature and its language remain a privileged site: for analyzing, comprehending, or performing ideological or cultural work; for thinking about racial, sexual, or gender identity; or for establishing and thinking hegemony or disclosing politics in some other fashion. "Altieri," in turn, rejects this sort of exceptionalism based on literature's language. Accordingly, the undertakings just identified can be situated along a line, on which he stands at one extreme and "Attridge" at the other.

A second fuller mapping thus looks like this:

History
"Cavell"		"Poovey"
Some Aesthetics	Marxian-quasi Marxian	Some Foucault
Ethics	Cultural Studies	Sociology of Lit
Neurobiology	Cultural Logics	Distance Reading
Sociobiology	New Historicism	Big Data
Some Narrative Theory	Posthumanism	
	Postcolonial	

Language
"Altieri"		"Attridge"
Wittgenstein (not Cavell)	Marxian-quasi Marxian	Deconstruction
Mimetic Approaches	Cultural Studies	Some Aesthetics
Sociology of Literature	Cultural Logics	Benjaminian and Other
Foucault (not New Historicism)	Ethnic Studies	Quasi-Messianisms
Distance Reading	New Historicism	Early Žižek/Lacan
Cavell	Posthumanism	
Neurobiology	Postcolonial	
Sociobiology		

This chart portrays perhaps only what many of us already know, conceivably in an unusually compressed or synoptic fashion. It does, however, cover a good deal of the activity of literary studies in recent years and some of its defining trends (also doubtless recognized in other quarters). Thus the growing prevalence of literature's being seen in tandem with some other topic, something other than literature, strikingly appears when the bottom staff in the second chart is read from right to left. Moreover, even as some capacity believed specific to literature continues to be retained at least in the middle ranks of both columns, literature's specificity on the first staff on the right hand extreme, as well as in the bottom left, appears to be dissolving, as is true more generally among emergent and cutting-edge approaches. Accordingly, within more recent tendencies, the very identity of literature as an object of study shimmers and threatens to disappear. Charting the contours of literary studies as a field at present, then, may exhibit, above all, a tendency on its part toward evanescence.

1.1 Discourse and Literary Form

Other reasons than their providing useful limit cases led to the choices of camps and authors currently in question ("Cavell," obviously, being an unlikely candidate for this sort of survey). Talk! or discourse is this work's major theme; it surfaces in all four of these initiatives, including those ranged against one other in the second mapping. By discourse, as noted, I intend, roughly, a view of language-related activity for which *use*, language's employment proves foremost in preference to language as such.

Discourse's paradigmatic instances are indeed sentences, and still more extended bodies of articulated expression, *as used*. Use—speech- and writing-acts, inscriptive and verbal performances—as opposed to signs, codes, signifiers, grammar, and words comprise talk! or discourse as here understood. Signification, the signifier, the sign, grammar, and also all illocutionary rules and other algorithmic conceptions, such as competency, at best remain secondary from my perspective.

Talk!, then, must indeed be distinguished from "discourse" as construed by Foucault (especially in the *Archaeology*), or in so-called discourse theory (doubtless more familiar reference points than the present one to most readers). Though such programs do share some roots with discourse as here conceived, they refer back to a structuralist linguistic context, extending, even as they transform (and at times doubtless contest) the latter's insistence on systems of signification. Discourse, in Foucault's and related senses, *looks to other rules*, such as those supposedly governing demonstratives, or ones that pertain to the *objects* of discourse, establishing regularities controlling both these and the statements about them across finite historical segments. Even such an ambiguous case as J. L. Austin, especially as interpreted by John Searle, falls short of discourse, insofar as new regulative and constitutive conditions—so-called illocutionary rules—are there believed to accompany talk! While all these perspectives attend to language's actual use, sometimes granting this moment relative independence, they ally discourse with determining principles, rules, or structures, not simply or always those of language.[6]

To be sure, within a non-structuralist, more Anglophone and analytic-oriented context, a spectrum of views on talk! still remains possible, stretching from authors that similarly harness discourse to language systematically understood (as happens in Searle's account of speech-act theory, upon which Foucault was able to draw at

---

[6] See my "'Signature Event Context'…in, well, context" for a deeper discussion of these matters, including a treatment of French discourse theory, its genealogy, and its implications.

one epoch owing to this isomorphism), to approaches that, as will be the case here, conceive discourse as standing apart from (and/or predominant over) the linguistic in any usual sense. In Donald Davidson's now famous account of malaprops, language's very *relevance to discourse* is questioned and language's function is ultimately folded into discourse, as is also the case here. Something similar, though perhaps less drastic, occurs in H. P. Grice's account of "speaker's meaning."[7]

Between these extremes (with Heidegger's account of *Rede* arguably going all of them one better, a contention that will return), one finds discourse, loosely construed, embraced to various degrees, and often mixed with a range of linguistic or structuring elements: words; intentions; propositionally formed utterances; language games conceived as actually existing socio-cultural phenomena, and so on. Thus we have the following mapping, which must remain both provisional and otherwise undiscussed.

Discourse	B	C	D	E	*Discourse/Talk!*
Foucault (of the *Archaeology*)	Bourdieu	Altieri	Cavell	Diamond	Davidson, Grice, Heidegger
Searle	Wittgenstein/ Winch			Wittgenstein/ Conant	Early Michaels and Knapp

All four of the critical camps initially mentioned, and especially their titular authors, display a tendency toward discourse or talk!, which again was one ground for their being singled out. Moreover, this impetus, I would suggest, connects with a broader emergent tendency in literary studies. Talk! represents the "flattening" of language: the denial of structure, depth, and so on, in that very area, language, where these have been claimed to operate most profoundly and continuously.[8] In the present context, discourse, then, is a wildcard. It joins all four stances together, intimating where the treatment of literature and language may be going, and thereby ripples the surface of the two prior mappings, without otherwise altering their relative orientation.

These authors—Altieri, Attridge, Cavell, and Poovey—share another trait crucial to their foregrounding here. Each explicitly discusses and, in fact, aims to model the practice of literary criticism. Each author reflects on literature's and literary studies' standing in the academy and what is involved in interpreting literature. (This is true even of Cavell, albeit in a distinctive and partially unanticipated way.) Moreover, not only do the standpoints in question provide such views, but, within their accounts, the notion of *literary form* or some identifiable substitute also proves central, albeit to a varying extent, such that a range of recourses to form or its avatars is at work. To be clear, none of these authors embrace form in its most familiar guises—as literary thing in itself, as organic unity, or as aesthetic ornament. All target and transform "form," and two camps border on its complete abandonment. Nevertheless *the place* of something

---

[7] Davidson's thinking thus plays a major role in the final chapters of *A New Philosophy*, albeit under certain major stipulations. See H. P. Grice, "Utterer's Meaning and Intentions," in *Studies in the Ways of Words* (Cambridge, MA: Harvard University Press, 1989): 86–116, and Donald Davidson, "A Nice Derangement of Epitaphs," in *Truth, Language and History* (Oxford: Oxford University Press, 2005): 89–108.

[8] On such flattening, again, see Bennet, "Sociology, Aesthetics, Expertise."

like form remains clearly discernible at least in the first three of these instances, with Cavell, who explicitly dismisses it in toto as a metaphysical lure, proving an extreme instance (though even here the matter proves less clear than it initially appears, owing to Cavell's affirmation of words and language alongside discourse).

Attridge, more specifically, explicitly embraces both the notion and the term "form," coming closest to using it in a relatively traditional fashion. Poovey, speaking of what she calls the self-referentiality of the literary text, and eventually also explicitly of "form," retains a version of it, yet only and wholly as *a disciplinary requirement*. Finally, Altieri, in line with his relinquishing of any linguistic specificity to literature, largely does without any explicit version of form. In his most recent work, Altieri instead offers something like a substitute for form from a standpoint that views literature as a belonging to a broader genre of (self-) expressions.

The four positions in question, then, may be set out thus:

Form
Closest to Tradition	Historically Specific	Reworked on Non-exceptionalist Terms	?
Attridge	Poovey	Altieri	Cavell

In what follows, attention will be paid to the intersection of the two tendencies just identified: that toward discourse and that toward form or some equivalent. Ultimately owing to the impetus of discourse in their work, these stances are compelled to question form, yet they, in part, also reconceive it. Accordingly, the accounts of literature and literary studies in question result from an interference pattern between the impetus arising from discourse and the more traditional reference points for working with literature that congregate around form.

The first problem faced by the present study, for its part, emerges from the first three author's take on the latter, on literature's supposed literariness. Is discourse as here conceived, it will be necessary to ask, compatible with literary studies in any of its traditional understandings? Can talk! be reconciled with the work usually attributed to attention to form, if not with form itself?

Of course, today form is a notion far less likely to be invoked than it once was. Its function of defining literature (as what uniquely possesses a certain sort of form) has long faltered, with the restriction of literary studies' attention to literature in its specificity largely losing whatever hold it once had (alternative approaches of course existing even in the heyday of the New Criticism). As previously registered, from surface reading to different sorts of description, numerous rejections of just this concept occupy the current scene (the New Formalism being a notable exception).

Nevertheless, not in any of its usual acceptations as found in structuralist, formalist, or New Critical poetics, but in a more generalized version, enjoining something like attention to the medium as such, thus in a wider and perhaps intrinsically undefined sense, a version of this conception, some remnant of "form" arguably remains at work in the accounts that contemporary literary studies gives of its own labors, even and perhaps especially when it insists on its brief to speak about topics other than literature. Accompanying its own skill set's migration into more distant fields, literary work seemingly cannot help but invoke some remainder or difference, some portion deferred or excessive, not recognized by the discourses found in such fields and not reducible to language's simple employment, as uniquely belonging to the literary and thus warranting literary criticism's own interventions. Literary criticism as practiced today almost continuously finds in discourses, documents, and other media, not simply or wholly what the discipline or region in question (social or natural science, economics or political theory) understands, something neither necessarily deep nor structured, but also not meant by its speakers nor discernible in its primary recipients' understanding. Thereby, implicitly or explicitly, these projects conjure new avatars of form, or of textuality, the sign, or the word to explain and justify their vantage points. Within this operation, something akin to form, accordingly, returns by its own practitioners' account—at the very least in the insistence on an *availability* of the spoken or inscribed to an analysis that travels beyond the bounds of common use.

Accordingly, the present project will eventually have to address both how the reading of literature remains conceivable, not to mention what might be its importance or urgency, when literature along with all other genres of discourse are viewed simply as talk!, without further structural or formal differentiation of any kind coming into play. Indeed, it is no accident that all of those authors here working in the literary field, while turning to discourse, also rework something like form. Yet not one of them arguably grasps how strongly the former tendency evident in their work—namely, their invocation of discourse—pushes in an opposed direction. Two different impulses on different levels simultaneously exist in their reflections, and this, no doubt, is neither the first nor the last time that explicitly articulated stances toward language, and the work done with literature and reflection upon it turn out not entirely to jibe.

Accordingly, what must be done first is to trace out the interaction of these vectors of talk! and "form" in the three authors situated entirely in literary studies. Ultimately a transformation and broadening out of the problems so far only provisionally posed will result (form, in particular, ceasing to stand in the foreground), as talk!'s conception increasingly emerges and becomes further refined. The inquiry into these authors also makes plain that Cavell's approach is at once the most aware of the possible tension at work here (in that sense, the most radical or fundamental), even as it continues to bear traces of this tension, and thus before Cavell's treatment of discourse and its relation to literary study is taken up, a first response to the question of how to approach literature and its interpretation without form will be brought forward on the ground of literature itself—namely, in an interchange with the poetry and essays of Charles Bernstein.

1.2 The Textual and the Imaginary (Derek Attridge, Mary Poovey, and Charles Altieri)

Before taking up the critics in question one by one, the most general intuitions concerning literature to which form (no matter how amorphous) continues to answer should be identified. When critics reflect on their own practices, two suppositions, in particular, still largely underlie their construal of literature, even if only implicitly. To these assumptions, a single notion of language corresponds, and this conception of language, some avatar or ghost of it, allied to literary form, is traceable in those writers about to be treated, albeit accompanied by varying degrees of effacement.

The two notions underpinning literature's broad understanding are (a) the textual and (b) the imaginary. The imaginary designates the made-up, the pretend; it differs from lies or mistakes, by being still further removed from the claim on the real that seemingly inheres in the former. Literature is believed to be a product, or exist in the space of the imaginary, thereby cutting ties to considerations of reference, to aspects of the world, or a concern with truth, falsity, or insight.

The textual informs literature in a different sense: now understood as what bears repetition, as what is able to be read multiple times, accessed and engaged on numerous occasions. Literature construed as text is not confined to the literature critics study, though the latter is often taken as its preeminent instance. Literature in this second sense is a verbal performance singled out by being lasting, in respect to its existence, its perdurance often including the singularity and importance of its expressions as well.

Mapping the various accounts of literature in terms of these two different notions—their combinations, variants, and overlaps—would require a distracting degree of detail. To glean a very rough overview, in the current context, one might provisionally place at one extreme deconstruction, for whom the textual component remains predominant. For Attridge and deconstruction, as is about to be made further clear, literature embodies an excessive (and singular) power of remaining (without cancelling the other aspect answering to the imaginary that Attridge calls "innovation"). At the other extreme, one finds those like Kendall Walton for whom the imaginary as such, the capacity for pretending, permits the production and reception of literature and the other arts, the textual assuming virtually no importance.[9] Between these fall possible world theories that see in literature the ability to trade on what is not, thanks to propositional forms capable of expressing strictly counterfactual and thus imaginary worlds.[10] Possible world approaches in their own way thus include, and to some extent, privilege, a version of the "textual," that is, the propositional, while recognizing the imagination's power. Finally, Aristotle's poetics begins from the power of imagining in the sense of *mimesis*, and isolates some mimetic performances as especially able to make a claim on our understanding and our affects; these latter stand as preeminently repeatable (in themselves and in their techniques) and only thereby become literature in the "textual" sense.

Accordingly, we find:

Textual	*Imaginary* *because Textual*	*Textual* *because Imaginary*	*Imaginary*
Attridge	Possible Worlds	Aristotle's *Poetics*	Walton

Now both features, the textual and the imaginary, are not identical, and neither in itself, it should be underscored, is specific to the literature of literary studies. I can

---

[9] Kendall L. Walton, *Mimesis as Make-Believe: On the Foundations of the Representational Arts* (Cambridge, MA: Harvard, 1993).
[10] See among others, Lubomír Doležel, Thomas Pavel, and Ruth Ronen.

imagine what I will have for dinner were I in Paris, or even a life story for the person sitting next to me on a train (as Virginia Woolf did in her essay "Mr. Bennet and Mrs. Brown"). Similarly, literature as what remains, as the permanent, is not isomorphic with any one medium (writing, audio tape, electronic switches, or html codes) nor is it restricted to products of the imagination. Oral epics and folklore, but also written histories, are all literature in this sense, while, again, the shopping list I made yesterday, even if inscribed on a pad or IPhone, is not.[11]

The divergence between the two criteria tends to escape notice, however, because literature appears to combine both, while seemingly exemplifying and perhaps extending the power of each. In addition, within both facets resides a vector toward a single readily recognizable conception of language. Language, on this understanding, is a reservoir of grammatical rules and words—of signs, signifieds, and signifiers, and of the syntax that governs their combination. Language, as so conceived, clearly a definitive counter-instance to discourse, supplies a storehouse of *meanings* (or signifieds), and rules for employing them, ones deemed wholly autonomous, independent of the rest of what is, of the existence of the world and things.[12]

Owing to the work of language so understood, the textual, then, can, be returned to again and again, since its meanings (or signs and signifieds) function in themselves apart from all possible contexts and users. The imagination's ability to trade on what is not, similarly, would flow from significations' independence from everything else, from its autonomous, linguistic existence. Saying what is not, what is merely imagined, on this account, is inherent in language's own being. Owing to language's independence, certain writings and speeches may stop short of the true or the false, of all belief or disbelief, trading only in meanings. Hence, what is not, including what might never be, can be expressed, not for the sake of deception and similar ends, but as something simply imagined. In sum, meanings (signifieds) found in language operate independently of contexts and purposes, making possible the textual and imaginary capacities often ascribed to literature. Language so understood explains the apparent ability of a story, play, or poem to trade on what is not, as well as the literary work's ability to remain legible beyond the moment of its production.

---

[11] Interesting to note is that the seemingly greater power of annotation represented by information technologies, their ability to record unprecedented amounts of data, coincides with the reforegrounding of the temporal dimension of all such recording, of all discourse, including written discourse. The problem of future generations of technology retrieving records, inscriptions, and other discourse registered by early ones captured in older formats is a relatively novel and intrinsically daunting problem.

[12] Ferdinand de Saussure's structural linguistics as set out in his *Course of General Linguistics* is often taken as offering a rigorously worked out view of such an autonomous language, though that reading sometimes has been debated (see, among others, Roy Harris, *Saussure and His Interpreters* [New York: New York University Press, 2001]). The issue of language's autonomous status as presented by Saussure, its removal at once from all diachrony, use (*parole*), and reference were, of course, central issues in its reception and debated by the structuralists themselves. Arguably, none of these problems were ever successfully resolved. For an overview of these developments, see chapter seven, "The Saussaurean Break," in Francois Dosse's *History of Structuralism* v.1 (Minneapolis: University of Minnesota Press, 1997), 43–51. I have previously treated these issues in my discussion of Derrida's *Of Grammatology* in my *Essential History: Jacques Derrida and the Development of Deconstruction* (Evanston, IL: Northwestern University Press, 2005), 258n218.

The stuff of poetry and literature, as informed by these twin assumptions, would, then, be language. To be clear, the suggestion is not that this somewhat simplified model of language, or of literature, operates in any of the authors about to be discussed nor in literary studies more broadly. It does, however, give a rough and ready idea of *a space* or a place recognizable in these endeavors, which, being only a space, although empty, stands ready to be *filled in*. The outlines of a formation resonating with this model of language, or some variation on it, show forth in these projects, projects that also assume a *greater and greater distance from this same template*, as is about to become clear.

1.2.1 Form as Arrangement of Words (Derek Attridge)

Two sets of tendencies render Attridge's *The Singularity of Literature* distinctive, accounting for its appearance here. First, Attridge presents literature's singularity throughout his text as tied to moments found in discourse. He indeed treats signification and literature as *events*—involving authors, readers, and what he calls "idiocultures."[13] "This is what a literary work is," Attridge exclaims, "an act, an event, of reading, never entirely separable from the act-event . . . of writing that brought it into being" (SL 59). Attridge repeatedly underscores that literature's singularity transpires solely in events that take place across writing and reading, between the "authoredness" of the text and its being "created" again by its interpreters (SL 87).

Measured against many accounts of literature, especially those associated with deconstruction, which supplies the context for much of Attridge's thinking, Attridge's approach is notable for incorporating this feature of talk! or discourse. For discourse here, as well, all speaking, writing, and understanding are individuated, or inherently singular, events in which persons, albeit loosely defined, play a role. Attridge's aim, however, as his title attests, and this is the second reason his work draws attention, is to reserve the singularity of discursive events solely for literature and the literary (and perhaps the other arts), thereby establishing literature's specificity over and against other genres of discourse. Attridge, in his own words, wishes to identify the "*literariness*" of literature on these new discursive terms (SL 3).

The notion of what Attridge calls "otherness" is central to Attridge's conception of literature so understood. Attridge's starting point is an intrinsic foreignness to our understanding and expectations of what we find in some literary performances, which he designates under the headings of "otherness" and "alterity" (SL2). "Verbal creation is a handling of language," he declares, "whereby something we might call 'otherness' or 'alterity' is made, or allowed" (SL 19). Though such excess and otherness, for Attridge, to be clear, *defines* "literature" rather than the other way around, nevertheless, for him it accompanies literature wherever and whenever literature appears.

With an eye to such "otherness," Attridge thus re-describes literature, offering his own versions of its imaginativeness and textuality. The first, imaginativeness, answers to literature's purported power to be constantly new or "inventive"; the second,

---

[13] Derek Attridge, *The Singularity of Literature* (London: Routledge, 2004), 52. Hereafter all references will be given in the text to SL.

textuality, corresponds to the capacity of this originality to remain legible across time (SL 2). Ultimately, Attridge invokes three features—otherness; literature's legibility that Attridge also deems its uniqueness (connected to its otherness); and literature's inventiveness, its unerodable power of "innovation"—which according to Attridge, comprise a "trinity" (SL 2).[14] These traits consistently inform each other in Attridge's analysis, and thanks to them, Attridge's model may be seen to rework the traditional understanding of literature set out earlier. Under their joint rubric, literature knows a virtually unlimited power of invention and a similarly unbounded capacity to present itself as an innovation. Together, this ability to appear as other and distinct, at once unique and novel, across numerous times and places, corresponds to "the singularity of literature" found in Attridge's title.

Attridge's reworking of literature's literariness in this relatively novel manner is at the least provocative; moreover, in the present account as well, the potential difference of what a discourse says from its reader's perspective and beliefs, while not of an unbounded or absolute scope, is also an important feature of literature's, and indeed all discourse's functioning. Yet setting aside the absolutization of such foreignness, and the delimitation of literature's imaginariness and power of repetition, what is perhaps most problematic in Attridge's account is the recourse it ends up having to quite standard notions of language and of literary form. At the moment, Attridge unpacks how this otherness determinative of literature dwells or appears in it, and with that, literature's novelty and legibility, a readily recognizable version of language returns to the fore.

Attridge, in fact, at one point himself shies away from standard views of language. He stipulates that literature's singularity is *not* a function of a "particular collocation of coded elements," and thus apparently *not* a matter of language as usually understood (SL 87). Later on, however, Attridge not only invokes literary form as such, declaring "a creative achievement in the literary field is, whatever else it is a formal one" (SL 107). Moreover, he further indicates that this formal moment indeed resides in "the selection and arrangement of words" (SL 107). Formal considerations are inseparable from literature's literariness, and form in turn relies on "the selection and arrangement of words for inventiveness, singularity and otherness" (SL 110).

The identity of any piece of literature as literature, its literariness, for Attridge, answers, then, to a fairly standard notion of form, despite what Attridge says elsewhere about the event—a form that recurs to words' arrangements and thus to language traditionally understood.[15] Attridge at this moment, to be sure, will insist that not simply

---

[14] Literature's excessive originality for Attridge indeed remains accessible beyond its current moment, thereby at once implying the textual, the supposedly superordinate lastingness specific to its mode of being. Attridge affirms, in the early going of his text, that "we can read a poem or watch a play written hundreds or even thousands of years ago and feel we are directly experiencing its creator's inventiveness" (SL 2). To be clear, Attridge's view of this capacity is somewhat nuanced. Though this singularity is in principle inexhaustible, and may thus always return, it does not, he claims, simply "transcend history," in the sense that the excess in question is necessarily able to appear in *every* historical epoch (SL 66). Nevertheless, literature as literature, for him, is the site of such otherness, and by definition retains the capacity to make its newness repeatedly felt across history and cultures.

[15] This contention is further confirmed by Attridge's affirmation of "meaning" and of the "work." (See chapter eight of SL, "Form, Meaning, and Context"; pp. 107–21.) Otherness and innovativeness turn out to be an elusive version of meaning, one that takes shape within the contours of a work, albeit

words are in question, but words as a "stage" for the sort of event that he previously described, including author and reader. Nevertheless, what remains and allows this piece of literature to be identified in its own right is that always identical "stage" that the work's words provide, a piece of literature's form in a fairly traditional sense.[16]

Attridge turns to form, then, and with it, a version of language that he elsewhere seems to question, in order to account for literature's literariness. The present account, of course, questions Attridge's reliance on words and language and the notion of literariness that attends it. No instance of discourse, including literature, on the present view, differs from any other by dint of harboring a unique capacity, such as instantiating radical otherness, nor does it glean its identity from any arrangements of language, no matter how determined.

Discourse's radicalization in the present work, consequently, prompts questions that Attridge's reliance on language and form and his fealty to literariness forestall: not only how are discourse or talk! to be conceived, but also what might be the urgency or necessity of working with texts usually deemed literary under discourse's rubric? *A New Philosophy* rejects that very space, shaped like language and form, on which even so much cutting-edge contemporary criticism continues to rely; how, then, does it fashion its own understanding of literature? Similarly, how can literature for it be both legible and significant, given the temporal, geographic, cultural, and other distancing it often implies? What is literature's fate as an object of study, once that language-based imaginativeness and the novelty believed specific to literature are called into doubt?

1.2.2 Form as Disciplinarity (Poovey)

Poovey's project appears inherently more immune to the temptation to which Attridge has just succumbed of falling back on form and language. Her avowed approach, historical description, is anything but formalist. In fact, at one point in her magisterial 2008 *Genres of the Credit Economy*, Poovey states that it was her dissatisfaction with the residual form and formalism at work in her earlier new historicist practice that led her to embark on the approach that she takes up in *Genres* (GCE 342).[17] *Genres* itself, then, emblematizes that turn toward flatness and the rejection of structures of any sort (including historical ones, as witnessed by her recantation of the new historicism), all of which obviously sit poorly with form. Should, then, recourse to fallbacks of this sort, to some avatar of the more traditional formalism, accompanied by an invocation of language otherwise unexplained also be at work in Poovey's project, that development

---

both are understood as requiring what might be called "supplementation" by authors and readers. By contrast, in the present account, the interchange between author, reader, and the world does away with both of these notions—no meanings as such, even in performance, and not necessarily any works, since what sort of slice into the body of literature is to be made here depends on the orienting question with which it is approached.

[16] To this extent, Attridge's account may be close to that of the Romans (Ingarden and/or Jakobson), for both of whom the literary text is a (linguistic) virtuality that fully exists only in its revivals and reenactments. Attridge has written somewhat extensively on Jakobson, so the latter's influence may be the major one here.

[17] Mary Poovey, *Genres of the Credit Economy* (Chicago: Chicago UP, 2008). Hereafter cited as GCE, references to which will be given in the text.

would go a long way toward attesting to these assumptions' continuing hold on literary studies even at this late date. Such a recurrence would also give cause to further wonder how a radically discourse-based approach operates, and whether it is even compatible with literary studies, given the fate of its intimations in the authors in question here.

Before addressing these issues, talk!'s prominent role in Poovey's initiative first must be registered. Poovey indeed explicitly traces her own analysis back to a version of discourse or talk!, not language. To be sure, in *Genres*, Poovey rarely addresses language-related issues; her reflections focus on literary history and its practice. Nevertheless, discourse, or talk! looms large, largely thanks to her self-proclaimed antecedents.

Poovey, for one, identifies Ian Hunter's work as decisive for her own thinking (GCE 20). In his *Culture and Government*, Hunter, in turn, repeatedly invokes Wittgenstein's understanding of language precisely against those models of meaning that Hunter finds operative in both the New Criticism and Cultural Studies. Long before the present venture, Hunter aims to set out a new view of meaning "as a 'dispersed' phenomena . . . *not determined by a single general form like language*" to contest the received understanding of semantics in a literary context.[18] So, too, Bourdieu, to whom Poovey often appeals, claimed Wittgenstein as central to his own conceptions, especially that of the "habitus."[19]

Now, neither Hunter's nor Bourdieu's interpretation of Wittgenstein are as radical as the those found in Cavell or in Altieri, both of which are soon to be discussed. Nevertheless, similar to the sociological treatment of Wittgenstein by Peter Winch, a version of Wittgensteinian language games, and thus language in *use*, proves critical to these thinkers and thus to Poovey's undertaking.[20] Viewing talk! in an institutional and ultimately sociological setting, Poovey herself, to be clear, prefers the term "function" to "use," and she further connects "function" to "genre," a correction that she traces back to John Guillory. Poovey cites Guillory, who, in *Cultural Capital* critiques Barbara Herrnstein-Smith's (sociobiologically oriented) version of use and affirms instead "a *finite range* of uses prescribed by the *social-classification* of an object," that is, by a genre or a conventional kind.[21] Yet Guillory himself here employs "use," and, as his usage attests, as well as his avowed source for this insight (Guillory footnotes Bourdieu), talk!, discourse, the linguistic as written and spoken by authors and readers at specific times and places, not language, remains the primary model at work in his text.

In *Genres*, Poovey, then, aims to provide a genealogy of the genre of fiction as we have come to understand it, on the basis of discourse so understood. Specifically, she at first traces literary fiction's emergence back to an originary differentiation of fictional from economic writing that also lays the ground for the introduction of paper *currency*. Form, as something literature is believed to intrinsically possess, follows on the heels of fiction. It enters at a next stage, thereby establishing an important constituent of Poovey's own critical practice. In line with the significance she assigns to genres of

---

[18] Ian Hunter, *Culture and Government: the Emergence of Literary Education* (Basingstoke: Macmillan, 1988), x (my emphasis).
[19] Pierre Bourdieu, *Outline of a Theory of Practice* (Cambridge: Cambridge UP, 1977).
[20] Peter Winch, *The Idea of a Social Science* (London: Routledge, 2008; orig. 1958), 23ff.
[21] John Guillory, *Cultural Capital: The Problem of Literary Canon Formation* (Chicago: Chicago UP, 1993), 294.

discourse or talk!, Poovey ultimately understands form and the attention paid to it in a literary context, as an historical achievement forming part of the *disciplinary functions* comprising her own *genre* of writing, that of present-day literary studies.[22]

Poovey, whose own work of course by no means is composed solely of formal or close readings, harbors a still greater ambition pertaining to form, however, within which her own recourse to it as a critic is ultimately nested. She would describe the conditions under which literary form and formalism first emerged in the literary practices of earlier times and their concrete historical contexts. Poovey thus will offer *an historical account of form* as it has been and as is still understood in the contemporary context by exhibiting its emergence within literature's evolving genres, all of which reference points, being historical and in flux, for her ultimately redound to talk! or discourse rather than linguistic forms or structures.

Accordingly, the final two parts of Poovey's book are organized in view of the following rather strikingly ambitious aim: to exhibit the nineteenth-century English *realist* novel as establishing the notion of form as it functions in the present-day literary critical context. The nineteenth-century development, to be sure, finds precedents still further back, in the differentiation between genres of financial and other kinds of writing set out in the first half of her work, when literary fiction becomes established as a category in its own right. In these final two sections, however, Poovey offers *a positive genealogy* of the matrix of literary concepts assembled around form (including self-reference and the aesthetic) in transformations specific to novel writing in nineteenth-century Britain. The development of the novel, specifically from Austen to Eliot to Trollope, according to Poovey, offers a pre-articulation of literary form, establishing those guises under which it continues to function as a disciplinary norm in literary studies today. Her last three chapters, accordingly, undertake the work announced in their titles: they sketch "Jane Austen's Gestural Aesthetic," the movement "From Gesture to Formalism," and finally identify "The Rewards of Form."

Birthed in this same sequence, perhaps not surprisingly, are both of the notions set out earlier: literature's textuality, its status as something to be read "again and again"— here in the concentrated form of multiple readings of the same text by a single critic—as well as the power of a supposedly wholly autonomous literary *imagination*. Everything in literature and literary studies that lays claim to being either a thing in itself (text) or a world in itself (imagination), Poovey's genealogy traces back to the burgeoning genre of literary realism, where both vectors, according to her, were initially fashioned as means of turning attention away from *specific economic crises*, ones that Poovey at times recounts in some detail.

Poovey's treatment of the first author in this sequence, Austen, suffices to make plain this more general drift. Both possibilities, textual and imaginative, are found in Austen's work, as well as their potential difference, according to Poovey. The imaginative, it should be noted, for Poovey, owing to its featuring a world apart from our own, largely lends itself to *popular* reading focused on pleasure; academic critical practice preeminently concerns itself with the textual, on account of the sustained attention, the repeated readings, academic readers give to a work.

---

[22] This point receives further discussion below; see esp. GCE 378, treated in n.25.

On the first score, imagination, Poovey portrays Austen as inventing, through her style, a new kind of novel, less given over to plot or suspense. This style, by deepening its fictional world, directs interest away from our common one and toward itself, thereby for the first time, according to Poovey, creating authentically imaginary *worlds*, worlds that claim to stand wholly on their own, without reference back to actual society (as, for example, Henry Fielding's *Tom Jones* or Jean-Jacques Rousseau's *Julie* do). "Austen's novels," she insists, "rendered their relationships to the actual world less important" in favor of "their ability to conjure up a self-contained, self-referential world . . . augment[ing] the pleasure of reading" (GCE 371).

In turn, mainly thanks to Austen's text's *plotting*, her works also lay the foundations for close reading and its corresponding *textuality*; they invent literature's superordinate persistence or legibility. "The complexity" of narrative that she has "been describing," Poovey indicates, "encouraged readers to re-read the novel"; it thus "anticipated the kind of Literary reading described at the end of the century by Ruskin and Dowden" (GCE 372). Austen, according to Poovey, fabricates a new kind of narrative possessing a self-referential form, thereby inviting and indeed effectively instituting the practice of a single individual returning to the same text again and again.

Poovey herself then, explicitly addresses both of those features to which form has customarily answered, and she is indeed savvy to the point of being suspicious when it comes to employments of form, including her own. Form would in no case, it appears, be a thing in itself, but instead a feature answering to historically instituted practices, ultimately recurring to discourse. Nevertheless, discourse (as function, genre, and related practices), thanks to which these analyses make their way and find their targets, encounters a disconnect in a recourse that Poovey herself will have to language. Despite the foregoing and her focus on history, Poovey, at times, in these same sections, views language, not history nor talk!, as ultimately subtending literature, including form so understood.

Poovey's reliance on an otherwise unexplained linguistic reference point first appears in her text's initial stages. Poovey apparently understands written linguistic expressions, and perhaps all such, as possessed of a power of "deferral of reference" as by definition somehow removed from the real (GCE 79). Such a power, on this account, only finds its greatest *amplitude* in the versions of the literary established by the nineteenth-century English novel. Accordingly, looking back toward a point before the differentiation of the trio comprised of fictional writing, financial instruments (paper currency), and economic writing (taken as factual and referential), Poovey claims that what initially held these together along a continuum is just this deferral in which they all necessarily participate, one that she associates with signification generally. All of these enterprises possess an ability to step back from what is otherwise taken as genuine or actual (from gold or silver, in the case of paper money), with the differentiation of illicit from licit versions of such representations in the case of currency proving the driving force from which the others, with their distinct identities—literature as fictitious and economic writing as factual—eventually emerge (GCE 79–80, cf. 399–401).

Yet positing such a power of removal from the real, Poovey leaves otherwise unexplained whence it comes that any signification on a socio-cultural level, in which she herself includes all three cases, can avoid or withhold itself from reality or actuality. Deferral exists as a capacity the effects of which are historically negotiated and registered; yet this potentiality as such for her stands back from all history. Positing such deferral at the root of a general continuum between fact and fiction, accordingly, only seems conceivable if the *presupposition* of linguistic and semiotic systems—a space or place answering to these—continues to lurk in the background, arguably in both the literary and the monetary cases.[23] Poovey's supposition of a general power of deferral indeed points toward and tacitly recurs to some sort of otherwise unidentified linguistic or semiotic systematicity, with its own semantic and representational powers, capable of standing apart from the world—and thus to some avatar of language in distinction from discourse or talk!

Language or signification (of this very general and otherwise undetermined stripe) also serves as the minimal condition for Poovey's analysis in the last two parts of *Genre*. To accomplish her genealogy of fiction, Poovey explicitly assigns to the works in question the ability to conjure a "world" entirely from "words," thereby granting these works a capacity to function autonomously, to operate in an explicitly *non-worlded* manner. Discussing Austen's style, Poovey speaks of the "textual" as "a world of words" resulting from the amplification of the imaginary owed to Austen's innovations in the craft of fiction (CGE 371). Similarly, Poovey credits Austen's novel with the ability "to conjure up a self-contained, self-referential world," when identifying Austen's invention of narrative techniques that yield "form" (CGE 372).

Of course, Poovey's treatment, as sketched earlier, ultimately aims to question these constructs—form and imaginary worlds—as things in themselves, including as ahistorical norms. Both notions are in some fashion the *target* of her descriptions. Yet the supposition that language or literature *could* at any moment in its long career break from the world and function as self-referential fiction, like her earlier invocation of a general deferral common to currency and literature, runs counter to discourse's present conception. Poovey goes this route, however, since she needs these phenomena to remain intact to accomplish her genealogy of contemporary critical practice, in order to tie the latter moment to the former. Such a possibility of literature at any point functioning autonomously invalidates the notion of discourse found in her own text, however, since talk!, or discourse entails that no performances of language are autonomous or self-contained, all being intrinsically *worlded*. Poovey's own tight linkage of literature's career to contingent historical events, after all, would come into doubt were any piece of language or literature to function in this way. Hence, to grant literature a genuine capacity to proceed on autonomous terms implicitly threatens her own historical references.

Poovey, to be clear, in *Genres* more generally, approaches her chosen works as embedded in contexts; she sees them as inseparable from social life and a world*ed* horizon (assigning them all dated historical references, some of which they defer, hide,

---

[23] Poovey footnotes Marc Shell's pathbreaking work on money and literature, but she misprizes its specific and arguably pioneering thrust; Shell's is in fact an essentially discourse-based account of money, focused on exchange, not one that views money and discourse as language (CGE 25n1). For Shell, see, among many others, *The Economy of Literature* (Baltimore: Johns Hopkins University Press, 1978). Discussion of Shell, now as a reader of Shakespeare and Oedipus and as an interlocutor of Cavell's, returns in Chapter 5.

or conceal). In the present discussion, however, Poovey seems also to credit Austen's text with the power *to operate apart from all such considerations*, thereby rehabilitating form, while more or less explicitly invoking that space of language previously sketched. Poovey indeed stipulates that, though some event must have spurred Austen's innovations in fiction writing, and even offers a candidate for that event, this occurrence *in principle* can never be pinned down and identified with any concrete historical one (GCE 358–9).[24] Not such an event, but Austen's "style," accordingly, gives birth to form. Not only owing to the absence of any historical record, but because of the new way that Austen herself writes, no one occasion could possibly answer to her innovation; this linkage between history and her innovation thus remains in a state of what Poovey herself deems "undecidability" (GCE 372).

Yet for this to be so in any fashion, something like a formal structure must indeed at this moment operate, and a self-referential world and text must genuinely appear. Poovey herself, as we have seen, does speak of "Austen's language" as providing the grounds for this new object of attention (GCE 359). Over against her own construal of literature as always occasioned, contextualized, or worlded (Poovey hypothesizes, even in Austen's case, that her invention was spurred by the banking crisis of 1815), a competing version of language as unworlded, as deferral, and as text bearing independent and autonomous forms, at this moment also informs her account.

To be sure, Poovey by no mean fails to sense this difficulty. Instead, throughout her work, she apparently views all such potential clashes as flowing from the necessity to apply working categories currently embedded in the genre of literary studies to the past, even as we distinguish the past's categories and genres from our own. Otherwise put, she understands this potential tension in her own conceptual armature at this and other moments as a problem of *historical* translation.[25] In this particular instance, her own reading of Austen, and her finding of form in it, would be, then, owed to Poovey's own genre of writing, to the contemporary norms governing her own literary critical labor.

Yet, this last claim ultimately sits uncomfortably. After all, if Austen's works are to serve as source and precedent of Poovey's own productions and of the discipline generally, must not the self-referentiality and non-worlded language Poovey finds in them genuinely belong to these writings themselves? The existence of these features cannot be *the result* of those same practices, simply a function of what her discipline *today* demands, if her *genealogy* of her own contemporary practice as stemming from these antecedents is to be persuasive. Making what she finds in Austen the product of her own discipline and genre obviates Poovey's discovering in Austen her practice's

---

[24] This stands in marked contrast to the variation of such plotting Poovey finds in Trollope (cf. GCE 397–9).

[25] At one point she avers how "difficult it is to give a historical description," since such a description must "recover" the "terms and categories that prevailed when the novels were written"; yet, at the same time, for this same description to "count as a disciplined description," it must "be formulated in the technical terminology used by today's professional literary critics" (GCE 378). The bite of the first, more general claim, for what it is worth, I am unable to wholly follow, as well as her conclusion. Poovey herself must already have some grasp on these past categories to speak of them at all, either as hewing to or resistant to present descriptions; yet if such categories can sometimes be grasped, as she herself must claim, no insoluble obstacles to such translation seemingly exist.

inauguration. Poovey's reading of Austen, while doubtless in some fashion a product of contemporary practice (certainly not available without it) thus must also affirm its antecedents in Austen's work, in a way that grants them legitimacy on their own terms. But if form, and these imaginary and textual worlds are indeed attributable to Austen's writings as such, Poovey's way of working throughout *Genres* comes into conflict with itself. There is no need, indeed no possibility of connecting these and other literary innovations to various historical crises; once imaginary and textual worlds are granted, such historical developments could only serve as *occasions* for discovering reference points and frameworks—such as imaginary worlds and self-referential plots—possessing genuine grounds and capacities of their own. Poovey indeed wants to have it both ways, to have her cake and eat it, too—doubtless because she herself is such a fine close reader. She wants a version of literature that still gives sufficient leeway to the practice of close reading, while also assigning that practice's possibility wholly to historical becoming. Her turn to nineteenth-century realism to provide a genealogy of her own literary practice instead, however, renders doubtful her underlying historical suppositions and her project's commitment to discourse or talk! Historical-discursive frameworks based on generic uses or functions and the founding of close reading in worlds of words and self-reference, despite her extraordinary efforts, seemingly remain incompatible.

1.2.3 The Expression and Model in Place of Form (Altieri)

Among those critics in question in this chapter, only Charles Altieri, then, wholly successfully dispenses with recourse to an autonomous imagination, one entirely divorced from the real, as well as with those residual appeals to an equally autonomous language that haunt the imagination's conception in Poovey and Attridge. Each of the former critics in their very different ways grants such a gulf between the imaginary and the real, and, as we have seen, both are led back to language in something like its customary guise. Altieri's *Reckoning with the Imagination*, by contrast, approaches literature on a fully *worlded* basis, and thus on a more fundamentally discourse-based ground than any of those positions previously met.[26]

Breaking with all traditional views of language, Altieri, accordingly, must himself confront one of the two leadings questions facing the present work: what sort of urgency, purpose, or necessity accompanies the study of literature once its formal character, and the view of language subtending it, has been ruled out. Altieri's project aims to respond to this problem, by way of a version of discourse that he attributes to Wittgenstein, as Altieri indicates in his book's subtitle "Wittgenstein and the Aesthetics of Literary Experience."

Altieri's importance in the current setting consists in his starting on this discursive terrain, and in his making a case for the aesthetic and for literature, without assigning any specialness or any species of ontological differentiation to literary language as

---

[26] Charles Altieri, *Reckoning with the Imagination: Wittgenstein and the Aesthetics of Literary Experience* (Ithaca: Cornell UP, 2015); hereafter all references will be given in the text to RI.

such.[27] Altieri does possesses a strategy, however, for making the case for literature, and this approach, it will be argued, encounters significant obstacles, albeit different ones from any that the previous two critics faced. Altieri's problem, in a nutshell, pertains not to literature's relation to language but arises in his appeal to what for him *explicitly falls outside* both language and discourse. Altieri, that is, does not call on an imaginativeness found only in literature and allied to literary form. Instead he proposes to distinguish two great genres of talk! or discourse, ultimately based on what such talk! can and or cannot make available in its own expressions. Literature, in turn, constitutes a subset of the latter, of expressions that pertain to a subject that can never appear as such in discourse or talk! itself.

In the early going of *Reckoning*, more specifically, Altieri views literature through the lens supplied by what he calls "avowals" and "display," notions that center literature's work in a particular conception of *expression*. Displays are a more general version of what Altieri calls "avowals." Avowals are statements such as "I am in pain," where an immediacy of apprehension is at work and no recourse to directly shared evidence is presumed available, with the result, according to Altieri, that no considerations of truth or correctness can enter the mix. I cannot inspect the other's pain as I would, let us say, a flower or a wedding ring, and for this reason, someone's being in pain is not of the order of a straightforward fact but an exhibition or showing that invites a response from its hearers different from registering the truth of what is being expressed.[28]

Display is still broader than avowal; it is not confined to first-person reports. Display includes all expressions that for Altieri essentially *show* rather than state.[29] Not only do a wide range of display phenomena exist, each with their own distinctive "grammar" (in Wittgenstein's sense), but Wittgenstein's own philosophy, according to Altieri, is also a kind of display, a showing of, rather than stating, its perspective. Literature and literary criticism, too, are examples of displaying, which, for Altieri, also includes affective charges and states, as well as aspect-seeing (grasping something as something in a way that excludes other equally well-founded possibilities). Literature thus engages in display and provides templates for those aspects of the world that may be seen in it, as well as for the attitudes taken toward the matters so exhibited.

---

[27] Altieri early on affirms that "the skills we need to engage art objects are . . . the same skills that we need to negotiate the many interpretive decisions we encounter in our everyday lives" (RI 6).

[28] Altieri cordons off avowals from any sort of insight or cognitive burden—while still insisting that they have their own grammar, and that they apparently do indicate or show something—by arguing that it would be inappropriate when I tell you "I am in pain," for you to respond to me "you are correct," (or as he puts it, "yes, you are right, I am in pain") (RI 70). But, to the furniture repair person coming to my apartment, I might well say "it's the chair in the corner that you want." And it would, of course, also be wrong for her in many instances to answer "you are correct," or "yes, you are right." Nevertheless, as I, in this case express a set of wishes or demands while also informing someone about something, so, too, on the present account, in the other case, I am describing my own condition of being in pain *and* reporting on something to my interlocutor, even while I also am requesting sympathy, assistance, and so on.

[29] In addition to the Ashbery poem cited in the next note, Altieri's primary example of display comes from Wittgenstein, who speaks of someone entering a room painted red and exclaiming red. Altieri, it appears to me, unlike Wittgenstein, must reject this declaration being both a statement and an expression of the subject's reaction or feeling. Though displays almost always pertains to beings other than the subject for Altieri, like avowals, they lack all cognitive or veridical bite (RI 26–7; 70–2)

Crucially, all of these capacities, according to Altieri, answer to practices available in everyday life. Altieri, consequently, founds his understanding of art, verbal included, on display; he explicitly "link[s] the functions of display in practical life" to "what artworks can be said to make present" (RI 66).

A more concrete idea of what Altieri has in mind can be gotten from one of his own examples. Altieri cites John Ashbery's poem "Instruction Manual," in which the speaker appears as someone who, while writing such a manual, becomes bored and daydreams of a visit to Guadalajara (RI 47-55). Altieri treats Ashbery's text as unequivocally depicting an actual situation and context. The broader point that he draws from it, in turn, is that it *displays* the power of the imagination to respond to fallow stretches of our everyday lives and transformatively fill them in. Literature's power, for Altieri, thus never simply stands apart from the remainder of life or of discourse. It depends on worldliness and dispenses with all veiled reliance on language as a system and all autonomous literary forms.[30]

Altieri, in sum, reconceives the work of the imagination in terms of discourse, by way of avowal and display. Accordingly, he attempts to embrace both options presently on the table: he indeed wishes to affirm talk! or discourse in its present radicality, but also to affirm on this relatively new ground (no longer that of language and form) literature with some of its customary specificity. Should, however, Altieri not be able to carry out the latter—or if he must pare down or retract the force of discourse in order to do so—his attempt would seemingly experience some turbulence, thereby rendering still more acute the problem of conceiving of literature's standing when understood entirely as discourse.

To delineate a space in talk! for the imagination's work, which literature thus will also occupy, Altieri, it turns out, finally has no choice but effectively to "aestheticize" (for lack of a better word) discourse more generally, in particular as presented by the later Wittgenstein. Altieri, to be clear, does not make of literature and literariness a separate language, performance, object, or even a disciplinary practice; rather, he carves out two dimensions or distinct genres of discourse, one of which is ultimately marked by a concern with value and specific to (*self-*) *expression*. This broad genre, set over against a second, comprised of veridical speech, harbors tendencies that permit literature to don something approximating its usual garb. So proceeding, however, Altieri draws back from conceiving of discourse in its full radicality.

In a nutshell, the major problem with his otherwise powerful account—notable both for its novelty and its insight—is that to arrive at it, Altieri finds himself assigning to *the subject of expression* a dimension *transcending* all discourse. To be sure, no construal of talk! can do entirely without the notion of persons. (Their standing, over against their status in collectives, is the theme of the final chapter of Part I.) Yet, Altieri explicitly makes the person (whether individuated or collective) into a new,

---

[30] At certain moments, something like form and language return, particularly when Altieri attempts to make sense of artistic expressions as works and thus account for the other facet of literature ultimately in question here, its textuality. In the midst of his discussion of the model, taken up below, he follows Hegel in seeing in expression a merging of "subject" and "substance" (RI 106-9). It is not entirely clear to me, however, that this treatment really is on all fours with the vector toward discourse emerging from Wittgenstein's thought that Altieri primarily embraces.

special kind of *absolute*, thus blunting discourse's apprehension by relating it to such a reference point.[31]

More specifically, Altieri recurs to what he takes to be the positing of a special subject in Wittgenstein's thought, initially in the latter's first work, the *Tractatus*. Wittgenstein, later, according to Altieri, adapts, but does not entirely abandon this standpoint in his *Philosophical Investigations*.

Wittgenstein himself, in the *Tractatus*, as is well known, likens the "subject" of discourse to the eye; just as the eye does not appear in the visual field so does the subject not appear in its domain (presumably that of life). Near the close of that work, in turn, Wittgenstein, with reference to this subject, speaks of "ethics" and deems it "transcendental," declaring that ethics "does not let itself be expressed (*aussprechen*)."[32]

Altieri, then, contends, first, that Wittgenstein genuinely affirms the (separate) existence of such an ethical subject in the *Tractatus* (one that is at the basis of all understanding and action but cannot strictly be spoken of or speak about itself); secondly, he takes that subject to play a role in Wittgenstein's later *Philosophical Investigations*, now, however, while simultaneously being integrated into specific social, cultural, and linguistic contexts and practices (*Reckoning* 119–20).[33]

Consequently, Altieri views everything that he identifies as display as necessarily incorporating what remains a "socialized subject," which, at the same time, harbors a transcendent dimension that makes itself known in various ways, including, importantly, its *style* (RI 119). Altieri insists that through its style of expression in displays, Wittgenstein's subject, necessarily positioned in a marginal and eccentric manner, makes itself felt, albeit not known (RI 122–3).

Style, in turn, contributes to Altieri's most thoroughly elaborated account of the work of literature. Literature for Altieri provides what he now calls "models" of various modes of display. Such models fix at once aspects of the world (various kinds of seeing something as something) as well as the perspective from which those aspects are registered and expressed. Literary models, for Altieri, accordingly, provide templates for other such subjects (or those who participate multiply in this single one), themselves also at once social and not. Ultimately, models permit *value* to be imparted to subjects'

---

[31] Though expressions obviously relate to individual persons and capture their perspectives, whether "the transcendental dimension of subjectivity," as Altieri sometimes calls it, is itself individuated or not is left unclear in his account (see RI 99–100, 122–20, and 141–2 esp.).

[32] Ludwig Wittgenstein, *Tractatus Logico-Philosophicus* (London: Kegan Paul, 1922); hereafter TLP. TLP 5.632; 6.421. The fate and sense of Wittgenstein's views of the subject in TLP are today the subject of enormous controversy, predominantly stemming from Cora Diamond's "resolute reading" of the early Wittgenstein, as it has come to be called, and that of her ally, James Conant. Cavell's early work on Wittgenstein is often seen as a sort of god- or grand-father of this position, a view of Cavell both endorsed and contested in Chapter 3.

[33] Proceeding thus, Altieri indeed adopts what is in effect a position precisely opposite to "the resolute" reading of Wittgenstein's corpus just invoked. The latter's main proponents argue that, for Wittgenstein, terms count as meaningful or not only in the individual statements in which they are found within actual events of talk! Accordingly, the nonsense Wittgenstein brands his own talk! at the end of TLP cannot indicate that he wants TLP's conclusions to be understood as a special kind of talk! or discourse but rather not as talk! at all. Accordingly, neither the *Tractatus* nor the *Investigations* can be said to affirm a genuinely world-transcending subject.

interaction with their own world and the things around them, both as at first found in literature and then when these models are taken up and deployed by their readers.³⁴

Literature, then, in Altieri's treatment, is conceived as providing models for expressions of various types of display; consequently, literature would have no specificity, nor indeed any task to perform, bar the status assigned to Wittgenstein's subject. Yet this vector toward a subject, transcendental and ultimately inexpressible, at the same time, clearly represents a paring back of discourse or talk! Positioned, by Wittgenstein's own avowal, at the "limit of the world," deemed inherently "marginal," this subject represents a last instance found neither in language nor in use. Understood on Altieri's terms, which are not the only ones possible, a unique, seemingly metaphysical entity ultimately informs all discourse, including that of literature. Rippling back across discourse *tout court*, it divvies up its operation into two radically distinct types.

To be clear, discourse concerning things and states for Altieri does radically diverge from that in which persons are central, along with their values, attitudes, and affects. Withdrawing all considerations of truth or insight from this last class, Altieri, in the end, then, conceives every display and all its models along "aestheticized" and perhaps even ultimately "imaginary" lines. For him, a moment completely neutral or immune to questions of truth or insight governs these domains of talk! from which literature's specific difference, in turn, descends.

The unavoidability of such concerns, of questions of truth or insight, can be gleaned from one important example: confession, where what is at stake for Altieri is expression as it relates to a "feeling for 'myself' that does not conform to criteria of public identity" (RI 22). Altieri begins, to be clear, seemingly necessarily, by crediting confessions with an aim at truth. Given his understanding of self-expression and literary self-expression, he soon swerves away from this characterization. Specifically, he cites Wittgenstein speaking of confessions as having both "truth" and "truthfulness" of a special sort, while distinguishing these from "any description of a process." Altieri himself, then suggests that confession knows only "truthfulness without truth." Next he goes still further, turning confessional discourse entirely into a matter of self-expression. Confessions, he maintains, are a matter of a "fit," fitting nothing itself specified in them, since confessions function ultimately only as a "form of taking responsibility," and "a revelation of painful individuality" (RI 124).

Yet as is also true of "I am in pain" (see n.28), confessional discourse, it seems clear, can be both *self-expression* and can bring to light genuine situations in the world, express some concrete truth: I really am in pain; I really have done someone wrong on this occasion. Altieri rejects this alternative, and must do so to establish literature's provenance as he understands it. To this degree, Altieri's stance ends up neighboring the prior two. To be sure, Altieri never claims that literature inhabits a world apart; instead he introduces such apartness into the world. He affirms a transcendentally inflected (self-)expressive subject, exceeding all worldly bounds, to account for

---

³⁴ For Altieri, any artwork offers both the direct presentation of the dawning of an aspect (something worldly taken in a certain way) but also the meaning and indeed meaning-making of that aspect for an (idealized) author/subject. This doubleness characterizes the model, which shows both some *thing* and *how* it is seen; as such it provides an example that exhibits how this com-posing can go to work in our lives (RI 126–7).

literature's specificity, and, consequently, views all expression and display, including confession, as lacking any veridical aspect, even one sui generis. An entire sphere of talk! is thus removed from truth, trailing in its wake a subject that exceeds it as such (while still enmeshed with experience and language games), a movement to which literature's existence as literature ultimately recurs.

Discourse as here conceived, however, does without any reliance on such a subject. So, too, for it, all talk!, including literature, not only is worlded but also, being so, is concerned with some sort *of understanding* or insight into some aspect of the world, including our own existence. To be clear, discourse and the veridical in the present case are by no means confined to statements or assertions; they ultimately receive a very different conception than is usual, not being restricted to this rather narrow region. Consequently, the radical separation of fact from value, clearly central to Altieri and also to Poovey, albeit in ways at present here not able to be further charted, is to be rejected. Similarly, the participation of all discourse in a perhaps unparalleled species of truth undermines its obverse: the privilege both Altieri and Poovey give to everyday or institutionalized knowledges—the sphere of fact, over against values—knowledges that each, albeit differently, distinguishes radically from literature and its pursuit.

From the present perspective, accordingly, Altieri steps back from talk!'s full conception, while standing on its threshold. So proceeding, his work and the two discussed before it, nevertheless bequeath important questions to the present study. How does discourse allow for literature and literary studies to retain any significance or importance? All versions of form, and Altieri's aesthetic imagination, having been contested, how can literature continue to be read as literature and how is such an enterprise deemed urgent, once literature's existence as a special form of language or discourse ceases to be viable?

2

Discourse as Literary Innovation
(Charles Bernstein)

What is here being proposed, then, is a self-consciously non-exceptionalist account of literature and literary criticism. No essential, structural, or generic difference on the present view distinguishes literature's talk! from talk! generally, nor will appeal here be made to any absolutes, be they in the guise of "otherness" or some variation on the transcendental subject. All discourse answers to the same reference points and takes place under the same conditions; all is worlded, and in some manner aims at a kind of understanding, albeit of a potentially unlimited number of types—from the selection of a tool to the "fictitious" depiction of an excellent or failed ruler, to the calculation of the sun's changing positions across the year.

The avowal of such literary non-exceptionalism doubtless triggers questions and objections, such as: What becomes of literature's aesthetic distinctiveness under this construal? Won't such non-exceptionality turn literature into philosophy? Alternatively, must not literature just to be literature remain removed from any aim at insight, however it manages to do so? These quite reasonable concerns may begin to be addressed by noting that the work of the imagination, understood as bringing novelty to literature's expressions and attention to their character, here need not be dispensed with, though this is also ultimately true for all discourse. Innovations in mode of speech, concerns with expressions, and an eye toward insight into what is being spoken about cohabitate in much talk! and are by no means exclusive to so-called creative writing.[1] Literature, like all talk!, can draw attention to itself and be "about itself," if one wishes, in the sense of being concerned with how it should or could be composed, in a manner related to its traditional understanding. This comes to pass, however, not despite of its worldly interests, but ultimately *along with* what literature takes as its subject matter. Literary writing, that is, does have truck with what under other construals could be classified as formal concerns; yet these aspects recur solely to talk! and its reception (and have no other existence or ground beyond these), while always being accompanied by something not themselves with which they engage, some matter to be disclosed or development to be understood. Any literary exemplar finds its shape as literature while at the same time reckoning on those aspects of the world

---

[1] Mary Louise Pratt in her early work had already brought this point powerfully home, though she retained a far greater generic and discursive formal apparatus than any found here. See her *Toward a Speech Act Theory of Literary Discourse* (Bloomington, IN: Indiana UP, 1977), 152 ff.

that concerns it on a given occasion. The two moments are ultimately inseparable in any given instance, as they also are for criticism or commentary. Criticism, too, is also always at once about how some stretch or stretches of literature are literature—it attends to their specific innovations and devices—yet with an eye to some worlded subject matter at stake in such articulations.[2]

Indeed, though literature more recently has been understood purely as the confluence of the textual and the imaginary, poetry and other literary writing (as Poovey also indicates), have for a longer time been envisioned in the fashion just suggested: with their expressions viewed as intertwined with some worlded matters of concern about which they offer a species of insight.[3] Literature most often has been believed *both* to express and to describe, to report and to invoke (or convoke or enjoin)—just as does the avowal "I am in pain," or a confession, or the communication that the piece of furniture in the corner is the one that wants fixing.

The main point of the present section, then, in addition to provisionally surveying how discourse actually functions, consists in recognizing the need to relinquish all literary exceptionality, while simultaneously realizing how much of what already takes place in literary, and literary critical, practice is not thereby precluded. Granting literature's exceptionality, affirming literariness, by contrast, as Attridge's project attests, inevitably results in embracing a dubious autonomy: assigned to literature's formal properties, to its generic functioning, or to the realm of (self-)expression more generally. Yet, today literary studies often approaches literature as proposing "genuine" or "valid" "insights" and "stances" or "problems"—about economics, race, technology, social institutions, and so on. Criticism, accordingly, already implicitly views literature as a version of discourse, despite not thematizing this practice, owing to its retention of more customary models of language and of literature in ways that here have begun to be sketched.

Cultural, ethnic, gender, or queer studies, however, obviously harbor concerns not confined to literature and believe that these findings matter—that they give insight into their themes, as well as their texts. Since, however, there never was, nor could there be any truly autonomous literature, or literary studies, the same holds good in every other instance. Thus, in those cases where appearances portend the contrary, such as the New Criticism, or deconstruction, "ulterior" subjects were also always also in play: deconstruction tracked a broader quasi-ontological excess, an absolute Other (and/or language as such and its forgetting), while the New Criticism, among other things, aimed at the methodology of literary studies and the proper manner of teaching literature, as well as fished for insights into the human condition more generally. Both schools pursued these issues, in texts where they by no means seemed to stand at the

---

[2] In a forthcoming essay, "The Silence of the Concepts (in *After Finitude* and Gottlob Frege)," I argue against identifying this coordination of subject matters and expressions with what Meillassoux calls correlationism, or at least argue for conceding that the proposed coordination is ultimately less correlationist than Meillassoux's own stance.

[3] For a fascinating recent account of more long-standing views of literature and the arts, with significant overlap and divergence from the present study, see Henry Staten, *Techne Theory: A New Language for Art* (London: Bloomsbury Academic, 2019).

forefront, in the Metaphysicals or in the Victorians, Hardy or Milton. Literature and literary studies thus always have been about themselves *and* about something else.

The setting out of these problems, as well as the foregoing response, nevertheless, remains too compressed, too "theoretical" or "abstract," to be fully persuasive. Accordingly, it proves worthwhile, to think these questions through *with* an actual piece of literature, while also simultaneously setting the present understanding *against* this same set of writings, for reasons that are about to become clear.

The instance of literature I have in mind indeed emerges from what is widely considered to be one of the most notable *formal experiments* in American literature in the last thirty years. A self-conscious successor to the modernist avant-garde, this movement at its outset designated itself as L=A=N=G=U=A=G=E (or L=A=N=G=U=A=G=E poetry).[4]

L=A=N=G=U=A=G=E as formal experiment indeed seems to render doubtful the present *denial* of the formal properties of literature and of language. With its morcelization of words, its apparent non-sequiturs, its near constant disruption of syntax, and its lists—to name but these—L=A=N=G=U=A=G=E's use of language aims at *language*, and seemingly never assembles into anything recognizable as discourse or talk! L=A=N=G=U=A=G=E pushes talk! to the breaking point, while making an explicit appeal to *language* in its difference from discourse. L=A=N=G=U=A=G=E undoes or reroutes just about every expectation, every contouring, associated with communication, the utterance, and the speech-act, and thus with discourse as such.[5]

This is doubtless why, for many, even today, L=A=N=G=U=A=G=E poetry most immediately signifies the incursion of a poststructuralist perspective on language into poetics. Actualizing the death of the author and implementing the insight that there is "no outside text," L=A=N=G=U=A=G=E, it is claimed, debunks notions of (self-) *expression* (bound up with the foregoing "myths"), ultimately to contest the role of art as commodity, and the operation of normed subjects (consumers and producers) within contemporary society.

Of course, such an account of L=A=N=G=U=A=G=E's operation, in particular its relation to poststructuralism's view of language, was always too simplistic, even if it may well map on to some of the more manifesto-like proclamations made by practitioners in its earliest phases (especially those proposed by Steve McCaffrey).[6]

---

[4] This designation descends from a narrowly circulated periodical, excerpts from which subsequently became more widely available in an anthology bearing the same title.

[5] Hence Ron Sillimann, introducing a small magazine that served as a precursor to the movement, declared "I hate speech" (cited in Laura Reinfeld, *Language Poetry: Writing as Rescue* [Baton Rouge: LSU Press, 1992], 1). Reinfeld's book is a nice treatment of the writings of the main figures associated with the movement, in addition, of course, to Marjorie Perloff's now classic discussions, some of which are available in her *The Dance of the Intellect* (Cambridge: Cambridge University Press, 1985) and her *Poetic License* (Evanston, IL: Northwestern University Press, 1990).

[6] See *L=A=N=G=U=A=G=E Book*, ed. Bruce Andrews and Charles Bernstein (Carbondale, IL: Southern Illinois UP, 1984), 159–62. Perloff, looking back on the movement, summarizes L=A=N=G=U=A=G=E's and, in particular, McCaffrey's work's "animating principle" as the insistence that "poetic language is not a window," and claims that their poetics "owes its greatest debt to poststructuralism," albeit, she, too, notes that Bernstein is an exception, as is about to be acknowledged here (Marjorie Perloff, "After Language Poetry: Innovation and Its Theoretical Discontents," in *Contemporary Poetics*, ed. Louis Armand [Evanston, IL: Northwestern UP, 2007], 18).

Each contributor to L=A=N=G=U=A=G=E had their own unique perspective on language (such as Ron Silliman's provocative privileging of the sentence). That singular perspective, in turn, fuelled their poetic practice, sometimes in more, and other times in less, obvious ways.

Such complexity proves nowhere more true, moreover, than in the poet (and thinker) upon whose work focus presently falls: Charles Bernstein. Bernstein has followed a path that repeatedly unfolds unexpectedly. Bernstein himself, at the same time, never viewed poetry or language simply through a poststructuralist lens, in part owing to having studied Wittgenstein with Cavell at Harvard. His 1997 *boundary 2* essay, a sort of introduction to Cavell's thought, indeed memorably concludes with an explicit critique of what Bernstein takes to be Derrida's positions on language.[7]

Nonetheless, Bernstein, like L=A=N=G=U=A=G=E more generally (though never in fact on one and the same ground), seemingly appeals to language and views it and discourse differently than presently construed. Bernstein, on various occasions, affirms language as such, and even at times borders on treating it as a kind of absolute. He insists that language is always "fronting" us (CD 43), its "shape" is all we have (for thought, expression, and understanding) (CD 49), and at least once even declares that there are "no transcendental signifieds" (CD 171).[8] While, to be sure, he also includes talk! and worldedness in his conception of language—maintaining that through "language" everything comes to us, without not necessarily thereby "limiting" what comes—Bernstein in his own fashion assigns a leading role to language, one centered on the word (anticipating a set of problems that will return when discussing Cavell). Thus, though we may not always know what language is when language is at home for Bernstein, we do at moments know how to find that home and at least some of what language looks like when it puts on its slippers.

Even from Bernstein's perspective, then, which stands closer to my own than many of his peers, language in L=A=N=G=U=A=G=E markedly deviates from what is presently envisioned. Nevertheless, it remains possible to *think alongside* Bernstein's poetry and texts in order to grasp literature's conception within the present framework. As will become clearer when Cavell's work is discussed, the assumption that the text interpreted (whether literary or not) either expresses or otherwise shares the critic's beliefs, or, barring that, is not to be bothered with at any length, is rejected here, along with the alternatives it trades on. Precisely because literary expression and

---

[7] It should be noted that throughout this inquiry I will be turning to literary productions, which, like Bernstein's, occupy extremes of some sort. Such choices should not suggest that the considerations to which they lead apply only to the authors or examples or texts in question; they function as the criticism chapter 1 focused on did there. At the same time, most, indeed all, of the literature treated proves not to be *exemplars* of my theory, especially not my "literary theory." Beside the range of material treated here being wider, the present work's relation to its literary texts varies from the presumed norm (though whether that norm genuinely functions as such in any case may be doubted), insofar as interpretation first and foremost here applies to larger segments of discourse, in which attention to the work (itself taking varying guises) plays a secondary and open-ended role. My "readings" thus function as much as notes in an ongoing melody as chords in a cadence.

[8] Charles Bernstein, *Content's Dream: Essays 1975–1984* (Los Angeles: Sun and Moon Press, 1986); references given in the text to CD.

interpretation are both talk!, a greater back and forth between reader and text than any model of the text's "genius" permits holds sway in the current context.⁹

Reflecting on some of Bernstein's performances, then, can exhibit how talk! does not exclude what are usually taken as experiments with literary expression without invoking structures, words, and so on, and while literature and interpretation continue to maintain some concern for insight and truth. Let attention turn, accordingly, to one very short work of Bernstein's, a "poem" apparently composed of a single sentence. Though written well after L=A=N=G=U=A=G=E's first upsurge, this brief "piece"— untitled, or simply consisting in its title—can be viewed, on account of its compactness and its exemplarity, as the equivalent in the context of the L=A=N=G=U=A=G=E movement to Ezra Pound's "In a Station of the Metro" and the role Pound's text played in imagism and modernist poetry.¹⁰ Just as Pound's single-sentence poem famously encapsulated imagism and *vers libre* at the moment these movement first came to the fore, so Bernstein's text arguably similarly incarnates L=A=N=G=U=A=G=E's poetics.

On page 121 of the volume, *With Strings*, stands the following, "this poem intentionally left blank," all in lower case, bolded, and, of course, without any quotation marks.¹¹ Accompanied, as it is, by a page otherwise blank, Bernstein's poem refers, as most literate readers will recognize, to an inscription that sometimes appears in various published volumes, usually found on one or two pages near their beginning or end: "This page intentionally left blank." Lifting this formulation from everyday life, Bernstein not only underscores its own apparent strangeness, but, of course, by replacing "page" with "poem," also transforms that stretch of discourse into a declaration of his own approach to poetry. As in the preceding everyday usage, in this case, too, "intentionally" ("this poem *intentionally* left blank") orients the phrase, providing its fulcrum, in a different way, however, than in the printer's case. Here, "intentionally" apparently emphasizes the self-conscious and stated refusal of Bernstein's poetry to otherwise make a statement—that is, to engage in more standard forms of poetic performance or of discourse generally.

Being such a (deliberate) non-statement, the poem as such, similarly, declares a break, cleanly and wholly, with just those aspects of the poetic enterprise that customarily are privileged: expressing oneself and speaking for oneself—capacities Bernstein now famously once associated with "official verse culture" (*Content's Dream* 246). His is thus a poem that appears to eschew self-expression, while being about itself, as well as poetry and language more generally.

More specifically, the poem doubtless states, in a voice not wholly its own or wholly "original," a refusal to be a poem, embodying that anti-romantic and anti-lyric thrust perhaps not simply wrongfully associated with the totality of this movement (even if this was never the entire picture). Yet Bernstein's text does more than that. It simultaneously recurs to a world other than literature's, that of a society in which texts, including those of poetry, are produced and consumed. Gesturing, by dint of its

---

⁹ Cavell's discusses a text or work's "genius" in his essay on Emerson and Poe, "Being Odd, Getting Even" (*In Quest of the Ordinary: Lines of Skepticism and Romanticism* [Chicago: Chicago UP, 1990], 105–29.). I comment extensively on this work and on Cavell's hermeneutics in Chapter 3.
¹⁰ Pound's poem originally appeared in *Poetry* (April 1913), p. 12.
¹¹ Charles Bernstein, *With Strings* (Chicago: The University of Chicago Press, 2001).

citationality, toward the printing and publishing industries, Bernstein's performance combines a refusal to speak poetically (as customarily understood) with a vector toward the social conditions of literary production, thereby tracing a transgressive arc across both. Hence, the poem left blank ultimately takes a stand against contemporary modes of social production and consumption, particularly in the case of literature. Putting both registers into play, the non-expressive declaration and its reference to its "source" in a broader social context, Bernstein's line emblematizes the orienting ambitions of L=A=N=G=U=A=G=E as a whole.

Yet granting this account (to the precise status of which I will return), the question can be put: Where exactly is *language* in all of this? Where in this piece of L=A=N=G=U=A=G=E poetry is language in any of its usual guises (setting aside the issue of extrapolating from this one case the unique features of which I by no means wish to deny)?

For many literary critics (including some of those previously canvassed), language will reside precisely in what remains the same across Bernstein's "poem" and its forebear: namely, the sentence seemingly composed of the words "this ... intentionally left blank," omitting its variable portion. Bernstein himself frames language in terms of "words," and these presumably would be what is common to both inscriptions and of course would also cover the more usual inscription's "page" and the newly added term, "poem."

But can any model of language, based on either the word or the sign, genuinely be said to operate here? Even "poem," after all, seems not able to bear its customary meaning—this being the point of Bernstein's own enterprise. The issue first and foremost hinges on their being, in neither sentence, a meaning strictly derivable from language at all (understood as composed of words or as providing signs, signified, or morphemes). After all, in each case, neither the page nor the poem actually is *blank*. Something appears on the relevant pages. Yet it would be wrong to claim, on this basis, that what these inscriptions *say* is false, self-contradictory, or somehow metaphorical (as is immediately clear in the first, publishing case). To *talk!* in this way, to refer in each case to the page as blank, in the relevant instances, seems just fine. And this is because what is being said, the sense of so saying, resides entirely in *use*; it depends on the context the expression as a whole provides (rather than on any feature of its individual words), as well as on the broader worldly one in which the expression operates.

Language as usually understood never enters into the matter; parsing this message word by word, or sign by sign, could never render what is said intelligible. Bernstein's performance is thus only understandable as an instance of discourse or talk! Each inscription, Bernstein's and the printer's, permits apprehension or understanding only as talk!—as used within the publication context originally, and again by Bernstein. The brilliance of Bernstein's invention on my view redounds to this aspect of his "poem": to its piggybacking on a prior instance of *use*, while giving that use a new, yet not entirely new, role of its own to perform.

Of course, it might be replied that the foregoing misses the point. To be sure, what Bernstein's poem says and does depends on context. Language comes into this performance, however, with the signs, or more properly the signifiers taken apart *from any and all sense,* from any signifieds; these are what remain the "same" (though whether Bernstein himself would go this route may be doubted). Yet whether there are such entities as signifiers apart from discourse can be questioned (a concern already posed, if not simply wholly met, within late structuralism, as I and others have elsewhere discussed). Remaining with the present instance, notions such as the signifier prove prima facie inadequate, however, since Bernstein's work cannot merely *be quoted* or cited, while this capacity remains the touchstone of the foregoing categories. And should such semiotic instances, for this reason, be shown not to operate in any instance of speech or writing, their purview more generally, of course, comes into doubt

Bernstein's poem cannot be cited, only reported on, since it *includes the page* on which it is written, as does the printer's inscription. To what this inscription refers ("this page," "this poem") must indeed (otherwise) be blank. Bernstein's poem, act, or performance necessarily includes the page on which it appears, and it thus cannot genuinely be quoted. Indeed, even were the whole "object" "copied"—a page with this citation inserted into the present text—it would still not be cited, since it would not in this case operate in the same way. Not only is this inscription's standing upon a page wholly blank necessary, but the appearance of such a blank in certain contexts, in certain works and in certain kinds of work, and not others—publishing ones or loosely speaking literary ones—also is required for its operation.

A still further redoubt, however, may remain: something like language and semiosis, something exceeding the event of talk! is required at the very least to account for this inscription appearing as the same in multiple copies of Bernstein's book, *With Strings* itself, and similarly for multiple copies of any book, in which one and the same inscription is presumably to be found. The force of some sort of formal excess, perhaps going beyond language as such (the latter indebted to it, rather than the other way around), must operate to speak of the text, the same text, in the present sense.[12]

The foregoing, however, establishes that these instances cannot belong to language as usually conceived, owing to their being otherwise non-reproducible, non-citable. Moreover, the denial of existence to something like a semiotic force, moment, or substance is not ultimately on offer here, in any case, though that moment's operation would remain *subordinate to use,* and thus offer no ground for understanding literature and what is said more generally.[13] Nevertheless, staying with Bernstein's performance, that a demonstrative, namely "this," occurs in it is not an accident. Demonstratives function essentially as occurrences: events for which can be substituted no other semantic or propositional function (such as "the place at which the speaker or writer of the current text points"), though both the general terms on which it operates and

---

[12] I am of course referring to Derrida's notion of iterability as set out in his "Signature Event Context" (*Limited Inc.*, ed. Gerald Graff [Evanston, IL: Northwestern University Press, 1988], 7; see my "Signature Event Context'... in, Well, *Context*," for further discussion.

[13] Claude Shannon's pathbreaking information theory is the account of the materiality of signification that I here have in mind. What counts *as information,* however, can never be decided by this theory itself, which takes that determination as a given. Accordingly, though signification can be formalized, indeed even quantified, this feature lends no intelligibility to the discourse that serves as its precedent. See Shannon, *The Mathematical Theory of Communication,* ed. Warren Weaver (Urbana: University of Illinois Press, 1998). Weaver's commentary at the end offers a valuable restatement of Shannon's theory for those who cannot follow all of Shannon's formalism.

its results may subsequently be able to be given such a form.[14] Thus even if what is apparently the same page with the same inscription is found in multiple printed volumes of Bernstein's book, that is only because in each instance that inscription operates *individually*; its individual "this" in each case goes to work in this way, and only after the fact is it extrapolated as for all intents and purposes "the same" in every instance.

Bernstein's "poem" and the printer's inscription, accordingly, operate as *discourse in their entirety*, within concrete contexts, the parameters of which are never themselves simply determinable in advance.[15] All that is sometimes said to belong to language—its words, its signs, and even its materiality—accordingly, in the first instance operate as talk!, or not at all. Without Bernstein's poem's movement across a single instance of discourse within a single context (trailing its own kind of *discourse-based* repetition in its wake), as well as the movement from one context to another (found in Bernstein's invocation of a different context), these inscriptions' intelligibility and even identity fail. Hence, they depend not on any structure or shape for their understanding and recognition, but ultimately on something closer to a *history*, on the specific traditionality or historicity inherent in these concrete events of talk!

Such traditionality is unfolded at length in Chapter 4. A further lesson pertaining to literature and literary studies' functioning on talk!'s basis at this moment, however, may also be drawn. Though a difference apparently exists between the perspective here set forth and Bernstein's view of language within L=A=N=G=U=A=G=E, that divergence effaces neither what Bernstein is saying nor his own texts' appeal to their subject matter and the potential insights about it they may offer. Since, in his or any work, ultimately what is at issue is neither a word nor a concept, nor even a single sentence, but discourse, what Bernstein aims to speak about continues to have force when revisited again.

More concretely, "language" has been teased out at once with respect to Bernstein's saying concerning it, as well as *to what is being talked about*, language's own status as a subject matter. So approached, "language" when Bernstein and others in L=A=N=G=U=A=G=E spoke of it, and at present, have ultimately not been finally grasped in the same way. At the same time, all of us continue to be speaking *of something*, albeit what it is is only nailed down in the back and forth between their talk! and the present treatment. The subject matter, the worlded topic at issue, emerges beyond each of our perspectives, and yet also across them, as a common, albeit virtual

---

[14] Indeed, John Perry long ago showed, following Héctor-Neri Castañeda, that the demonstrative's work in context cannot be fully translated into any sort of propositional terms, its operation thus being concrete and contextual, radically particularized, even if general formulations of that operation remained possible and the information it supplies can subsequently be given propositional form ("Frege on Demonstratives," *The Philosophical Review* 86, no. 4 [October 1977]: 474–97). Interestingly, both Attridge and Altieri for their own readings of literature to work need to offer very different accounts of the demonstrative, ones by which I myself remain unpersuaded (Cf. SI 110 and Altieri, *Reckoning*, 120–1).

[15] I might, after all, have written a different book like this one in which this poem could stand, and it is not clear, even in Bernstein's case, if his might be, or also be, a piece of theory. The blurb supplied by his publisher speaks of *With Strings* as a "A *companion* to the critically acclaimed *My Way*, his 1999 montage of essays, conversations, and poems" (my emphasis).

point of reference, while the terms on which it is presented change. Accordingly, what is spoken of, in distinction from the discourse about it, glimmers in such interchanges, here being confined to no (single set of) concepts, even as it always remains something taken up (again) in the relevant discourse.

In interpretation, as construed on discourse's basis, divergences and agreements together, like a one-time living lattice, permit glimpsing the item or matter being talked about; this cannot be doubted in the present instance, in Bernstein's case especially, since Bernstein already has some sympathy with a talk!-based approach, and he thus takes an allied view of these matters at moments, especially when defending *formal experimentation in art more generally*.

More specifically, in "Stray Straws and Strawmen," Bernstein insists that the production of all art, including, especially, art known for experimental and formal innovation, hinges on a *decision* (even when such works are said to arise from the subconscious or chance).[16] That declaration has obvious resonances to the role assigned to "intentionally" in the poem that I just discussed. The ability of modernist works, such as Gertrude Stein's or the late Yeats, depends on decision and intention to be recognized as art at all, according to Bernstein. Speaking of things like automatic writing, he insists: "Various formal decisions are made and these decisions shape the work" (CD 47). Bernstein himself thus here strikes upon a variant of literature as talk!, viewing verbal art in part as relying on persons and their doings. To be clear, on the present understanding, Bernstein's affirmation receives a somewhat different emphasis. What remains key is not so much that such undertakings entail decisions—that formally oriented events are fundamentally products of selection—but that such experiments are always after something, always pursuing a question, a problem, a possibility, and only in such contexts do they take hold, something Bernstein in part also suggests. Contra Bernstein, however, one *can* truly randomize a work, as do John Cage or Tristan Tzara, without endorsing (or not) any given sequence so produced. This very procedure, however, only takes shape within, and only functions *as* part of what is here being called discourse—it emerges within broader contexts than any single chance product, permitting this last its own identity as such, while being advanced with the aim, again, of disclosing some bit of the world or of life along with whatever new variations in writing or music happen to be generated.

In a discourse-based context, such is the final disposition or avatar of what throughout this chapter has been called "literary form." All such experiments with "form," from those of loners like Harry Partch to such gregarious types as Ezra Pound or Stein herself, take shape in broader, ultimately temporal contexts, whereby they necessarily imply a variety of worlded features and a range of problems or questions (for example, that of the subconscious, matter, or of chance itself). Insofar as from the first they are so motivated, these productions concern aspects of existence, and are thus never simply "formal." Correspondingly, a lens other than that of the work (while not simply leaving it or aspects of it out of the picture) accompanies their production, as well as subsequent encounters with them. A web or net more capacious than any single text or performance is always already in place, which does not overwrite any of these

---

[16] Bernstein, *Content's Dream*, 40–9.

individual instances, but instead encompasses and buoys them up. These adventures, and ultimately all literary exercises, accordingly, possess a larger and different weave than the work or any of its purported forms—the latter, the supposed forms, themselves always arising and disappearing within discourse, both in literature and in its reading, where formal features stand forth only thanks to momentary and often highly variable articulations and apprehensions.

Formal experiments thus still remain possible; the stick of talk!, as it were can always be picked up from the other end (and this relates, for example, to the spelling or sound of words or syntax, and the meters of poetry, all of which here are seen as housed in use). Such experiments, at the same time, take shape within a still wider compass of concerns and context, where these forms as such and these instances exist only in discourse, while appearing within a changing understanding that includes them *and* what is at stake in their various transformations.[17]

But if this is true in this case, within avant-garde work, in self-declared "formal" experiments, how much more will it prove to be so in instances such as the realist novel, the classical or romantic lyric (as well as the symbolist or modernist poem or story)? All of these finally exist only as discourse, if the foregoing is correct, and thus are always already worlded, and always about, or concerned with some thing or matter, as a part of what they take themselves to be and to do. They aim at questions, insights, and noticings—various kinds of commentary—both through what these literary endeavors choose to repurpose (as in Bernstein's case) and also on account of the innovations to which they subject these, their preceding occasions.

That it is to say, recurring to the theme of imaginativeness, citation or collage, and what is sometimes opposed to them, metaphor or figure (with their novelty), are but two results of a single possibility. Collage and figure function along one and the same spectrum without entailing any structural or generic difference in kind. Literature reworks usages from other walks of life *at the same time* that it invents new ones. All literature is thus like Bernstein's example: it is a repurposing of things we say or do, which harbors such recurrence even as it begets new variations, with a view to some sort of insight or disclosure or understanding (including that concerning and provided by feelings and moods).

This same repurposing, which includes, rather than fends off, aboutness, worldedness, and reference, finally, provides an opening for *criticism* (or interpretation or commentary). Criticism, too, repurposes; it repurposes literature's repurposing, in its own case also always with some issue, problem, or concern in mind, never simply with an aim at the literary or the text in itself.[18] This does not entail that reading becomes

---

[17] The example of metered poetry is, in some way, the most interesting, in fact, because it is the most difficult, as it seems to function without much regard to what any given instance of it is about. Before insisting that its existence necessitates language and forms, recall, however, that it is older than any conception of language and indeed, in some instance, the existence of scripts. Its practice precedes any version of its theorization, including the notion of meter as such; thus it, too, had to be and still is discourse-based, residing in that traditionality discussed below.

[18] The working of commentary or reading, especially as it pertains to those instances found in the Humanities, where imaginativeness or novelty, along with legibility and repeatability, are preeminently in question, is treated again in Chapters 3 and 4, and still more extensively and granularly in Chapters 8 and 9 of the present work.

impossible or nugatory. Just as Bernstein could not have chosen just any stretch of talk! from which to start his poem, the same is true of the critic. Accordingly, whatever critical discussion these prior literary articulations find, they emerge insofar as literature, too, is understood as talk!, and not from some point of view presumed above or apart from them—that of language or logic (of a syntax or a semantics of concepts), nor from that of signs or of words. As should be clear by now, this absence of governing formal constraints does not entail that one may just say anything (to some extent precisely the opposite) nor even that one cannot contest different treatments made in different contexts, since along with their being such different unfoldings of some text, these same unfoldings can be rehearsed and reorganized again on subsequent occasions. It does require, however, that whatever transpires within literature and criticism, as well as in any other textual interpretation, finds no other measure than the insight or understanding, the discovery or novel questioning it affords on that occasion, in respect both to the stretch of talk!—the text or texts—in question, and to the matters at hand—matters and texts already standing within an at least implicit repetition, and, hence, subject to always being revisited again.

3

From Persons to Words

"I am Stanley Cavell"

Earlier, the following chart was offered:

Form
Closest to Tradition	Historically Specific	Reworked on Non-exceptionalist Terms	?
Attridge	Poovey	Altieri	Cavell

After the preceding discussion of Attridge, Poovey, and Altieri, that chart may also be set out like this:

Persons
And Language	Socially Specific	Reworked on Exceptionalist Terms	?
Attridge	Poovey	Altieri	Cavell

The second template shows how persons in each case gain greater prominence as form's and language's autonomy becomes eroded and transformed. Though the novelty and imaginativeness thought to define literature can exist on new ground, their source retreats further from language and its structures. Such a movement away from language is already evident in Attridge. His emphasis on authors and readers, as well as on the event, as integral to literature's singularity, significantly departs from accounts of deconstruction that regularly proclaim the "death" or irrelevance of persons. Poovey, in turn, takes socially and historically specific practices as the basis for literature's autonomous (imaginary) worlds and self-reflexive forms. Persons, inserted in practices keyed to socially concrete genres, underpin her account. For Altieri, essentially worlded persons and their displays, bearing a vector toward the ineffable, install the imagination's operation across everyday life, literary expression emerging as a subset of this possibility. Persons, characterized by Altieri by their partial nonappearance, and for this reason inherently linked to the imaginary, give to literature and other aesthetic achievements their leeway.

In the present context, Cavell's work completes the foregoing trajectory. Influenced by J. L. Austin, and, above all, Ludwig Wittgenstein, Cavell, from his earliest publications on, rejects every customary or constituted notion of language, every attempt that would define language as any sort of autonomous system; similarly, he gainsays talk of literary form as found in the New Critics. Furthermore, those aspects or vectors of the person that unintentionally come asunder in Altieri, seemingly merely by dint of being mentioned—persons' worlded, socialized existence, and their transcendental/transcendent status—elude this fate in Cavell, where they function as one. For Cavell, personhood is inseparable from the concrete individual's empirical existence. Hence, Cavell's stance presents the most extreme version of the person's embrace.

Cavell's approach, similarly, shifts the ground on which discussion itself proceeds, calling into question the already etiolated notion of a "last instance" that functions in the other three accounts. In Cavell, the foregrounding of the role of concrete individuals in all expression and understanding leads to the withdrawal of finality from every account and the affirmation of philosophical and critical discourse's inherent open-endedness. Structural or really any sort of fixed grounds cease to be in question in talk!; hence, the burden of understanding falls entirely on individuals and their apprehensions. Conversely, what Cavell sometimes refers to as the plight of our being human, as it relates to each one of us, is bound up with this same open-endedness. That plight consists in both a desire for a final account of who we are and an encounter with this account's absence, the acknowledgment of the necessary lack of any identifiable necessity in human understanding.

Before turning to his earliest writings, where the significance of persons just claimed perhaps most readily appears, it is worthwhile to first give a broader look at Cavell's achievements. Even today the striking breadth and winding paths of Cavell's corpus remain relatively unknown, so that situating his first productions, to which attention is about to turn, in the context of the panoply of Cavell's accomplishments is useful.

* * *

I am Stanley Cavell. It is 1962; I am currently a fellow at the Institute for Advanced Study at Princeton, and have not yet arrived (back) at Harvard, where I will eventually be *Walter M. Cabot Professor of Aesthetics and the General Theory of Value*. I remain preoccupied by the problem of explaining the sort of philosophy I do, which I understand to be inherited from Wittgenstein and Austin. Though I have already deeply mulled a version of this problem in my recently completed dissertation, I will not publish that text, now known as *The Claim of Reason*, for almost twenty more years, and that only after numerous revisions and struggles with its final section.

I initially encountered John Langshaw Austin's thought when he lectured at Harvard while I was a Junior Fellow at the Harvard Society of Fellows, pursuing my second year of doctoral work. Upon hearing Austin lecture, I dropped the original plan for my thesis (devoted to ethics), and took over his way of doing philosophy for myself. I delved further into Wittgenstein's and John Wisdom's work, and, after securing an appointment at Berkeley in 1957, I was more or less forced by my department, at the close of the 1950s, to present a paper defending my and their approach. That essay became the titular one of my first book, *Must We Mean What We Say?*, a book that I only published at the end of the 1960s.

In 1962, in an address delivered to the American Philosophical Association, I took up aesthetics—the aesthetic judgment of Hume and Kant—but also the New Criticism and questions of form and concerns about whether poetry or metaphor can be paraphrased.[1] I will address the topic of aesthetics again, in a field with which I had been long familiar, music, my first love, a few years later at a conference held at Oberlin College. Monroe Beardsley, one of the leading New Critics, with whose work I do not engage in my earlier discussion, comments on that paper, "Music Decomposed," when I deliver it. I respond to his arch, critical, and systematizing response in the strong style that is already my own, in "A Matter of Meaning of It," published in the conference proceedings, and later as a chapter in *Must We Mean*.

Though addressing problems in literary criticism as such again but rarely, I remain throughout my lifetime a strong reader of literature. In *Must We Mean*, I already mount now seminal discussions of Shakespeare's *King Lear* and Beckett's *Endgame*. My *Claim* ends with an extended interpretation of *Othello*; throughout my career, moreover, I offer numerous interpretations of Thoreau, Emerson, and the Romantics. I am also perhaps the first in English to "theorize" film and engage in extensive commentaries on it, publishing an entire volume devoted to cinema in 1971. In that work, *The World Viewed*, I also set forth my understanding of modernism, modernity, and medium. I continue to offer readings of film, and the great Hollywood comedies of the 1930s assume a central place in my thought. A number of my texts, finally, especially my later ones, have an autobiographical aspect. My last major publication, *Little Do I Know*, yields an experiment in this genre, mixing extended discussions of the philosophical topics that have interested me throughout my life with recountings of my life's formative episodes.

Though in notable quarters of analytic philosophy my work, upon its appearances, astonishes and amazes (and many of my students become well-regarded professors in their own right), during much of my lifetime, it is not widely referred to or discussed—neither in philosophy nor in literary studies—albeit I am one of the very few non-continental US philosophers to address literature, the arts, and the broader issues attendant upon their interpretation. That larger stage proves occupied instead by a coterie of French thinkers, the attraction of which I at least partially understand, but the soundness of which I sometimes doubt. In the last ten years or more, the previous neglect has altered, and all signs suggest that this change of fortune will only continue.

* * *

First-person speech in the foregoing highlights the centrality of the notion of personhood for all Cavell thinks and writes; it thus intends no disrespect. Cavell's conceives of the person in part in overlap with the self in an existentialist context.[2] His

---

[1] Stanley Cavell, *Little Did I Know: Excerpts from Memory* (Stanford, CA: Stanford University Press, 2010), 411.
[2] An early essay by Cavell, "Existential and Analytic Philosophy," perhaps too blatantly attests to existentialism's influence on his own thinking. Only much later anthologized, EAP, as it will

version of these notions—alongside some others Cavell finds implied by them, such as the everyday—finally stand preeminent among all his reference points.

To take a step back: in the Anglo-American philosophical context more generally after the Second World War, persons and their attendant capacities prove inseparable from discourse's burgeoning conception. (This remains true up until the 1980s when a renewed push toward logical inquiry, in part made possible by Grice's work and also that of Richard Montague, as well as by advances in modal logic, takes hold—a tendency perhaps only very recently again waning.) In many of these writings, capacities viewed as intrinsically belonging to *persons*—beliefs, attitudes, intentions, and norms—are said to underlie discourse and its operation. A spectrum of positions (similar to the one offered in the previous section) exists, with Searle, and those who would advance various rule-governed conceptions (themselves specific to persons, such as rules pertaining to illocutionary acts), on one side, to Davidson and Grice (who in different ways do with less structure and rule) to still more radical pragmatics, or to Heidegger's early work, at that time not at all part of the discussion, on the other.

Even amid these developments, however, Cavell proves something of an outlier. He both radicalizes and rethinks the status of persons in the analytic context, in part owing to his interest in a wider range of philosophy, including existentialism. Cavell differentiates himself from all his peers, most of all, however, as, for him, personhood proves intrinsically *a problem*. For Cavell, personhood ultimately exceeds the authority and legitimacy of reason; it stands before, and to some extent beyond its "claim." The opposite vantage point that grants reason unquestioned primacy, to be clear, is more or less baked in to the pursuit of analytic philosophy, though there reason's limits at moments are also rigorously tested, in part owing to the depths of analytic philosophy's commitment to rationality.

Cavell questions the status of the person and personhood as a self-evidently given thing or consciousness or existent, and indeed conceives personhood essentially as a problem or question, rather than as a ground, or as a moment entailing structures, norms, rules, and other algorithmically reckonable capacities. Personhood, for him, does not, of course, prove problematic in the sense of failing to exist. Personhood and the person's existence instead know a special kind of positivity and experience all their own.

Another signature theme of Cavell's, worth getting out on the table with an eye to what is to come, underscores how Cavell stands at a decisive distance from persons as "rational animals" while still insisting on their centrality in their own positivity. This theme is skepticism. Skepticism is one avenue by which the ultimately unstable yet decisive status of persons in Cavell's writing becomes visible. Cavell's treatment of skepticism is, to be clear, unique. In a nutshell, Cavell questions those skeptical arguments so central to modern philosophy (those of Descartes and his successors), while also diverging from, indeed rejecting (more or less), all *refutations* of these

---

henceforth be designated, again receives mention in the present discussion ("Existential and Analytic Philosophy," *Daedalus* 93 [Summer 1964]: 946–74).

positions. Such refutations ultimately move on the same ground as skepticism itself, according to Cavell.[3]

By questioning both sets of views (both pro and con), Cavell loosens the notion of reason's hold on the person. Ultimately, for Cavell, only persons, embodied selves, can account for the authority of our practices and understanding, and that in the face of each other, with all the ambiguity and uncertainty to which such a circumstance leads, including the impulse to find a different more firm ground (the tendency toward a foundation or an "in itself" remaining inescapable).

Personhood as conceived by Cavell, accordingly, finally emerges, not as a problem, but as a *problematic* in Heidegger's sense: it always remains and must remain a problem or question. Yet this interrogation, as noted, indeed by no means results in *less* emphasis being placed on persons (or selves) in Cavell's thinking than in his peers. The person, myself, and others, in our concrete individuality, indeed furnish whatever last resort there is, while this entire layer or stratum, escapes all knowledge, instead grasped only in being "acknowledged," by other persons (and they by oneself), as Cavell now famously puts it. By combining a persons' acknowledgment and centrality with the absence of all ground or foundation, the person proves the focal point at once of Cavell's philosophizing and of his practice of philosophy.

These powerful insights of Cavell's will of course be further canvassed and set out. The aim throughout their exposition at no point, to be clear, is to foreclose or even to blunt them. Nevertheless, Cavell's disclosure of the person turns out to entail very specific notions pertaining to language and history. Accordingly, in light of these decisions—not only what they buy but also what they cost Cavell—the notion of talk! or discourse already introduced, ultimately different from Cavell's own, is further unfolded. Some of Cavell's reckoning with language and discourse, in particular his distinction between primary and secondary usages, and his related construal of metaphor, raise questions regarding what Cavell himself inherits or takes on board from that tradition in which he worked. These decisions, moreover, weigh most on Cavell's practice and conception of interpretation, his hermeneutics; in respect to this theme, the most significant distance between his endeavor and the present one results.

Viewing discourse preeminently in relation to time and temporality, the present construal, to be clear, ultimately neither severs talk! from people or persons altogether (though these will stand in need of reconception) nor places their existence, even as so problematized, at the center of what transpires within talk!, in the fashion of Cavell. Persons instead become subordinated to a more radical temporal dimension, a kind of becoming, that Cavell's own framing, it is here argued, ultimately downplays or even omits. On the basis of this temporality, the present account elaborates a more radically discursive, or talk!-based conception of expression and of understanding. This same view

---

[3] Cavell discusses philosophical skepticism in two swoops in *The Claim of Reason* (Oxford: Oxford University Press, 1999; orig. 1979), hereafter CR. He examines skepticism first in CR's section II, where its discussion is somewhat unusually divided by an excursus on Wittgenstein's views on language. Cavell returns to skepticism in Part IV, to which discussion turns at the end of *A New Philosophy's* Chapter 5. Whether, in his initial sally, Cavell himself wholly maintains the force of the skeptic's questions in the face of its purported refutation is not clear to the present reader. Skepticism's discussion is a central theme, of course, in the Cavell literature.

of discourse also entails a hermeneutics different from Cavell's, in part owing to its refusal to differentiate between ordinary and other usages of language, while Cavell, as we will see, perhaps following Wittgenstein, when discussing such usage, divides it into two great genres or classes, primary and secondary, to which only metaphors do not belong.[4]

3.1 Persons

"—It is impossible to say just what I mean!"
T. S. Eliot, *The Love Song of J. Alfred Prufrock*

Gleaning Cavell's account of personhood, along with the unique open-endedness it entails, is the first task that here must be tackled; the second half of Cavell's 1969 "Aesthetic Problems of Modern Philosophy" is the site from which this labor begins.[5]

As noted, in his earliest work, Cavell repeatedly attempts to account for his own approach to philosophy; many of his essays find him explaining his stance. At that time, competing initiatives were rife that also invoked discourse and language, some inspired by Noam Chomsky's work in linguistics. Their practitioners doubted the contents of, and the evidence for, the reports that Austin, the later Wittgenstein, and Cavell himself offered on those topics. The latters' descriptions of our language and usage, according to the former thinkers, lacked any scientific or genuinely empirical basis, while also not being argumentative, logical, or deductive—thus they were not philosophical (i.e., comprehensive and universal) in any recognizable sense.[6]

A relatively early instance of Cavell's confronting these worries is provided by AP. AP here further serves as a touchstone for Cavell's early thinking, because, in it, Cavell explicitly addresses issues of literary form and of figural and metaphoric language, matters that he will never again confront at such length, with the exception of an essay he wrote virtually at the same time as AP, EAP.

Cavell's focus on literature and art in AP has a much wider scope than would otherwise be anticipated. AP aims to account for Cavell's *philosophy's own way of working*, in part with an eye to the aforementioned critics, by *turning to literature*, to the aesthetic, and to the arts. Judgments concerning these latter topics provide the

---

[4] In Cavell's *The Senses of Walden* (Chicago: University of Chicago Press, 1992; expanded edition, orig. 1972), 15 ff., he draws a distinction between mother and father tongues that parallels the one that he makes between secondary and primary usages in *Claim*.
[5] "The Aesthetic Problems of Modern Philosophy," in *Must We Mean What We Say?: A Book of Essays* (Cambridge: Cambridge University Press, 2002; orig. 1969), 44–96; hereafter AP.
[6] Most notably, Jerry Fodor and Jerry Katz (both still under the influence of Chomsky) had echoed a criticism already made by one Benson Mates (to which Cavell's first writing on this topic, "Must We Mean What We Say?" is in part a response). The discourse of philosophers such as Wittgenstein or Austin about language, for these critics, fail of true access to either topic, since they do not yield genuine empirical knowledge—of the deep structures of our language, in the one case, or of the statistical frequency of our words and their usages, in the other. Cavell's "Availability of Wittgenstein's Later Philosophy," a scathing review of David Pole's *A Treatment of Wittgenstein's Later Philosophy* treats similar themes, as Pole offhandedly raised concerns much like those of Bates and Fodor and Katz.

model whereby Cavell responds to those erstwhile questioners of what now would be called OLP.

AP's greatest ambitions, accordingly, are encapsulated and arguably performed in the second half of AP at a moment when Cavell, ringing a series of changes on his philosophy's characterization, ends with an outburst, an anacoluthon, reminiscent of that voiced by the narrator of T. S. Eliot's "The Love Song of J. Alfred Prufrock." Cavell breaks off and confesses to an inability to authoritatively express his own philosophical standpoint, in intonations much like Prufrock's when pretending to speak to a comely woman about why he, Prufrock, cannot speak with her. Cavell's unusual remark at once signals that his and Wittgenstein's philosophy's mode of saying is a problem *for Cavell*, not just his critics, while also gesturing toward the unprecedented resolution of that problem to which he will come, entailing a shunning of all last instances, and an incompleteness or open-endedness, of the sort just mentioned.

Cavell, more specifically, had ventured that the understanding of language that his and Wittgenstein's observations supply, the status of their remarks about what we say, falls under the rubric of "psychology." Psychology may only serve this purpose, however, it can only identify the domain of his philosophical findings on language and its use, Cavell further stipulates, if psychology's "psychologizing" would be *undone*, along the lines of Frege's and Edmund Husserl's undoing of the "psychologizing" of logic (AP 91).[7] Confronted by the considerable difficulty of actually carrying out this task, Cavell next confesses that "I cannot describe to anyone's satisfaction what *it* is"— "it," referring to his own philosophical practice—thus echoing Eliot's narrator's cry: "It is impossible to say just what I mean."

Cavell, accordingly, is quite cognizant of the barbs of his critics, who ask for whom do you speak when you say "we" and who wonder how he gets further than individual belief or opinion. Cavell's demand for the depsychologizing of psychology attests to his awareness of the difficulties that he faces in rendering the individual and her concrete judgments a basis for reporting on our expressions and their use; it also, of course, speaks to the centrality of individual persons for Cavell's own thinking. Cavell's own philosophizing, he here intimates, depends on the perspectives of concrete actual subjects or persons (thus answering to a "psychology") while assigning these a more general or fundamental standpoint than is customary (corresponding to this psychology's depsychologization). His final exclamation, moreover, mirrors this conflict, while resolving it only in a negative manner, since the absence of satisfaction there recorded and assigned to "anyone" ("I cannot describe to anyone's satisfaction what *it* is") obviously includes Cavell himself.

To pursue these topics that Cavell's profession of inadequacy invokes, especially the role of persons and the potential incompleteness or open-endedness of his new philosophy, the text-based discussion in which Cavell is already engaged must be brought into view. In AP's second half, Cavell turns to Kant and his treatment of the

---

[7] Here by the way, Cavell's relative unfamiliarity with phenomenology, a term he may have taken from Wittgenstein or Austin, though also perhaps Heidegger, seems a hindrance, since Husserl in his late works actually attempts precisely what Cavell describes: the removal of psychologization from psychology. (See Husserl's *Phenomenological Psychology*; this text was important to the young Jacques Derrida, who comments on it in his Introduction to *Voice and Phenomenon*.)

aesthetic to fend off, or at least engage, those qualms about his own speaking voiced by his critics and in part himself. The second half of AP stages a sort of three-way dialogue—or perhaps better, two simultaneous duologues—with Cavell investigating aesthetic judgment by way of Kant, while simultaneously addressing criticisms of his own and Wittgenstein's philosophizing.

Cavell, in fact, draws but peripherally on Kant's own presentation of the aesthetic judgment's character in Kant's *Critique of Judgement*, and what Cavell omits or contests in Kant's account turns out to be as important as what he foregrounds. Cavell latches on to an aperçu, almost an aside, offered by Kant in a footnote. In it, Kant distinguishes between aesthetic judgments of taste ("Michaelangelo's David is beautiful") and those of merely sensual pleasure ("Canary wine is pleasant"). Kant further indicates that anyone who would take these judgments as equivalent and thus view the judgment "that something is *beautiful*" as saying the same as "something is beautiful *for me*" would assert something "laughable." For Kant, aesthetic judgments, judgments of beauty, unlike statements about sensual enjoyment, necessarily aim at *universal assent*, albeit in a different way from, and on different grounds than, statements of fact and other "objective" truths; that is the point of his aperçu.

Cavell takes up Kant's anecdote, then, both to unpack aesthetic judging and to shed light on his own philosophy's mode of speaking and philosophizing. Not only the model found in aesthetic judgments but also the *philosophical* judgment that Kant passes in his *aside*, which conforms to this same template, exhibit Cavell's and Wittgenstein's way of philosophizing. Kant's anecdote, *as an anecdote*, presents the kind of philosophical observation (or judgment) Cavell's own thinking about language employs and Kant's recourse to the self-evidently laughable shares this occasional and individual aspect found in aesthetic judgments themselves—in judgments about an artwork's beauty and value.

Accordingly, aesthetic evaluations and OLP's apprehensions about "what we say" possess an identical seemingly paradoxical status: these statements lay claim to going beyond a merely individual standpoint; they invoke some species of "necessity" and somehow speak for all of us; yet they rest on no argument nor on any other kind of demonstration beyond what seems obvious to the one making them. Cavell's most direct answer to his critics lies in this coincidence between the judgments made by his philosophy and those of taste as handled by Kant.

Cavell's or Wittgenstein's observations, to be clear, are not for all that unmotivated, as Cavell himself insists. Instead, they are based on a seeing, a "getting it" performed by individuals, just as when Kant deems the error in question *self-evidently* laughable. Cavell thus further lays out this remarkable "sense of necessity . . . we feel in such judgments"— his answer to critics like Fodor and Katz and Mates—by stating that it is essential that at some point that we be prepared to say, "don't you see, don't you dig" (AP 93).

Cavell's second-person address ("you"), at this moment, as well as his "dig" are indeed telling. In question, they underscore, is an *individual* perspective, not of persons, but of *these persons*. This speaker finds *this* necessity (here, that "beauty" not only be "for me") in her judgment. At the same time, being so individuated, this insight is one that each interlocutor must see themselves. Judgments about our words' usages are, then, of exactly the same sort as of the word "beauty" (as passed by Kant), as well as those that arise in concrete instances of aesthetic judgment.

Individuals and their seemingly contingent reports are central to Cavell's and Wittgenstein's philosophy's achievements; yet their thinking indeed also speaks for all in the singular manner of aesthetic judgments and of Kant's aperçu. How this intersection between individual personhood and "all" finally is to be conceived, upon what it does or does not ultimately rest for Cavell, becomes further evident in the closing pages of AP, where Cavell's Prufrockian outburst turns out to resonate.

Coming to his essay's conclusion, Cavell explicitly refers to OLP's talk of "what *we* say" when making reports on linguistic usage, and asks about its status (AP 95). There, he again emphasizes the non-fungibility of a first-person point of view—some person or self's perspective for his thinking—but also lays bare the terrain, ultimately more tenuous than Kant's, on which this first-person perspective operates.

Cavell, concluding AP, in fact questions those aspects of Kant's treatment that, for Kant, underlie aesthetic judgments' special type of universality and necessity: namely, the necessarily *shared humanity* at work in the making of such judgments. Speaking of OLP's own use of "we," Cavell insists: "This plural is still first person: it does not, to use Kant's word, 'postulate' that we, you and I, say and want and imagine and feel and suffer together" (AP 96).

Cavell, accordingly, sets aside what for Kant, specifically on side of the subject, ultimately lets aesthetic judgments speak for all. In judgments of taste, according to Kant, our agreement is assumed in advance by the speaker's positioning, even if it is not always achieved in its outcome. In the very tendering of such judgments, in expressing themselves thus, the speaker, according to Kant, posits his own standpoint as that of a universal judge. Each speaks in "a universal voice," which is itself subtended by what Kant calls a *sensus communis*, a common or shared sensibility, envisioned as operating in essentially the same fashion in every individual's encounter with beauty.

For Cavell, however, participation in philosophical judgments, as well as those concerning art, is never so secured (though neither is it constantly in doubt). Kant's universal voice and the *sensus communis* remain absent from Cavell's reckoning with Kant, along with that "play of faculties," which, on Kant's account, is occasioned by the object and responsible for beauty's experience. Accordingly, Cavell's philosophical and artistic criticism are more contingent and more tenuous than Kant's own. For Cavell, a permanent possibility exists that "you and I" may not "say, want and suffer together"—in which case, your philosophy and your aesthetics will be irrelevant to me and mine to yours. Nothing common to us all insures the "we." Hence Cavell grants a non-fungible open-endedness to our speech and talk that in part hearkens back to Wittgenstein's rendering in PI of the understanding of others and of the world as depending on the intersection of manifold strands of seemingly otherwise contingent circumstances.[8]

That is not to say, of course, as Cavell himself hastens to add, that the observations his philosophy makes, therefore, *are irrelevant* to others. Rather, pushing still further the aesthetic model, his philosophy's descriptions, he indicates, "like art are powerless to prove their relevance and this shows what sort of relevance they have" (AP 96). At this moment, then, Cavell's distance from the traditional self-understanding of philosophy

---

[8] This last phrase in effect summarizes what Wittgenstein, and Cavell following him, call "forms of life"; this notion is explicitly unpacked later.

attains perhaps its greatest amplitude. His thought mimes aesthetic *judgment*, but ultimately is like *art itself*: powerless to command assent. In this heretofore unparalleled view of philosophical utterance, any appeal to *reason* thus seems almost entirely lost from view. To be sure, confronted with the failure by another to see or understand, preparatory labor can be undertaken, Cavell states, both in art and in philosophy. Explanations can be tendered and relevant features of a work pointed out. Yet such judgments ultimately stand on nothing but themselves and their occasional being cobbled together.

Cavell's Prufrockian exclamation already discussed, correspondingly, anticipates this last version of philosophical discourse that AP tenders. Cavell's inability to identify to anyone's satisfaction his philosophy's character turns out not to be a bug, but a feature; it is built into his philosophy as one that is ever powerless to prove its relevance and hence this incapacity can never disappear. Just as Prufrock's declaration "It is impossible to say just what I mean" is redirected by Eliot at the end of his poem to his own poetic mode of insight and expression—when "human voices wake us and we drown," the entire poem being swallowed up—so Cavell's "it is impossible to say to anyone's satisfaction" characterizes his ultimate view of philosophical and aesthetic judgment in contrast to Kant's.

To be clear, in this section of AP, such silence itself affords a working answer to OLP's critics and interlocutors rather than a failure to provide a rejoinder. In his conclusion, moreover, Cavell continues to invite discussion and inquiry, insisting, in his final paragraph, on the character of his speaking as "a claim about our lives" that does not brook standard liberal forms of tolerance.[9] Cavell thus does not intend to simply be giving up on his and Wittgenstein's discussions of "what we say."[10] In fact, for at least the next twenty-five years, Cavell affirms that remarking on our usage is (his) philosophy's main *labor*; philosophy's task is in part the unearthing of logical, grammatical, and "transcendental" differences along the lines first set out in Kant's footnote, where the difference between aesthetic judgments and those of sensual pleasure are identified. Cavell speaks at that moment of finding a "metaphysical" or "logical" distinction. "Kant," he continues, "calls it a transcendental difference; Wittgenstein would call it a grammatical difference"(AP 90).[11]

---

[9] Cavell insists on all this in the final paragraph of AP, after also stating in his penultimate one, where his likening of philosophy to art is to be found, that "all the philosopher, this kind of philosopher, can do is to express, as fully as he can, his world and attract our undivided attention to our own" (AP 96). Whether these two affirmations are wholly on all fours can be left for each reader to decide.

[10] Cavell indeed continues to trade on observations and descriptions that, as in the case of "beauty," anticipate concepts' and words' relation to the world, as well to other aspects of our talk. Cavell's philosophy, as he puts it, captures "the difference" in "the kind of judgement in question," "the nature of the concepts employed," and "even the nature of reality," presumably of what is being judged about, here beauty (90).

[11] Thus, almost precisely twenty years after the first half of AP was written, in his 1983 "Emerson, Coleridge, Kant," Cavell explicitly repeats the construal of ordinary language philosophy's treatment of language here in question. He first refers to "Kant's ... Copernican revolution," and then picks up on his own earlier gloss of philosophy's work in terms of Kant's transcendental undertaking. "Kant's ... Copernican revolution," Cavell tells us in Cavell's own work becomes "radicalized, so that not just twelve categories of the understanding are to be deduced, but *every word in the language*—not as a matter of psychological fact, but as a matter of, say, psychological necessity" (my emphasis 38). Cavell, concluding this paragraph by mentioning that earlier instances in which he offered this sort of account of Wittgenstein' philosophy's work exist, thus proclaims: "Here I am, still at it" (38).

Even as Cavell never ceases to be faithful to these judgments, despite the complexity of identifying whence they are launched, the role of what cannot be said, of where talk ceases proves still more complicated: such silence, in a somewhat different guise, had already been a leading concern in part one of AP—now in respect to philosophy's aims as a whole and Wittgenstein's own innovations in philosophy's self-understanding. What is known, shown, or remarked upon concerning discourse or talk! by Cavell and Wittgenstein may entail certain stipulations as to the limits of its authority, thus bringing a breaking-off of its own discourse as found in part two. Accompanying that exposition is a second, doubtless related, silence about what this novel enterprise yields as a whole in respect to philosophy's traditional concern for disclosing fundamental truths about human life and human doings, about ourselves and about our world as a whole.

Grasping this earlier phase of Cavell's thinking in AP must be further pursued, then, since it lets be rounded out the standing of persons for Cavell, while bringing Cavell's own view of discourse, specifically philosphical discourse, further to fore.

On this second score concerning philosophy's *aims*, Cavell brings silence to bear still more radically in fact than at AP's end. His and Wittgenstein's new philosophy's point, Cavell insists, consists wholly in *a* dissolution and disappearance of problems, rather than in providing answers or persuading others about the rightness of some views— views being precisely what are not on offer on the present construal. That is to say, Wittgenstein's new philosophy is a kind of "therapy," according to Cavell—a claim that also presents obstacles to its acceptance as philosophy, ones perhaps even greater than the intrinsically vague status of OLP's reports on "what we say."[12] Speaking specifically of that version of therapy, psychoanalysis, which he maps on to the Wittgensteinian one, Cavell declares that in his and Wittgenstein's philosophizing "the more one learns . . . the less one is able to say what one has learned, not because you have forgotten what it was, but because nothing you said could seem like an answer or solution" (AP 85).

His and Wittgenstein's thought's labor as a whole, then, is attuned to a strikingly new and different end in comparison with that previously found in the philosophical tradition, bringing with it a still more profound silence about their philosophy's accomplishments. Their philosophical practice aims at a transformation or reorientation of the (self-) understanding of those participating in this exercise in a manner that eludes any stateable doctrine, the problems it engages being dissolved rather than resolved. Hence, though

---

[12] Therapy's introduction is unexpected and something of wildcard in AP's presentation; it is not anticipated as a theme to be discussed in Cavell's brief introduction that stands before his essay's two parts. AP as a whole has the following shape:

Intro   Part I   Part II
        "Two Problems of Aesthetics"   "Aesthetic Judgment and A Philosophical Claim"
        Problems in Literary Criticism   Problems Pertaining
        Problem/Expositions: To OLP's Talk!
        1) Metaphor   4) Philosophical and Aesthetic Judgment as
        2) Modernist Poetry   Transcendental-grammatical
                                                         5) As itself Aesthetic, "Art"
           3) Modernist Poetry and Wittgenstein's *Philosophy as Therapy*

various flies may be shown their way out of various fly bottles, potentially ad infinitum, the actual purpose of these exercises remains eccentric to anything found *in them*, and this includes everything that may be said about language and its use. Accordingly, within this broader context, the inquiries and observations of part two of AP themselves would be only *means*: ways of changing the perspective of each participant on their own world and existence in a manner that re-inspissates them, brings back their weight. Wittgenstein's and Cavell's philosophy fosters a change in (self-)understanding, a difference in a person's grasp of their own personhood and being-in-the-world, rather than purveying delimitable doctrines or standpoints of any sort.[13]

The presentations found at the end of each of AP's two sections are thus at once different and related. Cavell at the end of part one deems his philosophy's work as a whole therapy, entailing silence about philosophy's traditional orienting concerns, culminating in these problems' "disappear[ance]," and an inability to say what one has learned, rather than answers or solutions (AP 85). In turn, the judgments rendered by OLP concerning "what we say," a variant of Kant's judgments of, and on, aesthetics, entail a final breaking off or silence insofar as their relevance to their subject matter is similar to art's, rather than that of prior philosophy or even perhaps Kant's own version of aesthetic judgments.

These paired outcomes, though dovetailing, may raise questions, however—ones that eventually turn out to be central to the alternative account of discourse offered here. Acknowledging that therapy characterizes Cavell's philosophy's overall purposes, and granting his judgments' radically aesthetic character (their bordering on art, their being situated in individuals' perspectives, and their necessary openendedness), does not part two nevertheless trade on positive descriptions, some concrete account of what we say (and what we do), no matter how tenuous their base, in a fashion foreign to philosophy's characterization as therapy at the end of part one?[14] Kant's understanding of beauty may itself be returned to and repeatedly examined, as is also seemingly true of all those reports on what we say that Cavell deems grammatical or logical or transcendental. Though they may ultimately not be able to constrain consent, these discussions announce problems, survey subject matters, and mull findings, the shareable character of which never seems to be in doubt. None of these

---

[13] Similarly, it could be said Cavell's own thinking, at this early stage, aims to *reverse and undo* the arguably equally unique movement by which philosophy traditionally claimed to come to itself, to arrive at its own singular standpoint. From Plato's allegory of the cave up through Husserl's transcendental *epoche*, a radical change in perspective, indeed a process of self-conversion, leads *from* everyday life *to* philosophy and its concerns. This philosophical prelude often is figured as a vertical ascent. Cavell's thinking, by contrast, would trace *a descent*, back to everyday life, and to a new more "grounded" relation, as we say, to self, others, and our own existence. Ordinary language philosophy returns to the surface, indeed to the ordinary: a return ultimately without a concrete content, that brings us before our existence as embodied human beings.

[14] Cavell himself at moment may share these qualms. Specifically, at the end of EAP, Cavell declares that his and Wittgenstein's philosophical conclusions are effectively further from any stateable doctrines than even modernist poetry's figures since their expressions are open to two entirely opposed ways of being understood, without possibility of further disambiguation. Having offered this affirmation, which would seem to render articulating any fixed standpoint impossible, Cavell, however, appends a footnote stating that positive findings, indeed "doctrines" of some sort, after all do belong to his and Wittgenstein's philosophy, without in any way explaining how this and the earlier affirmation both may hold (EAP 970n14).

articulations, accordingly, seemingly suffer dissolution or silence about what has been learned. Though their ultimate significance, their reference and relevance, and perhaps their truth may remain unclear, what one has learned, or believes one has learned (about what we say) nevertheless can be expressed and discussed on multiple different occasions, as opposed to that dissolution of standpoints, that disappearance of problems, and of stateable resolutions modeled by therapy at part one's end.[15]

These qualms, of course, are close to the ones occasioned by Wittgenstein's *Tractatus*' so-called resolute reading, of which Cavell's approach to Wittgenstein's later work is sometimes taken to be a godfather or precursor.[16] Setting this concern aside for the moment—this reference point will return—the usual response to this issue should be noted, especially since it was originally offered by Cavell himself, when speaking in the context of PI and drawing on Wittgenstein's own avowals. That rejoinder suggests that OLP's *positive* talk of what we say (and do) takes the form of what are called "perspicuous descriptions" or expositions—"*ubersichtliche Darstellungen*" in Wittgenstein's German. Such descriptions rely on comments or observations with which *no one could disagree,* and their force thus consists in their staging and organization

---

[15] These concerns clearly dovetail with those raised in an exemplary interchange between Stephen Mulhall and Steven Affeldt, occasioned by the latter's review of the former's book-length study of Cavell's work. Affeldt, as I read him, unpacks a recourse to individual persons at work in Cavell's talk of philosophical grammar similar to the one just set out. His essay concludes by affirming that "if there is a ground of intelligibility, then I am (each of us is) that ground" ("The Ground of Mutuality: Criteria, Judgment, and Intelligibility in Stephen Mulhall and Stanley Cavell," *European Journal of Philosophy* 6, no. 1 [1998]: 1–31; 23). On this basis, furthermore, Affeldt finds Cavellean and Wittgensteinian criteria to always only be at issue in concrete judgments, never to float above them, or provide grounds for such judgments themselves. I agree there are never "full criteria" for Cavell in Affeldt's sense; nevertheless, I will soon suggest that Cavell's treatment of criteria is more double-sided and perhaps inconsistent than Affeldt allows, owing, above all, to Cavell's focus on words. To be sure, Cavell, at moments, doubtless does stress how much the work done by criteria depends on persons, contexts, and all that these entail. Criteria do not stand on their own; they do not supply assertability conditions, and they do not supersede the role of judgment in deciding what is true in individual cases. (See for example, "On the opening of the *Investigations*," where Cavell speaks about them as both trivial and important, weak and strong [*Cambridge Companion to Wittgenstein*, ed. Hans Sluga and David G. Stern (Cambridge: Cambridge University Press, 1996), 261–95; 285–6].) At the same time, in their discussion in *Claim*, Cavell attaches criteria to concepts (and thereby ultimately to words), viewing them as pertaining exclusively to our talk about our talk!, not to our talk! about the world. As Cavell puts this, Wittgenstein's are criteria for generic objects, and thus grammatical criteria, which do not "relate the name to an object . . . but various concepts to the concept of that object" (*Claim*, 73). Cavell at this moment, then, seems committed to some form of positive speaking about our speech, even as he himself also stresses that this talk never can function mechanically, nor can its necessity be adduced in a fashion that omits selves and others, so that it consequently can never overcome the skeptic's worry once and for all. The question presently at issue here, then, is *what* this positive component is, and how it relates to what Cavell says about philosophy at the end of AP Division One. Affeldt, by the present lights at least, also does not get fully to the heart of this matter. Though he identifies what is entailed by a psychology somehow undone, he leaves unaddressed how these analyses for Cavell also remain accessible in their own right and continue to maintain their standing—that a positive, repeatable appreciation of the grammar and logic of our language in some fashion is still to be had, ultimately with an eye to our words, even if these never function as determinative in the fashion Mulhall at times may suggest.

[16] Cora Diamond's "Throwing Away the Ladder" is now the locus classicus for resolute reading's statement, especially her talk there of "not chickening out" (*Philosophy*, 63, no. 243 [January 1988)]: 5–27; 8). For an overview of resolute reading, canvassing its various sides, see Silvio Bronzo, "The Resolute Reading and Its Critics An Introduction to the Literature," *Wittgenstein-Studien* 3 (2012): 45–80.

rather than their contents as such. Accordingly, if perspicuous descriptions stand at the heart of part two's judgments, this may not conflict with the impossibility of stating what one has learned and the disappearance of philosophy's problems as presented at the end of part one, since none of what the former says entails any special contents or doctrines of any sort.

This no doubt powerful account remains ambiguous, however, in regard to the status of such *Darstellungen* themselves, these organizations, or expositions as such. Is the organization or exposition of such self-evident observations itself wholly a one-time affair, with its corresponding perspicuity also being entirely occasional? Alternatively, do these *Darstellungen* have more "shelf life" and thus speak to matters imbued with genuine positivity (such as do judgments of taste), and does their perspicuity extend to a broader range of occasions and interlocutors?[17]

Toril Moi, it should be noted, who is a very faithful interpreter of Cavell, in her recent book, nicely registers this difference, without, I believe, entirely resolving it. Glossing Wittgenstein's "perspicuous descriptions," she likens them to "engineer's drawings" and further stipulates that they "won't do anything . . . unless they are offered in response to a confusion."[18] Yet "engineer's drawings"—schematics, wiring diagrams, and so on—actually depict machines *independently* of the specific problems that prompt their consultation. They accompany the construction and distribution of the relevant devices and may be returned to repeatedly. Such templates thus appear to embody the first alternative of a positive, intrinsically shareable *Darstellung*—one that sits uneasily, however, with Cavell's and Wittgenstein's more radical model of therapy and of their discourses' disappearance.

Part two of AP and by default most commentators nevertheless treat Wittgenstein's and Cavell's descriptions as drawings of this sort. They assume that these descriptions do maintain their contents over time and thus, to this extent, that "what we say" has some unequivocal sense and purchase of its own, including sets of circumstances repeatable and positive in their own right—contexts that may also be described, ones permitting joint, sustained, and continuous discussion.[19] By contrast, on part one's terms, those problems and the descriptions aimed at them would elude being voiced even in this minimally lasting fashion; Wittgenstein's philosophy in totality instead would prove entirely passing and occasional.[20]

---

[17] Ultimately, this question recurs to the problem that Husserl called sedimentation: the availability of a past instance of expression, and especially a written one, to have its meaning and subject matter retrieved—a problem especially acute in a discourse-oriented setting, where stand-alone linguistic forms are not available to do this work. More discussion of this issue is forthcoming.

[18] Moi, *Revolution of the Ordinary*, 182.

[19] Of course, the underlying implication may be that these problems, like Christ's poor, are somehow always with us, dwelling as they do in the depths of our language. That response seems question-begging, however, since what is at issue is the degree to which language, however understood, itself can be spoken about as having lasting, repeatedly recognizable features, necessarily including those that would account for these difficulties' reemergence.

[20] This set of question may map on to a split within the *Tractatus*' interpretation among resolute readers themselves. On the view of the most extreme swath, or so-called Jacobins, such as seemingly Juliet Floyd, the *Tractatus* engages one-time issues, an otherwise contentless exposition being embraced. See Bronzo, "Resolute Reading" (54–5) and Floyd "Wittgenstein and the Inexpressible" (in *Wittgenstein and the Moral Life: Essays in Honor of Cora Diamond*, ed. Alice Crary [Cambridge, MA: MIT Press, 2007], 177–234).

However this tension plays out in Wittgenstein's own work, crucial in the present instance is that certain features of Cavell's own thinking, not found in Wittgenstein, function so as to make Cavell's descriptions hold fast and retain their own positivity in a fashion Wittgenstein's may not. For Cavell, for discourse to take itself as philosophical subject matter appears unproblematic, at least at certain moments in his text. Moreover, the concerns that tilt Cavell's approach in this direction specifically pertain to his treatment of *words*, an investigation found only in Cavell, albeit at times based on Wittgenstein's own remarks.

At key moments, Cavell relates Wittgenstein's insights and experiments back to words as commonly understood, as found in our actual, or possibly existing languages and cultures—an identity that Wittgenstein himself seems never to embrace with this degree of positivity, albeit words, names, family resemblances among usages, and so on, of course, appear in his work.[21] Along with words, Cavell also gives great weight to a generic differentiation among their different kinds of employments and corresponding senses: specifically between primary, secondary and/or figurative, as well as metaphorical senses and usages, distinctions at points also drawn by Wittgenstein but never further unpacked. As married to a preexisting "philological" perspective, found largely in Cavell, Wittgenstein's expositions in his later texts, as well as these distinctions themselves, arguably coalesce and harden in Cavell's hands.[22] Cavell's approach renders these grammatical descriptions and verbal categorizations less transitory, more absolute and more authoritative than in the original—leaving aside to what extent they

---

[21] Frege's new version of logic, which effectively makes *the sentence* the smallest unit of thought, no doubt massively influenced Wittgenstein himself (as James Conant often argues); the same can hardly be said of Cavell, however. Conant's account of Wittgenstein's thinking is deeply indebted to its starting point in Frege. If Conant is right about the holism that he imputes to the later Wittgenstein, however, then words necessarily play at best a minimal role in Wittgenstein's thinking. Conant in his commentary extrapolates from the Fregean context principle, which applies to sentences, to the larger contexts furnished by forms of life; he claims that Wittgenstein "seeks to generalize Frege's context principle so that it applies not only to words (and their role within the context of a significant proposition) but to sentences (and their role within the context of circumstances of significant use, or—as Wittgenstein prefers to call them—language-games)" (James Conant, "Wittgenstein on Meaning and Use," *Philosophical Investigations* 21, no. 3 [July 1998]: 222–50; 233). Words in use in the late Wittgenstein being *twice contextualized* would thus not only lack significance in themselves but also cease being able to serve as reference points; they could not be "quantified over" in Wittgenstein's philosophy, as the logicians say. It should be noted that Diamond's genealogy of some of PI's treatment of knowing my own mind, and beetle in a box, while not altering the status of words, nevertheless, by dint of connecting Wittgenstein's conviction that language is fine as it is to Wittgenstein's earlier views that were influential on positivism, suggests that the distinction between kinds of usages or meanings of the kind Cavell will draw may well be Wittgensteinian and thus matters are ultimately neither as simple on this score nor perhaps as simply holistic as Conant's account suggests (Cora Diamond, "Does Bismarck Have a Beetle in His Box," in *The New Wittgenstein*, eds. Alice Crary and Rupert Read [New York: Routledge, 2000], 262–92); see also her "Throwing Away the Ladder," *Philosophy* 63, no. 243 [January 1988]: 5–27) and her treatment there of sentences', not words', statuses in TLP, as flowing from Russell's work rather than Frege's (15 ff.).

[22] See n.15 for Cavell's avowal of the centrality of words in his revised Kantian and Wittgensteinian account of what we say. The best account of words in a Fregean, and to this extent, Wittgensteinian, context of which I am aware is Diamond' "What Nonsense Might Be," *Philosophy* 56, no. 215 (January 1981): 5–22; 18ff. Though profound, as I suggest later, I think her own account of these distinctions runs into problems contiguous to those we will soon encounter in Mulhall's early account of secondary senses. Henry Staten has fully sensed, and in his own way, resolved this tension between talk of the logical grammar of our words and Wittgenstein's stress on their use. See his *Wittgenstein and Derrida* (Nebraska: University of Nebraska Press, 1984): 82–6.

finally are such there.²³ Accordingly, over and against the plasticity Cavell assigns to persons and their understanding can be set a hardness, a crystallization with which Cavell credits words when used and the philosophical discussions concerning them. The status of words for Cavell, thus, must be explored in order to arrive, first, at a more global understanding of discourse in Cavell's thinking, and, next on this basis, at an outline of Cavell's conception and practice of interpretation, including the role his understanding of the word plays there.

3.2 Words

Cavell's treatment of words is sometimes taken as one of his major contributions to what today is called OLP. That discussion, to which the division into kinds of usages is appended, arises in the section of *Claim* entitled "Projecting a Word," and will be shortly discussed. The conclusions at which Cavell arrives concerning specifically literary topics in part one of AP already introduce considerations pertaining to this topic, however, since they seem impossible to parse on their own terms without an awareness of the broader framework that Cavell reveals only later in *Claim*. In AP, injecting himself into what, at the time, was a hugely significant debate between the literary critics Cleanth Brooks and Yvor Winters, Cavell sides with *both* Winters' and Brook's, yielding a standpoint in respect to figural language that on its face is inherently perplexing.

The core of Winters' and Brooks' disagreement indeed concerns figures and their paraphrasability. For Winters, all figures are necessarily subject to paraphrase; all may be restated in what amount to assertoric terms, as claims or propositions. Further, because the figurations specific to modernist poetry (such as that famously found in Ezra Pounds' early poem "In a Station," sometimes labeled "images") seemingly cannot be so treated, for Winters, Pound's poem and virtually all modernist poetry lacks the requisite stuffing, ultimately, the rational and ethical contents, characteristic of truly lasting and valuable literary work.²⁴

---

²³ A conundrum regarding words' status can also be found in Diamond's writings. In her article, "Wittgenstein, Mathematics, and Ethics: Resisting the Attractions of Realism" (in *The Cambridge Companion to Wittgenstein*, ed. Hans Sluga and David G. Stern, 226–20), Diamond, following the Polish poet Herbert Zbigniew, speaks of giving due heed to certain words when it comes to ethics along with attending to other aspects of our language as language (249). Yet how this affirmation squares with Diamond's insistence on use at this moment and with her avowal later that no words are moral in themselves remains unclear (253). Though Diamond distinguishes between the uses in question in the two cases—as organizing concepts in the first and representing predicates in the second—not only why but also how, in the first instance, some but not all words may serve such a purpose remains unexplained. The present account, it should be noted, though it ultimately takes all discourse to be about something, as does the author Diamond criticizes, Sabina Lovibond, departs from Lovibond's *expansion* of the scope of indicative statements or propositions—in particular to ethics, a development which Lovibond takes to separate the later Wittgenstein from the earlier. "Aboutness" in the present instance instead comes in many guises and arises in many types of speech, in a way that includes the instances that Diamond presents as exceptions to Lovibond's account, most of which are literary (cf. 243).

²⁴ See Yvor Winters, "The Experimental School in Modern Poetry," in his *In Defense of Reason* (New York: New Directions, 1947), 30–74.

Now Cavell in AP's first half initially stands with Winters; he does so, however, solely in respect to one figure and its specific paraphrasability: metaphor. According to Cavell, metaphors are inherently paraphrasable, while all other figures are not. Hence Cavell may and also does endorse Brooks' position: specifically Brooks' denunciation of what he, Brooks, then famously, called "the heresy of paraphrase," which he mounted in part as a defense of modernist poetry and poetics.[25] Brooks argues that all successful poetry *as poetry* is constituted by essentially the same properties as metaphor and other figures, with all of them resisting strict paraphrase. Though Cavell clearly finds much of Brooks' talk of paraphrase muddled, and rejects out of hand the notion of poetic form upon which Brooks at moments relies, Cavell does affirm that figural usages *other than metaphor* cannot be paraphrased, and, on these grounds, he, too, eventually defends modernist poetry's achievements.

When placed in its explicit context, and confined wholly to what is said in AP itself, Cavell's own stance toward figuration seems rather opaque, however. Cavell never gives reasons as to why *only metaphors* are subject to paraphrase. Yet, Brooks and Winters, though agreeing on little else, do concur that metaphor's and the other figures' fate stand and fall together. Only Cavell singles metaphors out.

Cavell's unique situating of metaphor in AP, then, to which discussion returns later, really only makes sense within the broader framework through which Cavell approaches all words and usage, a framework that appears solely in *Claim*. That template is partially drawn from Wittgenstein, but functions differently in Cavell's hands, I maintain, owing to the analysis of words to which it is appended.

In *Claim*, more specifically, coming to the end of his discussion of what he calls words' "projection," Cavell introduces a distinction between primary and secondary senses, and their corresponding uses.[26] All that he has said so far about words and their projection, Cavell here somewhat suddenly informs his reader, *does not apply* to an entire class of usages he only now identifies. These latter "regions of a word's use . . . cannot be assured or explained," he insists, "by an appeal to its ordinary language games"; this class, Cavell further defines as "'figurative' or 'secondary' senses of a word," but only ones that "are not . . . '*metaphorical*'" (CR 189). [27]

---

[25] See Cleanth Brooks, "The Heresy of Paraphrase," in *The Well-Wrought Urn: Studies in the Structure of Poetry* (London: Dennis Dobson Ltd, 1947), 176–96.

[26] Robert Mankin in his "An Introduction to The Claim of Reason," *Salmagundi* no. 67 (Summer 1985): 66–89 also raises concerns about Cavell's situating of metaphor and the remainder of figures (77), and later in his own fashion connects this time, as I eventually do here (86–7). Mankin, however, focuses on the question of convention in Cavell, and his is ultimately a full-throated defense of the imagination and its capacity to exceed all worldly concerns, thus departing from discourse as here understood. Cavell penned a response to Mankin, which appears in this same issue, which, to me, seems to cede no ground on the point concerning metaphor (92). In that response, Cavell tells us that Mankin's piece influenced the work he was doing in *In Quest of the Ordinary: Lines of Skepticism and Romanticism* (Chicago: University of Chicago Press, 1994), hereafter IQO. His essay in IQO on Emerson and Poe is extensively discussed later in the present volume, albeit Cavell says it is the earlier lectures in this same book upon which he specifically was laboring when reading Mankin.

[27] Cavell speaks about senses in the last quotation and of usage earlier, when discussing poetry and deeming all of it a "second inheritance" (189); yet since he himself derives the former, senses, from the latter, usage, I do not think it too grave a latitude to identify the usages themselves as secondary. Cavell here, importantly, explicitly brings together talk of secondary senses with his own

Cavell, then, here isolates two distinct genres of verbal usages, with metaphor falling outside both. Metaphor, though usually taken as a figure, and thus appearing to be part of the second class, does not operate, according to Cavell, in a fashion found in either group. Presumably words as used in metaphors retain contact with their usual employments and primary senses in a more direct way than in other figures, perhaps because metaphors in appearance are most like assertions. *Only* metaphorical uses, accordingly, invite or sustain paraphrase, Cavell insists in AP. Metaphor's position with respect to this framework of the primary and secondary thus explains its otherwise opaque status in AP, where metaphor similarly proves exceptional.[28]

Setting aside any further analysis of metaphor itself for a moment (to which attention soon returns), equally extraordinary in the foregoing passage is Cavell's suggestion that an entire swath of usages exists for which "appeal to ordinary language games does not apply." This being so, how, then, do these so-called secondary instances say anything intelligible at all? Not answering to their primary employments, even as do metaphors for Cavell, how is what they express deemed by him available for understanding? For a potentially vast class of usages, a genuine unfolding of what they communicate seemingly is not in the cards, as attested by Cavell's ruling out their being able to be *paraphrased* in AP.

Cavell himself at this moment in *Claim* largely remains silent on these points. (One treatment by him of this difference is further addressed later on in this volume.) Some of Cavell's and Wittgenstein's best readers do offer glosses on these notions, however, and these accounts make clear what is at stake in this distinction between primary and secondary senses and uses both for Cavell and for the present reading. The suggestion is that there are uses of words different from our usual ones, ones which would not be possible were it not for the recognized set of uses, as when one says "Tuesday is fat, Wednesday lean," or "the vowel 'u' is purple" (as once Rimbaud did). In these cases, sense may be gotten, kenned, or not, and is not itself subject to further explanation or paraphrase.[29]

That such accounts may not be fully satisfying is immediately suggested, however, by the fact that the meaning or sense such secondary uses are said to possess is itself said to be secondary, to fall under the category at issue, *to be meaning* only in a secondary sense. Meaning or sense, used in this same fashion, secondarily, it is stipulated, is in question when considering secondary uses and their (secondary) meanings. This account thus seems question-begging, since one must already know and understand meaning as secondary for this explanation to function, while secondary usages and senses themselves are what are being investigated.[30] Nevertheless, this division between

---

speaking about a "second inheritance" of language, or of a "father tongue," as found in his writings on Thoreau, a usage first encountered in *Senses of Walden* (CR 189).

[28] A more granular treatment of Cavell's account of metaphor in AP in the context of a range of approaches to this figure is offered at the beginning of Chapter 5.

[29] I am in part following Diamond's account in her "Secondary Sense" (*Proceedings of the Aristotelian Society, New Series*, 67 (1966–7). (189–208.) The relation of secondary to primary meaning and each to their respective usages (the two not always dovetailing for her) is more complex than that set out here and in my next paragraph; yet Diamond's account arguably faces problems contiguous, if not identical to the one being identified.

[30] Stephen Mulhall in an early work entirely devoted to aspect-seeing, *On Being in the World: Wittgenstein and Heidegger on Seeing Aspects* (London: Routledge, 1990) gives an account of this

two types of meanings turns out to have more radical and decisive consequences than some might suspect. *Philosophical Investigations* (hereafter PI), after all, repeatedly counsels that the meanings of words, terms, and sentences only appear in their use, including their accompanying practices and contexts. Meaning, to the extent it exists at all, for Wittgenstein, as the last paragraph of part one of PI goes out of its way to underscore, is not a homogenous property or medium that words have or in which they participate in their own right.[31] Yet at the juncture when the distinction between primary and secondary meanings is at issue, the former understanding of meaning as use apparently ceases to fully hold sway and another appears—meaning, as it is in fact more commonly understood, as homogenous and assignable to individual words and expressions—now standing in isolation, or at least at one remove, from use. A more customary notion of meaning returns with the result that the distinction between primary and secondary meanings (and genres of usage) turns out to be a decisive one—so fundamental that it apparently cannot even be drawn or explained without the secondariness it should define being defining of it.

This impasse or conundrum, which here will only be followed out in Cavell's writings, takes on particular significance in the present context, moreover, when it is recognized that the bulk of writing and talk! found in the humanities must fall under this rubric of the "secondary." All "texts" (including oral presentations, things like spoken folktales and epics)—as well as works in philosophy, history, or even law—ultimately must be secondary as that notion is presented. In none are any identifiable "language games" immediately evident, so as to buoy up such usages and senses.[32] Owing at once to humanistic texts' inherent novelty (and/or foreignness) and to their extended length, such that their performances in part carry their contexts with them, no primary usages seemingly buttress the expressions of the texts in question.[33] Were *Claim*'s set

distinction between primary and secondary, which he himself in part explicitly differentiates from Cavell's, which also illustrates this problem. Mulhall, if I follow him, distinguishes *both categories of meaning* as they apply to words from any of what actually happens with words in discourse, such that any *direct connection* between meaning and *use* disappears. Both sorts of meanings are, as it were, secondary phenomena, the actual intelligibility of discourse being independent of them both (38; but cf. 41). Yet, what, then, a secondary meaning in Mulhall's sense proves to be, as well as its relation to primary meaning, remains difficult to parse. This is especially so, since Mulhall indeed understands the distinction between primary and secondary to apply to "meaning," taking "meaning" as such as an instance of *secondary* meaning (46–7). Mulhall's account, then, seems to presuppose rather than to genuinely disclose the phenomenon in question. For its topic, scope, and ambition, Mulhall's book nevertheless has been an important one to think with for the current author.

[31] *Philosophical Investigations*, trans. G. E. M. Anscombe (Oxford: Basil Blackwell, 1986), hereafter PI, para. 693.

[32] Law may appear to be an exception. When traced back to its constitutional foundations, where debate rages on both its meaning and the meaning of meaning, it becomes clear this is not simply so. (See, for example, Antonin Scalia and various commentators in Scalia *A Matter of Interpretation* [Princeton: Princeton UP, 1997].)

[33] This difference, as has begun to be seen, and as will be further confirmed, is what Cavell himself intends by speaking in all these instances of a "father tongue" in opposition to a "mother tongue." Stephen Mulhall, who generously read a draft of the present chapter, suggested that my insistence on the scope of these distinctions, especially in AP, might possibly involve "a fantasy of completeness" (Mulhall email, July 16, 2019). His answer struck me as genuinely Cavellean, which is in part why I cite it here. As I responded to him, these are nevertheless distinctions upon which Cavell himself rather consistently relies, nor does Cavell to my knowledge offer any other account of humanistic

of distinctions genuinely legitimate, accordingly, no discourse in the humanities, featuring new and extended writing thinking, would be genuinely paraphrasable or interpretable.[34] All humanistic discourses, instead, on the construal in question, would hearken to a life led solely by their individual words, and thus necessarily distinct from that found in the relevant texts.

In Wittgenstein's own case, to be clear, the perhaps problematic status of the secondary appears tied to his contention that about a whole swath of subjects, deemed the most important, we cannot properly speak, and thus must keep silent or at least not jointly pursue articulable insights, as opposed to what holds good in the natural sciences, or, differently, math. Wittgenstein's invocation of the secondary thus arguably is one with his thought's considerable distance from all working traditions in the humanities—as found in political theory, law, and literary interpretation, as well as in much of philosophy, particularly pre-modern philosophy, where, of course, investigations into all that Wittgenstein would disallow are regularly undertaken.[35] Cavell, of course, is himself by no means reticent in this fashion. In his work, correspondingly, the secondary's positing does not check, but *informs* his dealings with the humanities, literature included. This is all the more the case, since, as we have begun to see, the distinction between primary and secondary usage and sense is buttressed by Cavell's own distinctive focus on words as words, an analysis that, while potentially distancing him from Wittgenstein's treatment, implies on its own terms a reification of "what we say," as is about to become still clearer.

In the present context, by contrast, the generic distinction between primary and secondary, and Cavell's novel view of the word ultimately disappear in the face of the importance of greater swaths of talk than either words or even single sentences; as is clear in these more encompassing expressions a being in time informs all understanding, all usages—primary, secondary, and metaphorical ones—without distinction, thus cancelling these generic differences altogether. The alternative account of discourse here to be offered, moreover, can itself be provisionally glimpsed, thanks to a notion that Cavell invokes in the present section of *Claim*, to which fuller discussion is thus about to come: namely, "form" or "forms of life." In *Claim*, specifically in the twin sections, "Projecting a Word," and "Learning a Word," where words are indeed his focus, Cavell relates words' conception to the notion of a "form of life" central

---

discourse as discourse, except for ones based on words, with an exception noted later. Thus it seems to me reasonable to investigate what these distinctions imply, especially since they prove consistent across a considerable swath of Cavell's writings: AP itself, *Senses of Walden*, *Claim*, and "Being Odd," to mention just these.

[34] That such an outcome is in the cards is further attested by a footnote Cavell adds to AP in subsequent editions of *Must We Mean* in which he claims that *explication de texte* somehow differs from paraphrase and *is* possible, thus acknowledging that his stance suggests it may well not be (AP 79n). In the footnote, moreover, Cavell does not offer how or why this would be so, or the terms on which interpretation or exegesis would function. Cavell offers only a bare statement that it is the case, as in the note cited earlier from EAP.

[35] To be clear, noting the seeming distance of Wittgenstein himself, especially in TLP and PI, from these traditions is by no means to gainsay the work done in this vein in his thought's wake by G. E. M. Anscombe, Iris Murdoch, Cora Diamond, and others. In Chapter 5, this lacuna will be somewhat, albeit still scantily, filled in; one instance of Diamond's work in literary studies there is engaged.

to Wittgenstein's later work. In the one section, "Projecting a Word," Cavell presents words' relation to such "forms" differently than in his discussion in the immediately preceding section, "Learning a Word"; the explanatory or illuminating power of this notion of a form of life as taken up here, in turn, flows from the different treatment forms of life receives in these two portions of "Claim."

* * *

In "Projecting a Word," Cavell sets out his fundamental understanding of words as words. Addressing a topic that never receives sustained treatment by Wittgenstein himself, Cavell there declares any word as a word inseparable both from its explicit repetition *as the same word* and from its use on *different occasions*, thereby setting apart his perspective on words from any rule-based or algorithmic approach. Words, as used in the relevant range of situations, for Cavell, indeed inherently possess a twofold character; they exhibit both "an inner constancy" and an "outer variance."[36] One can *see* (though perhaps not always state) an "internal logic" inherent in all of our allied usages of a word (homonymy here being ruled out). Nevertheless, even as so allied, words within the usages and occasions accompanying them are variable, such that no algorithm can take us from this presumed intuition to a single actual instance of use. Speakers and persons, consequently, are never simply out of the picture, as I emphasized earlier.

Cavell, then, approaches words in terms of projections, or what he calls "projecting a word." Constancy and variation together, in turn, indeed comprise a "word's projection into contexts," a relatively novel notion of words that never separates them entirely from their use or from what is here called discourse and which thus is the mainstay of Cavell's Wittgensteinian, or post-Wittgensteinian, conception of the word.

The foregoing may appear uncontroversial on its own terms. Yet, the very making of words a theme, and approaching use on their basis, as has already been suggested, potentially poses a problem, while it also arguably deviates from Wittgenstein's

---

[36] His broader conclusion proves to be "that any form of life and any concept integral to it"— defining of a word in its primary usages and meanings—"has . . . both [an] 'outer variance' and an 'inner constancy'"(CR 185). At times in his discussion, when speaking of such projections, Cavell seems primarily to have in mind a subset or family of usages, as found in Wittgenstein's discussion in PI of our use of "game," which Cavell's analyzes on these terms; at other times, as in the earlier citation, actual individual instances seemingly stand front and center, as calling all these games "chess," albeit played on different boards at different times. Given how Cavell envisions this operation, the difference is not in any case grave, since both situations are mapped by it. Hilary Putnam in his "Attunement and Ordinary Language" suggests that shifts in science on the order of that from Newton to Einstein can be understood in terms of Cavell's notion of projecting a word (in *The Legacy of Wittgenstein: Pragmatism or Deconstruction*, eds. Ludwig Nagel and Chantal Mouffe [Bern: Peter Lang Publishing, 2001], 9–24; 18–19). Putnam initially cites a very powerful passage in *Claim* where Cavell suggests a scientist might affirm a radical change in her science for the sake of maintaining touch with the project of science, and parallels it to how one might at some point jettison perspective in order to maintain touch with the project of painting (13; *Claim*, 121). Though suggestive, it seems to me such leaps of understanding are foreign to Cavell's talk of projecting a word. All of Cavell's own examples refer to previously established, albeit varying usages and thus deeply speak against these sorts of radically new uses in science being instances of projection in the relevant sense.

treatments of discourse in PI.³⁷ Cavell, by contrast, indeed organizes his own analysis at this moment entirely on *verbal* lines. He chooses the English word "feed," to give an example of a word being projected, and cites different usages in which it appears, such as "feed the lions," "feed the projector," and "feed the meter."³⁸ "Feed," as used in all these cases, Cavell claims, shares some sameness or connection necessarily lacking from expressions in which it is absent. "Feed the meter," for Cavell, accordingly, differs from "put money in the meter," just as does, for example, "feed the projector" from "thread the projector." This perhaps only "felt necessity," then, is central to "feed's" *being* as *a word*.

Cavell's presentation, however, arguably strays from Wittgenstein's own thinking on these matters. Examined in context, in instances when such phrases are actually being used, "feed the meter"—said on the way to a restaurant or a show, for example—seems to differ not at all from "put money in the meter"; the two expressions express exactly the same request. They do the same work, just as in most cases do "feed the projector" and "thread the film into the projector." Moreover, these various "feeds," when they are actually being used, seem unconnected among themselves; in *use*, they lack any linkage, including a "felt" one. All the relevant usages, it appears, could easily have been expressed otherwise.

Of course, on some occasions, such differences in wording *can* play a role, by hearkening back to other already familiar instances of use. ("The meter is *hungry*," I say to my friend. "*What?*" "I am suggesting that you 'feed it.'") Uses *can* arise where the differences Cavell indicates become relevant, but this does not mean that they already are relevant when used. Cavell's examples, accordingly, do not display the variance and constancy that make words words in their projections. Indeed the supposition that in actual experiences of talk!, in actual usage, words appear as words at all is questionable; to the contrary, the entire expression appears and blends with talk!'s subject matters, its contexts, and its purposes. Neither words nor expressions present themselves in use, discourse not being something "present-at hand," as Heidegger would say. Cavell's here treating words as if they do appear, and thereby imagining that the wording of speech commonly makes a difference, for this and other reasons, is itself, then, arguably an instance of being "held within a picture of language," of the type Wittgenstein evinces, a retrospective recasting of what happens in discourse that departs from its genuine operation.³⁹

---

³⁷ Wittgenstein, of course, examines related set of usages, many of which contain the same word or set of words, such as "following a rule"; yet his inquiry seems never aimed at the word (or words) as such (PI para 82 ff.). Thus, he can and often does switch to usages that do not contain any of the same words (for example, in the case of following a rule, he turns to mathematical series and their continuation [PI para 145]). Wittgenstein's appeal to uses and their relatedness is thus not oriented by words as words; instead, it targets concretely situated philosophical problems and questions, to which, as noted earlier, even his invocation of distinct language games may be subordinate.

³⁸ His analysis thus again seems somewhat indeterminate, perhaps innocently so, between external variations such as "feed" used for giving a baby food on Tuesday and again on Wednesday (perhaps breast-feeding in the first and strained fruits and vegetables in the second), and the seemingly wider range of cases Cavell offers.

³⁹ PI para.145. Presumably, this is why Mulhall had such difficulty reconciling Cavell's remarks, and Wittgenstein's in part two of PI, with much of the rest of what Wittgenstein says about discourse.

Cavell at this moment in *Claim* maintains a questionable focus on words; at the same time, he also aligns them with what, without doubt, remains a crucial Wittgensteinian notion: forms of life.[40] *Lebensformen* is a key term of art in Wittgenstein's thinking; it introduces holistic considerations that also operate in the present context, which is its primary import here.[41] Disentangled from the word, life forms' functioning depicts much of what the holism claimed at work in discourse in the present instance entails. Accordingly, perhaps the most decisive issue raised by Cavell's discussion is whether a focus on words as words, even of Cavell's novel sort, is compatible with forms of life and the holism that this notion implies.

"Forms of life," more specifically, indicate the being combined together into a single greater whole of the following: (a) expressions as used (including at times, in Wittgenstein's analyses, gestures, and other "behavior"); (b) some aspect of the world (things, persons, other "existents," such as features or "properties" of things, and so on); as well as (c) outcomes that talk! so understood enables (requesting help, measuring lengths, informing someone one is in pain, and so on).[42] To evoke a form of life is thus different from offering an *explanation* of what we say or mean, or how we say or mean it, including of the kind still common in much analytic philosophy. In respect to the different vectors just mentioned (expressions, existents, and practices), speaking of a form of life insists that each aspect rests on all the others, such that no one of them can serve as an explanation of them all, nor, then, can anything else provide such a final instance. In this way, "form of life" embodies a holistic vector: an appeal to a greater context or whole, in which multiple registers are coordinated, entailing a forfeiture of the claim to offer any real ground or some other explanatory account for the phenomenon in question.[43]

Thus in one of Wittgenstein's own example of such an appeal, he asserts, at first glance surprisingly, that in the case of a visual sign in the shape of an arrow, no reason exists to look toward where the point of the arrow faces rather than the opposite way; our reasons for doing so are not genuine grounds or reasons. Instead our practice answers solely to our form of life, to the "application that a living being makes of [the arrow-sign]," which could well have been otherwise (PI para. 454).[44]

In this example, the significance assigned to the visual arrow (which may well seem "natural") and the use to which it is put, as well as those using it are thus brought together in a single implicit "form of life." Wittgenstein's appeal to (a form of) life, however, does not even pretend to explain the phenomenon in question. Instead it

---

[40] Albeit a relatively rare one: David Kishik's *Wittgenstein's Form of Life* (Continuum, 2008) chronicles its markedly infrequent appearances in Wittgenstein and discusses some of its possible antecedents.

[41] What is intended by "holism" and "holistic" soon will be made clear. My usage largely conforms to this notion's understanding more generally in philosophy of language: it indicates that meaning and reference cannot function apart from larger contexts and broader dispensations—hence holism— that themselves resist any ultimate parceling out and inventorying.

[42] Cf. Conant's account cited earlier for a similar understanding of this notion (n.21 in the present chapter).

[43] Holism is further discussed in the present study in chapters eight or nine, in part to distinguish what Hubert Dreyfus has called Heidegger's "practical holism" from Davidson's theoretical one.

[44] My presentation of the arrow combines Wittgenstein's comments in PI with his discussion in *The Blue and the Brown Books* (New York: Harper and Row, 1960), pp. 33–4.

underscores both *that* this phenomenon does so function and that it does so *in still broader contexts* than those to which we usually attend.

In the section of *Claim* now being discussed, along with keeping words in view, Cavell, then, suggests that they and their usage (their internal constancy and differences) answer to *different* forms of life. Cavell, that is, proposes to identify or at least distinguish forms of life on the basis of words *as words*. His account thus arguably moves in precisely the opposite direction of Wittgenstein's. Wittgenstein shows that no verbal usage or sign operates apart from the forms of life in which it appears; Cavell, by contrast, begins from the verbal usages, from the presumed signs and their organization, in order to disclose and identify *forms of life themselves*.

Cavell, more specifically, in this same section of Claim suggests that were one to encounter a speaker and a culture that used different *words* than we do on *the same occasions*, this would indicate that their *forms of life* are likely to be different from ours (CR 185). If, for example, when *feeding* different animals, a speaker did not use the single word "feed," but instead different verbs when different animals are being nourished, this verbal variation should indicate that a different form of life is at work. "Suppose we find a culture which does in fact change verbs [in these cases] ... won't we want to ask: why are these forms different?" Cavell declares, thereby marking what he believes to be a different holistic nexus comprised of words, world, persons, and their practices (CR181).[45]

Yet, it is far from obvious that the use of different *words* here, or in any case, says anything at all about the relevant speakers' forms of life. After all, we could use such expressions as "feed the drawers" of a dresser or of a file cabinet, or "feed a database," but happen not to (except, of course, when we actually sometimes do). Nothing seemingly does or should follow based on an expression's *verbal surface* with respect to the more comprehensive wholes engaged by its use.[46] Cavell's suggestion in fact really is no different from Edward Sapir's and Benjamin Whorf's once famous hypotheses, popularized in the chestnut about the Inuit having more words for snow than English speakers. Yet just as that "fact" about Inuit words did not show that the Inuit actually

---

[45] I am aware that Cavell's remark, seemingly correlating words and forms of life, takes the form of a question and that it is important to him, as sketched earlier, that no final *knowledge* of forms of life and their relation to words is at issue, the desire for such being itself a product of skepticism. Part of Cavell's thrust toward the ordinary is to turn away this concern, without substituting some other knowledge for it. (See "Availability of Wittgenstein's Philosophy," MW 52, where Cavell himself emphasizes this aspect of projection.) Yet at the same time, the notion of culture and of a culture showing its forms of life through its words, however pursued, seems to me to raise the questions here registered, both in itself and perhaps especially because the optics of a culture and what belongs to it already implies a *special perspective* different from that of the ordinary.

[46] On this issue of words, history, and national languages, see Paola Marrati's 2015 "The Fragility of Words, the Vulnerability of Life," *MLN* 130, no. 5 (December 2015 Comparative Literature Issue): 1055–66. Marrati, writing in a very different context than the present one, wishes to affirm the pertinence of history and actually existing languages to Cavell's and Wittgenstein's forms of life, and especially to the key notion of criteria accompanying such usage. It is not clear to me, however, that Marrati's overlaying of the radical contingency of our practices as practices, her claim that our nature is radically contingent (as witnessed by our understanding of how to go on in our calculations), which is clearly the case, can be understood in terms of what a given "culture expects" or the crises it confronts, as these must always bring into play explicit goals, aims, and intentions, features that by her own avowal are not characteristic of forms of life as such (1062).

understand weather in a different way than we do (or indeed offer anything probative about it—it is today, as it happens, largely taken to be false), so, too, it seems wrong to suggest that *anything* follows from "feed's" differing distributions in the aforementioned two cases. Similarly, Saussure's famous example of the French having one, but the English, two words for sheep—in the latter instance when being eaten and not—does not, of course, require that the English have a different *form of life* when it comes to their *sheep* than the French.

Cavell himself, moreover, presents profound reasons to believe that this last is the case—that words and forms of life remain disjunct—in the immediately preceding section of *Claim* "Learning a Word." In this section, he presents forms of life in what I believe is a far more faithful and fundamental fashion than in "Projecting a Word." Cavell's treatment of forms of life and words in "Learning" makes still plainer why forms of life cannot be mapped through the optics of words, and why word's identity as words, even as reconceived by Cavell, do not play a working role in actual expressions and their understanding.

Cavell in "Learning," more specifically, envisions a young child in some fashion "imitating" a parent's activity and labeling jars, while saying something like "I putting on labels." (Cavell similarly imagines a small child "pretending" to "pay" and to "use" money, and making the relevant sounds.) The verbs earn scare quotes, however, since at this moment Cavell himself suggests that the child in question could not be said to be using *the same words* as we do, albeit she says, "I put on labels" (transcribed by Cavell in phonological symbols) (CR 174). She does not speak the same words, because she doesn't yet understand the forms of life of the relevant activities, Cavell claims, in this instance, presumably, the *work of classification*. Similarly in the case of currency, Cavell questions if the child can be said to use our word "pay" or "money," not understanding how money works. Absent acquaintance with doing and saying the other things implied by the relevant form of life (classifying and commerce) with which we, her teachers, are presumed acquainted, Cavell doubts that the child employs *the same words or names* as we do, although she makes the same sounds and seemingly even uses the same sentences.

Cavell's analysis, accordingly, casts doubt that forms of life can be reckoned by way of words, since seemingly identical words or phrases are themselves deemed not to be such, absent the relevant forms. To be clear, in question for Cavell himself in these examples is a limit case, applying solely to someone first learning or becoming initiated into language and not already a native speaker of any. Cavell, above all, aims to envision a scenario before the words "word" or "name" have themselves been learned—to imagine someone not yet able to ask for the name of something or to ask about a word's meaning.

Nevertheless, so proceeding, though denying that in these cases their words would be the same as ours, Cavell, in fact, also rejects affirming that their words *are* different. Given that the affirmation and the denial of such identity both are possible, doubts necessarily arise as to whether any significant correlation exists between names or words as such, and forms of life themselves. If the identity with our own of the words in cases where acquaintance with a form of life is absent cannot be ruled out, how then can words' identities ever allow forms of life to be distinguished, despite Cavell suggesting just this in "Projecting a Word"?[47]

Cavell's own observations in "Learning," moreover, make still more evident why and how correlation between words and forms of life cannot be maintained, even when the discourse of so-called "masters of the language" is in question. In "Learning a Word," according to Cavell, not only would an acquaintance or initiation into a given form of life be needed for the identification of words themselves to be made but an awareness of the "relations" among forms would also have to exist, he insists, for the child's words to be deemed unproblematically identical with ours (CR 178). Even were a child able, for example, not only to pick out labels in her parent's drawer but also to affix the right labels to the right items, thus actually performing what we usually call labeling, the identity of a child's talk!'s with ours at that moment, for Cavell, could not be simply be affirmed. In addition, the child must also ken related practices in other settings, such as labeling in law offices or databases or certain types of mockery. Identity of words and names only "goes through," as it is sometimes said, for Cavell in "Learning," thanks not just to the presence of the right practices and forms of life but also to *connections* among forms of life, to awareness of these linkages among forms.

Yet, who among us genuinely grasps the various "forms of life" in which money today is enmeshed, or for that matter labeling (as in biology and genetics)? Such words and their use vary wildly across multiple contexts, some of which do not include the words in question at all, as is true with money (in cases such as the Federal Reserve selling or buying bonds).[48] Consequently, it seems impossible to map such relations on a grid offered by *words*. These relations can never appear through the optics of the *word*, as Cavell's own earlier analysis suggests. Forms of life defy such mapping in this, and arguably in any other way, although Cavell himself still insists at this moment that these intersections are "grammatical" (CR 178).

Cavell's presentation in "Learning a Word" thus indicates both that no one-to-one correlation between forms of life and words is feasible and also why this is so: because forms of life remain *latent*. They operate in the *background* on occasions of use. These

---

[47] Cavell here to some degree may be following Wittgenstein, who highlights the absence of any bright line between mastery and its absence. Accordingly, while within narrow bounds this observation indeed calls into question the centrality of words as words, and the ultimate philosophical importance of our reports made on occasion about them, on Cavell's interpretation, masters of a language might still possess the capacity to say what we *can* do with words in a way that differs from learners.

[48] In his "Declining Decline," Cavell distinguishes between horizontal and vertical understandings of forms of life, though he seems to view them both as one by the end of his essay, thanks to invoking Spengler's perspective ("Declining Decline: Wittgenstein as a Philosopher of Culture," *Inquiry An Interdisciplinary Journal of Philosophy* 31 [1988]: 253–64; 254). Owing to the considerations earlier set out, however, it is questionable whether the vertical sense of forms of life—which distinguishes at least some of our practices from those of animals and so on—can be mapped or gleaned in terms of words, especially words belonging to actually existing national languages. Cavell later in this same essay suggests that the view of words taken as outside of language (as things in themselves) be seen as a comment on "a culture" (261), specifically our own, thus answering to Spengler's naturalist notion of the decline of civilizations, and one that Wittgenstein, now modeled as potential "prophet," would remedy by diurnalization, by the return to the ordinary or the daily (274). My discussion of Cavell's 1983 essay "Being Odd" in the next section examines the status that Cavell gives to words specifically within modernity, as invoked by him here (48ff).

wholes are not in us, even in those of us deemed "masters of the language," but we in them. A sprawling network of understandings and interconnected usages with no fixed limits, distributed among uses and across distinct occasions backstops our discourse. Put otherwise, forms of life and/or other holistic configurations buttress discourse as *pre-judices*, never as actual (present) judgments. What accompanies talk, accordingly, is only ever "life," absent any true forms.[49]

In "Learning a Word," then, Cavell exhibits the contribution of something like forms of life to discourse in a way his discussion of words' projections as such occludes. Forms of life, from the perspective of "Learning," however, disappear as distinct items, as do words themselves, since their identity as same or different must always be confined to moments of actual use, regardless of who is master and who is initiate.[50] With words no longer being in the picture, however, the distinction between primary and secondary, or between everyday and purportedly established usages and ones deemed to work differently (i.e., secondary ones), obviously, also falls away. Use on every occasion goes where it may, without any large-scale generic differences governing its itinerary.

Chapter 4, "Nothing is Metaphor" will return to these distinctions, as they operate in AP, in order to suggest how metaphor, figures, and the remainder of the secondary may be understood, and, with that, all other usages, once the foregoing distinctions have been relinquished. In the meantime, as noted, these distinctions have consequences for Cavell's practice of interpretation and at least some of his reflections on it. Though the work done by forms of life in "making our sounds words," as Cavell rightly puts it, occurs only on concrete occasions of talk!, obviating usage's division into great classes, this schema, with its focus on words as words, remains central to Cavell's reflections on reading and much of the labor he undertakes in that vein. To this phase of his writings, attention thus must now turn, in order to sketch Cavell's hermeneutics and to begin to suggest an alternative one, based not on words, but entirely on discourse or talk!

3.3 UnBecoming

The stipulations or descriptions pertaining to kinds of usages met with in Cavell's account, it is maintained, have consequences for conceiving the practices of literary

---

[49] Though disputes on occasions arise and are often adjudicated about what is said or to be said, the terms on which they are resolved would here be as individual and as specific as the occasions themselves; they would not rest on nor disclose forms of life and their outlines. In "The Argument of the Ordinary," Cavell returns to the example of a child's learning a word and also the issue of criteria discussed earlier, while treating Kripke's reading of Wittgenstein (*Conditions Handsome and Unhandsome* [LaSalle: Open Court, 1990], 64–100). He stages a version of the ordinary's "argument" in which both voices, the skeptic's, denying, and the non-skeptic's affirming our criteria play a role. Though a powerful presentation, the ordinary's argument obscures the present concern. Cavell's treatment presupposes that there are words and that criteria (to be denied or affirmed) may be imagined in respect to them. Yet this entire nexus is here in doubt in a fashion not at all isomorphic to the skeptic's position, since talk!'s capacity to function is by no means questioned, nor that of the holistic configurations that backstop it.

[50] For example, I can read about "reverse repos" in the pages of a financial newspaper, and though I may still have only half an idea of what they are, I now know *that* they are, which is enough to get through the next stretch of talk! that concerns them.

studies and the other humanities. Accordingly, the present section follows out how words operate in Cavell's interpretations and in his own reflections on that practice.

To be clear, to examine and ultimately question Cavell's interpretative practice is not to call into doubt any single one of Cavell's *interpretations as such*, nor the profound and often important pathways and provocations that they have afforded numerous literary critics and other thinkers. None of that stands at issue, though what is set forth here perhaps may furnish some critics and philosophers with the opportunity to think more about their own readings and what they presuppose.

Moreover, Cavell's concern with words will be examined only in one text and in a single interpretative instance, which may prove something of an extreme case. Indeed, shortly after this piece's appearance, Cavell renewed his thinking on this subject under the heading of what he called perfectionism.[51] The latter, also announcing a new phase in his concern with other persons, doubtless alters the emphases of the text here considered, as well as of some other earlier works, though whether Cavell shifts ground entirely or simply expands on what came before is less clear.

Without, then, claiming to comprehend either all of Cavell's discussions of reading or all of his reading practices in what follows, it nevertheless remains the case that in the text about to be discussed, Cavell addresses reading and interpretation in a fashion he rarely does elsewhere with this degree of explicitness and detail. His 1985 "Being Odd, Getting Even" is self-consciously *about* these practices, while engaging in a version of them. Accordingly, it provides a look, offered by Cavell himself, at both the role played by words when Cavell reads and his explicit understanding of the word's status in interpretation.

"Being Odd" is in part a reckoning, a settling of accounts, or *Auseinandersetzung* of a kind, with both Jacques Lacan and Jacques Derrida, and a number of appendices pertaining to this aspect accompany its published version. Cavell's essay opens with an extended treatment of Ralph Waldo Emerson's "Self-Reliance," followed by a discussion of Edgar Allan Poe's story "The Imp of the Perverse"; only Cavell's engagement with Emerson is discussed here.[52]

Before he broaches interpretation as a theme, thereby offering his riposte to Derrida in particular, Cavell turns to Emerson's text, establishing the basis on which that

---

[51] See Cavell's *Conditions Handsome and Unhandsome*, especially its Introduction, for an overview of his complex presentation that returns to Emerson, turns to Saul Kripke's interpretation of Wittgenstein, and ends with a discussion of John Rawls theory of justice. Andrew Miller's *The Burdens of Perfection: On Ethics and Reading in Nineteenth-Century British Literature* (Ithaca: Cornell, 2010) offers an especially sustained development of this theme, that gracefully brings the possibilities Cavell lays bare into contact with other contemporary approaches to literature. See also, sections three and four of Mulhall's *Stanley Cavell: Philosophy's Recounting of the Ordinary* on redemptive reading (Oxford: Oxford University Press, 2010) and chapter one of David Rudrum's *Stanley Cavell and the Claim of Literature* (Baltimore: Johns Hopkins University Press, 2013), as well as Toril Moi's "The Adventure of Reading" in Eldridge and Rhie.

[52] Mulhall, in the correspondence previously cited, queried why the Poe portion of Cavell's essay is not addressed. As that part explicitly concerns words and their morcelization, his is a fair question. Yet Cavell's work on Poe does not seem to me to add anything new to Cavell's practice of interpretation (already focused on words) or his reflection on it, except perhaps for his concession that we do not usually notice words themselves, or at least their "cells"—presumably the etymological roots that we find configured in the words, which he also calls "word imps"—in our ordinary usage (IQO 125).

discussion, and its explication of interpretation, proceeds. Cavell's initial treatment of Emerson's "Self-Reliance," specifically, entails two basic characterizations of Emerson's goals in that work. Both of these emerge solely on the basis of *words* found in Emerson's text—in one instance a single word, in another two.

Cavell, first, contends that in "Self-Reliance" Emerson offers a variant, or indeed, as Cavell will later insist, a *reading* or interpretation of Descartes' *cogito* as set out in the latter's *Meditations on First Philosophy*; second, this reading, or what Cavell also calls Emerson's rewriting of the *cogito*, locates the *cogito*, the "I think," Cavell suggests, in a more "modern" register than Descartes himself, giving it in an existentialist, and indeed distinctly Heideggerean, flavor.

Cavell's first point, that Emerson offers a reading or rewriting of the *cogito*, it should be noted, flows entirely from Emerson at one moment, accusing his present-day readers of not daring "to say, I think, I am." Without commenting on the remark's context, Cavell identifies Emerson's mention of the I with Descartes' discussion of the *cogito* in *Meditation Two*, an identification thus based solely on Emerson's words. Though many readers "assume the *cogito* always to be expressed in words that translate 'I think therefore I am,' in Descartes *Second Meditation*," Cavell notes "that insight is expressed: 'I am, I exist'" (IQO 107). Hence, because Emerson in *Self-Reliance* employs the same words as Descartes, "I am" (preceded by "I think"), Emerson, by Cavell's lights, at this moment is reading Descartes and supplying his own version of the *cogito*.

Emerson, however, according to Cavell, not only recasts the *cogito*—including its performative dimension; Cavell, on this score, citing then recent interpretations of Descartes by Bernard Williams and Jaako Hintikka—but Emerson also envisions his *cogito* in a more thoroughly modern guise than Descartes. This claim also depends on a single word. The role played by god as creator in Descartes, according to Cavell, is taken for Emerson by the self, by the "I"—a suggestion that depends on Emerson's employment of the lone word "author." Noting that the English word "author" can translate the Latin word "*auctor*," Cavell recurs to Descartes usage of this Latin term when speaking of god as creator in *Meditation* III. Accordingly, Emerson's claim that we should be "authors" of ourselves, by Cavell's lights, refers to and indicates his replacement of Descartes' god as guarantor of our being and our thinking with that of our self.

Cavell himself, it should be mentioned, at this moment, remarks on the slender thread from which his interpretation hangs. "But surely," he states, "the idea of self-authoring is . . . the merest exploitation of the coincidence that the Latin word for author is also the word for creating" (IQO 110).

Individual words alone, words as words, then, by Cavell's own avowal, support his initial interpretation of Emerson's "Self-Reliance": his view of Emerson as reading and rewriting the Cartesian *cogito* in a more modern guise. Cavell next sets out his own understanding of interpretation on the basis of the gloss on Emerson that he has just tendered. Interpretation, Cavell eventually tells us, is a version of the practice that he has just identified: it consists in an existential or self-oriented *self-authoring*, by means of *the words* found in a text. Emerson's modern *cogito*, as understood by Cavell, demands that one "author oneself" both existentially and literally; it enjoins *existential* self-authoring through an actual or literal authoring. Correspondingly, reading or interpreting the productions of such self-authored authors (as Emerson or Descartes) consists in a parallel self-authoring of the reader, a (self-)creation, essentially the same as that act of (finite) self-creation that the author performed when producing herself and her own work. Such (self-)creation in the readers' case also attends to words, just as did Cavell in this instance, in his reading of Emerson. The "theory" or perspective on writing and reading that Cavell next gives, consequently, serves as an unpacking, a hermeneutic justification, of Cavell's own interpretative practice.

Cavell initiates this next phase of "Being Odd," in which his explicit hermeneutic standpoint comes to the fore, by way of reference to, indeed thanks to a barb tossed at Derrida, one that builds on the work Cavell's text has just done. Cavell wonders, more specifically, whether a tension might exist between Emerson's insistence on authoring *oneself* and this very injunction emerging by way of Emerson (putatively) *citing or quoting* Descartes. Caught between the one vector toward speaking for oneself (authorship) and a second vector toward quoting another, Emerson's stance, muses Cavell, may appear "undecidable" between "saying and quoting" (IQO 113).

Cavell resoundingly rejects this possibility, however. Declaring "whether I am saying ... or quoting" is equivalent to whether I am "saying ... first- or second-hand," or "thinking or imitating," Cavell draws on the demand for self-authoring that he has just set out in order to link the distinctions just mentioned (between "first- or second-hand" and between "thinking or imitating") to "the question whether I do or do not exist as a human being" (IQO 113). At stake in the difference between saying and quoting, thinking or imitating, for both author or reader is thus existence as a genuine (or self-created) individual, insists Cavell. At this moment, moreover, Cavell brings the distinction between words' primary and secondary senses surveyed earlier into his quasi-Cartesian/quasi-Emersonian/quasi-Heideggerean framework. The choice between saying and quoting is indeed *not* undecidable, and this is because it ultimately answers to "the difference between language and literariness," or "the difference between ... the mother tongue and the father tongue," as Cavell also here identifies it (IQO 113).[53]

What Emerson (or Cavell) has been doing, then, when he appears to be (re-) reading Descartes, is thus not, in truth, unfolding and explicating another's text and discourse, namely, Descartes' or Emerson's. The activity or reading, rather, concerns words as words, language as language, and the requirement to forge a father tongue from a mother tongue, just as the author originally did, both reader and author being similarly enjoined, by Cavell's lights. Indeed, in line with the role already granted to a "performative cogito," neither in the reader's nor in the author's case is the primary purpose of saying to express some concrete insight distinct from the performance in question; the main task is not to express something about something—neither as author nor reader—but to author oneself, and, while so doing, to restitute what has been lost in respect to language's words *as words*.

---

[53] See my previous discussion for Cavell's explicit identification in *Claim* of the "father tongue" and "secondary" sense.

This is the case, here the two necessities of self-authoring and the restoration of words converge, in part because the division earlier met between primary and secondary usage no longer is as straightforward as earlier now for Cavell. In "Being Odd," so-called primary usages and senses have themselves apparently suffered a certain displacement, specifically at modernity's hands, as is also true in Senses.[54] Accordingly, the vocation of "literariness," the point of forging "a father tongue," resides in *restoring* that commonness and everydayness *that words ought to have* (and in a fashion still imply), but which they have somehow ceased to fully embody, owing to modernity's advent.[55] Hence Cavell concludes his avowal of saying over quoting, and his parrying of Derrida, by affirming on the part of authors like Emerson, whom Cavell at points deems "secular prophets," "an inheriting of language, an owning of words, which does not remove them from circulation, but rather returns them, as to life ... the claim to existence requires returning words to language, as if making them common to us" (IQO 114).[56]

With the gordian knot seemingly posed by the tension between saying and quoting thus having been severed, thanks to the word's restitution being the task jointly faced by those who would, in writing or in reading, self-create, it is not difficult for Cavell to make still more explicit the status that reading or commentary in general holds for him. All textual interpretation indeed proceeds as Emerson is purported to have done, by Cavell's lights; it speaks rather than quotes, bringing about a claim to one's own existence, a self-authoring, that simultaneously forges a father tongue that presents words fully as words, as what they are already supposed to be, but somehow not fully are.

---

[54] Modernity, as such, is not explicitly mentioned at this moment in Cavell's text. Earlier, however, the very "need for the cogito," Cavell has had told us at the outset, arises "at a particular historical moment ..." (IQO 111), and he has indicated that what demands Emerson's performative *cogito* is "that man, the human, does not, or does no longer, exist" (IQO 112), a condition bound up, indeed perhaps ultimately one, with the absence of a truly common language here also avowed, since "the claim to existence," Cavell tells us, requires "returning words to language, as if making them common to us" (IQO 113). Emerson (or Poe) or someone, according to Cavell, accordingly, must restitute what modernity has removed; along with inventing themselves, they must make words as if common, and invent or reinvent man and the human—at least as an aim or a goal—as well as, while so doing, reconcile "the private and the public or social," since "genius," Cavell tells us, is "the name of the promise that they [the private and the public or social] will be achieved together," itself predicated on the "perception that our lives now take place in the absence of either" (IQO 114).

[55] Cavell thus insists that what he calls "Emerson's gag," (i.e., Emerson's rejecting quoting in favor of saying, while also seemingly engaging in the former) depends on the following, which Cavell lists in a single compendious sentence, here broken down and abridged as follows:

- a) "the fact that language is an inheritance, words are therefore before I am, they are common"
- b) "second, that whether I am saying them or quoting them, as it were saying them first- or second-hand, which means whether I am thinking or imitating, is the same as the question whether I do or do not exist as a human being, a matter demanding proof"
- c): "third, that the writing, of which the gag is part, is an expression of the proof of saying "I," hence of the claim that writing is a matter ... of life and death,"
- d): "and that what this comes to is the inheriting of language, an owning of words, which does not remove them from circulation, but rather returns them, as to life. That the claim to existence requires returning words to language, as if making them common to us" (IQO 113–14).

[56] For Wittgenstein as "prophet," see n. 48.

In fact, self-authoring under modern conditions, as set out earlier by Cavell, necessarily involves persons *who do not author themselves*, who remain, as Cavell calls it, "uncreated." The specifically Heideggerean overtones of Emerson's purported reinterpretation of the *cogito*, indeed, include "a view of the world, let us say a perspective on its fallenness . . . in which human life appears as the individual's failure at self-creation." Such failure at self-creation is "a mode of (uncreated) life" that "Emerson calls 'conformity,'" Cavell announces, again resting a complex interpretation entirely on a single word (IQO 111).

The watchword of Emerson's (or Cavell's) explicit "theory of reading," then, while including the aforementioned injunctions, since also established on this quasi-Heideggerean basis, finally turns out to be "mastery," a mastery once more existential and verbal. "Mastering [a] text," by way of mastering its words, and thereby simultaneously authoring oneself, is the overarching task of reading or commentary, as Cavell's hermeneutics explicitly envisions it in "Being Odd" (IQO 115).

To be sure, such mastery, at once of others and of words, for Cavell also involves a kind of obedience; it consists in discerning the "whim" (both accident and necessity) "from which at *each word* it [the text] follows" (IQO 116, me). Even as such, however, reading's focus remains words, ideally "*each word*" of a text, of which the reader aims to gain "command," as Cavell is also about to put it.[57] All interpretation is, then, a mastery, and a listening and obedience, aimed at a text's *words*, organized around the reader's self-authoring in the face of uncreated others, while also returning words to themselves. Such a complex movement, finally, is described by Cavell as attention to a text's "genius," attention to the moment when a text "*invariably* says more than its writer knows."[58]

A paradox or irony resides in Cavell's present characterization of interpretation, however—one worth noting now, although it will soon become clearer. Cavell's own interpretative practice, aptly sketched on these terms, is visibly isomorphic with, indeed turns out to be essentially a version of the close reading of the New Criticism. For both, interpretation consists in attending to a text's words in a manner that exceeds the intentions of its author, as well as any contexts attendant on the text's coming into being and its functioning. Previously unnoticed connections among all its words in the New Criticism provide a new view of the text as a whole—indeed its "genius"—a template that accords with Cavell's own account of a text's "mastery." The irony,

---

[57] "On the reading side, the idea of mastering Emerson is not that of controlling him exactly . . . but rather that of coming into command of him," an overtaking of his work, specifically its words, itself a matter of saying not quoting, just as in Emerson's own case (IQO 117).

[58] IQO 117 (my emphasis). Cavell, having likened his or Emerson's own reading practice to poststructuralism's, tweaks this present claim, by opting for what he believes to be a more nuanced version of authorial intention than the poststructuralists, affirming that the role played by such intention is neither "nothing," nor "everything" (IQO 117). Texts, accordingly, embody something like that purposiveness without purpose found in Kant; they retain a purely formal intentionality, or genius, in their verbal organization (see also EAP for purposiveness). In his *Conditions Handsome and UnHandsome*, it should be noted, Cavell returns to Emerson, and explicitly examines his intersection with Heidegger's later thought, through an interpretation of Emerson's "The American Scholar." While that reading is by no means a simple break with the present one—Cavell once more speaks both about "whim" and deducing words—it does also seem to be conducted with somewhat more concern for what Emerson himself says, for Emerson's own point of view.

however, is that Cavell, of course, rejects the New Critics' understanding of language root and branch, even as his reading, and theory of reading, ends up in nearly the same place. Conversely, one New Critic, in fact one Cavell chastises, Cleanth Brooks, as will be made plain in the next chapter, actually breaks with these parameters of New Critical practice, thereby coming to a version of interpretation more in tune with texts as instances of discourse arguably than Cavell himself, albeit Brooks, to be clear, possesses a much more naïve view of language than does Cavell.

In any case, whatever power or glory, or inadequacy or failure, attends on Cavell's or Emerson's endeavor—every reading needing to be confronted on its own terms—most crucially, Cavell's practice of reading, and his account of it, inherently eclipses that temporality which is here inherent to discourse or talk!; a consequence of this omission is that Cavell similarly omits the possibility, if not always the fact, of understanding another as setting forth a perspective decidedly different from one's own.[59] The insights Cavell credits to the texts or works he reads usher from words as words, as well as the necessity to author oneself, to engage in a performatively inflected *cogito* entailing self- and other mastery. Cavell's construal of interpretation thus entails what I will call here a species of Unbecoming: a freezing of talk!'s temporality, yoked to an inherently static verbal focus, albeit one also ultimately occasioned by modernity. By contrast, interpretation, even on its common or everyday understanding, makes explicit the temporality that on the present account informs all discourse. Interpretation, on this view, rather than to words, recurs to earlier instances of discourse as discourse. To be sure, this attention need not prevent anything fresh and new emerging from either side, both text and interpretation surfacing in a single inherently temporal movement. Cavell's notion of reading, however, leaves vanishingly little room for that negotiation; aimed at the mastery of a text's words in the service of self-creation, it forecloses grasping discourse as genuinely the discourse of another, as expressing thinking different from one's own, indeed thanks to overlooking interpretation's inherent temporal articulation to the benefit of the word—Cavell himself, tellingly, choosing for the guiding thread of his hermeneutics a version of *the cogito*.

To confront the discourse of the other as discourse, not words must be read, not even the necessity/whim that putatively accompanies and organizes them, but extended stretches of talk!, in part backstopped by earlier ones, with an eye to what these stretches *say*, and the topics *they* talk about—what they express about actual subject matters, articulations which on some occasions at least are also likely to be *different* than the reader's own. For Cavell's approach, which aims at words, such an understanding of another's discourse, finds no place, not even, it would seem, a dedicated space. In the

---

[59] Cavell's remarks on mathematical concepts in *Conditions* further attest to his overlooking time and traditionality. In his settling of accounts with Kripke, in the course of arguing that mathematical concepts are on the same footing as all others, which also "count" (91), Cavell nevertheless distinguishes them, asserting "that mathematical concepts have befores and afters, not pasts and futures; they are eternal ("I always meant this"). Jacob Klein, a student of Husserl's and Heidegger's, in his *Greek Mathematics and The Origins of Algebra*, trans. Eva Brann (New York: Dover, 1992) does, however, offer a history of our concept of number, which Klein at least believes has lead to confusions that still plague this conception. Apart from this, what such an eternal perspective would mean for all our concepts, given that they purportedly are ultimately on the same footing, as well as our powers invention (or discovery) remains unclear.

present essay, moreover, Cavell's actual interpretative practice fails to register what his hermeneutics as formulated also explicitly excludes: the acknowledgment of otherness, that shock attendant upon making contact with a new, powerful, and fundamentally foreign perspective.[60]

Finally, to take a step back, a strange symmetry turns out to frame Cavell's treatment of the word in *Claim* and his understanding of the word's consequences for hermeneutics across its broadest reaches in "Being Odd." Cavell's discussion of *primary* usage in *Claim*, thanks to stipulating to words' internal constancy downplays—without altogether eliminating, owing to the corresponding external variation—a moment of novelty and improvisation in all discourse. The very notion of a single word's projection, or projections, covers over talk!'s, or discourse's, appearance within tacit series or sequences, in what is here being labeled a historicity or traditionality. In *Claim*, what needs to be known to talk! or to understand a discourse comes instead simply with our words, with their "internal constancy" and "grammar," at least in the case of a "master of the language," putatively initiated into the relevant forms of life.

In "Being Odd," however, where *secondary*, not primary usages now stand in the foreground, Cavell's apparently different focus on the word nevertheless has essentially *the same effect*: namely, of eclipsing discourse's temporality. Discourse is once again removed from becoming, in favor now, however, of restoring words to the primariness they are supposed to have but somehow never fully possess. In the forging of a father tongue, the avowed work of secular prophet's and geniuses, discourse as discourse and thus its own temporal operation, is again discounted—but here because primary usage has somehow *faltered*. Not because words and their usage are projected and protected by a culture, but because in the present culture they fail fully to be such, and thus require a movement of self-creation purporting to return language to us anew, any acknowledgment of the temporality and historicity of talk!, and of talk! of the other *as other* ends up ruled out.[61]

In both instances, accordingly, no room remains for how a genuine interpretation *could* be conducted, how one *could* understand and comment on the thought and saying of another. Whether viewed as either primary or secondary senses, understanding of the sort central to the humanities falls out of Cavell's ruminations *in principle*, despite his own advancement in practice of it at least at times. An inability to carve out a space for reading (the other), in the end, is thus inseparable from Cavell's new, albeit still in part Wittgensteinian, focus on words.[62]

---

[60] Gerald Bruns identifies such shock as inseparable from hermeneutic experience (as indeed do I). Cavell, accordingly, as a reader, on my view, is an allegorist in precisely Bruns' sense. Bruns himself, of course, places Cavell in a different camp, having long viewed Gadamer's and Cavell's hermeneutics within a single frame. See Bruns, *Hermeneutics Ancient and Modern* (New Haven: Yale University Press, 1995), 218.

[61] For these reasons, it should be mentioned, for Cavell, in the final analysis the ordinary and the extraordinary are never simply wholly opposed. The ordinary in our (modern) context proves extraordinary, in part revealing the extraordinary power, of non-coercive, individuated agreement it possesses or should. In turn, the extraordinary is also ordinary, both in our own (modern) day-to-day life, but also owing to its non-independence from the ordinary, which is similarly revealed under these circumstances.

[62] The most notable exception to this in practice is, of course, Cavell's interpretations of Wittgenstein, but others doubtless could be included. Interestingly, Cavell's readers, including many who most

To discover a more satisfying account of interpretation, one that proceeds without any recourse to words and instead remains wholly within discourse and its accompanying temporality, it will be necessary, then, both to return to Cavell and once again to turn away from him. In the first part of AP, not yet much discussed, Cavell offers a view of metaphor that he contrasts to that of Cleanth Brooks; for the latter, metaphor provides a gateway to discourse as it is found in poetry and literature as such. Viewing this difference in the light of the other decisions about language, discourse, temporality, and interpretation that Cavell makes, as well as in the broader context of metaphor's interpretation more generally, a new understanding here will emerge of metaphor, figural talk!, and indeed, all talk!, as fundamentally tied, including at the moment of its understanding, to temporality and to becoming.

would acknowledge as his best, are not like him in this regard: they indeed read his writings as discourse, they look to what Cavell's works *say*, in the sense offered here, a project that they self-consciously undertake. By contrast, Derrida, whose thinking, like Cavell's, includes or depends on reading others to a great degree, at least in his first writings, is, by my lights, a consistently more attentive and persuasive reader of those he reads than is Cavell. Derrida's commentators, however, by contrast, believing they are following their master, adopt a practice more like Cavell's, and their interpretations, similarly, often focus on individual words or neologisms found in Derrida's own writings. Cavell, then, is arguably more of an overreader than Derrida, at least, claimed to be, while just the reverse is true of their respective commentators. Discourse as here conceived, in the final analysis, however neither affirms the "overreading" sometimes said to practiced by Cavell and by Derrida, especially in Derrida's later phases, nor falls in with that aim at one single final reading implied by the hermeneutic practice of more traditional philosophy, though doubtless preferring the latter to the former if forced to choose. (Colin Davis brings out this notion of "overreading" in his *Critical Excess: Overreading in Derrida, Deleuze, Levinas, Žižek, and Cavell* [Stanford: Stanford UP, 2010] and he is fully aware of the discrepancy I mention. Davis also turns to "Being Odd" for Cavell's general take on interpretation, albeit he arrives at rather different conclusions than I; *Overreading*, 135n1.)

4

Nothing Is Metaphor

Having come to grips with Cavell's understandings of persons, language, words, interpretation, and, in part, time, the present focus widens, eventually to fill in further that temporal aspect of discourse that Cavell downplays.[1]

A more multidimensional approach to Cavell's text, accordingly, now follows—one that examines what is said *by those he reads* in some depth, as well as by Cavell himself. Attention is paid, in particular, to a singular reciprocity that invests Cavell's encounter with the New Criticism. In the first half of AP, two very different approaches to language emerge, one seemingly emanating from literary studies' future (Cavell), and the other from its past (Brooks and the New Criticism). The advances that Cavell's work undoubtedly represent in conceiving of discourse in his own case, as just displayed, do not preclude shortcomings in envisioning the actual work done by discourse in the humanities, in the interpretation of literature and of similar extended discursive performances. In turn, Cleanth Brooks, a leading New Critic, articulates an original and profound view of reading and interpretation, although Brooks' conception of language inhibits him from grasping some of its most important consequences. The present understanding of interpretation and its practice thus ultimately differs from both Cavell's and Brooks'; its presentation is embarked on by turning to their encounter in AP's first half.

4.1 Metaphor and Time

Cavell's tamping down of the temporal features of discourse emerges particularly clearly when his account of metaphor in AP is placed in the broader context furnished by alternative conceptions of this figure. Then, and only then, do the advantages of Brooks' account of interpretation, and of metaphor and of literature more generally, taken up in the following section, become apparent.

[1] Cavell's limiting of temporality, in addition to the foregoing, is evident in his assimilating the past to the relation to another (Cavell's account of other persons will also come into question here; see Chapter 5). Near the end of his essay on *King Lear* in *Must We Mean*, "The Avoidance of Love: A Reading of King Lear," Cavell speaks of the past and of the historian's work; yet he brings these considerations forward in the context of understanding Shakespeare's characters, thus rendering the question of historiography equivalent to the problem of other *persons*. "The epistemology of other minds," hence Cavell avers, "is the same as the metaphysics of other times and places" (*Must We Mean What We Say* [Cambridge: Cambridge University Press, 2002], 267–353; 337).

As previously noted, Cavell's discussion of metaphor appears on its face to harbor a certain opacity. Rather than identify this obscurity in terms of Cavell's episodic focus on language in terms of words, as has been done previously, now, thanks to surveying a range of treatments of this figure, the difficulties inherent in Cavell's treatment of metaphor can be brought into view, including making visible how Cavell's understanding suppresses time's contribution to metaphor's workings and ultimately to all discourse. Metaphor, on the present account, indeed ceases to be intrinsically distinct from any other instance of discourse. Hence, this chapter's title: *nothing* is metaphor.

This much is clear in Cavell's approach to metaphor in AP: metaphors, as he understands them, demand or allow paraphrase in a way that all other figures do not—metaphor and paraphrase for Cavell perhaps somehow being "logical" (or "grammatical") correlates in some quasi-Wittgensteinian sense.[2] Yet, why this finally should be so, what Cavell himself at this moment sees and apparently sees so clearly remains difficult to discern. This insight, if it is one, moreover, is not further explained, nor appears genuinely available on the surface of his text. As noted earlier, the two New Critics in question, while disagreeing about so much else, view metaphors and all other figures as posing equivalent interpretative possibilities. Cavell's treatment of metaphor, then, may usefully be situated amid other possible approaches to this topic.

Metaphor's explicit analysis stretches back at least some 2,400 years in the so-called West. Accounts of metaphor, in this tradition, customarily are divided into classical accounts—Aristotle's *Poetics*, mid-fourth century BCE, predominantly being their source—and so-called modern ones; the latter seeing the light of day, it is generally claimed, with I. A. Richards' and William Empson's treatments near the dawn of the twentieth century.

Modern accounts of metaphor differ from the classical, which also includes the Port Royal grammar and similar endeavors, in that they credit metaphors with saying something distinctly new, as well as inherently different from anything that standard, non-metaphorical speaking can express. This dividing line is true even of Cavell and others who affirm paraphrase, which thus does not denote a complete word-by-word translation capturing the entirety of the figure's meaning (whatever else it may designate). "And so on" trails all explanations of metaphor, Cavell states in AP, an observation he rightfully credits to Empson.

By contrast, for Aristotle and other classical accounts, metaphors are simply and wholly *analogies* with some terms missing, all of which *could in principle be restored*. So construed, as compressed or elliptical analogies, any metaphor can be rendered *literal* simply by "working backward" through the analogy implied by the metaphor, yielding a now explicit statement.[3]

---

[2] Cavell's inquiry, it must be said, is very much a tentative, open-ended, and zetetic one, to its credit. Such avoidance of all theory building, he insists, is part of his new style of philosophizing, and Cavell makes plain that that he believes it needs imparting to the New Critics themselves.

[3] For example, in the metaphor "the evening of life," "evening," according to Aristotle, substitutes for old age, according to an underlying analogy between a life and a day—formulaically: evening : day :: old age: life (*The Poetics*, trans. W Hamilton Frye [Loeb Classical Library; Cambridge, MA: Harvard University Press, 1922], sect. 21, 79–85). The metaphor thus results solely from a

So conceived, metaphors are thus entirely "lexical"; they concern solely the arrangement and ordering and choice of words, with no inherent bearing on what is being expressed, on the metaphor's logos or contents as such. By contrast, for the modern account, metaphor's raison d'être consists in furnishing some kind of new "speech," an authentically new meaning or content. "Juliet is the sun," to recur to Cavell's chosen figure, represents an unprecedented expression, and what it says ultimately could not have been achieved in any other manner, the modern vantage point claims.

Accordingly, the challenge in a modern context is understanding how something fundamentally new and unexpected can come to be *expressed*, with language and its use being understood on the usual terms. If, for example, language by definition permits an unlimited number of new statements to be made from a finite set of rules and entities (words or signs), how *can* uses exist that say something new, yet are also *not* already extrapolatable from what language already provides? Metaphor's operation appears to reach beyond language, or push language beyond itself, while at the same time somehow still being a matter of language through and through. Language's workings (and perhaps its very existence) is thus at stake in accounting for metaphor in a modern guise, that being the reason metaphor's construal is central to so many reflections on language.

Cavell's position, also modern, may then be further specified, thanks to a charting of the different responses to this problem of yielding new meaning out of old language that modern accounts provide. More specifically, the range of modern approaches to metaphor hinges on the answer to two related questions: (a) In what precisely do metaphors' novelty consist, what sort of newness in respect to speech belongs to them?; and (b)How do metaphors *produce* such novelty—specifically, what roles do language and discourse play in metaphor's production? Treatments vary in regard both to how they understand metaphor's novelty—specifically, whether what *is said* in metaphor is itself new, or only what metaphorical expressions *show*, or both—and to how language and/or discourse contribute to that result. Three modern possibilities, with differing responses to both (a) and (b) for the present purposes thus may be set out, according to the following chart, with Cavell's providing an intriguing middle case:

Linguistic	Borderline	Discourse Alone
Saying	Saying/Showing	Showing
Language	?	Literal Sentence Meaning
Interactive Model		
Black/Richards	**Cavell**	**Davidson**

The first modern standpoint corresponds to that of the early New Critics. Neither Brooks himself nor all his peers subscribed to it. (Monroe Beardsley, notably, offers a

---

substitution of names or terms ("evening" for "old age"), where the literal alternative "old age" has been suppressed in favor of a different term "evening." The figure, then, can be decoded, the literal name retrieved, by working backward through the analogy presumed to have generated the metaphor in the first place.

view of metaphor that anticipates Davidson's in important respects.[4]) The early New Critical position may most economically be approached through its later presentation by Max Black.[5] For this standpoint, metaphors coin *new senses*; their uniqueness resides in what they say or express. Such new sense, for this account like all sense, derives from language. This first theory, sometimes referred to as an "interactive theory," accordingly, focuses on how *new meanings* come about in metaphorical expressions, purportedly through an interplay among the connotations of the various terms used in the metaphor. The putative "meaning cluster" adhering to the metaphorical term (e.g., "the sun") is said to present its subject ("Juliet") in a new way, redistributing the sun's and its subject's respective associations, yielding a novel presentation with a novel sense.[6]

On the other extreme, stands an effectively wholly *discourse-based theory* primarily associated with Davidson (who fashioned it a few years after Cavell's work and who occasionally cites Cavell's discussion). For Davidson, the work and novelty of metaphor consists entirely of *what it shows*, while what a metaphor *says* remains wholly literal. Metaphors, for Davidson, do not state anything new; they bear only their usual meanings or senses, construed in the complex fashion that Davidson construes senses generally.[7] Such statements, moreover, are false. Metaphors for Davidson are false literal sayings, which, in being said, occasion new perspectives or insights, ones not available any other way. For him, metaphors thus offer a new view of something as something; yet they only intimate, not state, that view.[8]

In the light of both of these alternatives, Black/Richardson and Davidson, Cavell's stance can be better grasped. His perspective, unique to him, as far as I can tell, falls between the aforementioned two stools.[9] Unlike Davidson, metaphors *do say something*

---

[4] Monroe Beardsley, "The Metaphorical Twist," *Philosophy and Phenomenological Research* 22, no. 3 (1962): 293–307.

[5] Max Black, "Metaphor," *Proceedings of the Aristotelian Society*, New Series, 55 (1954–1955): 273–94.

[6] For example, when Benjamin Disraeli, on his finally having been elected prime minister, exclaims "I have climbed the greasy pole," the putative "meaning cluster" around "greasy pole" now presents "getting elected," redistributing this phrase's associations. Brooks' claim, yet to be plumbed, that metaphors cannot be paraphrased, whatever else it does, pushes back against this perspective.

[7] Donald Davidson, "What Metaphors Mean," in *On Metaphor*, ed. Sheldon Sacks (Chicago: University of Chicago Press, 1978), 29–46. Davidson generally disallows any account of language that grants independent meanings to individual words; for him verbal meanings have no existence apart from the sentences in which they potentially may be used. His complex stance toward words, to be clear, does not simply deny a verbal dimension; rather meaning, including that of terms, emerges in the context of sentences as used, across which a working theory of the term's sense can be disgorged with an eye to those conditions that would make the sentences in which it appears true. Davidson's semantics, a theory of meaning which turns out "to make no use of meanings," as he once put it, is explored at some length in Chapter 9 (Donald Davidson, "Truth and Meaning," in *Inquiries Into Truth and Interpretation* [Oxford: Oxford University Press, 1984]: 17–36; 24).

[8] For Davidson generally, as further discussed, not words, nor language, but the logical form of the assertion—without doubt in use, uttered with an eye to the world and in intercourse with others—but still that form, effectively bears an absolute privilege. It constitutes the core of discourse, the keystone of all intelligibility and understanding, with all other usages, including and especially those of interest here, proving but penumbra. The proposition's status is the major factor differentiating Davidson's standpoint from the present one, which in other important respects takes its lead from some of this thinker's central notions.

[9] Richard Moran has pursued this problem independently, first in his article "Seeing and Believing: Metaphor, Image, and Force," *Critical Inquiry* 16 no. 1 (Autumn 1989): 87–112 and again over

new for Cavell. Metaphors alone, as has been seen, of all figures say something in their own right in a fairly strong sense of saying, bordering on stating, allowing paraphrase. At the same time, as is true for Davidson, for Cavell metaphors also *show* something novel. The two moments of novelty, stating and showing, moreover, do not entirely overlap or exhaust one another; metaphor's showing is never entirely exhausted by its saying.

For Cavell, metaphors both show and say, and they perform the latter in a strong sense. As he puts this in AP: "A metaphorical expression sounds like an ordinary assertion, though perhaps not made by an ordinary mind" (AP 80). What Cavell's text leaves unanswered or implicit (noted by the question mark in the earlier chart), however, is *how* metaphors do this. Unlike the other two approaches, in Cavell, the manner in which metaphor does what it does is not explained.

To be clear, the two other accounts, Black's and Davidson's, directly correspond to the two distinct understandings of language and discourse here at issue. Metaphor, for the New Critics, redounds to language understood as furnishing, among other things, words, accompanied by a relatively stable repository of meanings or senses. By contrast, for Davidson, metaphor's accomplishments bear no relation to language understood in this form; what metaphors do they do only in *their being said*; Davidson's treatment of metaphor is based entirely in discourse.

Metaphors alone of figures, then, for Cavell, apparently allow their primary usages to remain legible, while these usages and senses are in metaphorical usages, as it were, caught in the act of being turned away. In AP, Cavell himself thus states: "To understand the metaphor, I must understand the ordinary or dictionary meaning of the words it contains; *and* understand that they are not being used in their ordinary way, that the meanings they invite are not to be found opposite them in a dictionary" (AP 79). For Cavell, primary (or "ordinary" or "dictionary") meanings thus remain in question in metaphor, even as these usages and senses do not finally account for the sense of the metaphor itself; dictionary meanings are invoked in a manner that also brings us up short before them. As marked by Cavell's own emphatic "and," a moment of shock and deflection in metaphor produces a new flash of meaning and a new view of something as something, the two perspectives overlapping, without emanating simply or wholly from *the meaning* (as in the New Critic's case), and thus at the same time participating in that showing found in Davidson's account.

A question or concern raised by Davidson about alternative treatments of metaphor can, however, be lodged at the point to which the explication of Cavell's has just arrived. Raised to motivate the acceptance of his own theory, yet extending beyond this, Davidson's *objection* to existing theories of metaphor brings time squarely into

---

the following years. (Cf. his "Metaphor," in *A Companion to the Philosophy of Language*, ed. Bob Hale and Crispin Wright [Oxford: Blackwell, 1997], 375–400.) His "Seeing and Believing" uses Davidson's comments as a springboard for his own investigation, which in some respects is like Cavell's, but also comes near to some of the conclusions arrived at here, particularly in respect to the role of words and subject matter in metaphor's framing and understanding (cf. 105; 109). Moran's gloss on Davidson's central point, however, diverges from that I offer, as he believes Davidson's view can be contested by distinguishing "meaning-in-language" from "speaker's meaning" (Moran 95). In Davidson's thinking, however, these two are never strictly separable.

the picture, albeit Davidson's *positive* treatment of metaphor, in distinction from his objection, joins both of the other accounts in excluding temporality.

More specifically, Davidson suggests that what all other modern treatments of metaphor than his own entail, yet cannot account for, is the operation of *two* senses (or, in Cavell's case, two uses) *at once*. Conceiving this figure, as is almost always done, requires that two distinct senses operate *simultaneously*. Such simultaneity of meaning, however, is ultimately inexplicable, according to Davidson, on all standard accounts of language.

Davidson primarily posed this question to Black and the New Critics, and there it can be most readily grasped. For a metaphorical usage to be understood as *metaphorical*, on that account, not only the new sense of the expression but also the previous non-metaphorical one must be registered. The identification of a metaphor as a metaphor entails recognizing at once an old sense of the words in question and also a new one. Were the expression unable to be somehow referred back *to both*, were a metaphorical statement not legible as bearing an everyday or literal meaning *and* a metaphorical meaning, it would not appear *as* a metaphor. Without this dual reference, the purported "metaphor" would simply provide some other, single sense.[10] The novelty of the meaning metaphors possess must thus somehow appear *in them*; it must be able to be registered there, and that can only occur if its older, previous sense and its new one are active together.

Under Black's linguistic construal of meaning, however, as Davidson's also points out, that there would be two *meanings* successfully dwelling in a single utterance is prima facie problematic. Even if, as in the interactive account, the (new) meaning arises through a rearrangement of a prior set of connotations, for the utterance to remain intelligible, and intelligible as saying what it (now) says, it would seem this new meaning must simply already *be one of its possible meanings*. If all meanings are indeed housed in language and derive from it, then this meaning too must already potentially exist there, in which case, once framed, the metaphor, of course, disappears and the statement is again simply a literal one. What the metaphorical expression at that moment conveys is, then, either not itself a lasting *meaning* at all, the alternative for which Davidson opts, or it is, and some account, then, must be given of metaphor's retaining two temporally distinct senses—since metaphors are not simply ambiguous, or catachreses, or puns.[11] Black's construal thus fails to yield metaphor, since language cannot, on Black's own view of language (and indeed arguably on any), provide the resources whereby a metaphorical expression continually wears and exhibits two meanings that are also *temporally* distinguished, one old and the other new.

---

[10] Hence, in the course of a complex counter-example, Davidson writes: "Your purpose was metaphor, not drill in the use of language. What difference would it make.... ? With the theory of metaphor under consideration, very little difference, for according to that theory a word has a new meaning in a metaphorical context; the occasion of the metaphor would, therefore, be the occasion [simply] for learning the new meaning" (Davidson, "What Metaphors Mean," 37).

[11] Davidson explicitly discusses all three of these options and differentiates them from metaphor (Davidson, "What Metaphors Mean," 37–9).

Davidson's criticism of Black hinges on identifying a moment of *becoming*, of novelty in all figuration, for which most standard views of language and of meaning apparently cannot account. Figuration, including metaphor, would be an event, an innovation, one inexplicable on the classical linguistic terms broached by Black and the New Critics.

Cavell's account might, then, seem better able to handle such becoming than Black et al., to the extent that it, like Davidson's, is discourse-based and already views expressions as requiring events of a sort. Yet, as just reviewed, Cavell's own treatment of metaphor, like Black's, similarly rests on old and new *appearing together*, as his emphatic "and" just discussed attests. Indeed Cavell's stance invites the arguably still more difficult question of how on any *single occasion of use*, two *uses* can be sighted together. It raises and arguably begs the question of how distinct *usages* may continue to appear in *a single one*, in the same utterance, a possibility that seems perhaps even less likely than two senses so cohabitating.[12]

That this concern is genuine, not some kind of debating point, moreover, is attested by how Cavell profiles metaphor in AP's first half. Metaphor's portrayal at Cavell's hands notably omits the contexts in which it is used; instead it aligns with a model of talk! in which expressions can be understand simply on their own terms seemingly in isolation from the discourse-based and worldly contexts in which they appear.

That metaphors are being understood in isolation from context, that they are functioning lexically or as some equivalent, is visible in Cavell's now often-cited aperçu that metaphors appear not to be true or false but *wildly true or wildly false* (as if Cavell, in advance, was responding to Davidson's later claim). The mark of a metaphor, according to Cavell, is that it does not even pretend to say anything that could possibly be true. But this characterization is only compelling if utterances are evaluated on their mere sentential face and apart from context and use. To recur to Cavell's own example, if I say, for instance, at the start of some game, "Juliet is the sun," and then add "Josephine is the earth" and "Jill is the moon," the same expression claimed wildly false and hence inherently metaphorical appears as neither; it operates wholly without hiccups—wild falsehood or truth drop out of the picture.[13]

In context, what might be classified as a metaphor works just fine; thus not what these expressions purportedly *say* shows whether they are figures, but solely how they are used, which alone, then, determines what they actually express. Accordingly, all other determinations of meaning (or use)—proper, metaphorical, figural, and so on—at best classify speech *after the fact, in the wake* of these expression's use and understanding. They play no significant role in any expression's actual operation or reception.

---

[12] Cavell's own impatience or frustration at moments in AP's text, I believe, recurs to his sensing something like this problem. That impatience is registered perhaps especially when he would distinguish metaphors from idioms; he indicates the latter "I fell flat on my face" is "an appropriate one" (AP 79).

[13] Similarly, "I have climbed the greasy pole," would appear to be just a statement, when uttered by a fitter and younger Disreali, with nothing wildly true or false accompanying it. Cavell's own Shakespearean example, moreover, gets much of its force from Juliet appearing from the east (in a window), a feature Cavell at this moment neglects.

The problem of how metaphors can bear two meanings or uses in a single case, in this light, is thus dissolved or resolved. Contrary to these accounts, the distinctions upon which metaphor's identification as a metaphor depend never play a role in their or in any expression's intelligibility. Nothing, no expression, accordingly, *is a* metaphor. In those instances, as in all others, only participation in larger contexts, both verbal and worldly, allows these expressions to say whatever they happen to on any given occasion—albeit in retrospect, to be sure, calibrations may be made about how more or less usual than other usages with what are taken to be the same words the expressions in question may be.

Hence, though sometimes it might be possible or desirable to classify usages after the fact, that possibility exists only in the wake of use, to which meaning or usage as so divided into their respective classifications does not contribute anything. Such classifications are indeed not probative in respect to what these utterances express and say and show, with the result that how these expressions work differs not at all from any other expression, any other instance of discourse.

Put otherwise, by being returned entirely to use and use alone, the entire framework that allows for there to be metaphors collapses: no metaphors in any philosophically relevant sense exist, since no pre-formed semantics, even as capacious as Cavell's discourse-oriented one is available or *informs* their work. Indeed for most literary figures but also for most of them in life, it is in any case not the single sentence but some larger context, including other stretches of discourse (as in *Romeo and Juliet*) as well as other aspects of the world that render what is said understandable, just as with all other utterances, which only when grasped *in concreto* indeed mean or say anything. Put in the terms Davidson and Cavell share, all discourse includes a moment of showing; such showing, however, does not take place simply apart from what is said, but participates in the former's articulation. Showing of some kind is already at work in any instance of talk, "internal" to it, without being contained by it, since talk! cannot in the first place assemble itself or saying anything except alongside some reference, which melds with its own expressions. No talk is ever understood without an accompanying object or subject matter in view, while such viewing in turn also always remains open to (further) discourse.

By contrast, though insight into some subject matter also inheres in Cavell's account of figures, he expels the role it plays in these figures' articulation in favor of words and dictionary meaning. Cavell's treatment thus is shadowed (or haunted) by traditional accounts of metaphor and the sentence's operation. At the same time, the temporal element, to which Davidson points, when asking how two meanings or uses are at once at work, while also being temporally distinguished, proves inseparable from understanding these and all expressions. In metaphors and all other discourse, a historicity or traditionality of talk! operates, such that no recourse to language as a preexisting fixed entity, as a kind of permanent reservoir of verbal meaning is needed, nor may language as so conceived, as is becoming clear, take temporality's place in use.

4.2 Interlude on Words

Oddly, given the other views of language that Brooks holds, such a temporal, contextualizing worldly register actually stands at the heart of Brooks' account of metaphor, and also of "irony," which Brooks identifies, along with metaphor, as the basis of what he calls "poetic structure."

Brooks' insights have lain relatively fallow until recently, in part doubtless owing to this very terminology.[14] (Cavell, certainly with some right, dismisses Brooks talk of "structure" as "metaphysics," while, perhaps less aptly, also riding somewhat roughshod over what Brooks wishes to convey with this and related expressions—Cavell once more arguably attending too much to his author's individual words.) Brooks' own conception of language also accounts for his lack of recent reception; his understanding stands at some remove from discourse as here and elsewhere conceived. (Brooks explicitly attributes his views on language to Rene Wellek, whose account was itself an "adaptation" of Roman Ingarden's treatments of language and literature, the latter influenced by Ingarden's own early studies with Husserl.[15])

Despite all this, Brooks' own thinking took as its primary examples literature and literary discourse, of which he was also a highly able interpreter. His practice thus allows identifying features of discourse's workings that might escape philosophers who do not start from this region, including, in the most complex case, Cavell himself. When discourse becomes approached *primarily* by way of literary discourse, however, the importance of *time*, both to its understanding and to its production, inevitably emerges, for reasons pertaining to literary's novelty and imaginativeness that my earlier discussions of metaphor and literariness have already begun to suggest.[16]

---

[14] Douglas Mao's "The New Critics And The Text-Object" remains the go-to discussion of relatively recent ones concerning the New Critics, including Brooks (ELH Volume 63, Number 1, [Spring 1996]:227–54). For a newer study, see Audrey Wasser's "The Book of the World" in her *The Work of Difference: Modernism, Romanticism, and the Production of Literary Form* (New York: Fordham, 2016), 11–37. A few other recent treatments are discussed later.

[15] Brooks, *The Well-Wrought Urn*, 186 note. Ingarden's now rarely studied works had enormous influence on literary studies in the previous century. Not only did they underpin some of the New Criticism, but they also buttressed much reader-response criticism, including that of Wolfgang Iser. For more on Ingarden, see my entry on "Phenomenology's Intersection with Literary Criticism," in *The Routledge Companion to Phenomenology*, ed. S. Overgaard and S. Luft (New York: Routledge, 2011), 644–54.

[16] Joshua Gang in a recent study on I. A. Richards' behaviorism and its subsequent reception by the New Criticism, "Behaviorism and the Beginnings of Close Reading," notable for its detailed and careful treatments of its subjects, claims that Brooks, unlike Richards, viewed his own approach to literature as "subjective" and "impressionistic," and correspondingly that Brooks' unique understanding of metaphorical and literary form was primarily aimed at the "experiential" and "affective," to this extent being a translation of Richards' own practice (*ELH* 78 no. 1 [Spring 2011]: 1–25; 14). Brooks, to be sure, as is further discussed, pushed back against viewing poetry and criticism as being able to yield objective knowledge; he denies that they traded in assertions of any sort, in this way distancing himself from the scientism and positivism of his time, as Gang notes, citing Guillory ("Behaviorism," 14n3). Nevertheless, Brooks' notions of form and of metaphor are not simply subjective or affective, as Gang suggests, but "semantic," as he at one moment allows, or what I would call discursive ("Behaviorism," 15). Brooks himself begins *Urn* by insisting on the need to pay the closest possible attention to "what a poem says as a poem" (iii). It is, moreover, of course, thanks to such attention to what literature *says* that Brooks especially, as well as the other leading New Critics, gained prominence.

Granting for the moment, the appropriateness of time's importance and of literature's power to disclose discourse, the outline of discourse's operation, in the terms on which it has so far been presented, may also raise questions; on this account, too, Brooks' work proves worth taking up. For one thing, despite the difficulties alternative treatments of verbal meanings seem to yield in the case of metaphors, a very deep intuition arguably maintains that there is a difference between knowing *a word* and knowing or understanding *its use* on a given occasion. This distinction (itself bearing a marked temporal element) between what seemingly happens once (understanding a use) and what is repeated or lasting (a word and its meaning or perhaps its usage) appears unassailable, this presumably being at least in part why Cavell embraced "primary usages" to begin with. To be sure, what is here suggested is that ultimately there are no words in any philosophically important sense, but this suggestion may seem more problematic than the conflation of what may be a single use with a standing usage or sense.

At the same time, momentarily postponing this first problem (which is about to be addressed), a zone of obscurity remains in regard to the hermeneutics so far here sketched. A concern with past discourse, discourse that is temporally and otherwise foreign to the interpreter, emerged as an issue when discussing Cavell's treatment of interpretation. Yet, this emphasis arguably seems not to square with the insistence registered more than once, especially in the chapter on Bernstein, that discourse is *about* something, something of interest to its present-day readers, as well as its producers. Is not concern for, on the one hand, what previous instances of discourse actually *say*, and, on the other, for their subject matter, and to this degree, *the non-discursive presently informing their understanding*, in tension? Talk! construed as use renders talk! an *event*; yet this eventful character seems to imply that writing (or previous instances of oral performances, etc.), as *past* events, necessarily recede into the past and remain irretrievable, as Cavell's own practice of interpretation at moments borders on suggesting.[17] The present view of discourse may thus harbor within itself the same division between present discourse (and what it allows) and all past discourse that at times becomes visible in Cavell and in all other discourse-oriented thinkers (including, often, Davidson).

Two concerns, one with words as such (uses and usage) and another with the status of past talk and its present understanding are thus on the table, which to a certain extent dovetail. After all, given the denial of there being words in any ways that matter, it becomes still more opaque how *past* instances of talk! can "communicate," as we usually put it, with the present, since neither words nor signs provide something supposedly "the same" to fall back on. The remainder of the present interlude on words is thus devoted to showing that only the second hermeneutic problem is genuine—how interpretation can be both of the past and of another, while also speaking to the present (and the future) about a common matter of urgency. The issue concerning words as

---

[17] As in the pages from "Avoidance" cited earlier.

such, its cancellation in the present instance, ultimately gives way to the hermeneutic consideration, leaving only it to be further worked out.[18]

What, then, at the present juncture must initially be seen is that of all the different circumstances that arise in actual discourse that are commonly thought to require words (or fully fledged signs), one case alone is crucial.

1	2	3	4
Synonymy	Catachresis	Learning a Word	Metaphor
Familiar words/single usage	Familiar word/"different" usage	Unfamiliar word/ new usage	Familiar word/ new usage
Examples			
Duenna/Chaperon	"Chronic" for marijuana	"Ontology"	

The chart lists various instances where words or signs seem required; on the present construal, synonymy, catachresis, and, of course, metaphor, can all be factored out, leaving only "learning a word" subsequently to be addressed.

Our practice and practical acquaintance with discourse, it is here maintained, suffices to account for the first two instances. Worries about synonymy and catachresis may indeed be put aside, because with discourse, as here conceived, comes a working familiarity with use, and, to this extent, different usages. Insofar as speakers have always already been engaged in stretches of discourse, on the present view, where duennas or chaperones, bachelors, and unmarried males have been spoken about, not only can we use the terms without worrying about any further codification but we can also point to overlaps or coincidences among them as they appear in use, without having to worry, in the bachelor case, for example, what to make of ten-year-old boys or widowers—instances where we have "unmarried males" perhaps not bachelors. These cases would be a concern, and demands for the limits of bachelor's scope registered, if discourse derived from individual words that bore fixed meanings. Then we would indeed have to worry whether "bachelor" and "unmarried male" do or do not contain identical "semantic cores," as Husserl once put it.

On the present construal, however, synonymy, first, derives from discourse, from previous uses. Moreover, *claims about synonymy* are themselves an instance of discourse; they inhabit stretches of our talk! Like everything else found in discourse, synonymy assertions, too, then, are contextualized, situated; they are similar to saying on certain occasions that two reds are the same or alike. Pertaining to various instances of use and themselves appearing in uses where such instances are being talked about,

---

[18] It should be mentioned, though words are denied any probative role, the fate of signs in the present context is more complex. The existence and operation of signs in some fashion does subtend all talk; yet, as noted earlier, *signs* are to be understood *only* as they are identified in information theory, where they can be quantified as bits and their capacity for conveying information is statistically determined in a system. Information theory, however, *presupposes* that discourse is already at work and understood, in order that what is informative and what not in relevant contexts can be ascertained and its own analysis can go to work (letters vs. squiggles, words or code, entire pictures or their outlines, etc.). Accordingly, though signs and or information so theorized may be implicitly at work in all discourse—ultimately accounting for why I must cut my MLA talk to make it only twenty minutes long—what these notions designate makes no explicit, direct, or conscious contributions to my or any other instance of talk!'s actual workings or their understanding.

synonymy so understood thus does not entail the existence of words in themselves, identifiable in some fashion apart from use.

The same sort of contextualization holds good for catachresis, except in this case, reports on other, purportedly related uses don't actually matter; they are essentially pointless. Whether, for example, some demotic genius, recognizing certain features of habitual marijuana use, ironically dubbed that drug "the chronic" (the scenario I personally like to envision), is not necessarily more true than if someone or some group perhaps misheard the sound "marijuana" for "chronic," and after eventually realizing their mistake (or not), came to use the latter term. The point, however, is that neither scenario is in any way probative and that neither matters a wit, nor is relevant, fortunately, when it comes to actual uses. The term functions, it says what it says, solely in use, in actual stretches of talk, and how it came to assume this role makes no difference; many users of the term "chronic," of course, are not even aware that it has a character that could prompt these questions.

Hence, only the third case, that of learning a new word—actual names or words that subsequently will be used—seemingly requires that there *be words* to be learned apart from discourse.[19] When both a *new understanding* (or new "meaning" or usage proper) and an *unfamiliar* sign or word are to be brought together, a question pertaining to discourse's sufficiency as here understood genuinely arises. If a new meaning *and* a new sign, such as "ontology," let us say, is encountered by one unacquainted with it, this seems to entail that there be *words* independent of discourse—these also being cases, of course, where dictionaries and lexicons tend to be consulted.

In this instance, however, the primacy of discourse itself arguably emerges clearly. For, the confluence that appeared in the discussion of metaphor indeed again comes to pass: namely, understanding *a use on a given occasion* and understanding *a usage* (or a sense and meaning) turn out to be the same.

---

[19] In analytic circles, the requirement that languages be learnable and thus that there be finite units enabling potentially infinite discursivity is called compositionality or the composition principle (sometimes contrasted to the context principle, as in Michael Dummett's readings of Frege). A foundational early essay by Davidson, "Theories of Meaning and Learnable Languages," is often taken to argue for the necessity of compositionality (*Inquiries Into Truth and Interpretation* [Oxford: Oxford University Press, 1984], 3–15). Davidson is thus viewed as an adherent of this dictum, all his work being interpreted in this light, especially in recent Davidson interpretations that advance what is called "truth-theoretical semantics." As is discussed further in *A New Philosophy*'s final chapter, Davidson's subsequent revisions of his own thinking, especially his "A Nice Derangement of Epitaphs," arguably call into doubt the validity of employing language's learnability as a baseline for what occurs in use, though I am not denying that an implicit compositionality remains important to Davidson, one that would be confined to occasions between speakers and hearers already familiar with discourse, thus a compositionality that, within such boundaries, may also be affirmed here, since it ceases to imply any full-blown formalizable semantical theory. Whatever the correctness of my interpretation of Davidson may be, from the present perspective, as was implied in the earlier discussion of Cavell's treatment of learning a word, how a language is first learned is indeed not in question for discourse as here conceived, in part since the moment of its being learned and what may have then been learned are both obscure, even on Cavell's account. Employing a version of Heidegger's "always already"—the present perspective jibes with Heidegger's in fundamental ways—participants in discourse here are taken to have *always already* embarked on linguistic performances, always already begun to talk! That they have already done so in the past is crucial, in way that obviates concern for an idealized moment of initiation, and it is from such a timebound perspective alone that what expressions say and their understanding in use may be gleaned.

What I understand when I understand, or let us say learn, "ontology," is indeed how it is used in some given instance, though I may and usually can imagine more or similar cases.[20] Yet that *cases* still remain in question, that is, other instances of use, attests to there being nothing more at issue even in this instance than occurrences of discourse. Nothing more happens or can happen or is needed than such situated, occasional understanding, since neither I nor anyone, nor even anything, actually masters in advance the ways a term functions apart from discourse.[21] To be sure, two ends of a single stick may be in play, the single event often being understood from the point of view of the sign (or the word), as a moment of becoming acquainted with that sign, rather than, or, in addition to, understanding how it is being used on this occasion (thus with an eye toward some future use). But nothing more than this single use (and/or imaginary other ones), no genuine meaning or lawfulness thereby is at issue.[22] If one wishes, one can say a new "piece" has been provided and put into play, yet apart from its "initiating" employment, it awaits actual games (themselves an open-ended array), while by no means implying such games in their distinct existence in any probative way, as became clear when discussing Cavell's remarks on learning words and the inability to correlate them with specific language games uncovered earlier.[23]

Taking the foregoing at least as a working hypothesis, if not a settled account (which is not to affirm it will indeed ever arrive at simply being such), the issue standing beyond all four cases, the second, specifically hermeneutic question is, then, the sole pressing one. The salient question is not how words work, or come to be known, such that they prove the same in different contexts (since they may actually not function in this fashion sufficiently to warrant such an explanation), but instead how can words that are used in *contexts that their receivers appear not to share* address matters of

---

[20] My own example may appear to stack the deck by choosing "ontology," given its abstractness. But just these cases of exotic, complex terms prove helpful in that if one is not familiar with them, that is, does not already know how to *use* them, their dictionary meanings often prove of no help. Even an educated adult unfamiliar with philosophy, when provided with its dictionary definition, is likely to have no understanding of what "ontology" says or how it should be used.

[21] Even apparently so outlandish or illicit uses, say of "blueberry" as a verb, as "blueberry the nail" (which would doubtless usually be met with astonishment if not admonishment, and which was indeed initially conceived as an example or counter-example foregrounding the inescapable necessity of the sameness of signs) makes perfect sense when uttered, for example, in a nail salon.

[22] A point of clarification: to claim that there are no words indicates they always function and are what they are, within larger structures of talk and in contexts of use. There indeed exist, as noted, signs, but these have no *prescriptive force*. Thus one can speak of "dogs" as a verb or as one of my hounds or as any of a number of other uses—"those dogs." These terms only function as such in these stretches, informing others in part on the basis of sharing other stretches of discourse but never from above, neither exclusively nor determinatively.

[23] As noted earlier, Cavell's account stresses the difference between those who already know what words and names are and those who don't. Yet as was put forward there, the line between the two, on a radically discourse-based construal, by no means is as bright as Cavell suggests; indeed as his own examples showed, it may not be fundamental at all, since words in their own right cannot be identified significantly apart from contexts. "Ontology" once again is a good example, since not being the name of *something*, it makes clear that "knowing" what a word or a name is really contributes nothing to our use of them (since here at least we clearly don't know how to understand this even as a type or class of word apart from understanding its use).

concern to those same receivers, while also presenting understandings *foreign* to their recipients. Understanding discourse produced in circumstances different or foreign (ones novel, including the imagined and/or from other times and places) while still speaking about something, about a relevant subject matter, is the crucial issue for any discourse-driven account. The questions occasioned by discourse in the humanities, then, not in everyday talk, if there is such a thing, consequently, are the most decisive for understanding discourse as a whole.

4.3 Discourse and Time: "Free Balloons"

How the unity of past and present in discourse's understanding functions *in concreto*, and, with it, ultimately, some account of the current work's own manner of proceeding can be afforded by turning to Brooks' writings, specifically his reasons for rejecting what he called "the heresy of paraphrase," both in the case of metaphors and when it comes to literature more generally.[24]

Brooks objections to paraphrase take two distinct, albeit related, forms. The first worries that affirming the possibility of paraphrase results in obscuring literature's type of talk, its specific way of being literature or poetry, in Brooks' word, it's form. Consequently, in AP's first half, Cavell takes Brooks to task for claiming, as Brooks does, that paraphrase fails of "the real core of meaning which constitutes the essence of the poem." Talk of "essence," "core," and also "structure," Cavell insists, is profoundly misguided (AP 75). Yet, while Cavell's remarks on Brooks' words are doubtless apposite, not only does what worries Brooks also ultimately concern Cavell, but what makes both of them anxious—namely, the reduction of literature's way of talking to any other mode of speaking—overlaps with a worry that pertains to the hermeneutics in the course of here being proposed.

More specifically, Brooks' concern, as Cavell recognizes, resides specifically in some *statement or proposition* (or some set of them) being taken for what a piece of literature says. That "the absence of self-knowledge is both inevitable and dangerous" be viewed as what Jane Austen's *Emma* amounts to, or Keats' famous closer, on truth and beauty, held to be what *Ode on a Grecian Urn* has *to say*, indeed worries Brooks. Brooks is anxious about *claims or statements* offered as paraphrases of poems, and these paraphrases then being taken as equivalent to the poem's own speech. What he identifies as "the structure" of literary discourse is needed, for Brooks, to ward off this appearance, to explain why poetry is inherently rebarbative to being appropriated by statements.

Whatever they ultimately yield, these concerns with propositional renderings of literature may well appear germane in the present context, so much so that after a first look at them, consideration of this problem returns at this section's end. In the present account, truth or insight, of some perhaps new or broader stripe, into some

---

[24] The "Heresy of Paraphrase" piece stands at the end of *The Well-Wrought Urn*, where it is proceeded by a sequence of close readings of literary works and followed by three appendices. As is often the case in Brooks, the particular engagements in part take on their significance from their place in the whole.

subject matter (itself expansively understood) plays a role in both literary production and reception. Affirming such a place for insight, however, doubtless invites Brooks' fear that literature is being turned into a version of the statement or assertion, or some set of them, and thus is not being treated as literature, or as literary, at all.

Cavell's response to Brooks, moreover, in its own way compounds this worry. To be clear, Cavell questions Brooks' concern. Cavell suggests that Brooks' anxiety about paraphrase, and Brooks ensuing talk of literary form is misguided, insofar as it implies that paraphrase somehow could *be* mistaken for the literary speech-act, that the two may be enough alike that the attempt to show why literature and its paraphrase do not "approximate" each other is a worthwhile undertaking.[25]

Cavell's stance, too, then, while contesting Brooks', however, also intimates that a risk may be run, or a mistake made, by the present approach insofar as it denies any difference between literature (or the aesthetic) and more standard forms of expression. Though Cavell does not think paraphrase threatens poetry's own speaking, for him an art work implies an intrinsic manifestation of its own being as literature or art, one that the approach taken here would ignore.

Cavell's response to Brooks, however, insofar as it participates in the latter's perspective, again, however, envisions a species of discourse removed from its contexts, as did his previous treatment of metaphor. In some circumstances, after all, the *Iliad* just *is* a set of clues for pinpointing the historical Troy; in others, it furnishes an introduction to the behavior of gods, heroes, and of the rest of us. Generic distinctions, accordingly, appear not at all to be "baked in" in the way both Cavell and Brooks at points suggest.

Nevertheless, the underlying worry shared by Brooks, Cavell, and possibly some readers deserves a more fundamental response, one here afforded by questioning the assumption they share: namely, that the disclosure of truth uniquely belongs to assertions and statements. In the present context, to the contrary, propositions or statements ultimately function no differently, and indeed no more directly than any other modality of discourse, including when it comes to truth.[26] Accordingly, the grammatical form of statements lacks any ultimate privilege or distinguishing difference; in effect, *there are no statements* or assertions in the fashion that Brooks (and also apparently) Cavell conceive of them, just as there are no metaphors.

To recur to what was said in Chapter 2, literary and artistic discourse does indeed show something, showing is integral to expressing anything at all, since without concrete contexts, literature, like all other discourse, bears no sense—or says nothing. At the same time, what is shown and what is said *never exhaust one another*—not in the literary nor in any other instance, albeit in a fashion distinct from that Cavell exclusively assigns to metaphor. Saying has its own past, its own series, while what is shown, though participating in it, also remains oblique to that sequencing. Each aspect, discourse, and things, then, takes on their intelligibility from the other, as well

---

[25] Cavell's somewhat winding discussion of Brooks' talk of paraphrase's "approximation" rests on the conclusion that Brooks' own talk leads to the belief that poem and paraphrase could be equivalent; "he himself," Cavell states, speaking of Brooks, "furthers the suggestion that paraphrase and poem, operate, as it were, on the same level" (AP 76).

[26] Part Two of *A New Philosophy of Discourse* is devoted to a further working out of this admittedly bold claim.

as the surrounding contexts and preexisting circumstances within which they appear, thereby overlapping but never entirely coinciding.

Accordingly, *literature's* discourse also speaks *about* something and it recognizes or sees *something as something*, without these moments either simply coinciding or definitively diverging, leaving room at once for insights and their expressions that take shape in an open-ended array of styles in respect both to what is seen and what is said.[27]

How saying in a literary context operates—an operation deemed to be the same as in any other instance of discourse, though not necessarily are all the types of expressions found in it themselves the same—becomes visible in Brooks' own thinking, moreover, in particular, in his rebuttal of Winters in his "Heresy of Paraphrase." Though Brooks may misapprehend the status of the statement as such (in ways and for reasons examined in the subsequent portion of this section), nevertheless, Brooks insightfully sketches literature's and literary criticism's operation, revealing a set of circumstances applicable finally to all discourse, despite Brooks' own intentions. When Brooks' text is encountered in its context, when its discourse above and beyond its words is given attention, what is presented by Brooks under the guise of poetry's structure or essence indeed astutely indicates how literature, and criticism, and ultimately all discourse function.

Brooks' account can be so illuminating, since in examining an example of what he deems to be the heresy of paraphrase—specifically, Winters' paraphrase of a metaphor found in Robert Browning—Brooks doesn't primarily focus on "the metaphor," but on the larger context in which it operates. Brooks' concern at first actually is with what he calls the expression's "literal" meaning, not some metaphoricity that supposedly inhabits this expression in isolation.[28] Accordingly, what the belief that metaphors are paraphrasable gets wrong, for Brooks, does not pertain to metaphor as such, but instead to *the relation* of what a single expression says (however construed) to other relevant stretches of talk! (in this case ones found in the same poem), a relation that Brooks at times also dubs "irony."

More concretely, Winters, for his part, glosses the metaphor "so *wore* night" as simply saying "thus night passed." In response, however, Brooks refers the reader to the expression that follows: "The East was grey." Winter's paraphrase, Brooks insists, loses not the single meaning of the sentence or inscription that supposedly constitutes the "metaphor" ("so wore night"), but its connection to the subsequent portion of Browning's poem: specifically, how "wore" (said of "night") relates to "grey," said of the East. The two taken together, for Brooks, depict night as *aging and weary*, characteristics absent from Winters' paraphrase.

---

[27] The task of the final chapter, in particular, will be to make clear how this works more granularly than is at present set out.

[28] (*Urn* 201). This is not to suggest that Brooks himself denies all difference between literal and figural. His 1965 essay, "Metaphor, Paradox, and Stereotype" provides the clearest statement of his views on this theme, and there Brooks clearly retains this distinction (*British Journal of Aesthetics* [1965]: 315–28). In that piece, however, Brooks similarly stresses both the necessity for what he calls metaphors to be interpreted while viewing that process as a matter of relating them to their broader contexts, as he does here. This approach, as far as I can tell, was distinctive of Brooks; many different accounts of metaphor circulated among the New Critics, from Richards' and Empson's canonical views all the way to Monroe Beardsley's discourse-based one.

Yet this dimension, which, as Brooks claims, indeed disappears in Winters' treatment, clearly does not concern what is said in *either of the two expressions when taken alone*; it emerges *only* in the movement and passage across them both. Accordingly, at this moment, Brooks, treating metaphor's paraphrasability, sketches discourse in miniature as it is here envisioned more generally. Poetic discourse is indeed *in motion* for Brooks; it necessarily undergoes new contextualizations and recontextualizations at the hands of other sayings. Only through such movement, indicates Brooks, does what is said become available at all, as well as what this saying talks about, the insight or showing it offers—in this instance, most proximally, of night as aging and wearying both itself and the poem's speaker.

Such a conception of poetic speaking or discourse, as movement through contexts that constitutes and reconstitutes them, defines poetry for Brooks. Indeed, what Brooks calls "structure" in part names the necessity for such a passage through contexts that he believes is specific to literary discourse. In *Urn*, Brooks identifies "structure" with "paradox," and does so again in his late writing on metaphor; in his now much anthologized essay, "Irony as Poetic Structure," Brooks identifies it with "irony."[29] There irony designates the centrality of *contexts*, and of *movement across them*, for poetic speech.

More specifically, Brooks in that article, having previously established that none of "the elements of a poem" function on their own, defines irony as the "warping of statement by context" (Brooks 758).[30] Context at this moment, for Brooks, primarily designates other things said.[31] Accordingly, for Brooks, all that poetry and literary criticism and commentary can say and show depends on the surrounding circumstances of any given saying, of what comes before and after it, while what such saying says and its subject matter arrive only by attending to that movement. The force of any one of a poem's expressions, what it says and what it talks about, descends from this greater whole, from these greater contexts, and does not exist independently of them, to this extent being rebarbative to strict paraphrase. At least as far as poetry and criticism are concerned, Brooks himself, accordingly, already goes quite a ways in conceiving discourse on the temporal terms here envisioned.

Brook's invocation of structure does not, however, entirely escape the stasis that this notion usually implies. Brooks endorses a literary type of discursive stasis or stability, one that emerges from literary discourse's own motion and being-in-time, ultimately with an eye to his understanding of the difference between poetic and all other speech. In light of this difference, then, in the name of identifying and defending his version of literature's literariness, Brooks closes his structure, in order to give poetry and its interpretation a standing as cognitively respectable as that of assertions

---

[29] Cleanth Brooks, "Irony as a Principle of Poetic Structure," orig. in *Literary Opinion in America*, ed. Morton Zabel (New York: Harper and Row, 1951); reprinted in *The Critical Tradition*, 2nd edn, ed. David Richter (Boston: St. Martin's Press, 2006), 758–65.
[30] Poetic speech, including metaphors, stand "not as blossoms . . . in a bouquet," as Brooks puts it (Brooks, "Irony," 758).
[31] Brooks, for example, insists that Hamlet's declaration "ripeness is all" does not in itself differ from "boldness is all," or other such locutions (Brooks, "Irony," 758). Only through its relation to the other parts of the play does it take on its force and is its subject matter registered.

and propositions.³² Accordingly, if Brooks' vision of discourse in a poetic context is to model all discourse, his affirmation of the difference between the statement and poetry's saying must be questioned, eventually leading to discourse's more thoroughgoing conception, once Brooks' embargoing of a more radical becoming by way of structure has been lifted.

In the present context of paramount concern, then, is the constellation of notions Brooks assembles around stabilizing structure (most significantly, what he calls "irony as the invulnerability to irony," and also the now famous concept of "organic" form, which he shares with Wimsatt and Beardsley).³³ More pressing still is why Brooks believes it incumbent to look to such devices in the first place. That necessity indeed emerges from Brooks' beliefs about propositions and statements. Examining their status in light of these beliefs in the present context, ultimately makes plain, contrary to Brooks, that statements are simply another modality of discourse, rather than different kinds of expression; they are neither opposed to nor free from the movement and becoming Brooks reserves for literary discourse.

In the "Heresy of Paraphrase," Brooks expresses most directly the worry underlying his recourse to structure. Without such stabilizing devices, he proclaims, poetic speaking and its understanding would be only "a commitment to *a free balloon*" (*Urn* 185). Deprived of those moments when the movement of poetic utterance closes in on itself, of that stability structure (as ironic invulnerability to irony) or (organic) form provides, since not being composed of genuine statements, poetry, literary discourse, would exist as "untethered," wholly removed from any fixed or fixable sense and insight, according to Brooks.

To combat this possibility, accordingly, a further delimitation of poetry's mode of speaking is necessary, one that Brooks finds in these stabilizing devices, appealing once more to "the essential structure of a poem," which he indeed distinguishes "from the rational or logical structure of the 'statement'" (*Urn* 186). Not only, however, does Brooks at this moment assign to literary and poetic discourse a unique type of stability, ironic invulnerability to irony—an interactive, yet ultimately self-closing motion, which can operate as a selfsame "form." So proceeding, moreover, he necessarily rejects in the case of poetry those stabilizing features—fixed vocabularies, univocal concepts, and declarative statements that he grants to all other *instances of discourse*, especially as found in the scientific disciplines. Fixed correspondences between words, concepts, statements, and their referents (pertaining both to expressions and their possible truths) underpin discourse that is *not* literary, avers Brooks, including, preeminently *scientific* discourse. The proposition, the statement, and all they usually entail (the word and the concept) thus are finally central to Brooks' thinking. For him, however,

---

³² Walter Benn Michaels, as I discuss in Chapter 7, especially in his earliest essays, also identifies the search for a cognitive status on par with the assertion as fueling the New Criticism's formalism.

³³ As Brooks' memorably puts it: "Invulnerability to irony is the stability of a context in which the internal pressures balance and mutually support each other. The stability is like that of the arch: the very forces that are calculated to drag the stones to the ground actually provide the principle of support—a principle in which thrust and counterthrust become the means of stability" (Brooks, "Irony," 760). For "organic" form or "relationship" see Brooks, "Irony," 758.

their effects fall not within literature but instead define the line *between* literature and other kinds of speech.

Yet just this model of nonliterary speech, as Brooks' own account makes clear, employs relatively naïve templates of language and linguistics, a naïveté that contrasts with the sophistication of Brooks' interpretative practice, and its specific and often ingenious self-thematization. Brooks, to be sure, starts from discourse, from statements or propositions. Yet within this context, he recurs to words and to a distinction between what they talk about, their references or denotations, and their connotations, their meanings or senses.[34] While all words, according to Brooks, apart from those found in "mathematics," bear some connotations, assertions, especially scientific assertions, use language so as to purify words of their associations in order to attain a one-to-one fit, or correspondence, between an individual statements and a given fact. "A scientific proposition can stand alone," Brooks thus writes. "If it is true, it is true. But the expression of an attitude," as found in works of poetry and literature, by Brooks' lights, "apart from the occasion which generates it and the situation which it encompasses, is meaningless" (*Urn* 207).

Brooks, at this moment, embraces a view of propositions that positivism—as found in Rudolf Carnap and others—perhaps most of all attempted to justify, one also found in Wittgenstein's *Tractatus*. To establish such stand-alone propositions in a scientific context, in the face of the unexpected directions modern science, especially physics, had taken, positivism wagered that their seemingly quite glaring semantic inconstancy (Brooks' connotations) could be avoided by tying statements to observable, ultimately sensible, contents, which could allow their truth or falsity to be individually determined; in turn, that possibility, the statement's verifiability, would do duty for its meaning. All statements for positivism that are not verifiable by observations would thus be not false, but nonsensical, technically meaningless.[35] This tethering applied to sentential reports of what was observed would work its way up to the most abstruse theoretical formulations (for example, "the curvature of the universe or quantum coupling), which would acquire their own "sense" insofar they could be cashed out, or not, by some relevant set of observations.

Yet what is now called sometimes called the Quine-Duhem thesis showed that even the expressions found in the most straightforward reports, the so-called observation statements, were inevitably theory-laden; consequently, their references, their denotations, could never be kept separate from the meanings or connotations brought in by other aspects of their treatment, in this case the relevant scientific theories as a whole. No regimenting of the latter on the basis of the former, consequently, could take place. Hence, even in a scientific context, individual statements or propositions

---

[34] Brooks' specific reliance on words is also visible in the analogous portions of "Irony" (Brooks, "Irony," 759). Correspondence, as a view of truth, and the assertion's role in it is treated at greater length in the discussion of Michaels' work later. Michaels, it will turn out, has a view of truth, derived from Bertrand Russell, curiously close to Brook's.

[35] For an in depth look at the movement, see Michael Friedman, *Reconsidering Logical Positivism* (Cambridge: Cambridge University Press, 1999) and also his provocative comparison *A Parting of the Ways: Carnap, Cassirer, and Heidegger*. For a first-hand view of the endeavor, see Rudolf Carnap, *The Logical Structure of the World and Pseudoproblems in Philosophy*, trans. Rolf A. George (Chicago: Open Court, 2003).

are never able to stand alone, as Brooks maintains, nor are their words' meanings, their connotations, fixed by their denotations, their individual references. Instead, as Wittgenstein once feared, who indeed opens TLP with a model of statements somewhat similar to the positivists, understanding of what is said, any purported "statement" must rely on other things said, different expressions' understanding and being true— on negotiations with other instances of discourse and other possible insights and references. This sort of reliance, however, is just that Brooks uniquely assigns to *poetic discourse*; such relatedness is what Brooks believes gives literature and literature alone its own specificity.[36]

Scientific and descriptive discourse, then, do not ultimately operate differently from literature and other discourses; in all instances, discourse "apart from the occasion which generates it and the situation which it encompasses, is meaningless," as Brooks puts it. These discourses, too, speak from and recur to situations, established in part by the state of their existing theories, in part by other circumstances, including those that pertain to their always occasional observations. Scientific discourses, though following different protocols than literary ones and doubtless capable of truth in their own fashion, simply as discourse do not possess a system, structure, or fashion of functioning distinct from literary expressions or the rest of talk!

This being so, that identification must also extend to the insights or truths of which poetry and literature are capable; they, too, do not differ in nature as Brooks believes, from those found in the sciences. For Brooks, all expressions fall into two great genres, not only in regard to their functioning but also in regard to their aims. A first, as found in literature is concerned primarily with attitudes, what Brooks deems "subjective positions taken toward life." A second class, by contrast looks to what Brooks understands as "pure" descriptions, appraisals of *what is* apart from any subjective point of view.

For the present inquiry, this distinction is at best quantitative rather than qualitative. Since discourse does not possess distinct ways of operating at its most fundamental level, it is impossible to uphold an equivalent difference when it comes to truth or insight, including in the clearly subtle and advanced guise proposed by Cavell. Instead, every discourse involves attitudes as well as descriptions in the sense of something worldly or real it is about, each in the end operating as what Brooks calls a "free balloon" (apart from these and related circumstances).

The privilege, and ultimately the straightforward existence of statements, propositions, fixed vocabulary (words) and concepts being questioned (for reasons further elucidated later), the talk! of the sciences, too, indeed must involve attitudes, in fact a whole range of them.[37] To be sure, the concerns literature and poetry address

---

[36] Wittgenstein had a singularly vexed relationship with Carnap, as reported, I believe, by Ray Monk in his *Wittgenstein: The Duty of Genius* (New York: Penguin, 1991).

[37] This is true of "attitudes" as understood in a contemporary analytic context. In that context, beliefs and other perspectives accompanying statements (I believe that the earth is round or I hope that the cake is big enough) are distinguished, or intended to be, from the statements themselves. Ultimately, however, this divide cannot hold. Davidson, arguably, did the most to maintain a version of it, while also profoundly recognizing the unavoidable overlap. (See Chapter 9 for a further discussion of attitudes and the role of what is sometimes called "oblique contexts," in Davidson's approach to the problem of externalism.)

are often usefully distinguished along the lines Brooks suggests—for the most part these days, we turn to chemistry and not to poetry for our understanding of how to turn straw into biofuels, though importantly this was not always the case. Not only, however, do none of these expressions, or their insights, or the relations between the two, permit being distinguished at the most fundamental level—scientific discourse, too, being a free balloon, relying on other discourse and its temporal unfolding for the legibility of both itself and its insights—but they also involve attitudes that vary across a range or spectrum, ones that map standpoints also visible in literature.

Indeed discourse deemed scientific does not, as Brooks believed, imply the *absence* of *attitudes*, of situated, invested perspectives, in favor of pure observation; instead it enshrines *different* attitudes, some closer to everyday life and others further, some less, some more "anthropocentric," if you wish. Thus, in the sciences comprising medicine, for example, more everyday or anthropocentric attitudes hold sway over against those of physics (furthest), the chemical sciences proving an interesting intermediate case. Depending on where they stand on this spectrum, what counts as a scientific question and answer distinctly differs. For example, how the chemical compound in anesthesia works is still poorly understood by chemistry even today; yet anesthesiology remains a part of "medical science."

Literary productions, as well as other discourse in the humanities, however, exhibit precisely the same range. Alain Robbe-Grillet's novels or Joyce's *Finnegan's Wake* (or, for that matter, the political writings of Thomas Hobbes) stand at the greatest remove from an everyday or anthropocentric standpoint (thus paralleling " physics"), over against, for example, F. Scott Fitzgerald or Eudora Welty, "realists," who are closer to medicine, with Virginia Woolf, Laurence Sterne, and Toni Morrison, conceivably answering to chemistry. Here, too, variations within a range of attitudes arise, just as in scientific research.

To be clear, no one is doubting that in important respects types of discourse, roughly speaking, live different lives and play different roles in broader social, historical, and similar contexts. Differences in the relevant institutions in which their expressions emerge, and even differences among the genres into which they divide, doubtless in some fashion exist. In some basic working sense, not only genres but also institutions pertaining to the variety of discourse's apparitions operate, bearing varying expectations pertaining to what may be expressed, how it is spoken about, who speaks, and so on.

Without gainsaying these facts and often at times their importance, nevertheless— and this proves the crucial issue at present—no one-to-one mapping allows moving *from* these institutions and various other attendant formations *to* some actual stretch of talk, or vice-versa. Neither institutions nor genres *directly* determine or otherwise regulate actual articulations of discourse, which they doubtless always accompany. The former concerns remain distinct from discourse as it transpires, albeit institutions and genres find their own different bearings in the time that spans and organizes them, as well as in the often complex terms on which their participants, their circulation, and so forth, function.[38]

---

[38] This would include things like the book and its history, which prove the cloudiest and most difficult instances to assess.

What in this and other cases may be called their traditions, as opposed to discourse's traditionality indeed may assume different styles and configurations, corresponding broadly to different purposes. Yet, the embedding of any stretch of discourse in time remains fundamentally on the same footing in all cases; all these concomitant factors and variations are but styles or prevailing tendencies and never provide control over what some would claim to be their vocabulary or their statements—never yielding outcomes along the lines Brooks, Poovey, and so many others in different ways suggest. In the scientific setting these factors do not map directly on to what discourse and research may find at any given moment, nor even how such research is concretely and granularly performed in any given instance.[39]

Talk!'s own fundamental traditionality or historicity indeed allows that distinct genres of scientific and other kinds of discourse can arise, as well as that distinct institutions and sociuses may assemble around them—and these often quite serious differences on the appropriate occasions should be given their due. Yet assuming that our ability to invent does not in fact extend to successfully creating genuinely ideal structures—words, ideas, concepts, and thoughts—"entities" of any sort somehow truly self-subsistent and capable of standing alone, independent of discourse, none of these moments can, or do, determine talk!'s own operation or its aim at truth at the most fundamental level.

4.4 Traditionality

These last considerations pertaining to discourse's movement through contexts, and how it may be varied or constrained, introduce the final issue that merits address in this chapter. Discourse's always being related to other discourse has appeared; how, then, this connection operates—the explicit being-in-time or temporality of discourse (and thus its specific traditionality or historicity)—has yet to be directly addressed. Discourse is coeval with a kind of traditionality, as it has here been called, apart from the existence of any single, or actually existing, tradition; that aspect of discourse must now be further unpacked.

Pursuing this topic, moreover, allows what otherwise may seem two rather different views of discourse on offer here to be reconciled: discourse's radical occasionality, its functioning like "a free balloon" over against discourse's always arising amid other discourse, its appearing as one balloon among others. Similarly, traditionality's investigation should give a response to the still unresolved question posed at this chapter's beginning: namely, how insights into past instances of others' discourse and matters of concern of contemporary critics can both be at work in interpretation. That words and their meanings are not relevant to resolving that issue has become clear; the structures based on words that Brooks assigns to discourse, literary and nonliterary, do not in

---

[39] Ian Hacking's discussion of the scientific controversy concerning the compound dolomite, in his *The Social Construction of What?*, furnishes a fine example of the absence of any such controlling guidelines even in the so-called hard sciences (Cambridge, MA: Harvard University Press, 1999): 186–94.

fact hold. How, then, the temporality and becoming that Brooks' analysis of literary speaking highlights operates more generally must be addressed; that investigation must also indicate how the past and present (and possibly the future) comport with one another in the interpretation of literature and other discourses in the humanities.

Recurring briefly to Cavell's AP permits the stage to be set for a broader examination of these issues. In AP, Cavell, speaking of his own philosophy, introduces something akin to traditionality. As is indicated by his essay's full title, "The Aesthetic Problems of Modern Philosophy," Cavell deems his own (and Wittgenstein's) thinking "modern." The designation "modern" here bears two possible readings, one of which has been previously discussed: namely, that this philosophy, being "modern," raises essentially the same problems as do the modernist arts.[40] Philosophy, as well as the arts, share in modernity, according to Cavell; their functioning is specifically modern or modernist.[41] Because this is so, what philosophy as philosophy is (or sculpture as sculpture, and so on) is never settled once and for all under these conditions. Instead, being always open to a new "revolution," works in these fields must disclose what art or philosophy are *now*, a labor they perform amid an implicit series of other such showings and installations.[42]

Modernist works thus clearly remain subtended for Cavell by what the poet Sir Thomas Wyatt called the desire for "continual change" and the search "for newfangleness," modernism for Cavell recurring to modernity broadly understood. Yet though a temporal dimension and considerations related to change clearly play a role in these determinations, questions arise (and have already arisen) concerning precisely how large a position temporality and traditionality occupy in Cavell's account of art, literature, and philosophy. For Cavell, to be sure, every (modern) work or corpus emerges against a background of change, and thus within a sequence, Yet its insertion in such a series, its relation to a past (and future) for him falls away in the face of what any given work of philosophy or art says or does.[43] Not only does Cavell often interpret

---

[40] The second reading conforms to what is sometimes called the "objective genitive" rather than the subjective; it names not the aesthetic problems that modern philosophy itself instantiates but the aesthetic problems (such as judgments of taste) that are this philosophy's objects of inquiry.

[41] "Music Discomposed," also collected in *Must We Mean*, presents a more worked through account of these issues than AP, as does its follow up "A Matter of Meaning It." In those essays, Cavell focuses on modern classical music; while music operates in the same fashion, its legitimacy apparently remains somewhat shakier than contemporary sculpture's or philosophy's in Cavell's eyes.

[42] See AP 74, where Cavell indicates that Wittgenstein's thought represents "a revolution" in philosophy. Apparently, what Cavell insists on in respect to philosophy, that present production defines its being *as philosophy*, is also true in the other arts. For Cavell, in fact, as noted earlier, this is so much so that in all modernist works, rather than the medium standing in advance of the work and subtending it, the medium only arrives *in* the work: what a work is *made from* first becomes presented and experienced in and through the relevant work of art. Modernist works for Cavell show/invent their media each time anew, and only as such, as made present in these works, do the arts within modernism know or have media at all. Cavell states this reversal as follows in a now well-known passage in "A Matter of Meaning It," anticipating a standpoint he presents at greater length in *A World Viewed*: "What needs recognition is that wood or stone would not be a medium of sculpture in the *absence of the art of sculpture*" (221; Cavell's emphases).

[43] This is a feature of Cavell's early thinking that he shares with Michael Fried. For both Fried and Cavell, while artworks arise within a time and history—including other previous productions—(proper) works of art ultimately present themselves wholly on their own terms without reference to other works or their worldly existence. Thus Fried, for example, can write of Anthony Caro's sculptures that "they essentialize meaningfulness as such . . . as though the possibility of meaning

literary works in terms of their words, hence in a fashion inherently atemporal. Moreover, though Cavell recognizes that a traditionality, or sequencing of some sort informs their emergence, the relation of any given work to other works (in the same genre or even different ones) makes no direct contribution to what a piece of literature or art is about or why it is important—what it shows or says. Cavell's interpretations proceed as if aesthetic and literary expressions in themselves are *unaffected* by time and change; the latter furnish only their *preconditions*.[44]

Cavell's take on modernist literature (to confine discussion to it), however, contrasts with versions of tradition offered by some *modernists*. Certain modernist writers provide a more thoroughgoingly temporal, and hence an even more "modern" or "current" account of literature and what could be called its traditionality than Cavell. Ezra Pound's early writings, including his "vorticist" phase offer one example; the historicity of literature and of all the arts is central to Pound's writings, including the *Cantos*, albeit how this is so changes significantly over time.[45]

Tradition's conception, similarly, was explicitly undertaken by T. S. Eliot in his earliest critical writings, especially in his 1919 "Tradition and the Individual Talent," for which Pound purportedly served as model.[46] This, and other essays from that era (to which discussion will come), shaped the thought of the New Critics, including to some notable degree, that of Brooks, thus taking the present account back a further step and assembling for *A New Philosophy of Discourse* its own tradition, or *traditio* in the same sense presently being investigated.

Recent appraisals of Eliot's essay have emphasized the potentially static quality of his speaking of "*a*" or "*the* tradition"—Eliot thereby seemingly equating tradition with a canon—sometimes with an eye to some of Eliot's subsequent critical writings. Doubtless, there is something right about this. Eliot's growing fealty to *the* tradition is problematic. Though in his early essays, Eliot brings time more deeply into the sphere of art's understanding and production, he clearly envisions a single actually, existing tradition, one that in "Tradition" he already dubs "ideal." Eliot's later conceptions of culture and cultural history, in turn, are framed on the basis of such an idealized tradition.[47]

---

what we say and do *alone* makes his sculpture possible" ("Art and Objecthood," reprinted in *Performance: pt. 1. Identity and the* self, ed. Philip Auslander [London: Taylor and Francis, 2003], 165–87; 178; his emphasis) In this way, Fried's account differs from Walter Michaels' account of Fried's thought in his recent *The Beauty of a Social Problem*.

[44] As noted earlier, Cavell's treatment of modernist traditionality echoes, and perhaps even directly derives from Kant's discussion of the production of artworks in his third *Critique*, as apparently does Fried's. For Kant, all specifically aesthetic criteria, those indicating what a genre of art should be and how it should be produced, emerge in the form of unprecedented and otherwise untranslatable *examples*. Such examples are fashioned at the hands of "geniuses," the capacity for generating such being Kant's definition of this term. Exemplary works produced by geniuses are subsequently taken up by tastemakers and emulated by epigones until another genius come along, producing work that establishes the next set of aesthetic reference points. See *Critique of Judgment*, para 46–9.

[45] See James Longenbach, *Modernist Poetics of History* (Princeton: Princeton UP, 1987) for a fine treatment of both the early Pound's engagement with history and the transformation it undergoes.

[46] *Modernist Poetics* 152ff. T.S. Eliot, "Tradition and the Individual Talent," in *The Selected Prose of T. S. Eliot* (London: Methune, 1920), 37–44.

[47] In his later works, most notably *After Strange Gods* (1934) and *The Idea of a Christian Society* (1940), Eliot trades not only on the notion of the tradition but also on its status within a single culture,

Eliot at this epoch, nevertheless, also begins to conceive the operation of traditionality in its own right. In literary studies today, these essays, and especially "Tradition," retain the status of (rather stale) chestnuts; nevertheless Eliot's early writings exceed the embrace of stasis often assigned to them.[48] His account of tradition in the first half of "Talent" (from which he himself in part later drew back) depicts a genuine temporal interaction, and hence tradition*ality*, as central both to art's production and its reception.[49]

In an oft-quoted passage, Eliot writes:

> No poet, no artist of any art, has his complete meaning alone . . . . I mean this as a principle of aesthetic, not merely historical, criticism . . . . What happens when a new work of art is created is *something that happens simultaneously to all the works of art which preceded it* . . . . The existing order is complete before the new work arrives; for order to persist after the supervention of novelty, the whole existing order must be, if ever so slightly, altered; and so the relations, proportions, values of each work of art toward the whole are readjusted; and this is conformity between the old and the new.[50]

Eliot's conception of tradition pertains both to the critical evaluation and to the production of a literary work or corpus. For Eliot, a fundamental interrelatedness among individual works or corpuses, a greater temporal setting, informs both. To this extent, the young Eliot goes further than Cavell in bringing time into the picture. No single artistic product can stand on its own, Eliot insists, not just historically, but "aesthetic[ally]." The significance and force of each emerges with reference to a "*whole*,"

---

one that itself may be grasped in terms of clearly delineated periods, above all, that of modernity. Eliot's embrace and defense of English and even Christian culture is thus launched with the aim of continuing (or reestablishing) a specifically aesthetic tradition one capable of measuring up to the previous achievements of "the tradition." Though Eliot's conversion to Christianity obviously plays a role here, his argument is put not in religious but in aesthetic terms.

[48] Just those recent critics perhaps most rightfully concerned with the problematic features of Eliot's treatment, his reification of tradition and his elevation of "the talent" in a manner that gives way to a problematic cultural critique and questionable periodizations (as of course happened all the more to Pound), are themselves the ones most prone to join with the later Eliot in using these very same frameworks of culture and period. (Cf. Michael North, *Political Aesthetic of Yeats, Eliot, and Pound* [Cambridge: Cambridge University Press, 1991] and Jed Esty, *A Shrinking Island* [Princeton: Princeton University Press, 2004] who often follows North on these matters.) Raymond Williams was one of the most savvy about left and right cultural studies possessing a shared standpoint and heritage. Williams, *Culture and Society* [New York: Columbia, 1983; orig. 1958) is predicated precisely on the possibility of giving a suitable response to Eliot and his fellow travelers in a way that enables Williams' own thinking about society and culture. The temporality specific to discourse, on the present view, to be clear, resists all such appropriations, all talk of cultures and periods. (On the point, see my "Against the Period," *differences: A Journal of Feminist Cultural Studies* 23, no. 2 [Summer 2012]: 136–64.) To speak of a traditionality is to affirm not only that such traditions are always plural and never fixed but also that their intersections are always local.

[49] Attention to Eliot's essay, it should be noted has recently come from unexpected quarters. Robert Brandom, for example, cites this same passage in his *Tales of the Mighty Dead: Historical Essays in the Metaphysics of Intentionality*, a reference whose very existence is as unforeseen as the contents eventually assigned to Eliot's notions, along with the rest of the so-called Gadamerean platitudes in Brandom's interpretation (Cambridge, MA: Harvard University Press, 2002), 93–4.

[50] Eliot, *Selected Prose* (1920), 38.

a whole, moreover, to which "something happens" by dint of the new work, thus a whole effectively itself in time, subject to motion and change. "What happens when a new work of art is created . . . *happens* simultaneously to all the works of art which preceded it," as Eliot puts it.

In this inherent relatedness of a given instance to a larger whole surfaces *the unique temporality* that literary and indeed any discourse implies, a specifically discursive traditionality or historicity. A temporality, at once pro- and retro-spective, back and forth, or zigzag, informs traditionality. In any instance, an art or literary work's emergence not only refers to the past, to a preexisting context, but also *"changes* the past," as Eliot states. That past, to be sure, is the condition of the present's emergence and identification; yet, the present also reaches into the past, revives, and reconvenes it, presenting it in a different light, and to this extent altering or changing what has come before.

Eliot's study of the British Hegelians, as well as of Henri Bergson's oeuvre likely enabled his identification of the temporality of a tradition in its difference from "standard time." Traditionality's setting out in "Talent" ends up being riven, then, by a gap between its discursive and temporal operation, on the one hand, and Eliot's own insistence on *a* or *the* tradition, on the other. Across this same gap, further specification of traditionality is thus required, which will necessarily call into question Eliot's own affirmation of a single actual unique tradition.

The pertinence of a single tradition to Eliot's later forays into cultural criticism, as well as its conflict with his own temporal schema can be most economically gleaned and its consequences reckoned in another well-known essay by Eliot, written a little after "Tradition." This text, Eliot's 1921 "The Metaphysical Poets," launched a thousand readings of Marvell and Donne, being perhaps the single most important one for the New Critics themselves. In it, Eliot again invokes the tradition as he habitually understands it, as a single, somehow genuinely existing entity.[51] The key addition there made, however, is Eliot's insistence that a good deal of poetry in English *prior to the time of his own writing* does *not belong to that tradition at all*. Eliot, in "Metaphysical Poets," indeed once more refers to a supposedly actual, albeit ideal order; simultaneously, however, Eliot insists that a falling away from that order on the part of some of the most notable writers usually taken to belong to this tradition has occurred—that pretty much all of British poetry, from John Dryden up through the Romantics and the Victorians, fails to form a part of it, of *the* tradition.

To support and explain such a failure or default, moreover, Eliot has recourse to a set of periodizing and cultural claims that anticipate many of his later pronouncements on "Western culture." Specifically, he identifies what he calls a "disassociation of sensibility" as setting in at the end of the seventeenth century.[52] The long eighteenth century, Eliot avers, brought a new social organization and a new parceling out of human practices that transformed sense and sensibility, and, along with them, poetry itself. Milton and Dryden were both the first victims and the enablers of this transformation, which,

---

[51] T.S. Eliot, *Selected Prose of T. S. Eliot* (New York: Harcourt, 1975), 59–67.
[52] Ibid., 64.

according to Eliot, caused the bulk of English letters to move away from what Eliot here designates as "the direct current of English poetry."[53]

In "Metaphysical Poets," Eliot thus resorts to a single actual tradition, now viewed as beholden to, and situated in still greater frameworks of culture and history. That tradition, its "direct current" (whether hydrological or electrical) disappeared or broke off, owing to a shift in "culture"—thanks to what Eliot (and also the young Georg Lukacs, a connection made by Michael North), as well as Cavell himself, understands in similarly broad terms as modernity.

When it comes, however, to the discrete, specific context pertaining to the kinds of discourse that most interests Eliot (who, in this same essay, is in the midst of both excavating and plumping for his own poetic practice), a very different notion of traditionality, with the same relation to time as found in "Talent" appears. The Metaphysicals poets may indeed, according to Eliot, represent the "direct current" of the tradition that concerns him. From the point of view of poetic technique, however, the contemporaries of these seventeenth-century writers turn out to be the French poets Charles Baudelaire and Jules Laforgue, quintessential products *of an even later stage of modernity and its disassociative dissolution*. Laforgue and Baudelaire, according to Eliot, rediscover, or newly invent poetic mechanisms akin to those of the Metaphysicals poets and of course of Eliot himself.

This last affirmation, obviously makes little, indeed no sense, however, in relation to Eliot's broader cultural-historical ruminations on modernity and also in terms of any concept of *the* tradition, its currents diverted or otherwise. Baudelaire, Laforgue given their presumed positioning in history and culture, should stand further removed, not less, from the mainstream of (British) poetic tradition and its practices. At this moment, accordingly, Eliot sketches not *the* tradition, but instead the existence and operation of traditionality in its specific talk!-or discourse-related acceptation, the operation of which shapes itself in that zigzag charting also brought forward in "Talent"—a temporality not reckonable in cultural, historical, or social time *en bloc*.

To be clear, Eliot's situating of his own poetic practice is largely persuasive: Baudelaire, the Metaphysical Poets, and Eliot himself, within certain limits, do write in a similar fashion (one leading more or less directly, as it happens, to Brooks' claim that all successful poetry at bottom is unparaphrasable "metaphor" and "irony"). They dispose of an overlapping poetic toolkit, constituting a tradition in this specific sense.

Yet tradition viewed as it is usually understood and as Eliot also here suggests—namely, as a previously established, recognizable historical lineage, as *the* tradition—is *not* nor can be deemed relevant to these considerations. Tradition instead functions solely as it emerges *practically* for Eliot himself: namely, as a sequence of past instances convened on a concrete occasion, in this case with an eye to that style of poetry that Eliot wishes to write—the future, as well as the present and past, at this moment, all playing a role. Eliot in "Metaphysical Poets," as at once a critic, and a poet investigating certain relatively novel capacities of expression and thinking, assembles a sequence into which his own work falls, installing a series that reaches from the present to the future and back into the past. Eliot himself here thus "changes the past" (in the sense

---

[53] Ibid., 67.

of rejecting or ignoring a large portion of it), while also making it appear as such.[54] Thereby, he carves out an otherwise previously unrecognized tradition in the service of his present and future concerns—concerns that only can be articulated thanks to that past and his own insertion into it.

By way of summation, the following chartings of tradition may thus be set out:

Cavell	TSE I	TSE II
Background	Whole and Part	Whole and Part
Change/Sequence	Unique Temporality	Unique Temporality
Installation in the now	Single Tradition	Worlded Insight
(Kant)		Multiple Traditions Occasionally Convened

What is found under the heading TSE II exhibits the traditionality belonging to discourse or talk! In discourse as found in the humanities, traditions only exist insofar as they are convened or assembled in tandem with an insight, nascent, or aborning. A single, albeit transient, tradition manifests itself and functions on an occasion provided by a problem or question, an obstacle or anxiety, a concern most broadly understood (as in Eliot's case, one pertaining to his way of writing poetry).

This worldly concern, as in Eliot's interest in poetic invention, in turn, emerges in an already greater context, on the basis of an already given *background*, including prior talk and life and forms of life, as set out earlier. Solely because such a background is already in place can some actual sequence, some single given tradition, be assembled at such junctures. On occasion, though not necessarily on every one, an *explicit* appeal to a one-time tradition can take place, for the sake of the matter at hand's further understanding and articulation, including of the discourse in question; the past, already at work in an amorphous and otherwise latent form, at that moment, is taken hold of in a back and forth temporality in the way just sketched.

Accordingly, the critical question posed earlier—of how insight into discourse of (past) others and into some worldly concern of the present reader/writer can cohabitate—begins to find a response. *Worlded matters*, it turns out, along with the discourse concerning them, arise within a context and against a background, permitting some traditionality relevant to them to be unfolded. Any feature of the current world is always already accompanied by a possibility of setting out *some* past discourse with its truth, insights, but also relevant lacunae, in respect to that matter at hand, the understanding of that matter changing—shaping or

---

[54] This stipulation concerning the past's changing character is treated further in part two. What has occurred in the past, to be clear, as Arthur Danto once argued, is no more nor less accessible, no more or less capable of being grasped than any other aspect or region of the world. What pertains to it is not inherently more spectral than anything else; yet the temporality by which it is accessed, at work in all talk! and thus in all understanding, does diverge from our more common plotting of time as a straight line. (See my "Document and Time," *History and Theory* 53, no. 2 [May 2014]: 155–74, where I sketch the workings of such temporality and its consequences for history, in part in relation to Faulkner's use of bookkeeping ledgers pertaining to Afro-American slaves in his story "The Bear.")

being shaped—in the course of being discussed.⁵⁵ Discourse, being already contextualized, standing within an implicit sequencing (if not a sequence) for its own articulation and understanding, can retrieve and make explicit aspects of its background, and thereby allow the worlded matter in question and that past to be unfolded together.

So does it prove in Eliot's case: in "Metaphysical Poets," Eliot exercises a concern for others' discourse, in this case other poets' poetry (and what may be true both in them and about them), alongside the concrete worldly ongoing topic he aims to understand and explore (his own poetics). Not only may his own findings, but the sequence Baudelaire, Laforgue, Donne, Marvell, Eliot prove persuasive, insightful, true (or not) in the relevant context, where alone it has any capacity to be, or to be understood. What is sighted in the discourse of others, of a Baudelaire or a Laforgue, emerges along with Eliot's own concerns, from which perspective it may also differ (witness Milton's and Dryden's fate). All of these imbrications and implications, moreover, may be visited again, as in the reinterpretation of romantic poetry (for Eliot marking the greatest falling away from the tradition), for example, as undertaken by M. H. Abrams and pursued within the so-called Yale School, which eventually would topple the New Critics' outlook and canon. Because a traditionality, a being-in-time, accompanies every discourse, a past can be explicitly unearthed and revisited, while the present concerns that occasion this excavation are pursued. Thereby, an understanding arises, at once new and old, bearing potential insights at once into present subject matters *and* past discourses.

Discourse in the present context, particularly in the current chapter, clearly pursues this trajectory. With an eye to truths and insights concerning discourse presently being sought, a similar one-time tradition has been convened and unfolded. Talk!, the present inquiry's subject, is explored at once on its own terms and through others' talk!, followed out in, and sometimes against, the authors in the traditions here convened— Cavell, Brooks, Eliot—authors whose thoughts thus can register as differing from the present treatment as well as coinciding with it.

To be sure, all these distinctions are ultimately relative. The entire sequence is finally but a free balloon, one indeed composed of other balloons, since no subsentential parts, no words or concepts exist except within these movements of discourse. Past and present discourses and their subjects appear as phases in the motion of a single discourse, which itself, in turn, cannot be identified without their contribution.⁵⁶

---

[55] One consequence of this movement is that the work done by what in other contexts might be called concepts, say that of "the aesthetic judgment," on the present account proves wholly performed through such traditionality, since such contexts always accompany and at least tacitly inform use. Thus, when a question arises, let us say, as to why aesthetic *judgments* are a concern rather than aesthetic observations or descriptions or reports, the unfolding of an already operative traditionality into a convened tradition can and usually does occur. Compare my "Silence of the Concepts (in *After Finitude* and Gottlob Frege") for a further view of this matter.

[56] The emphasis here on what a text says might well be genuinely questioned by asking about what a text or a stretch of talk! *does*, or the feelings it provokes, the affect it generates. These dimensions are by no means being denied; yet they, too, are about something, are themselves a kind of talk! and interwoven with their interpreted capacities. Though they indeed may show as well as say, and show in a different fashion than they say—no denial here of being moved by Jane's marriage or by Malcolm X's coming out of prison—in their case, too, saying and showing are interdependent, though not mutually exhaustive.

Lacking not only any anchoring terminology or words but also ultimately even stand-alone stretches of discourse (such as works), while nevertheless channeled through other sayings and showings, humanistic discourse, and *potentially* all discourse, makes visible passages in previous discourses, while simultaneously establishing its own. In the end, what results, what appears, is a discourse both one and many, others' and one's own, along with that discourse's occasioning worlded concerns, subject matters, and possible insights—all held together in a motion at once unitary and multiply divided.

5

Yet It's Personal

The Politics of Personhood (Martha Nussbaum, Cora Diamond, and Stanley Elkin)

An alternative hermeneutics and a relatively novel functioning of traditionality have begun to be set out, in part in contrast to those implied and sometimes advanced by Cavell. Substantial lacunae remain, however, that it will be the task of the final chapter of this first part to address.

For one, the positive contribution of Cavell's thinking to literary studies by no means has been sufficiently taken into account. The considerations occasioned by his work and practice are wide-ranging, fecundating critical work from studies of Renaissance literature to theatre, from romanticism to film. So, too, whatever concerns it may interstitially raise, his reconstrual of persons and personhood, as exhibited in Chapter 3, continues to give an ever-growing impetus to literary criticism and some endeavors in philosophy. Pushing back against all received ontologies and epistemologies, Cavell's work opened the door to viewing literature as perhaps *the site* where the most appropriate access to persons, their relations, and their existence could be addressed. His thinking builds a bridge that spans philosophy and literature that many other scholars have since crossed.

Cavell, in *Must We Mean*'s culminating essay on King Lear, "The Avoidance of Love," pays extended attention to the question of the existence of other persons, treating this issue in terms of avoidance and acknowledgment. Cavell takes up these themes again, and expands upon them in *Claim*, especially its fourth and final section, to be discussed a little later. The question of others' existence and what could roughly be called the ethical, though Cavell to my knowledge rarely uses this word, thereafter takes a relatively new direction in his thinking, when Cavell sets forth what he calls "Emersonian perfectionism," which also lays the ground for a new treatment of interpretation and reading. Coming to grips with the unstable status of personhood (in the context of modernity), for Cavell, includes re-envisioning various kinds of personal relationships (marriage, friendship, etc.), and, with that, coming to recognize the other's exemplarity for my own self-understanding. In "perfectionism," I learn about myself, come more into a genuine appropriation of my own personhood, through another's example, which thus provides a way of navigating the essentially unsecured space of being a person.[1] Reading and interpretation, in turn, can be understood roughly on the same terms: as coming to a better understanding of one self through intimacy with an exemplary text.[2]

Cavellean "ethics" and its modified or deepened approach to reading have not yet here been taken into account, however, despite providing fertile provocations for much literary scholarship and having affiliations with other important current approaches.[3] A second lacunae within the present endeavor also can be identified, related to the first.

The preceding treatment of traditionality and perhaps especially the depiction of discourse as a free balloon may have but exacerbated a concern some readers felt as early as my discussion of Poovey's work. Does not the balloon, especially designated as "free," encapsulating a broader withdrawal of primacy from language, structures, and rules, discount specifically *communal* aspects of existence, the centrality of *the collective* for discourse and for life? Discourse, as so far presented, may well seem to weight too heavily the individual and what might be called his or her or their occasions, to this extent dovetailing with that focus on individual persons and their prerogatives that invests leading Anglo-American conceptions of discourse (Austin, Grice, and Davidson), and, in a different fashion, that phenomenology and existentialism (including at moments Heidegger, though his is doubtless the most difficult case), which, taken together, have recently resulted in the embrace of "normativity" in some philosophical circles.[4]

This lacuna and the previous one, moreover, ally, since the collective's role in the present account and the standing of others in Cavell both concern how persons in the plural are to be conceived. The present chapter, accordingly, addresses both issues together: it inquires into the modeling of persons and their relations with and to others in literary interpretations close to Cavell—albeit not primarily his, but within

---

[1] "Perfectionism," states Cavell, is "something like a dimension . . . of the moral life that . . . concerns the state of one's soul . . . that places tremendous burdens on personal relationships . . . and on . . . the necessity of transforming oneself and one's society" (Cavell, *Conditions*, 2).

[2] In the foregoing discussion of Cavell's hermeneutics, at issue, to be clear, was not any claim simply opposed to this later stance (Cavell's newer thinking by no means representing a simple break with his earlier in any case); nor was it maintained, it must equally be emphasized, that Cavell *believed himself* unfaithful to or simply unmoved by the other's text (which is in part why his specific interpretations did not come into doubt, especially since what being true or faithful entails here is not known in advance, and does not necessarily always and only pass through the figure of the author in any case). Instead, owing to Cavell's charting of language in terms of the division between primary and secondary usages (including the exceptionality of metaphor and the implied retention of the assertion), the leading edge of written discourse, it was suggested, remained for Cavell *words*, thus damping down (if not wholly foreclosing) the relevance of what the other was *saying*, the other's *discourse* as another's and as discourse, as well as the becoming and the traditionality implied by all discourse and subtending Cavell's own writing and thinking. The model of intimacy found in perfectionism, of "being read" by the other's text, as it sometimes put, though powerful, does not, in the present context, at least, allay these concerns; with its ultimate reference point remaining *my* self-discovery, my as yet "unattained *self*," it may even further fuel such worries (cf. Cavell, *Conditions*, xxix).

[3] Mulhall, for example, characterizes Cavell's interpretive practice as one of "redemptive reading," a notion with interesting overlap with Eve Sedgwick's "restorative reading," so influential of late in literary studies. See Miller's *The Burdens of Perfection* for more on this topic.

[4] Of course, just such a convergence of existentialist and discourse-related tendencies informed Cavell's own work from the start, and the question of the collective touches it as well, as discussed near the close of the present chapter.

an approach sometimes deemed that of OLP more broadly—while simultaneously addressing how conceptions of the interpersonal and the collective stand within discourse as here presented.

Literature's ability to aid in understanding persons and their interrelations will be examined in a specific subset of what today is spoken of as OLP and its approach to literature. These critics, influenced by Wittgenstein and sometimes Cavell, frame or invoke versions of discourse, while commenting on literature, especially the novel, with an eye to moral concerns. They thus treat *the self's being with others* explicitly as a matter of *ethics or morals*, while turning to literature to pursue these themes, thereby engaging with versions of what might be called a *moral imagination*.[5]

Such philosophers, critics, and thinkers extend from Iris Murdoch to Alice Crary. Of present concern is a specific interchange between one of the leading commentators on Wittgenstein of the present day, as well as a preeminent thinker in her own right, Cora Diamond—among other achievements, the originator of the *Tractatus*' resolute reading—and Martha Nussbaum, herself not really a member of this school or coterie, but whose project overlaps with some who are in her advancing of what is sometimes called virtue ethics, a perspective on the ethical descending from Aristotle that eschews all formal rules and algorithms. Neither Diamond's nor Nussbaum's work thus coincides with Cavell's, nor could either properly be called a Cavellean; yet both turn to literary fiction, as did he, to investigate the status of persons in a supple, non-rule bound way, and they explicitly conceive literature, as opposed to philosophy, as the primary place to consider morals and ethics. Both critics look to literature for an ethics "beyond moral judgment," as Crary, herself another notable practitioner of this approach, puts it in the title of one of her books.[6]

5.1 The Spirit of Realism

Before turning to Diamond and Nussbaum, another author must be brought into the mix: the still relatively obscure, albeit much lauded recently deceased writer of fiction, Stanley Elkin. Elkin shares with these philosopher-critics and with Cavell a fascination with the everyday, as well as an existentialist-inflected concern for the self and its necessity to "show up" for its life (as Cavell himself sometimes puts it).[7]

---

[5] "Moral imagination" may be familiar from Edmund Burke's writings and in the previous century had a certain cache in conservative political thought. It is not being used here in this sense. David Bromwich, recently, has reexamined and reworked the notion in a series of political meditations, and his usage does overlap some of the work here in question.

[6] Alice Crary, *Beyond Moral Judgement* (Cambridge, MA: Harvard University Press, 2007).

[7] In an interview, Elkin praises "the extraordinary of the everyday," a phrase that echoes Cavell's talk of "the extraordinary of the ordinary." Moreover, his appreciation of the everyday is a consistent theme in the literature. (See Larry McCaffrey's "Stanley Elkin's Recovery of the Ordinary," *Critique: Studies in Contemporary Fiction* 21, no. 2 [1979]: 9–51, DOI: 10.1080/00111619.1979.9935204, and the third chapter of Peter J. Bailey's *Reading Stanley Elkin* "The Sound of the American Ordinary" [Urbana, IL: University of Illinois Press, 1985].) As to existentialism, one of Elkin's best and most famous early short stories, "A Poetics for Bullies," models Elkin's approach to writing in terms of just such an insistence on one's self; specifically, it presents Elkin's authorial project in the guise of

Elkin's main pertinence to the present discussion relates to the question of realism, at once as a genre of literature and as a way of approaching texts deemed to fall under it. Diamond and Nussbaum, despite the radicality of their philosophical perspective, privilege realist literature as a genre and adopt realism as a reading practice, seemingly without further reflection and account. They interpret solely realist fiction, and both read novels realistically, assuming that people in such fictions are of the same order as those found in life, that characters in these fictions comport themselves to those around them and to their nonhuman surroundings in a manner exemplary for individual human existence.

Elkin's writings to some degree also participate in this realist strand; they attend to what Diamond, following Iris Murdoch, refers to as "the texture of being" or life.[8] Yet Elkin's stories and novels cannot finally be contained within these optics, as is about to be made clear; they display some central feature or aspect rebarbative to realism.

Elkin, it should be noted, despite having a reputation for being one of the leading authors of his generation, somewhat like Cavell himself, failed to fully find the audience he wanted during his lifetime; moreover, in Elkin's case this lapse persists.[9] Elkin's obscurity may ultimately be irremediable, the absence of audience for his work possibly offering an indication of how his fiction itself operates. Although possessing a realist veneer, something in Elkin's writing prevents seeing his stories as finally being about persons like ourselves; his works, accordingly, apparently lack that kernel or nucleus of realist identification that permits an audience to assemble around novels that fall into this genre. Elkin's fiction starts in realism, but his texts then swerve away, distancing them from the expectations associated with the genre and apparently held by most readers. As will later be suggested, this aspect of Elkin's writing is also where the collective, in its difference from individuals and what they ken, becomes available.

The interchange between Diamond and Nussbaum is instructive, then, in the present context, at once for identifying the realism found in Elkin's novels, as well as for marking that realism's limits. Their interchange, moreover, is gripping in its own right; when it took place, it arguably established the furthest advance that discourse-based approaches had achieved in treating novels. Indeed, Diamond and Nussbaum's criticism is in part *about* why literature rather than philosophy is the preferred manner to *philosophically* address persons and their comportment toward others, why literature is the best means to approach what are usually called ethics or morals.

Nussbaum, in her piece, "Flawed Crystals: James's *The Golden Bowl* and Literature as Moral Philosophy," to which Diamond's "Having a Rough Story About What Moral

---

the doings of a twelve-year-old bully named Push (Stanley Elkin, *Criers and Kibitzers, Kibitzers and Criers* [New York: Plume Books, 1973], 197–217).

[8] Cora Diamond, "Having a Rough Story about What Moral Philosophy Is," *New Literary History* 15, no. 1 (Autumn, 1983): 155–69, 162.

[9] Elkin's failure to find an audience, like the ordinary, is foregrounded in the literature on his work as well as by Elkin himself. Elkin's biography, by David C. Dougherty, is entitled *Shouting Down the Silence: A Biography of Stanley Elkin* (Chicago: University of Illinois Press, 2010) and Peter J. Bailey, an Elkin stalwart, as were, however, also Helen Vendler, William Gass and many others, entitles his discussion of Elkin's *Dick Gibson Show*, "I Think I Know Most of My Readers by Name: Dick Gibson, Stanley Elkin, and the Issue of Audience" (*Dalkey Archive Casebook* on *The Dick Gibson Show*).

Philosophy Is" is a response, indeed presents a powerful case for understanding James' *Golden Bowl* as demonstrating the limits—further still, the ultimate irrelevance of every rule- or theory-governed form of ethics.[10] In her piece, to be clear, Nussbaum first nicely captures *the lived attraction* of rules and guidelines for measuring right and wrong, something she believes is evident in James' character's Maggie's initial standpoint—an attraction that does not finally seem entirely foreign to Nussbaum herself. In the end, however, Nussbaum plumps, as she believes James' Maggie also does, for an alternative to rule-following keyed to concrete situations. Nussbaum embraces a radically situated ethics that goes so far as to recognize that in some situations no "good" outcomes of any kind may be available.[11]

Diamond, in turn, in her response, pulls off the rather remarkable trick of appearing at once more modest in her conclusions than Nussbaum, while simultaneously seeming to question more deeply the philosophical framing of the ethical than her interlocutor.[12] Diamond suggests that the terms on which Nussbaum understands moral philosophizing, Nussbaum's "rough story," are themselves still too beholden to the philosophical tradition that Nussbaum herself criticizes. Insofar as Nussbaum views morality in terms of action (and choices related to it), and offers an account, a "rough story," about what moral philosophy genuinely is, Nussbaum herself remains gripped, according to Diamond, by that same traditional philosophical understanding of the moral that Nussbaum questions.

On the back of this criticism, then, Diamond proposes a still more capacious notion of ethics, emerging from her own profound encounter with Wittgenstein's writings—hence, one notably rooted in discourse. For Diamond, ethics indeed individuates, not only action, as in Nussbaum, but also understanding; along with what we do, what we see, notice, and appreciate is ethical or moral for Diamond. Over and against "moral philosophers" who "have been obsessively concerned with action and choice," Diamond thus advances texture of being or existence as central to the novel's work (again, borrowing from Iris Murdoch), and, with it, all "morals." "Texture of being hardly gets a mention; and yet it is surely enormously characteristic of many novelists that that is what they give us—and out of an interest we may properly call moral."[13]

---

[10] *New Literary History* 15 no. 1 (Autumn, 1983): 25–50.

[11] Thus Nussbaum concludes her reading of James in "Flawed Crystals," by noting that "Maggie, in the last sentence of the novel, recognizes that the keen vision and acknowledgment of the good tragic spectator are themselves values which can . . . collide with other values" (Nussbaum, "Flawed Crystals," 38).

[12] Given Diamond's proximity to Wittgenstein in these matters, it is in fact unclear whether she would accept the radical impossibility of being ethical and/or happy in the tragic situation that Nussbaum posits arising at the conclusion of James' novel.

[13] Diamond, "Rough Story," 162. In her "Wittgenstein, Mathematics, and Ethics," Diamond gives a related, albeit slightly different view of moral discourse that would *not* deal in moral predicates or be capturable in statements of any sort. There, also, she turns to literature for her examples, stressing how these stories purvey a moral understanding while technically being about something else (243–45). Even when a seemingly telling feature, Andrew Ramsey's death, for example, is being presented, the reader is curious why it is being presented and being presented in Woolf's fashion. Yet Diamond's own distinction between this kind of moral talk and statements proper (e.g., a report on Ramsey's death), on the present account, as previously discussed in Chapter 3, may not finally hold up, as suggested by something like story, or a vector toward narrative pertaining to all discourse, including the factual statements that Diamond would differentiate from moral ones.

"Moral philosophy," for Diamond, thus consists in revealing persons as individuals by way of what they find important in the world around them—what is appreciated and what not, what counts and what doesn't, thereby composing the "texture" of their lives. Her endeavor observes what individuals notice and what they fail to, yet also includes what these correlations *show* about the character of the person in question, being in this sense "moral." Novels and their readings exhibit what the world is for individuals like these, ultimately advancing reflection on what sort of lives may be lived by certain sorts of persons.[14]

In turn, Elkin's writings, too, trade on such texture and often in memorable ways. The description of a contemporary small town, with which his novel *The Franchiser* opens, is one such instance—Diamond herself counts noticings of furniture and architecture as examples of texture—and numerous other textural observations are to be found in his works.[15] Elkin's own enterprise as a novelist to this extent accords with Diamond's suggestion. Similarly, when embroidering on texture, Diamond insists on the intelligence of those appreciating it, that "the intelligent description of such things, is part of the intelligent, the sharp-eyed, description of life, of what matters, makes differences, in human lives," here building in part on Nussbaum's recognition that both Maggie and James possess a high degree of intelligence and moral sensitivity.[16] The bulk of Elkin's stories, which are handed over to first-person tellers, or at least heavily focalized, by his own avowal, possess these same traits. His central protagonists are indeed gifted in just these powers of intelligent observation and sensibility, of which both Diamond and Nussbaum speak.[17] Both aspects, the intelligence of his narrators and their realist devotion to the texture of being, separate his fictions from "experimental fiction" and from "postmodernism," a differentiation upon which Elkin himself often insisted.

Elkin's fictions do deviate, however, from Diamond's and Nussbaum's template. Specifically, his works' precise and evocative observations of the texture in the end never coalesce into *a single, stable, identifiable viewpoint* that reveals something unequivocal or even significant about the narrator or focalizer who tenders them,

---

[14] Diamond, "Rough Story" (62). Tolstoy's description of "Stiva's silly grin," offers for her an instance of such texture that makes clear its moral vector. Diamond herself, accordingly, appears especially close to the recent turn to description in literary studies (albeit writing in 1983), as well as to Altieri (in a way that goes one better Altieri's Wittgenstein, which retains the fact/value distinction, though their accounts are kissing cousins of a sort). Diamond in a later essay, it should be noted, provocatively suggests that the interest in a *theoretical ethics* may itself be motivated on these same grounds, owing to the same difference between "moral outlooks" among persons (Cora Diamond, "Henry James, Moral Philosophers, Moralism," in *Mapping the Ethical Turn: A Reader in Ethics, Culture, and Literary Theory*, ed. Todd F. Davis and Kenneth Womack [Charlottesville, VA: University of Virginia Press, 2001], 252–70; 266).

[15] *The Franchiser* begins with the following description that turns out to be focalized within its protagonist: "Past the orange roof and turquoise tower, past the immense sunburst of the green and yellow sign, past the golden arches, beyond the low buff building, beside the discrete hut, the dark top hat on the studio window shade . . ." (Boston: Nonpareil Books, 1980, 3).

[16] Ibid., 162–3.

[17] See an "Interview with Stanley Elkin in St. Louis," *Studies in the Novel* 16, no. 3 [Fall 1984]: 314–25 where Elkin and the interviewer, Richard B. Sale, discuss the "high intelligence" of Elkin's characters, including George Mills, "a shoveler of shit" (324–5). Elkin made similar remarks in some of the other numerous interviews that he gave.

nor about those he encounters. No genuine "attitude toward life" in Diamond's sense emerges in Elkin's work; accordingly, these stories cannot be construed as ethical or moral explorations, even in terms of Nussbaum's or Diamond's already capacious construal of morals. Elkins' writings finally elude the realist reading of realism that Diamond and Nussbaum at moments take for granted, and they do so precisely at that spot where such perspectives are gathered together and supposed to yield a replacement for or version of the moral by giving access to the genuine individuality of a character/person.

How Elkin does this, the feature of his writing that prevents any moral or ethical perspective from finally assembling itself, in turn, lets be pinpointed a problem that Nussbaum's and Diamond's own presentations face, as at once the overcoming and the continuation of moral *philosophy*. All of Elkin's novels pass through a personage, often an "I," that occupies a deeply skewed, inherently foreign place in respect to the society, world, and other persons, upon which and upon whom he (usually he) comments. Thus the titular character of Elkin's first novel, *Boswell*, not only is an orphan (like many of Elkin's storytellers) but also is an erstwhile professional wrestler and body builder, otherwise uneducated, and thus hardly an expected site or source for the nuanced and hyperarticulate registrations of persons, places, and things that he nevertheless serves up. In other works, a bail bondsman, handcuffs and black shoes shining, plays a similar role, as does a talk radio host consigned to the most minor of markets, as well as, in another, the owner of a string of KFC's and similar franchises. All undergo and deliver numerous epiphanies on their surroundings and the people (the other characters) they encounter, seemingly of just the sort that matter to Nussbaum, and, especially, to Diamond. The perspectives from which these observations are ultimately sighted, and thus the actual point of these reflections nevertheless remain elusive; they tend to convey attitudes contradictory in themselves, while the authorial and narratorial vantage point from which they are presented does not appear fixable as belonging to a genuine person or embodying a moral perspective.

Indeed, though Nussbaum's and Diamond's commitment to the realism of realistic novels goes all the way down, Elkin's does not. Because, however, the former treat all characters, but especially James' narrators and focalizers, as virtually indistinguishable from actual people, Elkin's practice helps identify a problem with their approach: namely, the double and seemingly conflicting valence Nussbaum and Diamond as readers give to "persons" (characters) viewed realistically, including Maggie, or, for that matter, her author, Henry James.[18] In Nussbaum's and Diamond's realism, not only are characters genuine people but what they understand and disclose sheds light on human beings *as human beings*, most obviously in Nussbaum's treatment, but also in Diamond's (albeit her lesson may ultimately be that humanity or human being is itself comprised solely

---

[18] Unexpectedly, such a realistic stance also seems to me true for many of Cavell's literary interpretations, despite his very different handling of so-called other minds' skepticism, discussed near the close of the present chapter. Albeit Cavell, seemingly unlike Diamond or Nussbaum, takes such skepticism seriously and believes it in some fashion irrefutable, often his interpretations, for example of Lear, never really draw into doubt that these characters are persons with problems, often about other persons, and to this extent like you and me. (Cavell's reading of Samuel Beckett's *End Game* in *Must We Mean* is one notable exception to this.)

of individuals—her negative conclusion nevertheless not cancelling the broader point). Their endeavors being avowedly the successor to, and perhaps fulfillment of, a specifically philosophical interest in ethics, theirs being an attempt to write a new modality and chapter in moral philosophy, Nussbaum and Diamond necessarily address human being on its own terms: what it is to be or act like one, what is best for persons as persons (at least these persons *as* persons), what might make them happy, and so on.

At the same time, owing to their departure *from philosophy proper*, from philosophical *argument*, and because these questions are now being pursued in literary texts, the characters in question hail from specific times and places, and bear other more limited identities, such as those of social class, race, and ethnic background. James himself, of course, really was like his characters in many of these respects. Hence, Nussbaum and Diamond, turning to novels of a certain genre, must take as their starting point for approaching persons, individuals belonging to an already existing society and to limited groups, ones who in these respects are like their authors and indeed like these critics themselves—not just in intelligence and sensitivity, but also in social situation, educational background, race, and similar aspects. Yet neither Nussbaum nor Diamond explain or even consider how these two vectors of their meditations are related, how their view of these characters as persons *simpliciter* comports with their portrayal within particular, limited historico-sociological situations. Pursuing something like an ethics or morals, yet attending to a distinctly narrow swath of types and situations of people, their latent philosophical perspective, their focus on morality or ethics, sits uneasily with the unavoidable social and historical vectors, especially to the extent that the latter remain unaddressed. A notion of the person, of human beings as human beings inform their work, overlaid by the very different optics of presumably more limited collectives or groups, yet the relation among these two sets of characterizations finds no account in their thinking; instead the non-appurtenance of the latter, and, with it, the human's absolute supervenience are taken for granted.

To be clear, this concern is not in the service of the gesture diametrically opposed to Nussbaum's and Diamond's: the affirmation of a perspective keyed to the sorts of "identities" Nussbaum and Diamond overlook—a perspective, where, at least at times, essentially the same question fails to be asked now in the other direction: how such identities (of race, class, and so on) pertain to persons as persons. Instead, the problem on the table at the moment consists in how persons are to be charted in terms of the collective as such, be it human being, class, race, or some other historical or social category. This issue, moreover, the question of a collective identity per se, is a question or a problem for *any discourse-based account*, including the present one, again as may have been clear to some readers as far back as Poovey's discussion.

Part of the power of Diamond's and Nussbaum's endeavor, after all, consists in their avoidance of the traditional treatment of existing social-historical reference points, thus keeping their distance from all hypostatizations of history and society. They refuse to grant these and other third-person perspectives any regulative power when it comes to (literary) discourse as such.[19] Such distance from the third person is itself,

---

[19] This is not to say that social problems, such as factory farming and the eating of animals are not raised, as Diamond at moments suggests in other texts, but this will again be through the perspective

however, inherent in any discourse-based approach, since discourse or talk! rejects those conceptions on which such third-person perspectives usually trade. Linguistic and all other structures being out of the picture, the ability to embed discourse in supposedly stand-alone cultural, social, or historical determinations also evanesces.[20]

Nevertheless, as Diamond's and Nussbaum's examples illustrate, the discourses of literature and criticism also cannot entirely avoid invoking collectives of various sorts, nor can finally discourse itself. Not only is it the case that such determinations may always be introduced from a first-person perspective, though what they entail at that moment perhaps may not always be clear.[21] Moreover, avoiding the question of the collective runs the risk of leaving the person or humanity as an unreflected fallback position, as to some extent both Nussbaum and Diamond do.

The horizon and scope of this problem, the challenge to all discourse-based thought posed by considerations pertaining to the collective, can be further gleaned, by bringing another example of recent criticism into the mix, one that eschews what is here being called discourse (and eventually also establishing a third intermediate case), before turning back to Elkin's work. The critic Nancy Armstrong in her *How Novels Think: The Limits of Individualism from 1719-1900* employs a perspective decidedly different from that of discourse, thereby aiding in making plain what approaches that embrace discourse share. Her contribution can be positioned at the far end of the spectrum from Nussbaum and Diamond, with the stance of another recent critical approach, the new sociology of literature, which employs both discourse and a third-person optics, falling between.

Armstrong's recent meditation on the novel treats realism's rise—the literary genre upon which she, like Nussbaum and Diamond, focuses—from an unapologetically third-person perspective. Armstrong's book offers a genealogizing history of the novel that coordinates realism's emergence with *capital's* and *capitalism's* growth and transformation. Armstrong differentiates herself from others who have trod this same ground, such as Ian Watt, as well as Poovey (a more complex case), in that she does not merely *correlate* realist literature's growing ascendancy with capitalism's emergence and expansion, but assigns to realist novels a unique role in that development: namely, the *invention of persons or individuals*. Novels, according to Armstrong, indeed *construct* persons more or less of just the sort in question in Diamond and Nussbaum's account. Her title *How Novels Think* could well stand above their work; in Armstrong's case, however, this phrase does not designate how literary fictions shed light on persons and their moral dilemmas and status. Instead, it signifies how realist novels as a *genre* produce persons and subjects, who then believe themselves capable of such labors,

---

of similarly situated individuals, understood as advancing understandings wholly and simply moral and human.

[20] This does not meant that these concerns—with race, class, nation, gender, and so on—disappear—only that access to them must be rethought; they cannot be advanced simply or wholly on the basis of a text's words.

[21] In an earlier draft of this work, I exhibited how such identities might be positively understood by way of a contestation of Walter Michaels' presentist criticism of concerns related to racial identity, in particular his misreading of Toni Morrison's *Beloved* in his *Our America: Nativism, Modernism, and Pluralism* (Durham, NC: Duke University Press, 1995), 137. Unfortunately, that discussion could not make it into my final draft.

along with the historical limits of this project. (Armstrong claims these limits have now been reached, adducing genre fiction and other developments beginning in the late nineteenth century to buttress her case.)

Hence the following chart:

OLP Ethical Turn	New Sociology of Lit	Third person social-historical
(Diamond/Nussbaum)		(Armstrong)
Individual perspective (affirms)	Individual perspective (affirms)	(invents)
Society/History (does not address)	Society/History (affirms)	Society/History (contests)

(Further subdivisions, it should be noted, also prove possible. Eve Sedgwick's work, importantly often dips into this same Jamesian realism, while using James to invent or disclose structures or formations at least adjacent to those found in Armstrong, ones Sedgwick herself in her late writings came to question.)

In the present context, as should be clear, Armstrong's analysis remains unavailable, since it employs otherwise unexplained forms and structures as devices explanatory of what realist novels do and say. Though discourse, again, does not entail the simple invalidity of the categories Armstrong invokes, it does necessitate that these do not directly determine discourse's operation, especially not en bloc, as it does in Armstrong's work, where these third-person formations produce persons and their understanding.[22]

Yet, echoing with what was set forth a few paragraphs back, Armstrong's concern also cannot simply be set aside. To be sure, discourse does not and cannot be conceived without there being individual persons—though they need not prove central for all varieties of literary interpretation, nor, as we shall see, are they to be identified simply with selves or subjects.[23] Their invocation, however, as has become clear, necessarily raises questions pertaining to Armstrong's most pressing and legitimate concern: the collective and its status.

The account of discourse so far given does indeed leave unexplained an irreplaceable *radically non-individual dimension* of individual existence, whether that of society or humanity, or determined in some other form; this is problematic, both because, as so far canvassed, discourse seems fated nevertheless to invoke these notions, but also because without any acknowledgment of the collective in its radicality, the status

---

[22] If and how perspectives, such as that of an economic one, are compatible with discourse remains to be worked out; only after the present view of discourse has been set forth can its relation to these reference point be tested. Some of the writings by those who participated in Louis Althusser's and Etienne Balibar's *Reading Capital*, notably Jacques Ranciére and Alain Badiou, give some indication of the possibilities of how this kind of thinking of discourse and the social may be joined—not surprisingly, given that Althusser's own program at that epoch arguably remains the most rigorous and far reaching investigation of third-person reference points for approaching society and history among those framed after the Second World War.

[23] As conceived in the present text, persons prove fundamentally interwoven with discourse; accordingly, they do not necessarily coincide with full-blown subjects, selves, or, of course, consciousnesses, while the identities they do possess map on to functions sometimes different from those associated with the foregoing. Thus in the appropriate setting, my dog may be a person, insofar as she is a fine interlocutor when it comes to the question of whether someone has entered my house when I am gone.

of politics, indeed any conception of the political, cannot be framed. If the present perspective of discourse were, however, unable to admit of politics in its specificity and to afford its operation due leeway, that fact would necessarily be delegitimating of what it advances. Thus though talk! as surveyed seems unable to offer any satisfactory account of the collective, the complete absence of this dimension also cannot simply be countenanced—not to mention that features of the collective, as is about to be further clear, do enter into discourse itself.

5.2 Collectivity in Elkin

How, then, to recognize the force of the collective beyond the personal, given that no third-person viewpoints may be authoritatively invoked at the level of discourse? Elkin's own unseemly narrative practice allows progress to be made on this conundrum.

The gyrating positionings of Elkin's narrators, alluded to earlier, begin to suggest how the collective in some fashion may be registered. These narrators—again, body builders, franchisers, and bail bondsmen—have a marked, and, in the context of Jamesian realism, markedly odd, social positioning, such that Elkin's writings seem not to entirely dispense with considerations of collectivity, with sociality, or with the question of humanity's status. At the same time, the stories that unfold from these narrators' seemingly unstable perspectives prevent any known collective from being identified and thus any real or implied assembly of (like) persons from being convened. Why this is so, how such lability of viewpoints manifests itself in some given case, in some actual Elkin story has yet to appear. Examining one of his texts, accordingly, can show how this instability operates while also exhibiting how these tales may invoke a collectivity deprived of any phenomenality in its own right, arguably the sole fashion that the collective *can* appear at the level of talk!

Elkin's way of registering the collective in a unique manner can be seen in an early short story, "I Look Out for Ed Wolfe."[24] The title character, Wolfe, from whose vantage point the tale is told, initially appears positioned to offer nuanced vistas on what today we might call "consumer society," thus falling in line with the realist vector of Elkin's fiction. Wolfe works for the debt collection service "Cornucopia Finance," and the story opens with him transposing the first word in the name of his employer, "Cornucopia" into the question "can you cope?"[25] This word play, like the titular Wolfe's monologues addressed to those from whom he attempts to collect, indicates Wolfe's insight into our present-day society's operation: Wolfe clearly grasps how, for the working class, the roses of consumption hide the thorns and snares of financial ruin and exploitation.

Wolfe soon loses his job, however, and subsequently begins to practice what he has previously preached: he does not borrow money nor purchase things on time, but instead sells, for cash, everything he does not need, which proves to be everything he owns, while he also gives up his shabby rental and starts to live out of his car. Following this extension of what appears to be the story's life lesson, an incident appears at its

---

[24] Elkin, *Criers and Kibitzers*, 37–66.
[25] Ibid., 37.

end, however, that strips away all of the reader's confidence in Wolfe's perspective and in Wolfe's own take on the collective and present-day society.

Wolfe's commitment to non-consumption, more specifically, culminates in an extraordinarily unsettling scene, set in a nightclub that is run, and predominantly frequented, by African Americans. There, Wolfe, in the face of the advances of a welcoming African American woman, despite his intense loneliness, rather than requiting her interest, begins to auction her off to the highest bidder. Wolfe announces: "Brothers and sisters, I tell you what I am not going to do; *I'm no consumer*"; and slightly later, correspondingly, he declares: "So I tell you what I am going to do. What am I bid? What am I bid for this fine strong wench?"[26] While seemingly entirely blind to its social and historical ramifications, Wolfe's final invitation, of course, aptly, induces horror in those assembled, who become so enraged that Wolfe ultimately must give them all his hard won cash in exchange for his own life (in effect buying *himself* back from *them*).

Wolfe, however, as the story's readers are aware, has only continued to act on his previous commitment to non-consumption—"I'm no consumer," as he says—and his aim at monetizing all that comes within his ken. Accordingly, though there is also an obviously allegorical aspect to Elkin's plot, one treated later, which accounts for its racialized cast in its specificity, the narrative, thanks to its conclusion, clearly pushes to an unexpected extreme the story's initial take on society, rendering its first, anti-consumerist perspective problematic. Just what would seem prescribed by dwelling in a consumer society—non-consumption—in the end is profiled as even more misdirected than what it was to remedy. Accordingly, though the dimension of the collective as such by no means has passed from view—quite the contrary, it has arguably now become felt still more forcefully —the register of the collective loses its previous shape and form, and discards any recognizable identity.

Elkin's narrator's perspective, then, seemingly offers no coherent view on either the human (implied by the slave allusion) or the social. Yet, throughout the story, Wolfe indeed finds himself amid a collective dimension that goes beyond him or any of the other characters. Elkin's story's spiraling deflections—and other instances in other works could be detailed—consequently, exhibit a collective factor at work, and that factor's force, while the collective as such remains withdrawn and removed from any direct identification. These texts, by failing to convene a *recognizable* social dimension, thereby register the collective *in its difference* from persons—this being the only sort of acknowledgment that the collective in its full radicality *can* receive at the most fundamental level of talk! Elkin's narrators and plotting ultimately embody no particular fact pertaining to such groupings—though kilted toward specific contexts, they also eventually elude them—but gesture toward a collectivity or sociality extending beyond the mastery and understanding of any individual, that precedes each one of us, and in some fashion proves both precondition and resource for discourse, as well as for all other practices and their spheres.

Collectivity so understood, moreover, dovetails with an aspect of discourse here previously mentioned: discourse's emergence as already within a world and within tacit traditions that furnish its backdrop. To the extent that such background traditions are

[26] Ibid., 64–5 (my emphasis).

already at work, the force of a collectivity beyond the individual invests any actual stretch of discourse, albeit that collectivity solely registers there *as prior* and *as already* at work, without revealing any inherent characteristics of its own.[27] Neither of the two alternatives between which Diamond and Nussbaum and others toggle, neither some specific social group nor, alternatively, humanity (to the status of both of which discussion again will come) are thus given in person; instead a collectivity or communality already convened, in which other persons, things, and prior instances of discourse have been joined together leaves its mark on any event of talk! and its understanding.

Talk!'s *factical* existence, to take a term from Heidegger, thus in part entails that any stretch of talk! appears within a world and implies a collective already there. Such facticity makes it possible to account for those differences found in discourse normally understood in terms of languages (or sign systems). Already communalized instances indeed preexist any single act of understanding and expression, as their joint resource and condition, without themselves being able to be further identified or accounted for so as to present them as directly shaping talk!

5.3 From Collectivity to Politics

To grasp the collective's characterization better, including in respect to other approaches to discourse that have already been discussed (as well as to prepare for the political aspect of this problematic that Elkin's narratives ultimately highlight), briefly returning to Cavell's corpus is useful. A major through line in Cavell's thinking, after all, has here yet to be broached in any detail: his treatment of skepticism. Not only is this topic important for his thinking, but skepticism also speaks to a version of the present issue: the status of others, and thus of any collective, from the point of view of discourse.

Cavell among those practitioners of OLP here cited arguably goes furthest in wrestling with the notion of the collective in a discourse-based context; unlike Nussbaum and Diamond, he by no means simply leaves unaddressed the other's possible social or historical situation, nor does Cavell stint, of course, when it comes to the status of the person or human being. Cavell explicitly asks about the recognition of the other and those others for whom they are others. In this way he reflects on groupings or collectivities within which persons as such seemingly are situated.

Cavell pursues these themes throughout *Claim*, but especially near its end, when he further unfolds his approach to so-called other minds skepticism.[28] Near the beginning of *Claim*'s last section, more specifically, Cavell invokes two figures central to the skeptical problematic: the first, he calls the *outsider*; the second, the *outcast*. In the present context, the status of Elkin's narrators echo in both characterizations.

---

[27] Chapter 8 explores this mechanism in more depth in the context of the opening portions of Heidegger's *Being and Time*, along with some of its consequences for the philosophical problem of realism.

[28] Part two of *Claim*'s four parts, which is interrupted by the chapter on language and words discussed in Chapter 3, is entitled "Skepticism and the Existence of the World." This question had already appeared in Cavell's opening discussion of the status of criteria in Wittgenstein, and, following on this, of Austin's use of examples.

Cavell brings forward both these figures in the service of distinguishing what is sometimes called "other minds skepticism" (skepticism directed to the existence of other *persons*) from "external world skepticism" (skepticism directed toward things, their properties and relevant states of affairs). Cavell is here ultimately interested in the former; he wants to expose how others do (and do not) present themselves in our experiences, in part by contrasting their way of becoming and of being present to that pertaining to the externality of things.

Cavell frames the *outsider* first.[29] In the case of *external world* skepticism, in situations where, for example, one person doubts that another may really be seeing what he or she believes that she has apprehended (a snake on that tree, for example), a perspective can be entertained outside of, or apart from both persons. An *outsider*, some third party able to successfully decide between my and another's perception, able to render an authoritative judgment about which of us is right, in these cases is at least imaginable, if not actual. Cavell deems this party an *outsider*, both because they stand apart from either one of us and also because they are depicted as endowed with some knowledge that each of us may not possess.

A similarly situated "outsider," when it comes to skepticism about *other minds or other persons*, remains inconceivable, however, according to Cavell, and so, correspondingly, does the possibility of an authoritative adjudication of such disagreements. No observer can even be imagined as able to correct my outlook about what I take to be the contents of my mind or another's—one capable of determining, for example, that the pain I feel is not pain, but that the one that another feels is. Other minds skepticism does not admit of a third, enhanced position—a conclusion that births "the outcast."[30]

With "the outcast," the standing of the collective as construed by Cavell comes into view.[31] Because the relation of an individual to her experiences of herself only can be

---

[29] To be clear, Cavell's own presentation is quite a bit "thicker" than my account here. On his understanding, the perspective of the outsider as it relates to the external world devolves from the concerns of philosophical skepticism, concerns that Cavell neither simply refutes nor fully endorses. The outsider's present invocation thus continues a discussion Cavell had mounted in chapter six and again resumed in chapter eight of *Claim*, where in various ways, he wants to suggest that the philosophical skeptic's worry that he is closed in on himself is a serious one, while also indicating that his questioning of (external) thing's existence is misplaced, albeit in a different way than philosophers such as Austin and Moore suggest (*Claim*, 158–67 and *Claim*, 234–41). Cavell's discussion of the role played by the generic object, which emerges from his discussion of Austin, and in part appears to borrow from Thompson Clarke, is one tool he uses to navigate this complex self-situation. (See Cavell's summary of his argument at *Claim*, 191; for Clarke, see Thompson Clarke "Seeing Surfaces and Physical Objects," in *Philosophy in America*, ed. Max Black [Ithaca, NY: Cornell, 1963], 98–114.) Despite all this, though Cavell later in *Claim*, accordingly, indicates, that such an "outsider" is a fantasy based on the skeptic's concern (relating to that "seeing of ourselves as outside the world as a whole" he had spoken of earlier, *Claim*, 236)—his own stress nevertheless will be on this authoritative position's imaginability as opposed to its being unimaginable in cases involving other minds (*Claim*, 417).

[30] Cavell makes the transition from the outsider to the outcast (a designation he uses but does not select out and define), writing: "A difference emerges in these two cases. If the Outsider discovers that what we see when we each say we see red is not the same, then it seems to make sense to ask which of us is right. I can tolerate the idea that the other might be right because I can tolerate the idea that neither of us is. But if I and the other do not feel the same when we sincerely exhibit pain, I cannot tolerate the idea that the other might be right and I not. What I feel, when I feel pain, is pain. So I am putting a restriction on what the Outsider can know" (*Claim*, 418).

[31] Ibid., 419, where Cavell does employ this term.

rendered doubtful by other persons from "within," as Cavell puts it, the deprivation of such recognition by others (but also possibly finally by myself) produces *outcasts*—a figure that I, or some self, refuse to acknowledge as a person—usually an object of horror to others, in extreme cases even such an abject object to the outcast themselves.[32] The outcast is one whom one or more insiders do not recognize as one of them, and thus remains unacknowledged as having experiences meaningfully like theirs. For example, Oedipus emerges as solely body (in *Oedipus Rex*) and perhaps solely not (in *Oedipus Colonnus*), according to Cavell.[33] In either case, these vicissitudes are negotiated by *others* capable of having genuine experiences of their own personhood, who, by contrast, view Oedipus himself initially with horror and later with awe.

Elkin's narrators, in turn, might, then, be deemed *outsider/outcasts*; they judge authoritatively about the world around them, even as their own personhood and ultimate likeness to each and any of us remains in doubt. For Cavell himself, however, there can be no confusing or merging of the two positions. Indeed, his contrast's ultimate takeaway is that the one skepticism, other minds, can *be lived*, albeit only in particular cases, while external world skepticism, though it would apply to external things' existence in its entirety, finally cannot. While external world skepticism as a philosophical position indeed cannot be disproven, it is also true, as Hume long ago conceded, that it is impossible to *act or behave* as if skeptical doubt pertaining to all of *the things in the external world* genuinely holds. By contrast, the personhood of other individuals can, and often genuinely is kept in suspension by oneself, or other individuals. Because the relation to the other involves only ourselves, and matters only in some sense "within" each of us, with one or more persons' experiences serving as a gauge of the other and of their "mind," in practice defaulting on recognizing others as others always remains possible.[34]

For Cavell, to be clear, this asymmetry between the two sorts of skepticisms entails a situation of the utmost ethical urgency. It implies both that there exist persons that we do not treat as such, as well as the difficulty of *consistently* acknowledging the personhood of individuals we do so count. The personhood of others, being so precariously positioned, may lapse both in its scope, as to whom it includes, as well as in our everyday relations with our familiars, with those whom we regularly do so recognize as other people.

Despite its arguable advance on all other approaches to this issue in the context of discourse, Cavell's treatment does not, however, finally get beyond that default in respect to collectivity seemingly inherent in every discourse-based approach. After

---

[32] Ibid., 423.
[33] Ibid., 419.
[34] Cavell states: "Am I to realize that no other (other than the one in question) could be in a better position than I for knowing the one in question; or that no other would be a better test of my knowledge; or both together—that no other can be in a better position, or have a better instance, for knowing any other, than I am, and have, with respect to this other? I suggested, in speaking just now of a 'limited skepticism'—one which states that we can never be skeptical enough—that the other in question may or may not vanish, depending upon some philosophical point of view, or thesis. But even if, at the extreme, he does vanish, even if there is just nothing there of the right kind to call a human being, this is a disappearance only to me, not to all others; and it is a disappearance at best only of him, that one" (Ibid., 426).

all, for Cavell, the other's *being*, including whatever collective guise it may seemingly conjure, still depends on a *person-oriented* optics. In his account of others, including those collectives that generate outcasts, such determinations operate exclusively on a first- and second-person basis. The very difference between the two instances, his distinction between the outsider and the outcast, and his contention that I can live my skepticism toward others in a way I can't toward worldly things, assumes an inherently personal and individual framework; it recurs to how these matters appear to *the persons* experiencing them, indeed to a first-person standpoint, as does that "inside" by which outcasts and genuine others alike receive their status.

Perhaps no treatment emerging from OLP, then, is able to untie the knot of collectivity. Fortunately, however, this question of the collective, on much the same terms, was previously broached within a different philosophical tradition. Grasping the collective's status in that discussion can begin to unfold its singular mode of surfacing in Elkin's texts, setting the stage for soon examining Elkin's fuller profiling of the collective in some of his other literary work.

Specifically, the German philosopher and sociologist Alfred Schutz, in the context of a debate in Husserlian phenomenology, in his 1957 "The Problem of Transcendental Intersubjectivity in Husserl," pursued the question of the collective as collective, along with the status of other minds skepticism. Just as Cavell investigates these questions from the starting point furnished by skepticism, so did phenomenology's founder, Edmund Husserl, as attested by the title of the work Schutz focuses on, Husserl's *Cartesian Meditations*.

Cavell, as just reviewed, believes that a certain skepticism was inherent in our experience of other minds, including those instances in which whether some individual is one of us are decided. Schutz himself, however, insists in his essay that the conception of a genuine collectivity can never be arrived at from a starting point consonant with skepticism, while examining Husserl's claim to do otherwise. Such a beginning, Schutz maintains, can "not yield a community, unless we were to define community in such a way that, contrary to meaningful usage, there would be a community for me, and one for you, without the two necessarily coinciding."[35]

The derivation of collectivity from skepticism's essentially first- and second-person perspective is always fated to miss it, according to Schutz; at best, it might result in distinct "communities," different groupings, for each of us. Since other minds skepticism entails looking for the collective on the basis of what an *individual* experiences and encounters, from their "inside" perspective, it checks any genuine or radical collectivity from emerging at any point along the line. Only a community that exists for *me* (and for you, only accidentally at times perhaps coinciding), as also happens in Cavell's account, and thus not a genuine community at all, is conceivable, if the difference between self and other skepticism is retained.

Schutz, then, would characterize the collective's standing still more profoundly, and with his next point, his work's pertinence to Elkin's becomes clear. Schutz not only contends that no genuine collective can be derived from a skeptical viewpoint but also

---

[35] Alfred Schutz, "Husserl and Transcendental Intersubjectivity," in *Edmund Husserl: Critical Assessments of Leading Philosophers V.5* (New York: Routledge, 2005), 90–116; 109.

further affirms that without a collectivity *already in play*, no genuine other can appear at all, including in presumed face to face confrontations (and thus in instances such as those that for Cavell pertain to the other's acknowledgment). By giving priority to the individual person and their perspective, the skeptical consideration etiolates the personhood of the other, whether it turns out to be acknowledged or not. If others *can be* the object of a *lived* skepticism, according to Schutz, then they can never have been *genuine others* at all.[36]

A collectivity from which such determinations emerge, for Schutz, then, must instead stand *in advance* of any individuals, if they are ever to be recognized *as persons by one another* with their existence remaining on equal footing. Personhood, accordingly, necessarily recurs to a region beyond single individuals and their perspectives. It is indeed not given, but pre-given before the question of the other on any distinct occasion arises or any confrontation among "possible persons" takes place.

After all, remaining within the terms of Cavell's account, his outcast, should by rights, completely pass out of view *even as a candidate for personhood* when *the recognition* Cavell specifies *ceases*. Personhood should stop being an issue altogether in this instance, once recognition has been withdrawn in the way that Cavell suggests, if it depends entirely on my own (or like others') recognition or acknowledgment. How others remain in question even as *possible others*, ones able, like Oedipus, to come to be recognized again, in Cavell's account, accordingly, remains opaque.

What is key in Schutz's treatment, then, to put it perhaps paradoxically, is that it shows how the collective as *pre-given* must already be *given* in our encounters with other persons, that pre-givenness alone genuinely making those encounters possible. Personhood as such is thus unthinkable apart from an already operating collectivity and discourse's factical pre-insertion into it in the way that Elkin has begun to sketch and Schutz further unfolds. In turn, this pre-givenness of the collective is critical for recognizing where Elkin's stories take us, as well as reckoning how his writings sketch the domain of *politics*, the second task the present chapter has set for itself.[37]

5.4 Discourse and the Political

As Elkin's texts begin to show, and as Schutz's account helps make still more plain, a moment of the collective always makes felt its weight or force in discourse while that collective

---

[36] Schutz's argument, presented in Husserlian terms, is that the empathetic identification that, according to Husserl, yields an analogously appresented other, presupposes the possibility of both of us being aware of our inhabiting the same world, something that only the lifeworld's preceding both of us supplies. Were this not the case, an other aware of one and the same world as I, in which we both are together, would not be possible. Schutz at first makes this argument in technical terms and returns to the lifeworld's role more generally and categorically at the end of his paper ("Transcendental Intersubjectivity," 105; 113).

[37] Schutz finally also finds inadequate, it should be noted, a scenario along the lines Diamond suggests, where skepticism happens not to be in play, but a first-person perspective remains. Diamond indicates that a community or group may appear within a *personal* perspective, as itself a kind of *individual* with a species of personality. ("*Moral reflection* may be directed not just towards individual human beings but towards forms of social life," as she puts it [Diamond, "Rough Story," 163].) Schutz, however, on the foregoing grounds, refuses "the completely untenable theory that social communities correspond to personalities of a higher order" (111).

otherwise proves undetermined.[38] Such collectivity does, however, bear one distinguishing mark, one feature (not despite, but thanks to its being so withdrawn); it gives rise to one specific region or area of existence. That region, which thus appears to toggle between humanity and the social, and similar seemingly more restricted determinations, while answering to none of them, as has already been intimated, is the political. The factical collective dimension that marks discourse destines all determinations of personhood to know an irreducibly political dimension, one that the social, the historical, the identitarian, the cultural, and the human, in their various guises, do not themselves contain, but in which all those just named instead *participate*. The radical collectivity found in discourse at once subtends, but also volatilizes these alternative identifications, prompting them to enter into a curious entanglement that exceeds each of them, while rendering their relation, and thus the collective itself, sites of politics.

This, at least, appears to be what Elkin's texts suggest when taken together, at that allegorical level that informs them along with their variations on realism. In a number of Elkin's stories, a movement toward or away from one of these termini (of the social or of the human) leads back to whence it came, like a kind of mobius strip, even as these termini remain distinguished. His narratives come to repeat an initial construal of a more limited collective and of the human (as at once opposed and intersecting) ultimately in the sphere or sector at first purporting to be the opposite of the collective in question, thereby differentiating the two, while both categories continue to inhabit and inform each other. Transitioning across sites in part named or identified through these questionable distinctions, Elkin's narratives call these very identities into doubt, exhibiting not only the inseparability and instability of the social and similar categories over against the human but also how all such identifications are functions of the ultimately political character of the collective in its facticity.[39]

This allegorical dimension emerges as early as "I Look Out for Ed Wolfe"; it becomes more prominent as Elkin's oeuvre accumulates, crescendoing and also further complicating itself in *George Mills*.[40] Though the site on which this admittedly difficult

---

[38] Of course, Schutz was himself a practicing sociologist (albeit one quite philosophically savvy) and thus he believed that he could access different frameworks than the personal and was capable of addressing this collectivity or sociality on their own terms, in his case through variations of Max Weber's notion of ideal types. On another occasion, his own attempt to identify a specifically social collectivity on the basis of temporality would doubtless be worth investigating further.

[39] Just to be clear, at issue here is not that everything is political—many things are not; or even that "the personal" is always somehow "political." It is being suggested, however, that the "personal" or "personhood" as a conception remains inseparable from politics, insofar as personhoood's determinations seemingly involve reckoning at once on the limits and mutual relations of (a given) society or other sort of group and on humanity (as such) in a fashion that proves unstable and unmasterable. Personhood in the present context, moreover, is understood as deriving from discourse, and thus in a fairly capacious fashion. As already noted, my dog, for example, under certain circumstances, can be understood as a person. At the same time, to place animality said not to be human, at the center of the political conception stands at some remove from the present meditation, which focuses first on the identification of the person and the problems it poses, though that this problematic also opens on to the issue of humanity and animality will become apparent at the present chapter's end.

[40] *Boswell*, Elkin's first novel, does not embody this matrix. Instead, taken as whole, *Boswell* may be read as tracing a kind of afterlife of what some might call the modern self, a movement from belief in human being, already emptied out and fixed on the social, that ultimately arrives at some beyond. Boswell, after dedicating his life to body building—the body itself, dedication to it, proving to be

aspect of Elkin's writing will ultimately be pursued is a story from Elkin's middle period, "The Making of Ashenden," discussion recurs first to "Wolfe" to make this movement's basic outlines clear.[41]

Elkin's title, "I Look Out for Ed Wolfe," echoes its character's opening situation. "I look out for" expresses an intention to protect or safeguard; it thus implies the existence of a threat and a resolve to protect against it. Wolfe, an orphan, is thus said to look out for himself, indicating his situation within society as threatened and also potential threat. That society, at the opening moment of the story, then, is itself portrayed in terms of only partially and imperfectly socialized *need*, as the site of (ultimately forced) labor and consumption, a contained version of the war of all against all. This first pole, in the broader context of the story, however, will ultimately be ranged against a second, one of *desire*, of genuinely human want, collectivity here now answering to humanity. This second pole is similarly implied by the tale's title. "Looking out for" may also indicate a search for something or someone, in this case, Wolfe himself. The claim "I look out for Ed Wolfe," accordingly, implies Wolfe's *absence* up to this point, his being so far missing as a genuine person or human being. Elkin's story's title thus evokes both potential collective poles of a given existing society with its constraints and of achieved humanity.

In turn, the events taking in Wolfe, homonymously named for an animal of prey, exhibit the following allegorical movement: from imperfectly socialized need (at the story's outset) to the genuine humanity and sociality featured at the end, when Wolfe is confronted by the specifically human desire of another person, rather than the war of all against all from which he sets out. As is characteristic of this strand of Elkin's narratives, however, coming to the pole of the human, the story reinstates the opposition from which it began, thereby drawing the stability of the entire matrix into question. At the beginning, need implicates Wolfe in an interplay of excess and threat, captured by the mantra "cornucopia/can you cope."[42] By tale's end, Wolfe faces the same predicament, now, however, initiated by the purportedly opposite situation. Wolfe, that is, again faces cornucopia, this time, however, in the form of specifically human desire, the bounty of another individual. Wolfe himself, at this moment, however, is indeed unable to cope; he mistakes a person for a commodity, repeating the misstep that defined his starting point.

Ultimately, then, neither Wolfe nor perhaps we, Elkin's story suggests, can distinguish or keep separate the twin stations across which Wolfe moves, need and desire, "consumer society" and true humanity. Wolfe takes the one for the other, and the threat in both cases is presented on the same terms. Nevertheless, the story, by dint of its movement *also* differentiates the two poles, even as it draws this difference into

the last form of credible radical transcendence— eventually rejects this stance. Recognizing his own non-recognition of any version of transcendence, Boswell becomes resigned to the world of professional wrestling where ethics are only fake and scripted. There, however, he confronts death in the guise of another wrestler and for all intents and purposes actually dies, finally to be redeemed as one wholly given over to chronicling his encounters with the famous, a vocation against which he also eventually turns.

[41] Stanley Elkin, "The Making of Ashenden," in *Searches and Seizures* (New York: Random House, 1973), 129–88.

[42] Elkin, *Criers and Kibitzers*, 41.

doubt. Where the human ends and where society starts remain in question throughout Elkin's text, with the result, however, that the difference between humanity and present-day society, and the status of their relation, turns out not to be a matter of society, nor of humanity, but appears instead as a specifically *political* issue.

That is why Elkin's story concludes by invoking the vexed history of race relations in the United States. No history makes more plain that the conception of humanity (the specification of who and what is human and what not), and the determination of the social in light of such an understanding together carry a profound *political charge* and yield similarly grave *political* consequences. A given form of society and the question of the boundaries of the human as such are indeed in this case at once wholly implicated in one another, while also of course remaining distinct. This holds good generally: the two poles (that of the human and of the social, or race, gender or class) are never simply identical, but their differentiation also always remains imperfect. These conceptions and their interrelation thus turn out to depend solely neither on the one factor nor the other, but instead are themselves finally political, intrinsically sites of contestation.

A collectivity withdrawn, unnamed, and seemingly unnameable, yet active and having force, thus underlies the allegory found in "Wolfe," itself functioning as the bearer of these various identifications. A communality, preceding Wolfe and all other persons, emerges at times as social and otherwise determined, at other times as human, while necessarily extending beyond the limits of both, even at it lacks a specific phenomenality of its own.

A parallel, yet still more enigmatic movement, shapes Elkin's later story, "The Making of Ashenden," where the collective and its inherently political status become newly evident. "Ashenden" recounts, ultimately in the third person, but initially in the first, the attempt of a philanthropic heir to a *matchbook* fortune, the titular *Ash*enden, to come into contact with the one truly suitable "match" he knows to exist for him—in this case, a woman, equally wealthy, gifted, intelligent, and philanthropic. Ashenden's jokey lineage—each of his four grandparents answer, we are told, to one of the old four elements, "earth, water, fire and air"—as well as his own self-avowals make clear that what it is at stake in his quest, or at least initially appears to be, is something like that pole of humanity, fully humanized nature, at which Wolfe unsuccessfully sought to arrive at the end of his tale. Ashenden's struggle consists not in meeting "the hard task of living," as James Joyce called it in "Two Gallants," but, as is often true in high realism, in propagating his own already seamlessly socialized personhood and humanity, by means of finding and marrying a similar, suitable mate.

"Ashenden," in contrast to "Wolfe," then, begins from the perspective of a wholly humanized desire, one where elemental and natural gifts—"air, earth," and so on—are now entirely one with their social functioning, yielding something like a non-coerced human existence and human being. Ashenden indeed emblematizes achieved human nature; the social dimension has been entirely successfully subordinated and all material necessity apparently removed, much as in many of James', Diamond's, and Nussbaum's characters' case.

Yet though Ashenden's story starts in the vicinity of where Wolfe's ends, a parallel movement, albeit still more enigmatic, drives Ashenden's tale. Ashenden transits from his starting point, desire and an already successful socially embodied personhood (a *nature* that is also wholly *human*) to something somehow still more perfectly socialized, at once entirely *art* and *nature*, there to find, not, like Wolfe, a jarring dissatisfaction, but an equally *jarring satisfaction*. That is to say, the balancing of nature and society in Ashenden, his already *coping* successfully with cornucopia, in Elkin's story, becomes repeated, hyperbolically repeated, in a fashion that, as with Wolfe, draws the initial standpoint into doubt, and once more destabilizes the relevant oppositions.

This motion, this procession into an unparalleled landscape, arguably one of the strangest to be found in all of literature, hinges on a singular articulation of life and death that confronts Ashenden at the moment when his quest for a mate appears about to succeed. Life (and life-making powers) first explicitly arise as a theme, when, after months of searching, Ashenden tracks down his potential fiancée, sheltering at the estate of a British mogul, and proposes to her. This proposal, to Ashenden's own surprise, is rejected; the cause, Ashenden soon convinces himself, is that he is not suitably "pure" in the sexual sense (he has not been chaste, while his potential betrothed has).

Though lost virginity would seem to be an irremediable condition, Ashenden attempts not only to undo it but, in unexpected fashion, actually succeeds. At first, recalling his earlier promiscuity, "shame" comes upon him "like a thermal inversion," reports Ashenden, who nevertheless goes on to proclaim "innocence is knowledge."[43] Knowledge of his previously unknown former condition, Ashenden's realization that even in his extreme youth he was already impure, as registered by shame, here, Ashenden claims, newly engenders innocence. Ashenden's is not, then, an innocence that once existed and subsequently was lost, but an innocence that never previously was in place and only at this moment appears. Coming to terms with what might be called the embodied self, and its powers of life, now fully "owning" them, as we say, Elkin in this way depicts Ashenden as recovering or inventing, in unprecedented fashion, the specifically human, as having given new shape to fully socialized desire, discovering in it or reinventing for it a now completely achieved freedom. Ashenden fully confronts his own embodiment, and, at this moment, he appears to hold total sway over it, the two coinciding in his current self-knowledge. Ashenden's previous blending of the human and the social, accordingly, is raised a notch, proffered as existing in a now unprecedentedly purified form, with all the consequences of having a body seemingly sublimed and overcome thanks to his achievement of self-knowledge.

This stunning perspective that Ashenden appears to attain is further enhanced and unfolded when Ashenden transitions into a *natural* landscape that is at once, simultaneously and seamlessly, also "art"—a transitional moment still more complex, however, owing to the role played by death, along with life at this instant, life and death at this juncture being paralleled and intertwined. Death is introduced as a theme, thanks to a fact of which the reader at this moment is only retrospectively made aware. While occupied with his fiancée, Ashenden had noticed a wolf-like shadow around her eyes; he now informs his reader that his fiancée suffers from lupus and cannot, then, be awakened at 3:00 a.m. (the hour to which his just completed spiritual exercise

---

[43] Elkin, "The Making of Ashenden," 167.

has brought him) to be informed of Ashenden's innocence, of his new condition, as Ashenden would otherwise wish.[44]

By way of the appearance of the wolf (with echoes of Wolfe!) and the naming of lupus, mortality and death are, then, explicitly brought into consideration alongside life. The regaining of bodily innocence and virginal purity that somehow succeeded, thus will now dovetail with a similar overcoming of mortality, including a terminal illness, conceived on virtually the same terms. Ashenden overcomes this new drawback to making a successful match—clearly the more obvious and relevant one, were a realist marriage plot actually in question—again through knowledge, in a fashion akin to how he overcame virginity's loss, in this case, however, through knowledge and intimacy with an appropriate other. The two vectors, life-making powers (chastity and sex) and death (lupus, disease, and mortality) are thus entwined and ultimately treated as one at this juncture.

Ashenden, speaking of himself and the life he imagines for him and his potential fiancée, consequently, proclaims that "there was no need to survive her . . . . They'd have their morality together, the blessed link up between appropriate humans, anything permissible between consenting man and consenting woman."[45] The binding of two "appropriate humans," the addition of another self to a self, itself already other or allergic to itself—lupus being an autoimmune disease—in consenting humanity here will undo mortality, first of all in the form of his fiancée's impending death, but also finally Ashenden's as well ("there was no need to survive her"). Hence, the body somewhat mysteriously refashioned or reborn, once again, takes center stage. The kernel of mortality, that inherent otherness, or allergy, arguably intrinsic to having a body at all, emblematized in an autoimmune disease's allergy of a self to itself, is said to be overcome by the addition of another self, a different other, through intimacy with another person (at once bodily and intellectual), "*morality*" thus effectively vanquishing and replacing mor*t*ality, not by removing the latter, but by wholly taking it on board and in this way undoing its sting. A superordinate now mutual understanding will overcome death, just as it permits Ashenden's sexual profligacy to be turned into innocence, at the same time it unites the two.

Yet Ashenden's attempt to discover or invent a specifically human morality and intimacy, a new sort of absolute, undergirded by the interplay and substitution of life and death does not prove stable, and it, along with its terms, ultimately turn out not to be a matter of a human nature, sublimed and fully embodied, at all. Why this plot turns out so, and how ultimately the powers of life and death, generation and mortality, relate to the issue of the political and the collective—in a more fundamental way than so-called biopolitics, albeit the imbrication in question arguably makes the latter possible—can be gleaned by recurring to another work of literature where the same sort of plotting in the course of being encountered in Elkin is found: Sophocles' *Oedipus Turannos*.

---

[44] "It must have been three or four in the morning. I couldn't wake Jane, she was dying of *lupus erythematosus* and needed her rest" (Elkin, "The Making of Ashenden," 167).
[45] Ibid., 169.

This reference, no doubt surprising, is in fact at least somewhat apropos, since the features of Oedipus' story about to be evinced actually were once brought to Cavell's own attention, in the course of a similar literary discussion, by the scholar Marc Shell, as recorded by Cavell himself.[46] Oedipus' story, on the interpretation to which Shell alludes, one that originates with the Classics scholar, Seth Benardete, indeed also involves the sort of plot movement in question here, a version of which came forward in "Wolfe," while, furthermore, foregrounding the potential interchangeability of birth and death that has just appeared in "Ashenden."

Oedipus' tale, to be clear, starts from the level previously disclosed in "Wolfe": imperfectly socialized, and not wholly human, need. More specifically, the Sphinx, a *hybrid* of human and animal, according to Shell, following Benardete (who here follows Hegel), represents existence as subordinate to need and thus as only partially human, as standing within a still not fully achieved humanity and sociality.[47] The Sphinx, moreover, executes her sacrificial victims at the moment of copulation, treating life and death as effectively one, thus providing a parallel to Elkin's broaching of birth and death simultaneously in "Ashenden."

Oedipus' doings in response to the Sphinx, his famous solving of the riddle, and what follows upon it, in turn, sketches a plot movement similar to that found both in "Wolfe" and "Ashenden," as the Oedipus story, of course, also culminates in error. Oedipus, faced with the city of Thebes' subordination to the Sphinx, again by knowledge, in fact by self-knowledge, would perfect and purify need, while dissolving the identity of birth and death inherent in the Sphinx's reign of terror. Parallel to Ashenden's conceiving of a new morality, Oedipus aims to confront and overturn the reign of the Sphinx, here, however, by *organizing* birth and death and *distinguishing* them in the compass of a single human life. The solution to the riddle that upends the Sphinx and knocks her from her pedestal, recall, is "humanity," *anthropos*, human being, achieved by rendering distinct the newborn (a creature on four legs) and old age (one with three legs, who uses a cane, a prosthetic device). Oedipus, who himself has a distinctive gait and feet, owing to having his ankles punctured at birth (his name means "swollen foot"), through self-knowledge thus aspires to establish humanity on its own terms and let it stand on its own "two feet," as we say.[48] Oedipus' capacity for

---

[46] Cavell, in the introduction to his *Disowning Knowledge: In Seven Plays of Shakespeare* (Cambridge: Cambridge University Press, 2003) refers to Marc Shell's interpretation of *Oedipus Turannos*, specifically to Shell's highlighting to him in conversation both the Sphinx's manner of killing its victims and the path that Oedipus takes toward the creature (15n2). Shell seems to me, somewhat as I have done here, to have been suggesting that Cavell's thinking, specifically, his *Hamlet* interpretation does not adequately deal with the political dimension, though it is not clear whether Cavell took this to be Shell's lesson.

[47] Shell communicated to me the importance of Benardete's Oedipus essay for his own thinking. That essay's epigraph is from Hegel's *Philosophy of World History* and concerns Oedipus' overcoming of the hybrid sphinx as the beginning of "spiritual clarity," a clarity, however, still mixed with "*Grueuln*" (abominations), and thus needing to come to true self-knowledge and genuine ethical transparency "through "*bürgerliche Gesetze und politische Freiheit*" (bourgeois laws and political freedom) (Seth Benardete, "Sophocles' *Oedipus Tyrannus*," now in *The Argument of the Action: Essays on Greek Poetry and Philosophy* [Chicago: Chicago University Press, 2000], 71–83; 71).

[48] Cf. Benardete, "Sophocles," 75.

insight thus should overcome the residual naturalness of society emblematized by the Sphinx, in order to found the genuinely human and the truly and fully social together.

Oedipus himself, in his very person, however, of course also embodies *the confusion* of these same moments, the very ones just distinguished, now within the confines of the presumed sphere of the "human" itself. Sleeping with his own mother, after killing his father, Oedipus recombines and confuses life and death, copulation and mortality, just as they were previously combined and confused in the Sphinx, albeit at a new and supposedly "higher" level.

Accordingly, in *Oedipus*, as will also be true in Elkin's story, an initial configuration of birth and death gets reenacted on different grounds, grounds that come about through their presumed differentiation, even as their repetition scrambles them once more. Death and birth, being confused in the purportedly genuinely human sphere of Oedipus, as a repetition of the prior confusion found at the tale's beginning, calls this difference of sites (Sphinx/need and Oedipus/humanity) into doubt without wholly effacing it, just as happened in "Wolfe." Accordingly, these reference points themselves, the partially socialized need of the Sphinx and the purely human one of Oedipus turn out to be intrinsically insecure, while also connected, and, as so disposed, they are once more revealed preeminently as sites of the *political*—Oedipus himself, the one in whom they are confusingly distinguished and combined, indeed being first and foremost *turannos*: tyrant, ruler, king.

Similarly, in Elkin's text, where human being begins, how it relates to its own embodiment, and to the capacity for both birth and mortality, emerge as *political* questions. Elkin's story contains essentially the same problematic and a similar movement as Oedipus (and "Wolfe"), albeit in a different direction, in this case from established or reestablished humanity toward some other still more unprecedented standpoint, some still more novelly socialized nature (which also perhaps in its own way ultimately proves Sphinx-like). Indeed, since Ashenden has already purportedly reached, or at least believes he is about to, the achievement of humanity in consummated interpersonal intimacy, the next phase of his tale is set by Elkin in a space in which every difference between art and nature, human convention and its others, is overcome.

Ashenden, sleepless owing to his excitement at his achieved self-understanding and his prospective wedlock, wanders "outside," on to his host's, Freddy Plympton's, grounds; yet, as the narrator (now third-person), nuancing this description, puts it:

> It was not "outside as you and I know it. Say, rather, it was a condition, like the out-of-doors in a photograph, the colors fixed, the temperature unfelt, simply not factors, the wind stilled and the air light, and so wide somehow he could walk without touching it. It was as if he moved in an enormous diorama of nature."[49]

Ashenden, corresponding to his attempted ascension to a new morality and a new human nature, now inhabits a space at once natural and entirely artificial ("an enormous diorama of nature"). His situation thus seemingly does away with any distinction between human artifice, its products—especially, between fine arts and

---

[49] Elkin, "The Making of Ashenden," 167.

natural beings of any kind. Consequently, his host's grounds, upon which Ashenden now strolls, are both a sort of zoo or natural habitat, where Ashenden encounters wild beasts and their remnants, while simultaneously placing Ashenden entirely "in art," as he soon gleefully puts it.[50]

More specifically, his late night wanderings lead Ashenden to a tableau that he recognizes as corresponding to Henri Rousseau's painting *The Sleeping Gypsy*; Ashenden takes notice of various aspects of the corresponding scene, including, perhaps ominously, that in it the lion has since eaten the formerly sleeping gypsy. Similarly, Ashenden passes through a version of *The Stag Hunt*, and numerous other animal paintings, eventually ending up in a space that Ashenden identifies, in this case wrongly, we are told, as *The Peaceable Kingdom*, which its supposed occupants (the lion, ox, and so on) have also recently left.[51]

The landscape Ashenden now inhabits thus embodies that conception of a new humanity to which Ashenden has just come, one where all differences that would insert human being into a restricted society by way of its body have disappeared. Ashenden is at once in art, in nature, and fully himself, as he puts it at one point.[52] Yet Ashenden's subtle misprisions about his own setting suggest that the narrative, no longer told by him, has shifted in ways of which he is unaware. Correspondingly, Ashenden's passage through this singular space culminates in a repetition of his earlier situation, in a denouement again hyperbolically outrageous, where Ashenden indeed receives the fulfillment from another he has anticipated, one that he has yet to actually experience with his fiancée, in a fashion that takes a wholly unexpected form, thereby calling Ashenden's own understanding of his situation into doubt.

Indeed, at this moment, "The Making of Ashenden" offers arguably the single most outrageous development that may be found among the tales belonging to the already highly provocative genre of "bear stories"—Elkin's novella, it appears, among other things, being a response of sorts to William Faulkner's "The Bear." (Elkin, who taught for decades in Washington University's English department, wrote his English Ph.D. thesis on Faulkner.) Elkin, narrating in the third person, and using Faulkner's rhythms and italics to show individual point of view ("This was the first time that he thought of the bear as *bear*, the first time he used his man's knowledge of his adversary"[53]), stages a version of Faulkner's text that retrieves and reworks his predecessor's charting of human nature by way of ursine existence, while bringing to a conclusion the plot just sketched.

Ashenden, believing himself dwelling in a Utopian tableau where the difference between art and nature has been erased, at this instant indeed encounters a bear. He at first believes the bear male, and, hoping it is tame, attempts to soothe it. His appraisal, however, is distinctly wrongheaded: the bear is not tame, and it is also a female, indeed a young female bear, newly menstruating and in heat, whom he has unwittingly erotically aroused. Consequently, in some extraordinarily detailed pages

---

[50] Ibid., 171.
[51] Ibid., 174.
[52] "But I am in art, he thought, and thus in nature too" (Ibid., 172).
[53] Ibid., 175.

that follow, the bear forces Ashenden, at first to satisfy her with his arm, and then eventually to arouse himself, and to copulate with her, at which point Ashenden moves from reluctance to avid participation and his own eventual satisfaction.[54]

"Ashenden's" conclusion, whatever else it may accomplish, thus conforms to the pattern already sighted in "Wolfe" (and in *Oedipus*). Ashenden's mating with the bear returns the story to its starting point and to its initial presuppositions, while staging a repetition that calls this entire movement into doubt, without simply effacing the differentiation it implies. Ashenden, after all, though in effect initially mistaken, as presented in the story, actually *accomplishes* his original intention: he finds a mate (he will add the bear to his family tree, placing "honey" alongside the other four elements), one who, moreover, was herself a virgin, as he was, too, now also in some fundamental bodily sense. Noticing a cut on his penis from which he bleeds, Ashenden indeed affirms both his own virginity and that of the bear.[55]

The story's outrageous conclusion, then, fulfills all that leads up to it. Ashenden indeed takes greater "possession" of nature at this moment than even its depiction as diorama or art could have suggested; he reoccupies it unprecedentedly, and "socializes" it all the more, by coupling with the bear and leaving his stamp and seed in her.

Equally, clearly, "Ashenden's" closing twist calls these same preceding moments and their supporting distinctions into doubt. These attainments are ultimately *forced on Ashenden*, at least at first, by the young bear, and occur in a sphere that obviously also *exits* from the human. Ashenden previously sought to renegotiate the very terms on which birth and death are confronted, overcoming them in a new morality, in effect subliming the human body and all it entails. By the end, he accomplishes something like this, but the *allos* (the other) that is to resolve self-allergy, turns out to be more *unlike* than Ashenden anticipated: indeed, an animal, a bear.

Elkin's denouement, then, reintroduces those differences upon which this movement was initially predicated and which it seemed to have overcome. The establishment of both the human and the social are at once undone, as well as the determination of a third term, nature, by what one cannot help but label the story's "climax." The initial embodiment of personhood in Ashenden and his final coupling with and in the bear thus exhibit the instability of any sorting out of human nature, nature, and social existence on their own autochthonous terms. Questioning these differences (first and foremost in respect to the human animal itself), again, without simply effacing them, the plot's movement, when taken as a whole, points to that otherwise withdrawn collectivity removed from any single univocal determination previously encountered, and indicates that the character of that collectivity, again, is inherently political, intrinsically a site of contestation.

To be clear, this is not to say that society, human intimacy, personhood, or animality are somehow effaced or that these terms (or any of the others) should be simply erased

---

[54] Elkin initially broaches Ashenden's sex with the bear in Faulknerian italics: "*And of all the things he said and felt that night, this was the most reasonable, the most elegantly strategic: that he would have to satisfy the bear, make love to the bear, fuck the bear*" (Ibid., 181). Five pages later, the narrator informs us: "And they went at it for ten minutes more and he and the bear came together" (Ibid., 186).

[55] "Maybe *I* was the virgin. Maybe *I* was," he remarks (Ibid., 188); also for "honey."

from discourse. Rather, what Elkin's allegory indicates is that every one of these references finally proves unable to perform the work of centering personal or political existence they remain called on to do in projects like those of Diamond, Nussbaum, Cavell, or, alternatively, those of the New Sociology or Armstrong's, or Latour's, not to mention the posthuman and animal studies, these last references here obviously also being apt. Such attempts end up withdrawing from the collective *its withdrawal*, and assigning it some genuinely distinctive feature—sometimes a novel one, other times not, sometimes explicitly, in other cases no—thus tamping down, if not wholly effacing its radically *political* character, including in those instances where they combine and recombine these reference points (nature, body, society, and humanity), as in Latour, in a manner reminiscent of Elkin's plots.[56]

To be sure, many of these projects aim at political outcomes themselves. From within discourse, however, the political as a register precedes and thus can never be captured in these or any sort of stable frameworks and models; instead, first and last the political is negotiable only *practically* and on occasions. The political is inherently practical, thus never masterable by theory, including the envisioning of a new, or an everyday, a fulfilled, or even a post-humanity, all of which options Elkin's story seemingly anticipates and to which it alludes. Not that there cannot be theories pertaining to aspects of politics, or tactical stratagems and strategizing, but what is not viable are theories of the political as such (as in Carl Schmitt or John Locke), including ones that determine it on grounds other than itself (such as is found in Marx). Because the political is coeval with discourse's own conditions in the fashion just sketched, because it rests on this withdrawn collectivity, the determinations of, and relations between humanity, society, nature, art, and invention must be reconceived and negotiated anew on every occasion and traced through their own historicity with an eye to their concrete political implications.

This too—politics' rebarbativeness to theory—finally, Oedipus' story exhibits, as it happens, as alluded to in a second reference from Oedipus that Shell offers Cavell, one also drawn from Benardete's essay. Oedipus unwittingly kills his father, Laius at a crossroads, as is well-known. The play itself, however, offers two importantly different descriptions of the intersection where this takes place. These accounts, when compared, provide what Benardete calls a "metaphor of political theory."[57] More specifically, Oedipus' account of the crossroads where Laius is murdered when set off against the different characterization offered by Jocasta makes plain the impossibility of charting the political from a position beyond it or outside it—from the standpoint of humanity, as apparently desired by Oedipus himself, or, conversely, through notions wholly redounding to society, or to politics as theorized as simply natural or conventional—not to mention, through the body, life, animality, technology, or some other similar theoretical perch.

---

[56] For more on this reading of Latour, see my "Neither a God nor ANT Can Save Us: Latour, Heidegger, Historicity, and Holism," *Paragraph* 40, no. 2 (July 2017): 153–73.
[57] Benardete, "Sophocles," 79.

The crossroads to which he comes, Oedipus identifies, specifically, as *threefold*.[58] So characterizing this site, Oedipus, however, describes his own path from *a point outside it*, above the fray, from the perspective of someone not themselves coming upon that crossroads, where in fact only two options remain. Oedipus' characterization, accordingly, contrasts to Jocasta's who claims her husband Laius was killed at a "split path," thus presenting the intersection as twofold, dual, rather than as triple. Jocasta's version, then, is really more apt; it captures the vantage point of the one actually travelling the road—in this case, Oedipus himself—who, coming to such a juncture, indeed only finds a single decision to be made, having already traversed one of the three legs in question. Accordingly, as Benardete nicely states, "Oedipus" himself seems to believe that "he has one more degree of freedom" than he has.[59]

Discourse, too, however, is situated within a kind of becoming and historicity, as has been more than once noted; discourse is thus also always already on some path, stretched between a concrete past and future. Accordingly, the political can never be theorized in talk! from above, by being enframed in some other conception—nor, apart from the crossroads specifically encountered, can some mastery over and some navigation of the political's tensions be attained, ultimately because the collective, to which politics necessarily pertains, ultimately precedes discourse and escapes all final and unequivocal identification. Discourse instead operates from within specifically political situations, where these various reference points—the economic, the social, the human, and ethnic and racial identities—may, then, be strategically invoked. Neither the scope of these alternatives—humanity, society, nature—is therefore known in advance nor, however, is some Schmittean Realpolitik thereby enjoined. Not real politics, but a politics in and of the real discourse demands, a politics that operates from out of a situation and recognizes that an otherwise anonymous factical collectivity has always already engaged society and its others (other persons and other nonhuman living beings), with discourse always being *practically* positioned in respect to this matrix and its momentary carving up.

"The undifferentiated beginnings . . . the nonanthropomorphic *archai* [first principles]" of human beings, as Benardete puts it, and as Elkin's bear story shows, indeed require that, along with discourse, it is politics all the way down.[60]

---

[58] With respect to the depiction of Oedipus' path of which Shell speaks, Cavell, as it happens, never furnishes its actual description. I am, however, able to indicate it, being already familiar with this same sketch, not only because I was once briefly a student of Shell but also because I already knew of its source. Though the interpretation of Oedipus already embarked on is indebted both to Shell and to Benardete's still landmark interpretation, its overall thrust as well as some of the particulars, doubtless are mine and may mark a deviation from both viewpoints.

[59] Ibid., 79.

[60] Ibid., 81.

Part Two

Discourse and Text

6

Can the Text Be "Saved" in Discourse? (The Early Walter Michaels)

Introduction: Questions?

Steven Knapp's and Walter Michaels' "Against Theory" and "Against Theory 2" were the first essays to bring a conception of discourse nearly as radical as the present one into a literary context; in these works, Knapp and Michaels cast aside all structures and frameworks believed to attend language, as well as questioning much of that "theory," then "reigning," which, of course, they were "against."[1]

In the first ATs and later in his own work, Michaels contends that forms, and linguistic conventions of any sort, contribute nothing to a text's understanding. If discourse is not already at work, then neither can *language* be.[2] Language thus does not precede discourse and cannot be identified on its own terms, no less serve as a guidepost or anchoring point for textual interpretation.

Such a wholesale dismissal of language as a reference point was especially pathbreaking at the time the first AT appeared. It flew in the face of all that then seemed most pressing in literary studies. No one contemporaneously aware of it can forget the enormous impact made by AT 1; the debates and controversies that swirled about it, captured in various documents and archives, attest to this excitement.

After all, the singular problem to which Derrida, de Man, and Lacan, had all devoted their attention, pertained to the *givenness* of language. None of these authors, it should be noted, unquestioningly accepted the existence of language or its conventions as determinative for discourse, including de Man. Instead, the fundamental *question* these thinkers pursued was that of language's very existence and how to access it— language for them at once being mediated by discourse, while remaining distinct from it and prior to it in the *ordo essendi* (order of being), if not the *ordo cognoscendi* (order of knowing). Language was not a thing, a spirit, a conscious convention, or a product of nature; hence, these and other writers inquired concerning language's necessarily

---

[1] Steven Knapp and Walter Benn Michaels, "Against Theory," in *Against Theory: Literary Studies and the New Pragmatism*, ed. W. J. T. Mitchell (Chicago: University of Chicago Press, 1985), 11–30; "Against Theory 2: Hermeneutics and Deconstruction," *Critical Inquiry* 14, no. 1 (Autumn 1987): 49–68 (Hereafter AT 1 and AT 2.)

[2] As they put this, "we have demonstrated that marks without intention are not language either," playing off their criticism of the philosopher P. D. Juhl (AT I 21); the terms of this equivalence, their specific understanding of discourse as involving "intention" receives further attention later.

sui generis ontological status and the epistemological contortions necessary to arrive at that status' apprehension or approximation.[3]

To this extent, poststructuralism did, however, refer to a language in its own right, and that possibility Knapp and Michaels questioned and indeed denied, thereby calling that inquiry, or "theory," into doubt. Such pushback against the thematics of language arguably was the genuine force of their stance "against theory," given the notable amount of theory that Knapp and Michaels otherwise did.

A second understanding of "against theory" does, however, surface in their essay, in tandem with the *positive* side of their inquiry, one that, in the end, ultimately preserved, rather than hastened, the departure of the linguisticism they sought to reject. In language's place, Knapp and Michaels opted for intentionality, specifically authorial intentionality. Just this equivalence, of (textual) meaning and (authorial) intention, however, had long been in doubt in literary studies and in theory itself. Nor did Michaels and Knapp offer anything new to allay those concerns; they did not address what intentions themselves might be (so-called mentalese or something else); whether they exist apart from speech and writing; and so on.[4]

Hence, just when linguisticism of any stripe was facing the firing squad, last cigarette between clenched teeth, it found a reprieve (as actually happened to another author deeply involved with this same problematic, Maurice Blanchot), thanks to Knapp's and Michael's invocation of intentionality and their silence about what it implied. To be sure, such non-responsiveness may have been intentional: aimed at a cessation of inquiry rather than its (eventual) satisfaction. The second reading of their slogan "against theory" corresponds to this strategy: it expresses the conviction that further reflection on the status of literature and literary criticism ought not be undertaken (AT 30). Intention in Knapp and Michaels' hands thus served to signal that the concerns of *other* critics, theorists, and philosophers were somehow not legitimate.

This penchant for short-circuiting inquiry, rather than wholly participating in it, arguably never serves Michaels or his insights well. In the present study, his questions, not his answers, however, are taken to be the most powerful and important aspect of his writings. His work registers as unavoidable, not only because he remains an original thinker of discourse in a literary context but also because behind Michaels' multifaceted arguments, that at times seem made solely for display, lie questions posed that go to the heart of the matter at hand: profound concerns pertaining to language (and discourse) and the interpretation of texts.

More narrowly, because Michaels holds a view of discourse quite near to the present one, his questions can serve as a springboard for the investigations that *A New Philosophy of Discourse* undertakes in its second half. In the ensuing discussion,

---

[3] This is most readily evident in the case of Lacan who identifies the unconscious with language. Discussed later in this chapter is an instance of de Man's work that makes clear how he engages with this same problematic at one phase of his thought. Seeing Derrida's early corpus in this light for philosophical readers may be more difficult, since themes other than language, such as radical alterity, there seem to eclipse its role. In my *Essential History* I argue that this sort of engagement with language can be discerned as well (168–97).

[4] Henry Staten nicely pinpointed this problem in his review of *The Shape of the Signifier* (*Modernism/modernity* 12, no. 2 [2005]: 362–4).

the same touchstones will be canvassed as in Part One—discourse, its historicity, its involvement with matters not discourse—in order to account for each phase more granularly than Part One's more provisional sketches allowed. The central question pursued, across various authors and texts, one bequeathed by Michaels' early thinking, will be this: how can texts, especially as found in the humanities, retain any integrity as the same, and some understanding of them, of what *they say* be sought, if they are wholly discourse and thus exist entirely as *events*.

6.1 Discourse and Representation

Michaels early work proves worthy of engaging with, then, on two scores. As a pioneer of discourse in a literary context, his writings are unavoidable for an endeavor that arrives at its own insights in part by exploring relevant undertakings implicit in its background. Moreover, what Michaels thinking yields, beyond a laying out of discourse (and a set of provocative readings and arguments tied to some of what it entails), is the formulation of a decisive problem with which Gadamer's work will be approached that eventually carries over to Part Two's subsequent discussions of Heidegger's and Davidson's writings.

This question or problem can be more fully set out by registering an early turn in Michaels' thinking that results in AT 1. Michaels performs a number of "conversions" in the course of a long and storied career. As is widely known, he initially worked in a deconstructive vein, and was featured as a rising academic star in Jonathan Culler's *On Deconstruction*.[5] In the meantime, Michaels had switched to an analytic approach to philosophy of language and to theory. Michaels' first works penned from this standpoint differ from AT and succeeding ones, however. In these first non-deconstructive pieces, Michaels' way of approaching his texts is more like that employed here. He glosses the thinkers in question in part through their intellectual context, and Michaels' focus is on modernist theory and literature, as well as the early New Criticism.

Michaels' writings with Knapp, accordingly, revise a still earlier phase of analytically inspired thinking on his part. Michaels previously, more specifically, not only was sensitive to traditionality as here conceived but also dismissed *authorial intention* as a reference point for interpretation. Michaels thus *first* turns to intention in AT and this notion informs Michaels' subsequent work up until its final transformation or conversion to date: when Michaels rather unexpectedly embraces that formalism he had denounced from the beginning of his analytic period, while treating works of photography and of literature with an eye to re-envisioning on these newly avowed formalist grounds contemporary social problems.[6]

---

[5] Jonathan Culler, *On Deconstruction: Theory and Criticism after Structuralism* (Ithaca, NY: Cornell University Press, 1982), 229ff.
[6] See Michaels, *The Beauty of A Social Problem: Photography, Autonomy, Economy* (Chicago: University of Chicago Press, 2015). Michaels views on society have also changed; once an advocate of the market and the logic of capitalism, he would now submit "neoliberalism" to critique and

Michael's turn to intention in AT itself, however, already yielded a relevant set of problems. Michaels and Knapp, though affirming discourse, there view it through the lens of *representation*. In Michaels' essays prior to AT, by contrast, discourse is paired with reference, and interpretation's starting point is the reader not the author. In the earliest, analytic Michaels, as in most discourse-based conceptions—for example Davidson's, Gadamer's, Heidegger's, and the present one—*the interpreter's standpoint* is central to a text's understanding. Since language's conventions do not render discourse intelligible, written discourse's operation depends on a *pre-acquaintance* on the part of *the interpreter* with discourse and what it concerns, as well as with things in the world more generally.

Such situatedness of readers neither Knapp nor Michaels credit in AT 1, however; instead they treat discourse as rooted in authors' or speakers' intentions and view talk! as a medium for expressing these intentions' representations. Making discourse representational in this way, however, as is about to become plain, ultimately results in the restoration of the sign and a new affirmation of its autonomy, at just that moment when these shibboleths were to be drawn into doubt.

That Knapp and Michaels view discourse through the lens of representation rather than with an eye to talk!'s subject matters becomes clearest in a text composed soon after AT 1, where the second, worlded alternative also surfaces. This text, the unrevised version of AT 2, is devoted entirely to Gadamer's thinking.[7] Both AT 2's, it may be noted, diverge importantly from AT 1, when it comes to *theory's* status. In AT 1, the authors repeatedly insist that theory as a project simply *is* the mistaken attempt to govern and command critical practice. In AT 2, however, they acknowledge that there is a whole swath of theory, hermeneutics (and, in the second version of AT 2, Derridean deconstruction), to which this vocation does not apply. Knapp and Michaels specifically exempt these reflections on literature and language from harboring an aim at methodology or governance of practice thus cancelling their own earlier definition of theory and effectively undermining the entire "takedown" of theory AT 1 had performed on its basis.[8] If some theory does not aim at such governance, then, if not all its answers, at least theory's questions may be legitimate after all.

However that may be, the passage in which they favor authorial representation over the text's and interpreter's being in a world emerges at the end of AT 2_1, in the discussion following their talk proper—specifically, when the philosopher Richard Wollheim questions the moment of intention they invoke. Wollheim asks what *sort*

---

analysis by way of the foregoing attention to form. (For the earlier view, see the introduction to his *Gold Standard and the Logic of Naturalism* [Berkeley, CA: University of California Press, 1987], 18.)

[7] Given as a talk in a colloquium setting, *Against Theory 2 : Sentence Meaning, Hermeneutics: Protocol of the Fifty-second Colloquy, 8 December 1985* precedes the AT 2 published in *Critical Inquiry*, though it only made into print after the latter (Berkeley, CA: Center for Hermeneutics Studies on Hellenistic and Modern Culture, 1986). The total publication, in addition to a draft of AT 2, contains commentaries by Daniel F. Melia and David Couzens Hoy, and a transcript of the question period that followed Michaels and Knapp's presentation. Henceforth it will be designated AT.2_1.

[8] AT 1's opening pronouncement "by 'theory' we mean a special project in literary criticism: the attempt to govern interpretations of particular texts by appealing to an account of interpretation in general" (AT 1 11) should be compared to this one from AT 2: "The denial that meaning is determined by intention is central to projects *as indifferent to method* as hermeneutics and deconstruction" (AT 2 49–50; my emphasis).

of intentions lend discourse its significance for Knapp and for Michaels. Knapp, in response, declares that "the intention to *represent* one's intentions" is the "intrinsically linguistic" one.⁹

Discourse, accordingly, is here characterized by Knapp as a domain where representations that recur to a speaker or author receive expression. Wollheim himself underscores the import of this response. At issue, Wollheim himself believes, would rather be "an intention directed toward the world" (AT.2₁ 45), and he tartly comments a few pages later that the difference between the two alternatives—his and Knapp's and Michaels'—is "pretty substantive and not terminological" (AT.2₁ 47).

Not merely intentionality, but an intentionality represented and removed from the world, as Wollheim indicates, stands at the center of Knapp and Michaels' views in AT. On the relevant alternative construal, however, discourse's articulations arise only alongside those subject matters central to an interpreters' concerns. Expressions such as "that is too yellow" or "it is cold," say what they do in such contexts, where they may turn out to be commands, descriptions, or any of a number of other speech-acts, the contents they express appearing only insofar as some subject matter—vichyssoises or icebergs, irises or acts of courage—is already in view.¹⁰ Knapp and Michaels, however, eschew such contextualizing, and opt instead for intentionality as something that either directly inhabits signs or not. For them "this is yellow" has what meaning it has not owing to its use in contexts, but to the meaning-endowing or expressive acts of its user.¹¹ Accordingly, the sign and its "ontology," as presented by them, remains intrinsically removed from discourse's capacity to say something about the world and in part by this means be understood.

---

⁹ Knapp indicates, to be sure, that this level of generality broaches new territory for him and Michaels. Nevertheless, on this notion of "expressive intention," an intention aimed at articulating some intentional state or feature of an agent's perspective, both Knapp and Michaels settle (AT.2₁ 46). Michaels, who is otherwise notably quiet, avers that "here the intention is to express" (AT.2₁ 47). Both may be thinking of H. P. Grice's work, which on other occasions they explicitly identify as a source for their own. See Grice "Utterer's Meaning and Intentions" (*Studies in the Ways of Words* [Cambridge, MA: Harvard University Press, 1989]: 86–116).

¹⁰ Semantics' dependence on context, on some topic for the ability of a stretch of discourse to say or express something, was treated in Chapter 5, where it came to light along with a provisional framing of the text's historicity or traditionality. The present inquiry, unlike the earlier one, not only foregrounds the interpreter's role in its specificity but also eventually aims to answer precisely how a historicity specific to discourse and its interpreters' concerns with contextualized things' or subject matters' are to be conceived as operating together, such that the text may retain its foreignness, or "be saved," as Michaels somewhat sardonically puts it in the title of an early essay soon to be discussed.

¹¹ As noted, Knapp and Michaels may here have in mind the work of another theorist of discourse, H.P. Grice, whose writings they later claimed in interviews influenced their own. Grice famously said that part of understanding what he called speaker's meaning was understanding not only what an utterance conveys but also understanding the utterance as having been so intended by the speaker or author to convey it. Yet for Grice, as for Wollheim, for whom intention also is not simply out of the picture, intentions of these sorts are not self-contained, but simultaneously directed toward the world. Grice is thus often said to be the founder of pragmatics: the study of discourse's capacity to communicate in contexts beyond its purported logical and semantic characteristics, in cases such as saying "great" in front of a sign declaring that the restaurant where I wished to eat is closed. Again, see "Utterer's Meaning and Intention" as well as Grice's "Utterer's Meaning, Sentence Meaning, and Word Meaning" (*Ways of Words*, 117–37), as well as Kates, "Semantics and Pragmatics and Husserl and Derrida," *Philosophy Compass* 10, no. 12 (December 2015): 828–40.

The thought experiment central to the first AT displays their commitment to just such an understanding of signs. That experiment consists in imagining traces in the sand that initially appear to be a stanza or a poem by William Wordsworth; subsequently, these markings, which seem to be a poem, are said to be effaced by a wave and replaced by a second stanza from the same poem.[12] At this moment, the one witnessing that event, according to Knapp and Michaels, must decide whether these lines have natural causes (such as same strange form of sedimentation), or not.[13] If natural, they are not discourse at all, but then they are also not language, insist Knapp and Michaels. Thereby, the authors aim to show that no daylight can appear between discourse and language—if it's not discourse, it's not language either—and, thus, that the priority (temporal and ontological) of language over discourse cannot be maintained.[14]

From the present perspective, however, the problem with their account, is not too little language, but too much. Understanding or using discourse, including written discourse, for one thing, never occurs in this sort of isolation from the world—suitably emblematized by the vision of a stanza of poetry encountered on an empty expanse of beach. Books and anthologies indeed have their reasons, and seasons, and, as will soon become clearer, Knapp's and Michaels' exercise works only because they and their readers are already familiar with poetry, Wordsworth, and so on. Indeed, their gloss on their own thought experiment makes clear that discourse and its understanding never concern a phantom intentionality that imparts itself to signs or somehow fails to (in the latter instance begetting shapes that only resemble signifiers).[15] After all, the first stanza purported to appear on the beach is unquestionably *legible*, and remains so (as in fact does the second), regardless of any of the considerations they raise—no decision ever being reached even in *their text* as to whether these supposed "signs" are or are not natural by Knapp and Michaels themselves. Accordingly, whatever understandability resides in these expressions (or, then, in any stretch of discourse, written or spoken) does not and cannot bear any relation to the absence or presence of intentions per se. Instead, as in the more standard hermeneutic account, the legibility of these and other writings derives from the pre-acquaintance of their *readers* with already existing instances of discourse. Pre-acquaintance with the genre of poetry and with similar stretches of the expressions found therein *on the reader's part*, along with readers' acquaintance with their presumed subject matters (beloveds, stars, and so on) informs this and every instance of textual understanding. To be sure, this hermeneutic perspective does not entail that persons or something like their intentions play absolutely no role in understanding—including, at points, a potentially disqualifying

---

[12] "But now suppose that, as you stand gazing at this pattern in the sand, a wave washes up and recedes, leaving in its wake (written below what you now realize was only the first stanza) the following words" (AT 1 15).

[13] "You will either be ascribing these marks to some agent capable of intentions . . . or you will count them as nonintentional effects of mechanical processes," they conclude.

[14] Thus the marks or words in question "are not, after all, an example of intentionless meaning; as soon as they become intentionless, they become meaningless as well" (Ibid. 16).

[15] This last difference, between the signifier and its "shape," of course, became the focus of Michaels' *The Shape of the Signifier: 1967 to the End of History* (Princeton, NJ: Princeton University Press, 2004), a portion of which is discussed a bit later.

one. Person-oriented and intentional considerations, however, always operate within this preexisting broader context supplied by discourse's traditionality, rather than signs being transformed into signs by authorial acts.

Moreover, it should now be clear, Knapp and Michaels, at this moment, have really only pushed back one step the sign's (or the signifier)'s reification on to the intentions themselves, now necessarily thing-like and able to be somehow absent or present *in* the signs. Accordingly, Knapp and Michaels' focus on signs as bearers of intentions permits texts once more to signify under their own steam—since no actual author is in sight even in their own case—and this, again when the autonomy of texts (and language) is supposed to be in doubt.

The error they identify on their terms' basis, consequently, turns out to be impossible to conceive or imagine, thus attesting from a different direction to their own illicit reification of intentionality and signification. The taking of genuine signs (because intentionally informed) for ones that are not so endowed, in cases where Wordsworth's poem would be *naturally caused*, can in the first place arise for Knapp and Michaels on account of a *resemblance* or *likeness* between the two cases, between genuine signs and what only *appear* to be such. About these inscriptions under the hypothesis that they are naturally caused, they declare "they will merely seem to *resemble* words" (AT 16; their emphasis).

Yet, how *likeness* in this instance is imaginable remains wholly unclear, given that in Knapp and Michaels' account the two inscriptions are entirely indistinguishable from one another in any observable way. How can an inscription in appearance wholly identical to a poem's text be said to *resemble* that text? Is this a likeness of a physical order, as between a photograph and what it portrays (but where, then, does the physical difference in this case lie?); or is it a wholly intelligible one, in which case how is such a resemblance to be conceived (what does an entirely intellectual likeness itself *look like*?). It is one thing, after all, to say that these *paint drips* on a shop door read from afar appear to say "open," only later to discover that they are but random drips. It is another, ultimately impossible, scenario to approach them and find that they have changed not at all, yet still affirm they only resemble such a message.[16]

These paradoxes, accordingly, show why, on the present account, discourse is always necessarily already underway, with interpreters *encountering* and understanding instances of discourse thanks to their acquaintance with prior ones, there being no origin of discourse as discourse in intentionality nor in anything else. By contrast, Knapp and Michaels, as their recourse to resemblance underscores, reify signs and intentions, effectively rehabilitating pure or autonomous language. They ultimately

---

[16] Michaels at this same epoch, it should be noted, seemingly aware of the dicey character of such resemblances, confronts these paradoxes explicitly and chews on them further, without, however, in my view really resolving them, in his *The Gold Standard and the Logic of American Naturalism*. (See especially, the title essay "The Gold Standard and the Logic of Naturalism.") In *Beauty*, moreover, resemblance again returns, now to coordinate the relation between formally autonomous artworks and social problems: the former emblematize, or picture, the kind of being accruing to the latter (the problems), this being just about all Michaels has to say about the issue that so bedeviled structuralism Marxism (and later Jameson): namely, of the relation of the aesthetic to social and historical formations, as well as the status of the latter in their own right (Cf. xii; 42).

turn discourse into "a piece of language," as they sometimes put it, by making the presence or absence of intention constitutive of the sign as sign, rather than looking to discourse itself for such legibility.

Nevertheless, in the present context, these considerations are but prelude to the central event: the problem that Knapp and Michaels identify pertaining to discourse and (textual) interpretation as such. To believe that no genuine difficulties accrue to discourse in the contexts that concern Knapp and Michaels would indeed be mistaken. They restore signs, and give the signs' power to represent intentions such a role, doubtless, with an eye toward those instances here of primary interest: literary and related ones. In these cases, common contexts and worlds seem *lacking*. Intentionally endowed signs with their relative independence thus seem necessary to account for the being of the text *as a text*, as readers of the Egyptian Book of the Dead or Wordsworth's poetry do not in any obvious way share their current situations with those in which these works were produced.

To be sure, an outline of how discourse might operate in this kind of instance was offered in Part One; nevertheless, obstacles exist for accounting for such cases at the more granular level at which discussion now arrives. What texts are and how they can in any way be conceived as having authority, indeed have anything new to say for the critic, prove questions once discourse without language or signs comes on the scene. As previously emphasized, discourse, as here envisioned functions wholly in time; talk!'s way of being is that of an occasional event. But what texts are in the *register of time*, and how they articulate understandings on their own terms, assuming they are capable of doing so at all, is not yet evident and hence demands further investigation.

6.2 Losing Belief and Saving the Text

It is worthwhile continuing to sojourn with the early Michaels in order to better grasp the current problem's terms. In AT1 and 2, Michaels and Knapp recognize intentionality, it may be said, only when they *don't* see it, just the opposite of the supreme court's renowned dictum on pornography. Their argument is indeed entirely negative, and intentionality, located in the difference between signs and what only resembles them, while simply present or absent, at the same time remains inherently unobservable. An irony, however, lurks in this criticism that complicates the current picture: namely, that Michaels himself once voiced these same worries about the elusiveness of intention and the potential re-objectification of the text, while hewing to an approach closer to the present one. Michaels, when he first conceives of discourse, in his earliest analytic writings, explicitly argues against *objectifying* texts, by way of signs, languages, or forms of any kind, and that issue, of whether texts are things, will serve as a throughline throughout this work's second half. Michaels' criticism of such objectification is itself, then, a powerful result, especially since a similar insistence on the de-objectification of the text is common to all the thinkers subsequently surveyed, as well as to my project here.

Perhaps not surprisingly, in this same early work, Michaels opts for construing textuality (and discourse) not by way of intentionality or representation, but as emanating from readers or interpreters along with references in contexts—hence, again in a fashion more proximate to the path taken here. This last feature, reference, to be sure, for Michaels is aggregated around beliefs and thus understood somewhat differently than in the present context. Nevertheless, Michaels' earliest analytic stance is proximate to the present one and to that of hermeneutics more generally, owing to the foregoing two points: his critique of textual reification and his focus on the interpreter.

The reasons why Michaels changed his mind, then, why he abandons a hermeneutic approach in favor of expressive intentions in AT1 and 2 (and subsequently) can indicate the questions that the present inquiry, operating on similar terms, must itself confront. To grasp these issues, Michaels' early proximity to the present viewpoint must first be more closely examined, however.

Michaels' "Saving the Text" was published about three years before AT 1.[17] Its central contention is the non-viability of "epistemological realism," as Michaels calls it. Under this guise, Michaels sets his lance against all attempts at objectifying the text.

Epistemological realism when it comes to texts consists in taking the text as equivalent to a thing or a state of affairs, as a "hard fact," as Michaels puts it, borrowing a phrase from Bertrand Russell.[18] Such realism informs I.A. Richards' program, and indeed virtually all of subsequent American literary criticism up through Paul de Man, according to Michaels. For Richards, Michaels insists, when "attempt(ing) to escape the perils of propositionalism," ended up affirming textual interpretation in the form of "an encounter with pure propositionality."[19] By this Michaels seems to mean that Richards, to find a place for literature as speaking in non-propositional terms, turned the literary text itself into the *object* of propositions, into a thing capable of answering to true or false claims about *it*, in this way inventing literary *form*. In "Saving," Michaels, accordingly, stands wholly removed from the construal of a text as object or thing, as an independent entity able to stand apart from the contexts in which, and the occasions on which, it speaks.

In "Saving," Michaels, rejecting all objectifications of a text, as does hermeneutics and the present account, instead assigns a text's legibility to discourse *as an event*, one in which the things texts talk about and the contexts in which they do so enable the text's own speaking and its own identity. Only as *occurrences* of this sort are there *any* texts or may they be understood, none of the usual props—signs, structures, words, and language—entering the picture.

Intentions, then, at this epoch, for Michaels, do not and cannot play any central role in textual interpretation. Intentions, as Michaels puts it, to the contrary, encounter the same problems as textual interpretation itself. "Intentionalists like E. D. Hirsch," Michaels affirms in "Saving," "are perfectly correct in insisting on the relevance of authorial intention to literary criticism; their mistake is to imagine that there can be evidence of intention which is not itself subject to . . . the interpretive problems that the texts are."[20] Accordingly, intentions depend on *broader* interpretative contexts; they

---

[17] Walter Michaels, "Saving the Text: Reference and Belief," *MLN* 93, no. 5 (Comparative Literature; December, 1978): 771–93.
[18] Ibid., 776.
[19] Ibid., 778.
[20] Ibid., 783.

emerge within those circumstances surrounding texts. What is said about intentions functions *within interpretation*; interpretation does not follow the reverse course and function *within intention*, as Michaels later maintains in AT.

With intention downplayed and the entitative text out of the picture, Michaels in "Saving" finally also affirms that what a *text talks about*, or *reference*, is key to its being understood, as is also true here. What a text speaks about for Michaels plays this role, once again in typical hermeneutic fashion, thanks to the subject matter's *already* being at hand when a text is encountered. Unlike the scenario suggested by Wordsworth at the beach (which of course ultimately relies on Michaels and his readers already being familiar with texts, poetry, and aspects of the world, possibly including Wordsworth and his Lucy poems), a pre-understanding—not only of the text and of its author but also what will turn out to be its *topics*—precedes any encounter with a given piece of writing, while interpretation proceeds by articulating what the text says or shows or wonders in respect to it.[21]

The earliest analytic Michaels, then, unlike the author of AT, thoroughgoingly resists the text's objectification, while foregrounding both the interpreter's role and a pre-acquaintance with a text's subject matter as central to the text's understanding and to its existence as a text. The reasons Michaels seems to have had for changing his mind should, then, bear on the current project, given the proximity between his approach and the present one. Having approached the text in a manner so different from Richards and subsequent formalisms, why did Michaels relinquish this perspective? So, too, how do his motives relate to the possibility of construing texts apart from all objectification, a goal that Michaels seems to have abandoned by the time of AT, insofar as intentions themselves now bear this load?

The initial question, concerning why Michaels changes his vantage point, clearly needs treating first. Fortunately, the answer comes quite readily to hand. The price paid by Michaels for saving the text in "Saving" was indeed *a changing text*, and this price apparently he later judged too high. Michaels in "Saving" explicitly affirms just such radical metamorphosis on the part of any text: "A text has meaning for us only against a backdrop of beliefs we hold and assumptions we make about literature and about the world, and when these beliefs and assumptions change, the meanings of our texts, the texts themselves, change too."[22]

Michaels worries, then, that were discourse given freer rein than in his later story about intentions informing sign-like shapes, it would, in effect, render texts wholly non-self-identical, entirely "free balloons," as it might here be put. There would not be a single text, but only *different texts*, different stretches of discourse varying on *each occasion*, ones corresponding to each of their readers.

---

[21] As discussed in a moment, Michaels approaches this feature practically. After surveying two different readings, of Henry James' *The Turn of the Screw*, Michaels concludes that each recurs to the contexts in which the work appears, contexts that bear references to previous encounters and understanding of a specific topic—in this case, what the critics in question understand as "love"—textual interpretation thus depending on what Michaels himself at this moment calls "the world," Ibid., 784.

[22] Ibid., 784.

To be clear, for Michaels in "Saving," our beliefs still provide a sufficient anchor for *practical criticism*. Beliefs, however, obviously alter from critic to critic. Consequently, the rejection of Richards' and related epistemological realisms, for Michaels, ultimately entails that there can be no text, no selfsame text on any terms. Michaels rehabilitates authorial intentionality in the AT's, then, in a nutshell, because the text in "Saving" was not sufficiently saved.

Despite his subsequent solution being doubtful, substantial questions for hermeneutics and the present approach fall out from Michaels' worry. In fact, the very charge that Michaels tacitly brings against his earlier self, he later levels explicitly against Gadamer and his hermeneutics. Michaels insists that Gadamer, too, lands in the untenable position of embracing an always changing text. In AT 2, Knapp and Michaels quote Gadamer as speaking of a text being "understood in a different way each time," and just this affirmation, they insist, amounts to there being *no text* at all, only different texts for different readers.[23]

Of course, the possibility Gadamer himself affirms when speaking of the text is not thereby ruled out: namely, that the text might be *both* same and different, both changing and identical. Though he does indicate that the text appears differently on different occasions, Gadamer also insists that the text furnishes criteria for adjudicating disagreements about its interpretation and to this degree remains identical across its readings. In *Truth and Method*, he at one point states this on his terms, by insisting that if one is not talking about the same thing in a conversation this will inevitably make itself known.[24]

Why the text cannot be viewed as Gadamer indeed does, as at once same and different, has a different reason than any Knapp and Michaels suggest; not only because they misread Gadamer's stance toward language upon which the text's sameness depends but also, especially, because Michaels in "Saving," while there in fact closer to Gadamer, had already ruled out this possibility.[25] Hence, seeing why for Michaels in "Saving," a text at once same and different is impossible can help introduce Gadamer's actual views on this matter, while at the same time permitting a first look at the problems Gadamer's own account may still confront.

In essence, Michaels' denial of a text both changing and not in "Saving" rests on the role there played by belief (where Michael's later representationalism already finds a footing), and belief's radical difference from insight or *truth*—truth, of course, being Gadamer's hermeneutics' watchword as set out in TM. For Michaels in "Saving," the text's "constitution," or "construction," as he calls it, depends on belief,

---

[23] AT 2 52.
[24] *Truth and Method*, 2nd revised ed., trans. Joel Weinsheimer and Donald G. Marshall (London: Continuum, 2004); hereafter all references will be given to TM.
[25] In AT 2, they offer an account (and rebuttal) of Gadamer's affirmation of the text being the same that diverges from Gadamer's actual one. Knapp and Michaels assert that the text's identity for Gadamer rests on linguistic "convention": the text's embodying stable conventional units and rules—words, signs, signifiers, grammar, and so on—over against its ever changing incarnations as discourse. Convention allows for the text's sameness; discourse its difference (AT 2 54). Gadamer, however, no more is this sort of conventionalist when it comes to language than are Knapp and Michaels themselves, so their argument against a text's in some fashion possessing identity for Gadamer does not genuinely hold.

not truth.[26] Belief, for Michaels, in turn, is an autonomous starting point, a kind of brute given, enclosed at once in itself and in its time. Stanley Fish's influence at this epoch on Michaels thus is evident, albeit for Michaels, belief is primarily *individual*. Hence, what this yields is that for Michaels *a single critic's* beliefs underpins his, her, or their interpretation, while belief as such does not allow for translation into any other contexts or permit any manner of correction.

Michaels distinguishes belief from truth in "Saving," specifically in terms of what is called a *correspondence* theory of truth, in this case as presented by Bertrand Russell, whose views, Michaels claims, originally influenced Richards. Correspondence theories, as previously met in Brooks, who also embraces them, view truth in terms of a one-to-one mapping of propositions (third-person reports expressed in sentences) on to state of affairs, facts in the world (the classic instance being "the cat is on the mat" as said of some cat on some mat).[27]

Correspondence theories contrast with coherence theories of truth; in the latter, truth consists in agreement between statements themselves, an internal consistency *across* sentences or propositions. Russell, Michaels relates, argues against coherence theories in favor of correspondence, on the grounds that distinct sets of statements might each be internally consistent, while still contradicting another. (My talk of Jupiter as a gas planet may be consistent with the rest of my astronomical theory. Another theory may hold that Jupiter is comprised of discrete chunks of solid matter separated by empty space. The second "fact" about Jupiter could be consistent with the terms of that theory, though both would not be correct.) Only correspondence, not coherence, then, is an adequate index of truth.

Michaels himself seems to have been convinced by a form of this argument, albeit the terms on which Russell draws this distinction are no longer relevant, something of which he is doubtless aware. Nevertheless, Michaels, like Brooks, affirms that truth can only answer to independent propositions, and is wary of calling true anything that looks like coherence, that operates in clusters and depends on larger wholes.

A version of just such holism, however, as will soon be plainer, is central to the present account, so it is indeed worthwhile pursuing further Michaels' account of belief and his qualms in respect to truth. For, on this basis, thanks to the distinction between correspondence and coherence, Michaels in "Saving" similarly distinguishes belief from truth. Clusters of beliefs, varying critic by critic, for him, indeed "constitute" the text; as so constituted, there can be no question of comparing either these beliefs or the corresponding texts they engender with one another. Beliefs being holistic and not propositional stand apart from any concern with truth and thus each text fashioned by each critic is bulletproof, while bearing no relation to any other of its presumed instances. In "Saving," Michaels thus offers an example of two different, yet purportedly self-consistent, interpretations of what otherwise would be the "same text," James' *Turn of the Screw*. A first critic reads James' text as portraying the nanny in *Turn* as mad (himself once having had a mad nanny); another, with more positive experience of caretakers, believes that the nanny represents a paradigm of a more than worldly love.[28]

[26] Michaels, "Saving," 791.
[27] Cf. Chapter 4, pp. 28 ff..
[28] Michaels' two critics are Robert Heilman and Harold Goddard; see Ibid., 780 ff.

For Michaels, neither of these interpretations nor the different texts they invoke can be further contested, nor can one be said to be more true or legitimate than the other, since only coherence not correspondence is question, interpretation and textuality answering to merely (holistic) belief. Michaels insists: "We couldn't justify it [rejecting one interpretation] by saying that the essay doesn't account for all the evidence. It clearly does, and indeed it is almost a commonplace to note that particularly aberrant readings will often be particularly thorough as well."[29]

Different *texts*, accordingly, are constituted each time by the relevant beliefs of the individual critics whose interpretations cannot be evaluated either in respect to what they claim the text says—they read different texts—or in regard to the world, the subject matters that the critics and their texts speak about (here the affection or hatred of nannies toward their charges). Both in respect to James' story and to its themes, interpretation bears no relation to truth, thereby spawning an everchanging text.

Michaels' account, whatever else it does, furnishes a powerful clue to a consideration that will soon take center stage. If, as the early Michaels affirms, a radically non-entitative, de-objectified text is to be embraced, then, it turns out, truth of some perhaps new sort also must be able to be affirmed, if the text is to be not always different but also the same. For hermeneutics, the text indeed appears as something about which there can be disagreement; insights concerning what the text says and also what it talks about are both possible and necessary. The text and the critic can speak about the same thing while saying different things about that subject and/or agreeing on some points, just as different critics do, all these possibilities requiring that some form of insight or truth in respect to some subject be at work.

Critical in the hermeneutic case in making this possible, moreover, is the radically temporal character of both the text and its interpretation. What the text says can be discussed, and its subject matters understood and insight about them gleaned, ultimately, because the reader's grasp of such subjects do not themselves precede the text being read, as beliefs are positioned as doing in Michaels' account. Texts, what they concern, and the relevant beliefs instead appear together in a single act of understanding; the text, its topic, and its interpretation emerge in a single event, both unified and diverse.

Indeed on both the hermeneutic account and the present one, a subject *already* in possession of his or her beliefs never *constitutes* a text; instead, their opinions, beliefs, and knowledge have the status of *pre*-judgments, pre-understandings, prejudices. Such prior understandings only click into gear and appear on the scene, however, in the same context and at the same moment in which the text stands forth, the two coming to light together. Such pre-acquaintances thus do enter the space of inquiry, but they are at that moment *in question* along with other possible viewpoints—namely, those of the text and competing interpretations of it. To stick with the present instance, a given critic, after all, might have had a crazy nanny *and* also a beloved one, or could have loved the crazy one, and so on. What transpires is thus not the critic making (or making up) the text—constituting it, in Michaels strong sense, by way of belief—but rather a two-way interchange. My pre-judgments, not just about the text I am reading (James, his time

---

[29] Ibid., 787. I myself do not find convincing Michaels claim that aberrant readings can account for all the evidence, in part because I doubt his "all."

and people, their relation to me), but also the subjects it concerns (terror, love, partial understanding) become explicit through *the text*, and can be questioned *by* it, even as James' text and what it says come to light on *these same assumptions'* basis. Gadamer calls this interchange the dialectic of question and answer.[30] As in a conversation, texts and their interpretations, *not being objects*, can emerge together, in a movement in which the articulation and understanding of each proceeds from both quarters at once.

Michaels, falling back on a less advanced philosophical model (constitution) and hewing to the distinction between belief and truth, denies truth to (talk about) texts and what they talk about, thereby obscuring the role truth plays (even merely as goal or desideratum) in the event of understanding. The Gadamerean alternative, by contrast, envisioning the text as an event of truth (in the broadest possible sense) sketches how there can be a radically temporal text, at once same and different, that comes to pass entirely as *discourse*—thus without conventions, algorithms, idealities, intentionally informed signs, or their traces. Only if texts speak along with their interpretations in a single dynamic movement can the text be understood at once as saying things different from and the same as their interpreters about a shared topic. As complex events of this kind texts are indeed compatible with discourse.

Yet, though pushing back against some of Michaels concerns or prejudices, this sketch only deepens the question of what texts, as so understood, actually may be and how they may be said to *exist*. A text may allow for insights about what it talks about, and about itself, thanks to appearing as itself in the movement of interpretation. In what sense, if any, does the text exist as the *same* across time, beyond its occasional appearance, even if it may genuinely show itself there? Or is this question not a question, as Gadamer sometimes intimates—but instead the remnant of an objectified and entitative construal of the text?

The text's inherently temporal way of being indeed remains difficult to grasp, arguably even more so, once the limits inherent in Michaels' and similar models based on constitution have been shed, these templates at least having the advantage of clarity. Accordingly, a final provisional light on the present alternative and the problems it faces can be gleaned by following out one last thread in Michaels' writings, one that emerges at the end of "Saving" and that happens to foreground another important instance where Michaels understands truth as pertaining only to the correspondence found in assertions.

6.3 Text and Time

In "Saving's" closing portion, Michaels offers the first of several interpretations he pens of Paul de Man's essay "The Purloined Ribbon." "Ribbon" initially appeared in the now defunct journal *Glyph* and it later became chapter nine of de Man's *Allegories*

---

[30] See TM 362 ff.

*of Reading.*³¹ Michaels returns to it almost obsessively over the years, with slight, yet potentially important, variations in his readings.³²

The text of the "Purloined Ribbon" at least, would, then, appear to be both one and many, the same and different across multiple readings for Michaels himself.³³ Michaels' interpretation of "Ribbon" in "Saving" is arguably his clearest account of this essay, however, and perhaps his most powerful, since that reading makes evident the central role of both discourse and reference in de Man's own work.

In "Saving," Michaels indeed contends, and rightly in my view, that de Man endorses Michaels' position that textuality is inseparable from there being something texts talk about, a worldly subject that in part allows for texts both to appear and to speak. De Man, however, at the same time that he finds reference non-fungible, according to Michaels, is yet another critic who yearns for an objectifiable, entitative text. De Man thus posits language, in addition to the text construed as discourse, thereby falling into what Michaels calls "hypothetical realism."³⁴ By "hypothetical realism," Michaels intends that de Man is a realist, in Richards' sense, in respect to *language itself*; yet Michaels further insists that de Man's realism in this regard remains merely "hypothetical," since no encounter with language, on de Man's understanding of discourse, can ever take place. Discourse's operation is unavoidable, and, with that operation a reference to *something nonlinguistic* always occurs. De Man's realism when it comes to language is aimed at a language conceived as distinct from all beings, however; thus language as such can never be accessed by discourse, and de Man's realism in respect to it must remain entirely and purely hypothetical.

Michaels' account, to be clear, offers some genuine insight into de Man's project; it faithfully maps the stages of de Man's argument. It stumbles, however, at this last juncture, in Michael's assigning to it a purely hypothetical realism, in a way that ultimately proves telling both for Michaels' work and for the present conception. Rather than pursue such *realism* (equivalent to formalism) in respect to *language*, de Man, early, and, at least implicitly, late, affirms *a radical temporality* of texts and of his own readings. Thus, Michaels is right that for de Man language is a sort of last instance, and also that for him *no propositions* about language can be framed. Nevertheless, the point of the de Manian exercise lies in language's being accessed *in some other* way, in a fashion at once non-propositional, while being implicated in time and becoming.³⁵

---

³¹ Paul de Man, *Allegories of Reading: Figural Language in Rousseau, Nietzsche, Rilke, and Proust* (New Haven, CT: Yale University Press, 1982).
³² It may be apt to note at this juncture that I myself have previously published work on Michaels and AT; see "Literary Theory's Languages" chapter four of my *Fielding Derrida*, esp. 97–105.
³³ Michaels, of course, treats de Man's essay again with Knapp in AT 1 and recurs to it in *Gold Standard*. He discusses "Ribbon" once more in *Shape of the Signifier*, along with some other de Man texts, including "Phenomenality and Materiality in Kant," which henceforth takes on a similar centrality in Michaels' commentary.
³⁴ Ibid., 790.
³⁵ This last holds at least up to "The Rhetoric of Temporality," when de Man famously abandoned phenomenology's nomenclature in favor of one derived from the theory of tropes (Paul de Man, *Blindness and Insight: Essays in the Rhetoric of Contemporary Criticism*, 2nd rev. ed. [Minneapolis: University of Minnesota Press, 1983], 187–228). The latter had the effect of obscuring the complex stratification central to all de Man's writing, especially the fashion in which language only emerges on the basis of discourse, a central feature of de Man's thinking that Michaels also affirms. Everything

Despite misprizing de Man's intentions at this moment, Michaels, in his later writing, does offer his own version of de Man's resolution of the problem of accessing language in non-realist or non-objectified modes, when treating an essay (written earlier than "Ribbon") in which de Man also happens to discuss two of the present work's main critical reference points: the New Criticism and Gadamer's hermeneutics. In *Shape of the Signifier*, once more about to comment on de Man's "Purloined Letter," albeit now in an intriguing pairing with the art of the earthworks sculptor Robert Smithson, Michaels comments on de Man's essay "Form and Intent in the American New Criticism."[36]

In "Form," de Man himself questions what Michaels contests in "Saving" when it comes to the New Critics: their treatment of the text as a thing, as "a hard fact." Michaels recognizes that de Man faults the New Critics for in essence objectifying the text, and Michaels further notes that de Man also endorses the *intentional character* of textuality, which de Man indeed claims the New Critics overlook. Michaels, however, differentiates de Man's earlier position from Michaels present one, by doubting the central development of de Man's essay, one that, among other things, separates de Man's talk of intention from Michaels' construal of it in AT (and subsequently). In "Form and Intent," de Man maintains that the New Critics, though indeed mistaking the text's "form" for a thing—like a "stone," adds Michaels (opening the door for his Smithson reading)—nevertheless, thanks to their mistake, arrive at a crucial *insight* concerning the poetic text, and, ultimately, into language. This insight de Man positively sets out, by way of an operation in which truth rather than belief is central, and a blind spot, or blindness is transformed into *insight*. This signature movement on the part of de Man—the title of the work in which de Man's essay is now found, after all, is *Blindness and Insight*—Michaels however, rejects.[37] Michaels claims "it's hard to see how it [this transformation of blindness into insight] is possible."[38]

In the very citation Michaels offers from de Man, however, where this conversion of blindness into insight appears, Michaels ignores that moment in de Man's account that explains how such a shift from blindness to insight is to occur. The nucleus of this movement, which Michaels omits noticing, moreover, is specifically hermeneutic: it recurs to the "hermeneutic circle of interpretation," as de Man himself says. Michaels indeed cites de Man declaring: "Because such patient and delicate attention was paid to the reading of forms, the [New] critics pragmatically *entered into the hermeneutic circle of interpretation*, mistaking it for the organic circularity of natural processes."[39]

As in his treatment in "Saving," Michaels, in *Shape*, thus again severs insight and truth from interpretation, here omitting the most classically hermeneutic feature

---

seeming to be figures, such as metaphor and allegory, readers wrongly took them to operate on the same, single level and readers also believed they could simply replicate de Man's use of these terms, something de Man had already indicated was impossible near the end of his essay on Derrida "The Rhetoric of Blindness" (de Man, *Blindness and Insight*, 140).

[36] De Man's essay originated as a lecture presented to "The History of Ideas Club" at Johns Hopkins University and was published for the first time in de Man's first book (de Man, *Blindness and Insight*, 20–35).
[37] Michaels, *Shape*, 109.
[38] Ibid., 109.
[39] Ibid., 109 (my emphasis).

of hermeneutics: the hermeneutic circle. Michaels gives no notice to the circle of interpretation—a decision that clearly recurs to his construal of truth in terms of correspondence and his allergy to any holistic understanding, attesting to the major role both of these conceptions play throughout his thought.

The circle, as presented by de Man in "Form," does furnish a possible response, however, to the question that plagues Michaels (and hermeneutics and the present account): of how to conceive of the text as different and the same in an entirely temporal register, while avoiding both epistemological and hypothetical realism. This is owed to the fact that the circle, in de Man's repurposing, ultimately is, as de Man says, "ontological." "The hermeneutic circle mentioned by Spitzer, of which the history has been traced by Gadamer in *Wahrheit und Methode*, and whose ontological significance is the basis of Heidegger's treatise *Sein und Zeit*," to quote de Man, makes available a disclosure of the text's own ontological character—the text's kind of being— including that intentionality that belongs to the text, as well as how this disclosure can be accessed.[40] The target of this disclosure, its subject matter, and the manner of its accessing, in this unique case, moreover, are *the same*, thereby affording an articulation at once non-propositional and temporal.

That is to say, in the instance in question, according to de Man, the New Critics entered the hermeneutic circle *pragmatically*, by way of their mistake about form— this mistake, the taking of the text as a thing, at some moment never being entirely avoidable. Doing so, however, they discovered that literature had already addressed the question of its own mode of being and of textuality as such. Hence, enacting the circle, first literature's, and now the critic's "answer" remains immanent to this sequence of interpretations, to the movement of the circle itself, thus disclosing the essentially temporal character of understanding, while also sketching the text's specific style of existence, the two, understanding and text, ultimately converging. Interpretation discovers its question has already been asked and answered, in de Man's case now twice, in literature and in criticism, and in so doing, criticism both enacts and embodies textuality's temporal "shape." Such repetition, which simultaneously entails *the withdrawal* of what it repeats, and marks its recession as well as its apprehension, is at once the manner of accessing the text's being *and* a description of it. Hence de Man states, building on Heidegger's description of the circle, the "foreknowledge" of what a text is, is supplied by the "text itself," even as that text always remains "temporally ahead of the explicit interpretative statement that tries to catch up to it."[41]

De Man in "Form," thus sketches a version of what has here been sought: a thoroughly temporal and temporalized text at once the same and different. De Man's account, at just this strongest point, however, also encounters a problem, one that sheds light on the different, yet parallel path, Gadamer takes. That problem Michaels in his own way also indicates: namely, that this movement, as spelled out by de Man, indeed depends on, and concerns not only textuality but also language. Much as was the case with the critics discussed in Chapter 1, de Man, too, wants to give literature a role different from all other kinds of discourse. For this reason, de Man isolates literature

---

[40] De Man, *Blindness and Insight*, 29.
[41] Ibid., 30–1.

and privileges its non-objectified "form" with an eye to what he insists is literature's *unique* relation to language. For de Man, that is, *literature's* circularity—its "form," albeit now understood as a phenomenon both temporal and intentional—is a sign of it's being "engaged . . . in the fullest self-understanding," centering on an awareness of language and language's mode of being, an awareness that the critic goes on to repeat.[42] Correspondingly, in "Form," what ultimately allows for talk of the same text across these events is the repetition of the same insight into *language's* character. Without having as their mutual aim, language, here in its difference—a difference not only from all discourse but also from all existence and every existent (de Man speaks of language as standing beyond "the void" furnished by "the inauthenticity of the existential project"[43])—the text's sameness across these repetitions, its repeating an earlier insight, albeit one removed in time (and thus also new), would not be able to be assigned either to literature or to literary criticism. The identity and difference of the literary text for de Man at this epoch can be sustained only if both interpretation and literature share an aim at language, which itself is deemed to have a unique mode of being, different from everything else that is, that can serve as their insight's "target," or "object."

Gadamer, who, contrary to de Man's claim, did not merely write the hermeneutic circle's "history," does not go de Man's route, which in some aspects may be closer to the (later) Heidegger's.[44] Gadamer does not reduce all literary or poetic discourse into a quest for a single insight, nor does he view language, for its part, as standing on the far side of a radical void. Doing away with these reference points and any special kinds of forms, even temporalized ones, Gadamer's account stands nearer to discourse than does de Man's; nevertheless, Gadamer's approach, in its own way, forces the question of the text as discourse to be reopened.

In fact, as will soon be further seen, a parallel issue pertaining to language haunts Gadamer's undertaking, his project ultimately falling between de Man's endeavor and Knapp's and Michaels' presentation of it. Gadamer's conception of the text incorporates something like the temporality of interpretation that de Man identifies, and it does invoke language, as Knapp and Michaels suggest, but a language not only temporalized but also historicized. Gadamer, that is, identifies language with a special version of history, envisioning it as both itself and as what he calls an Ur-tradition.

Accordingly, the text's temporality, for Gadamer, is not specific to literature, but ultimately belongs to all discourse. At the same time, the text continues to answer to something it is about, thus eschewing commerce with existential voids or any other radical negativity. The text's relation to existents, however, for Gadamer, in turn, recurs to handed-down languages and their *words*, as newly conceived in part on discourse's basis, in a way that necessitates that every one of these traditions and all these languages be capable of bringing one same, single *world* to light.

Whether, however, this vector to one world and thus to one language and an implicitly shared traditionality is sustainable on Gadamer's terms will turn out not to

---

[42] Ibid., 31.
[43] Ibid., 34–5.
[44] See de Man's "Heidegger's Interpretation of Hölderlin," for de Man's own reckoning of his singular proximity and distance from Heidegger's project of reposing the question of Being (Ibid., 246–66).

be clear. For Gadamer, things, while in a complicated way always standing in discourse, are also given in languages and in their words. If the aim at truth that animates discourse is not to be undermined, accordingly, multiple linguistic traditions with their mirroring words must ultimately answer to a single common understanding and tradition. Such multiplicity and unity are inseparable from Gadamer's view of texts' and their interpretations' mode of being. The following chapter, however, after unpacking these and related conceptions, questions whether this conjunction is successful on Gadamer's terms, whether the ultimate intertranslatability of languages and linguistic traditions can be maintained, thereby reopening the question of the text's status.

Nevertheless, owing to Michaels' work, as well as his treatment of Gadamer's and of de Man's writings, the text's intrinsically temporal character at least has been glimpsed, as well as that holistic standpoint in regard to truth the text entails, albeit the latter is denied any standing by Michaels himself. Michaels' *questions*, nevertheless, here continue to resonate: How can texts be deemed at once different and the same when conceived as events? Is such an understanding compatible with Gadamer's construal of language, and, if not, how should texts be understood? Gadamer's more discourse-based hermeneutics may ultimately outstrip both de Man's and Michaels' standpoints; yet Gadamer, alongside discourse, does invoke words and language in a relatively novel fashion (to this extent his work being reminiscent of Cavell's). For Gadamer, words in a special way give access to things, to the text's, and all discourse's, references. Apart from words' contribution, then, even understood on Gadamer's own discursive terms, how can discourse be said to be accompanied by worlded subject matters at all? That last question will initially prove the central one, and its resolution will allow for the text's standing as same and different finally to be addressed.

7

Why Language Can't Help (Discourse in *Truth and Method*)

In the course of Chapter 6, the problem of the text's identity took shape. Precisely because texts, like all discourse, are events, envisioning their sameness and difference over time poses seemingly insurmountable difficulties. Gadamer's account of the text came to the fore, as making inroads on these obstacles. His notion of question and answer overcomes Michaels' static model of the text's constitution, and exhibits the text's identity and difference at work in any given single instance of interpretation. How the text can be conceived as the same *across* such acts, if it indeed may be so, still remains not wholly clarified, however.

Gadamer, as noted, does have a response to this problem, albeit one that is not direct. Language, newly conceived, for him, sits athwart the difficulty. Much like Cavell, what remains the same for Gadamer are not only texts or stretches of discourse but also words, albeit Gadamer understands the word on the basis of discourse, and, at the same time, views words and language as inseparable from becoming and from what he explicitly calls a tradition. Gadamerean textuality in the end thus stands at the intersection of three vectors; discourse (and the movement of question and answer), language (and its mirroring or speculative word), and tradition.

Gadamer's standpoint, it should be noted, in this way, goes furthest of all those so far treated in de-objectifying the text. Gadamer explicitly insists on the non-objective character of the text at a moment when he also models the priority of what he calls the interpreter's word (above that of the author)—not, however, as a form of usurpation, as Knapp and Michaels claim, but as a version of what every employment of language entails.[1]

Gadamer's model and the issues it may encounter, it also should be mentioned, bear on the approach here eventually taken to Heidegger's corpus. Gadamer's hermeneutics, more specifically, involves a decision concerning what many consider a break in

---

[1] "What is true of every word in which thought is expressed is true also of the interpreting word, namely that it is not, as such, objective" TM 469. Jens Kertscher, drawing on Ruth Sonderegger, thematizes this non-objectifying aspect of Gadamer's approach to language, ultimately in the name of mounting a critique of it, based on Wittgensteinian premises, albeit, his account, to my eyes, also is objectifying on its own terms ("Gadamer's Ontology of Language Reconsidered," in *Gadamer's Century: Essays in Honor of Hans-Georg Gadamer*, ed. Jeff Malpas, Ulrich Arnswald, and Jens Kertscher [Cambridge, MA: MIT Press, 2002], 135–56) (136 for the "de-"; 156 for the "objectifying").

Heidegger's thought, albeit one that finally may be more a matter of emphasis than a straightforward rupture. After Heidegger makes his now famous turn, or *Kehre*, his standpoint in respect to discourse and language seemingly shifts away from his earlier one in *Being and Time*.[2] In BT, Heidegger assigns *discourse a fundamental priority* over language. Discourse (Heidegger's "*Rede*") articulates itself through singular events of understanding, from which, in turn, flow language and its words. Hence, Gadamer's views on language, discourse, and tradition in TM somewhat deviate from Heidegger's early ones; to the extent they give language a privilege equal to or greater than discourse, they map, or perhaps better, extend those of Heidegger *after* he made his *Kehre* or turn.[3]

Appeal to Gadamer's thought, in the last quarter century, has come from unexpected quarters, albeit his stance's parallelism with Cavell's may account for some of this confluence. In particular, the analytic philosopher, John McDowell, in *his Mind and World*, invokes TM, while providing what McDowell intends to be a correction of a position of Davidson's.[4] (Eventually, a contextualization of Gadamer's thinking that includes Davidson's perspective on these same themes, as well as McDowell's will be offered, allowing Davidson's and the *early* Heidegger's approaches to be aligned.) McDowell's philosophy, to which extended reference here will not be made, credits our capacities for knowledge and understanding with (a) being open to examination by empirical science (compatible with, though not reducible to, modern *naturalistic* accounts of the human animal), while (b) simultaneously operating within "a space of reasons." For McDowell, even our simplest perceptions inhabit such a space, with the result that perceptions come as *already conceptualized*, and implicitly rational, and thus able to provide grounds for our more complex knowledge, while remaining a form of *receptivity*.[5]

For McDowell, then, Gadamer's project explains how we can possess what McDowell sometimes calls a *second* nature that makes possible such already *conceptualized* "deliverances of experience," as McDowell likes to term them.[6] Gadamer's work accounts for how we, as empirical embodied individuals, are initiated into language

---

[2] Martin Heidegger, *Being and Time*, trans. John Macquarrie and Edward S. Robinson (New York: Harper and Row, 1962) (hereafter BT). Heidegger's 1963 "Foreword" to William Richardson's *Heidegger: Through Phenomenology to Thought* (The Hague, Netherlands: Martinus Nijhoff, 1974): 7–17, is the locus classicus for *Being and Time's* relation to the so-called Kehre, which Heidegger first spoke about publicly in his 1947 *Letter on Humanism* (cf. xvi). Heidegger in the Foreword expresses a marked impatience with how this notion was handled even then (xvi–xvii).

[3] As will become clearer, Gadamer folds discourse into language, and he clearly thinks that his notion of language remains near to Heidegger's intentions rather than diverging from them. Nevertheless, Gadamer speaks of the word as both preceding speech, and itself creative, the source of (living) concept formation in ways that seem to me not on all fours with BT (Cf. TM 427; 433). Christina Lafont in her *Heidegger, Language, and World-Disclosure* trans. Graham Harmon (Cambridge: Cambridge University Press, 2000) recognizes this difference; yet she mounts a powerful case that Gadamer's reading of Heidegger is needed to render BT itself coherent (42-3n40, *inter alia*). While the present interpretation obviously proceeds against the grain of Lafont's own, not only does her work, then, also, register the differences between Heidegger's early stance and Gadamer's in TM but, owing to its detailed attention to Heidegger's text, in the case of discourse especially, it has been an important interlocutor for the present one.

[4] John McDowell, *Mind and World*, with a new introduction by the author (Cambridge, MA: Harvard University Press, 2002).

[5] McDowell thus states that his "framework *precludes* supposing that sensibility by itself yields content that is less than conceptual but already world-involving" (McDowell, *Mind*, 114; my emphasis).

[6] Ibid., 114.

and practices somewhat akin to Wittgensteinian language games, thereby founding an inherently rational, common understanding of the world on the level of perception.[7] Gadamer's presentation of language as tradition enables McDowell to construe the relevant "languages" and "games," as emerging from empirical actually existing historical languages, without losing their disclosive and rational aspects.[8]

McDowell, then, questions the rejection of *common sense empiricism* seemingly implied by Davidson's stance.[9] On the present view, it turns out there is something right about this criticism, though the reasons McDowell gives for it, specifically those aspects of Gadamer's thinking on which McDowell relies, themselves here also come into doubt. Accordingly, on the key issue of how worldly things may accompany discourse, Heidegger's account of the givenness of things, which dovetails with Davidson's perspective solely when it comes to discourse's status, while otherwise differing from it, rather than McDowell's or Gadamer's, later will be central. What Heidegger calls the hermeneutic "as," and worldedness not only at a pre-propositional but also at a *non*-propositional level, exhibits things' ability to show themselves such that entity's and other subject matter's appearances no longer correlate uniquely to propositions or statements of any kind, whether those of straightforward perception or of first-person reports. Despite their differences on this point, for the early Heidegger and for Davidson, unlike McDowell or Gadamer, discourse, language in *use*, not *language* as such, no matter how novelly construed, has primacy for understanding and its interactions with the world. Only in that context, in discourse's inherently individuated or singular domain, accordingly, will the status of the worlded subject matters accompanying discourse be resolved and the question of the text's identity and difference finally be able to be pursued to its conclusion.

7.1 Language as Discourse and Tradition

Though Gadamer's construal of discourse together with language will be questioned, his conception of language, as noted, by no means coincides with its more familiar

---

[7] McDowell's appropriation of Gadamer in this respect dovetails with his criticism of Davidson. As further discussed at the start of Chapter 9, Davidson takes what is given in perception as the *cause* of our belief about it, without what is sensed as such providing a ground or reason for that belief. Because I have a perception that I take to correspond to a rabbit, *I believe* that I *saw* a rabbit, but my claim "there went a rabbit," finds its ground or rationale in my perception-statement ("I saw a rabbit"), not in the perception as such.

[8] "Gadamer," as McDowell states, lets "what impinges on us" be conceived in terms of "free, distanced orientation" ibid., 116 (the last two quotes are from Gadamer); for Gadamer and tradition, see ibid., 126 and 126n16. McDowell discusses Gadamer further in his "Gadamer and Davidson on Understanding and Relativism," in part a response to Michael Friedman's criticisms of McDowell's and Gadamer's positioning. Friedman's concerns overlap with some of those expressed here. ("Gadamer and Davidson on Understanding and Relativism," in Malpas, Arnswald, and Kertscher eds. *Gadamer's Century*, 173–94.)

[9] Davidson's scheme, according to McDowell, misprizes both language and our inhabiting of it, and thus our "second nature," as highlighted by the artificialness of the scenario of radical interpretation that Davidson in part shares with W. V. O. Quine.

avatars; language and discourse in his work never stand entirely opposed.[10] Language, for Gadamer, is not a system of signs nor any other kind of conventions, nor can it be approached apart from its being at work in use, as well as ultimately from its functioning as a tradition or history. Gadamer's standpoint hence goes furthest of all of those so far treated in de-objectifying language and, with it, the text.[11]

Accordingly, it is no easy matter, to state how language differs from discourse in Gadamer's thinking, nor how becoming, or tradition, operates differently in the two cases. These questions do find responses near the end of *Truth and Method*, in a section aptly entitled "Language as the Medium of Hermeneutic Experience." Across its tortuous presentation—Gadamer moves from Plato up through the Church Fathers to von Humboldt, to Hegel and back to Plato—the trio of themes identified earlier can be further fleshed out. Gadamer there advances a de-objectified notion of language along with discourse, and he understands language so conceived as a tradition, indeed as a basic or "*Ur-tradition*." In turn, his construal of language as tradition rests on a revival of the word and a version of holism centered on the latter. Gadamer's appeal to holism in the context of the word, finally, brings with it the problem of worldview (*Weltansicht*) and world; this last topic invites the more critical engagement with Gadamer's text indicated at the close of Chapter 6.

Gadamer's opening discussion in "Language as the Medium of Hermeneutic Experience" immediately makes clear how far removed his construal of language stands from our usual ones and how closely tied together language and discourse are for him. Gadamer first addresses the topic of *translation* (*Übersetzung*).[12] Translation, of course, is customarily understood as the substitution of the words or expressions of one language for equivalent ones taken from another. Gadamer, from the first, however, views translation as a species of *interpretation*; interpreting a text *in a single language* and *translating* a text from *one language to another* answer to a single problematic for him. Moreover, translation and interpretation must be so allied, because in both cases attention to the subject matter a text or stretch of discourse talks *about* is required for grasping and articulating what its expressions *say*, either in the same language (interpretation) or in different ones (translation).

In both instances, accordingly, the relevant expressions are viewed as discourse along the present lines, as saying what they do owing to their speaking about something. Gadamer affirms that "even in the most extreme situation" in translation of foreign expressions, "the subject matter can scarcely be separated from the language."[13]

---

[10] On this phase of Gadamer's thinking, in both its proximity to and difference from the early Heidegger's see also chapter five of Jean Grondin *Sources of Hermeneutics* (Albany, NY: SUNY University Press, 1995), "The Hermeneutical Intelligence of Language," 141–56, esp. 148ff.

[11] Gadamer's distance from standard, formal views of language is often found emblematized by his use of the term *Sprachlichkeit*, linguisticality or even speechedness, which stresses the relation of language (*Sprache*) to *sprechen* (to speak), and which in TM is translated either through periphrasis or simply as "language." (See translator's preface to TM for more on this, TM xvii, as well as Nicholas Davey's treatment of this notion in his "Hermeneutics, Structuralism, and Poststructuralism" (in *The Routledge Companion to Hermeneutics*, ed. Jeff Malpas and Hans-Helmuth Gander [New York: Routledge, 2015], 660–73; esp. 660, 672.)

[12] TM 386; Hans-Georg Gadamer, *Wahrheit und Methode: Grundzüge einer philosophischen Hermeneutik*; Gesammelte Werke Band 1 (Tubingen: J. C. B. Mohr, 1986), 388.

[13] TM 389.

Performing a translation and an interpretation both require attention to what is to be disclosed, such that both activities are discourse; they can never lose sight of what they talk about, even in the case of translation, which, again, would be the most likely instance where appeal to a stand-alone or autonomous language might be found.

Gadamer's notion of interpretation as question and answer, to which he here recurs, also rests on discourse, in this case the text being construed as inseparable from the subject matter about which it speaks. Texts say something in an interpretation, by Gadamer's lights, not because they contain verbal expressions understandable on their own terms, but thanks to a shared subject matter talked about. As Gadamer puts it, although in these cases "the text speaks only through the other partner, the interpreter," nevertheless "the subject matter of which the text speaks itself finds expression—as in a conversation, the common subject matter is what binds the two partners."[14] The interpreter's posing of a question, allowing the relevant subject matter to emerge, makes possible the articulateness of the stretch of talk in question, including the possibility of its registering disagreement with the interpreter's own viewpoint.

Language, then, never is an *object* for Gadamer, since it only *is* language insofar as it articulates a subject matter other than itself, and this holds true not only in interpretation, contra all formalism but, indeed, also in translation.[15] Gadamer's exposition in the section in question takes a further step, however, one with which language as such begins to come into view. For Gadamer language indeed only is language when being about something, when functioning as discourse. This worlded vocation for Gadamer is *defining* of language's role not only in hermeneutic experience but also in all thinking and understanding, which for Gadamer are ultimately themselves hermeneutic—an affirmation that eventually leads him to thematize language in its own right. "It is the medium of language alone that, related to the totality of beings, mediates the finite, historical nature of man to himself and to the world," Gadamer thus declares.[16]

Accordingly, while Gadamer affirms that language only is itself when being about something else, in the end, he is not in fact suggesting that there is no language, in any philosophical or hermeneutically relevant sense, as opined here. The instances just discussed instead foreground *language as it is in itself*, the mistake of its more common construal being the failure to understand that language as language always involves bringing forward something other than language. Language's role in interpretation and translation, for this reason, is ultimately the same as in all thinking, speaking, and understanding; in all these instances, language is at work, yet not as a tool of any kind, but as what lets the matter at hand be at hand and appear. Gadamer, accordingly, does not abandon language, but radically revises its conception, never simply presenting

---

[14] Ibid., 389. Translation, as well, then, redounds "to the dialectic of question and answer" (Ibid., 391).

[15] Walter Benjamin, famously, it should be noted, takes matters the other way; language appears as language with the different historicity Benjamin assigns to it, only in the work of translation. Gadamer, by contrast, insists that translation ultimately remains no different than first order discourse.

[16] Ibid., 454.

it as an existent in its own right, but always as standing in relation to other things, to nonlinguistic subjects.[17]

With language thus radically conceived, its relation to discourse at this moment shifts, at least in emphasis, and quite possibly in understanding. Though discourse and language are effectively identified by Gadamer, language as medium, indeed "as universal medium," at this moment assumes a certain priority for him.[18] This priority is framed not simply synchronically, however, but also diachronically, not in terms of language as reservoir of structure preceding discourse, as is usually done, but thanks to language's function as tradition or *traditio*. Owing to its contribution to all thinking, speaking, and understanding, language, a medium with universal import, is deemed by Gadamer the most radical form of tradition.

This development—de-objectified language becoming reconstrued as tradition and perhaps ultimately re-objectified in turn—can most economically be sketched by attending to a key notion of Gadamer's throughout TM: belonging, *Zuhörigkeit*. Belonging emerges earlier in TM as pertaining specifically to historical dwelling and it returns again in its closing section devoted to language. A term initially found in Count Yorck's philosophy of history (referred to by Heidegger at the end of II.5 of BT), "belonging" appears at first at the pinnacle of Gadamer's tracing of specifically modern attempts to found the human sciences.[19]

Modern hermeneutics, from its start, according to Gadamer, is marked by the search for an objectivist methodology for understanding. For Heidegger, however, that understanding, *Verstehen*, with which his predecessors had been concerned, ceases to be a technique of the human sciences and instead is viewed as rooted in a fundamental historicity—indeed characterized as a "belonging" (to history), on which all attempts at purportedly more "objective" knowledge also rest. Hence Gadamer concludes: "The fact that Yorck contrasts 'homogeneity' with belonging reveals the problem that Heidegger was the first to unfold with full radicality: that the historicity of human Dasein . . . is the condition of our being able to re-present the past."[20]

Heidegger, for the first time, then, according to Gadamer, frames an adequate response to the issue of how the work of the human sciences is to proceed. That response, "belonging," identifies how every understanding of the past (and the texts that issue from it) emerges from an active, living traditionality, a fundamental historicity that informs our existence from the ground up. We understand the past because we are already a part of it and it a part of us, because we live with and through the past, along with the present and the future.

---

[17] See Davey's "Hermeneutics, Structuralism, and Poststructuralism," 672, cited earlier, for a similar affirmation. Gadamer's singular construal of language is perhaps clearest in the extraordinary treatment of written discourse in its specificity that Gadamer mounts soon thereafter. Written texts, issuing from the past, he insists, speak immediately in a fashion distinct from all other historical remnants. A text "becomes part of *our own world* and what it communicates can be stated directly" (TM 392; my emphasis). That capacity for "being stated directly" finally is owed to language being understood as what always brings something other than itself into view.
[18] TM 390; Gadamer, *Wahrheit*, 392.
[19] TM 252; Gadamer, *Wahrheit*, 266.
[20] Ibid.

Late in his text, however, when Gadamer recurs to belonging, he indeed changes his emphasis, albeit he presents this alteration in the guise of a clarification. "Above we spoke of the way the interpreter belongs to his text and described the close relation between *tradition and history*," he writes. "We can now define more closely the idea of belonging on the basis of the *linguistically constituted relation to the world*."[21]

Previously in TM, discourse, texts in interpretation, all language *in use*, had been tied to belonging and tradition, as registers equiprimordial with discourse's own operation. In line with the role that language has begun to play, Gadamer now instead models all interpretation as a dialogue not simply or primarily between an interpreter and a past stretch of discourse, but between that interpreter and *language*, the latter becoming identified with and taking over from traditionality. Gadamer's speaking about the "ancient insight" concerning hearing's priority over the other senses brings home this change. "The *language* in which hearing ('*Horen*') shares is not only universal in the sense that everything can be expressed in it; the significance of the hermeneutic experience is that language opens up a new dimension, the profound dimension from which tradition comes down to those now living."[22]

Tradition, then, is itself invested by and thus now already taken up *in* language. It is language through and through; correspondingly, "belonging," now names belonging *to language* as tradition. Consequently, transacting with a given text is first and foremost transacting with language. Speaking of the dialogue between tradition and its interpreter, Gadamer states that what occurs in it is "made possible only because *the word* that has come down to us as tradition . . . encounters us."[23] Language, the word, is thus the universal and primary site of all tradition, of all "handing down," that medium through which all that has been handed down comes and all our understanding of the world emerges.

Gadamer's rethinking of tradition as language, accordingly, reconfigures the conjunction of discourse and language first sketched. While it remains true that for Gadamer all interpretation and translation continue to bear on worldly matters—and not simply or solely on language and text—it also turns out that what interpretation and translation concern has always *already entered into language*, and only because this is so, does the former prove to be the case. No interpretation or translation for Gadamer without attention to the things themselves; yet no things themselves without there already being language and a specifically linguistic traditionality. Hence discourse, accompanying the being-in-the world of each individually existing Dasein, has ceased to be the fulcrum of understanding, of *Verstehen*, and of the *Da*. That power now resides in language, including "natural languages" in their factual givenness, as Gadamer himself insists.[24]

---

[21] TM 454; Gadamer, *Wahrheit*, 462.
[22] TM 458; Gadamer, *Wahrheit*, 466–7.
[23] TM 457; Gadamer, *Wahrheit*, 465.
[24] Gadamer makes plain throughout TM that language as it is in question is to be understood in terms of actually existing historical languages—German or French, and so on. In a development that proves important later, he speaks of a factualness (*Sachlichkeit*) inherent in language, seemingly owed at once to language's own mode of expressing things and to its actual existence. Factualness thus effectively takes over in regard to the accessing of matters of fact (*Sachverhalte*) from the

7.2 "Word/World" and "Word/Word" Holism

Through combining language with discourse, Gadamer, then, reasserts the former's priority as universal medium and fundamental tradition, tilting language's understanding in an absolute direction, while never canceling out its relation to the being of what is. The brunt of this reconfiguration ultimately falls on the word, though what the word designates in a Gadamerean context, as about to become evident, is complex, owing to language being conceived as inseparable from some subject matter. Nevertheless, on this last account, as will become clearer, the problems that Gadamer's version of the word pose for his own thinking accrue, not, as they did in Cavell, from a word (and a text) possibly bereft of genuine expression, but rather from the side of what is talked about, from Gadamer's conflicting characterizations of those worldly instances that for him words bring to light.

Tellingly, especially in regard to the problem posed by existents other than language, Gadamer himself broaches the word, its being and its powers, in the context of what he calls "absolute idealism," while gauging the closeness of his own standpoint to Hegel's.[25] McDowell, it should be noted, relies on precisely this phase of Gadamer's thinking; he explicitly invokes Gadamer's reworking of it.[26] Correspondingly, the ability of Gadamer's project and of McDowell's to capture the real that perception is supposed to deliver, while so construing the word and its capacities as permitting perception's conceptualization, here will emerge as questionable.

The status of the word for Gadamer can begin to be gleaned on the basis of a now famous remark that comes at the beginning of the final subsection of the final portion of TM, "The universal aspects of hermeneutics." At the outset of this development, building on conclusions earlier drawn, Gadamer announces that "Being (*Sein*) that can be understood is language" ("*Sein, das verstanden kann, ist Sprache*").[27] This easily misunderstood phrase first and foremost emphasizes language's tie to things, to what it is about, along the lines sketched earlier. It is not an expression of any kind of linguistic idealism, as Gadamer makes clear. "What comes into language," he insists, "is something different from the spoken word itself," nor does language's foregrounding entail that "a second being is acquired" by what is presented.[28]

At the same time, in Gadamer's formulation, language and its word do receive some sort of heretofore unprecedented priority. This preeminence rests on what Gadamer earlier identifies as the *speculative structure* of language and its words.[29] This structure lets the word maintain itself not only through but also *as* this difference from "what comes into" it.[30]

---

facticity (*Faktizität*) of Dasein found in the early Heidegger (cf TM 442-3; Gadamer, *Wahrheit*, 449).

[25] TM 453.
[26] McDowell, *Mind and World*, 155 n4.
[27] TM 470; Gadamer, *Wahrheit*, 478.
[28] Ibid.
[29] A "speculative element," in common with that of "Plato or Hegel," defines language, states Gadamer, despite Gadamer's own distance from their "dialectic" (TM 461).
[30] TM 470; Gadamer, *Wahrheit*, 478.

More concretely, Gadamer approaches such "speculation" through its root meaning of "mirroring."[31] As with a table reflected in a lake, the mirroring work of the word, when it appears, disappears, since in discourse focus falls on *the mirrored*. The reflecting medium's own existence nevertheless is itself enacted with such reflection.[32] The givenness of things in their mirroring, in their verbally endowed appearance (or in that appearance with which they endow the word, as Gadamer might himself say), indeed answer to the thing's own being, while the reflecting of such being is the vocation of words as such.[33]

Nevertheless, though the thing itself, not some representative of it, comes to the word, Gadamer *also* maintains that this *difference as such*, between a thing and its appearing, ultimately falls on the side of *language*. For Gadamer, the difference between what comes forward in language and that worldly matter itself is *established through* language, Gadamer's own proximity to Hegel thereby entering by the backdoor. Hence, Gadamer affirms: "everything that is language has a speculative unity, a difference in itself, between being and its own presentation, which also straightway is no difference."[34] Being, then, is language for Gadamer, as quoted three paragraphs ago, *both* insofar as things find their own presentation *as themselves* in language and *also* because the difference between things and their appearance *belongs* to *language*. Hence, language, as the seat of Gadamer's holism, though neither simply separated from the things themselves nor isolated from its role in things' understanding, can be distinguished from a discourse-based construal, where existents are expressed solely in a temporal and individual register.

Recurring to a concept introduced in part one can shed further light both on what Gadamer contemplates at this moment, as well as on those alternatives he omits. As was earlier noted, *holism* designates the *inability* of sentences or words to mean individually, apart from other words and other sentences. This may be called "word/*word*" holism. Over against it, stands another type: "word/*world*" holism. If words or sentences cannot mean individually and autonomously, suggesting an incapacity of meaning to fully coincide with itself, this may further indicate the necessity *of the nonlinguistic* to contribute to their operation. Though Saussure, for example, only affirms the first, both the early Heidegger, and Davidson, while advancing forms of word/word holism, also endorse the word/*world* variety; they affirm the inability of discourse to

---

[31] TM 462; Gadamer, *Wahrheit*, 470.

[32] I am here compressing a long development in which the work of "the poetic word" and that of "everyday speech" are both shown to function in such a mirroring fashion, through "speculative reflection," albeit the former does so in an especially exemplary fashion (TM 465). The contrast with Cavell's stance on this point, Gadamer's affirmation of the identity of the poetic and the everyday, is striking.

[33] TM 461; Gadamer, *Wahrheit*, 470. As will later become clearer, such mirroring is a variant of an aspect of Heidegger's thinking about discourse and the assertion. For Heidegger, things show themselves in our talk, initially with their ready-at-hand significations or meanings (*Bedeutungen*), though these appear *as belonging to the things*. This capacity, rooted in the ready-to-hand and thus in a *practical* holism, backstops statements' ability to show things as themselves. Gadamer, by contrast looks to language for this ability; accordingly, the ready-at-hand context and the individual being-in-the-world on which Heidegger insists drop out in favor of language's newly universal power, reconceived as absolute in the fashion here being set out.

[34] TM 470.

operate apart from the contribution of a specifically nonlinguistic subject matter. Or, as Davidson briskly puts it, "linguistic phenomena" are "supervenient on non-linguistic phenomena."[35]

Now Gadamer's holism, to be clear, is also of both sorts. In his case, however, as the discussion just concluded began to show, "world/word" holism is finally subordinate to "word/word," unlike for Davidson and for the early Heidegger, where the order is indeed the reverse, albeit once again Gadamer understands something quite novel by the word, which never entirely departs from discourse as event. Gadamer can characterize language's operation in his own thinking as adjacent to Hegel's idealism owing to his privileging of a holism of the word/word type. To be sure, Gadamer puts distance between himself and Hegel, insofar as the speculative or mirroring meaning (*Sinn*) that for Gadamer language as medium permits is not exhausted by statements, and, consequently, cannot be exploited dialectically, in the way Hegel intends, to yield (absolute) knowledge.[36] Nevertheless, this meaning through which being may be caught in the speculative mirroring of language, for Gadamer, involves an interplay *of the finite and the infinite* proximate to Hegel's own—Gadamer adapting Hegel's terms at this moment.[37] Genuine meaning and genuine mirroring of beings, for Gadamer, indeed entails an interplay of the infinite and finite, understood respectively as the infinite unsaid and a finite said. In language, a finite saying, capturing beings as they are, is accompanied by the infinity of what remains *unsaid*, according to Gadamer. That unsaid, in turn, answers to everything else that at this moment remains unarticulated, at once in respect to what *can be said* and also concerning *the beings in question*, thus marking the difference between these beings and their appearance within discourse and language themselves.[38] The presented, the beings, show themselves, then; yet their identity and difference from discourse ultimately recurs to language's *own potentiality*. Language indeed implies an other; that other, what is *not language*, registers, however, within the interplay of what is said and what is not *in* language's own domain and operation, thus attesting to language's own unlimitedness.[39] Worldly beings, for Gadamer, accordingly, remain *transparently* caught in language's speculative play. Their expression has only an internal limitation that recurs to language and its events,

---

[35] Donald Davidson, "Reality Without Reference," in *Inquiries into Truth and Interpretation* (Oxford: Clarendon Press, 1984), 215–26, 215.

[36] Gadamer, *Wahrheit*, 472–3.

[37] When discussing the moment of speculation just treated, Gadamer indeed explicitly aligns his account with Hegel's—the latter's discussion of speculative reflection in his "Preface" to *The Phenomenology of Spirit*, in particular, speaking of language, on his understanding, engaging both the "finite" (*endlichen*) with the "infinite" (*Unendliche*) (TM 464; Gadamer, *Wahrheit*, 473). Again, Gadamer breaks with Hegel, not in respect to whether the speculation characteristic of language is absolute, but whether, as absolute, it is also *absolute knowledge*—questioning Hegel's fealty in the "Preface" to a dialectic rooted in *statements* (*Aussage*) (TM 462ff).

[38] Part of Gadamer's point, to be clear, falls on the difference between the stabilized meanings found in statements (a model ultimately owed to the "Greek logos philosophy") and the genuine meaning that comes about in understanding; the latter's occurrence, which takes the form of an event where words or the word never stand apart from discourse, Gadamer characterizes as speculative in the sense here being unfolded.

[39] Cf. TM 454, 464.

resulting in an idealism of an absolute sort, albeit one not intended to be incompatible with a species of realism.[40]

Gadamer's word/world holism, consequently, stands within a greater, more encompassing "word/word" holism, proximate to Hegel's own; Gadamer's interplay of the infinite and the finite gives the last (albeit always silent) word to language. Making language so central, again a language radically reconceived, whose own being never wholly splits off from events of understanding and speech, Gadamer's thinking in TM finds its culmination in a region nonetheless finally foreign to the early Heidegger and also, arguably, to Davidson. In the case of their holisms, as will become clearer, language of any sort, and with it, word/word holism, emerges on the far side of word/world. The existence of the nonlinguistic is there recognized, without ever appearing wholly removed from discourse, while the nonlinguistic also never fully recurs to expressions as such. For Davidson and Heidegger, too, to be sure, no moment arises when things show themselves wholly free from all understanding; nevertheless, in its entirety, the work of language, or better discourse, relies on, and is in some fashion even outstripped by, what it lets appear. For Gadamer, by contrast, though language is never simply separated from things, world/word interactions finally are taken up within language and its singular mode of being, language itself thus being deemed at once novelly universal and *absolute*.

The status of those beings, things, or matters of facts that language or discourse make available for Gadamer, consequently, raises a question, especially insofar as Heidegger's and Davidson's unprecedented sort of realism contrasts with Gadamer's absolute, albeit finite idealism. Things' speculative apparition, their givenness in their immediacy and transparency, in the end, for Gadamer, after all, recur not, or not only, to language as such, *die Sprache*, but also to various actually existing languages with their distinct historical traditions. By Gadamer's own avowal, moreover, *each* distinct language presents and expresses worldly things *differently*; it offers a different *Weltansicht* or world-perspective. Accordingly, it is not obvious, how the absolute and universal character that Gadamer imputes to language comports with there being multiple linguistic traditions and languages each with its own world-giving power.

Of course, the alternative to Gadamer at issue is not that of approaching language, discourse, and their operation from some point outside them all, assuming that such could be found.[41] Rather what is at stake is whether rendering words and languages part of his account, even as supply as Gadamer, does not ultimately renew the opposition

---

[40] This contention is buttressed later by Gadamer's contention that different languages each distinctly schematize experience, as also by Gadamer's declaration that *Sein* that is understandable is *Sprache*, as discussed earlier.

[41] Christina Lafont nicely traces Heidegger's arguments in his essay "Language" for why language cannot be approached from without, that is, objectified (*Heidegger, Language and World-Disclosure*, trans. Graham Harman [Cambridge: Cambridge UP, 2000], 99–100). For her, however, Heidegger, too, insists on language's specifically world-disclosing function, which she equates with its giving of meaning, thereby bringing Heidegger close to von Humboldt and in her eyes landing his project in insurmountable difficulties. The sketch of Heidegger's early thinking of discourse offered in Chapter 8, however, argues that reference (broadly understood), not meaning, is fundamental for Heidegger's account in BT, which does not, then, simply fall prey to the problems Lafont finds in the later Heidegger's views.

between realism and idealism that Gadamer himself strives to overcome. What critics have often claimed answers to relativism in Gadamer's thinking, it should by now be clear, in fact rests on Gadamer's affirmation of language's absoluteness; it is only because the one conception (language or linguisticality) as medium of all understanding cannot be kept apart from the other (multiple existing languages) that Gadamer opens himself to this charge.[42] Yet this very coincidence suggests that, with language posited in any guise alongside discourse—language grasped as singular and universal, as well as multiple (the former necessarily raising the question of the latter)—the problem of the differences among the worlds that language potentially gives inevitably resurfaces (as it also does in Cavell in a different way), and with these different worlds the standing of *what is* in discourse.

By contrast, discourse as presented here, operates in advance of the assembly of language as any sort of site. *A New Philosophy of Discourse*, in fact, for this reason, ultimately cannot be said either to make or not to make the "linguistic turn." In the present instance, discourse's work takes place before language and all its attendant frameworks—thus before these questions of whether language is one or many can arise. No reference point emerges, either on the side of beings or of expressions, for such questions to take hold. Instead, only the existence and disposition of those matters and the status of those expressions actually involved in discourse's always singular events can be adjudicated. Since for Gadamer, however, distinct languages ultimately make available a grasp on things as they are, his work opens the door to asking about the difference among languages and how each one, as well as all in their multiplicity, may be said to genuinely grasp things.[43]

7.3 Discourse Alone: World versus Worldview (*Weltansicht*)

Gadamer, to be clear, offers a response to the concern just stated; he furnishes an account of how languages can be conceived as multiple, while genuinely giving one and the same world. In a discussion that falls near the beginning of "Language as Hermeneutic Experience," entitled "Language as Experience of the World," Gadamer affirms both of the foregoing points: that every language and every actual tradition offers *its* own worldviews, and that each of these linguistically and traditionally inflected world-perspectives ultimately refer to the same single world, to what Gadamer calls "the world in itself." "In every worldview the existence of the world-in-itself is intended," he

---

[42] See Morton Thaning, *The Problem of Objectivity in Gadamer's Hermeneutics in Light of McDowell's Empiricism* (The Hague: Springer, 2005) for a good summary of those who make this charge (Thaning 39). Thaning's book proceeds in the opposite direction from the approach taken here: Thaning recognizes problems implicit in Gadamer's account of language, when it comes to accessing the world, but to resolve them looks to McDowell, Sellars, and a first-person notion of responsibility he identifies with Gadamer's conception of self-presentation.

[43] Walter Benjamin's corpus, as attested by some of his earliest writings, also confronts this problem faced by language-oriented accounts, even novel ones, as his also is; in his unique (and to my mind, unrepeatable) way, Benjamin alone perhaps comes closest to resolving it, albeit thanks to a messianicity that remains inherently futural. See especially Benjamin's "On Language as Such and the Language of Man," in *Early Writings 1910-17* (Cambridge, MA: Harvard UP, 2011), 251-69.

writes. "The multiplicity of these worldviews does not involve any relativization of the 'world.' Rather, the world is not different from the views in which it presents itself."[44]

Gadamer's contention ultimately supports two distinct strands of thought to which reference here already has been made. As noted, McDowell's invocation of a second *nature* draws on Gadamer's notion of language giving "the world in itself" to support the thesis that our perceptions arrive as already conceptualized. The universality and absoluteness of existing languages, as modeled by Gadamer in TM, underwrites that inherent reasonableness, at once of our speech and of things (of perception), that McDowell requires to sustain his viewpoint. As has also been indicated, however, the affirmation that some actual existing language performs this labor inevitably raises questions concerning Gadamer's and McDowell's *confidence* that a given language can and does relate to one and the same *single* world, while potentially modeling it differently from others. Since any language embodies a distinct tradition and has its own world*view*, the assurance that it and every other possible one share in understanding the same single world, as assumed by McDowell's talk of our second *nature*, may appear undermotivated.

Second, however, not from the side of nature, world, and language as *unitary* reference points, but in respect to their avowed *multiplicity*, concerns also surface. Gadamer and, certainly at points, Heidegger, speaks of the world-giving powers of languages, languages now understood as existing in concrete times and places (Attic Greece, Medieval Europe, and so on), and thus conceived as inherently multiple. Different worldviews are housed in *different* languages, Gadamer talking of a "human, linguistically constituted view of the world" in this regard.[45] The possibility of incommensurability among these perspectives, that one linguistically inflected worldview might not always successfully communicate with another, consequently shadows this framework, as Heidegger concedes, or perhaps at moments even celebrates.[46] Gadamer, however, clearly affirms the reverse: world being genuinely given for him necessitates that all *worldviews* refer to one same single world. Accordingly, both aspects of Gadamer's accounts, both his talk of each language authentically giving a world, and his talk of distinct worldviews in their own right invites further reflection. Owing to Gadamer's advancing language, *die Sprache*, not discourse, as answering to the inherent intelligibility of things, perspectives on *world*, not some aspect of it, by him are said to be *multiple* (as in the later Heidegger), even as world as a singular reference point is retained. How can Gadamer's affirmation, now, of multiple worlds be sustained, however, alongside his insistence on these worlds' ultimate compatibility and unity? How can Gadamer affirm both genuinely multiple, historical-linguistic world-perspectives and their all giving onto one same single world?

Gadamer's approach to this question starts, not surprisingly, from a discussion of Wilhelm von Humboldt's philosophy of language; Humboldt views language

---

[44] TM 444; Gadamer, *Wahrheit*, 451.
[45] TM 444; "*menschlich-sprachlich verfasste Ansicht der Welt*" (Gadamer, *Wahrheit*, 451).
[46] Davidson, famously, offers an argument against a version of this claim at the end of "On The Very Idea of a Conceptual," in *Inquiries Into Truth and Interpretation* (Oxford: Clarendon Press, 1984), 183–98, 197; yet that argument does not concern language and languages—it instead works from Quine's notion of radical translation and makes discourse fundamental.

both as world-giving and as in history. Initially, however, Gadamer reverses von Humboldt's position, and in this reversal, the core of Gadamer's own understanding lies. Von Humboldt indeed claims that each language embodies a worldview or world-perspective (*Weltansicht*); for Gadamer, however, this statement first and foremost expresses language's unthinkability *apart from world*, seemingly contrary to von Humboldt's own outlook. "Language has its real being only in the fact that world is presented in it," Gadamer writes, once more affirming language's aim at world.[47] At the same time, at this moment, the two-sidedness of Gadamer's own stance emerges, since, after stressing the difference of a world from the things in it, Gadamer also proclaims that world, after all, "is world, only insofar as it comes into language."[48]

Gadamer, then, indeed wants both: multiple natural languages and their different worldviews relating to that one world whose appearing he also foregrounds when discussing von Humboldt. Moreover, presumably it is because every language genuinely gives world, and thus the same world, because each veritably shows what is, that there finally can be no question of whether languages are related to one world and through that one world understandable to one another.

The question arises at this moment, however, of from what vantage point such an affirmation is made: How does Gadamer himself have access to this presumed insight? In what linguistic tradition and what worldview does he himself stand? Of course, in each language or linguistic tradition, one world may be and indeed no doubt is *intended*, since aim at *the world* is inseparable from its corresponding worldview, its *Welt-ansicht*. Nevertheless, there seems to be no way of reckoning in advance whether the world thus sighted will be reconcilable with any, not to mention with all of the other perspectives on world that other linguistic traditions may afford. Of course, it is similarly easy to maintain world *is only ever single*, and that only *some aspect* or *part* of that world is ever in dispute among languages.[49] This scenario, in which a genuinely single world has already been assumed *rules out*, however, a multiplicity of *world-perspectives* in Gadamer's (and Humboldt's and Heidegger's) sense. Thus, Gadamer indeed genuinely needs both: a veritable multiplicity of world-perspectives on one nevertheless genuinely single world.

Gadamer's most concrete response to this concern and the example he evinces to illustrate it are thus telling for the entirety of his project, especially as accessed by McDowell, as well for any historiography that would speaks of worldviews of any sort. For Gadamer does indeed insist that *communication* among them all is possible; though inherently multiple, each linguistically informed view of the world (worldview) is from within itself capable of communicating with and potentially taking up all of the others. "Each worldview can be extended into every other," he writes. "It can understand and comprehend, *from within itself*, the 'view' ('*Ansicht*') of the world presented in another language."[50]

---

[47] TM 440; Gadamer, *Wahrheit*, 447.
[48] Ibid.
[49] This is effectively Davidson's point: only some aspect of the world can be in question, the rest being assumed largely aligned, albeit finally talk of "the rest" in this instance does not have any genuine sense or reference, owing to language's marginal role in Davidson's thinking.
[50] TM 445; my emphasis; Gadamer, *Wahrheit*, 452.

How this is to be conceived, in turn depends on a schema that Gadamer has just sketched. That model, putatively explanatory of how multiple *worldviews* within themselves communicate so as to give a single world, arguably makes plain, however, the deepest difficulty that Gadamer's account faces. Gadamer's response, in the present context, consequently, leads to despairing of McDowell's perspective and his core concerns, a point of further importance later.

For Gadamer, wishing to craft a template for how multiple languages and their worldviews bespeak one same world, appeals to *Husserl's* analysis of a thing given in visual perception in his *Ideas I*. Husserl there speaks of the thing as appearing through various "perceptual shadings" (*Abschattungen*), and Gadamer likens these perceptual "adumbrations," as they are also sometimes translated, to the linguistic perspectives through which world is given. "The relationship is the same in the perception of things," writes Gadamer. "Seen phenomenologically, the 'thing-in-itself', as Husserl has shown, is nothing other than the continuity with which the various perspectival adumbrations of thing-perception lead into one another."[51]

For Husserl, the thing in visual perception indeed presents itself through various adumbrations and viewpoints, while not being reducible to any of them. It appears as itself across these perspectives, yet, within each one as also being different from any single one of them. More specifically, *multiple adumbrations* (*Abschattungen*) of some one thing are given, pertaining to its shape, color, and so, on, and these lived sensed qualities in turn give different perspectives (views, *Ansichten*) on some specific thing—parts of a table lived through from this or that angle, for example. These shadings and their views (*Ansichten*—the same word Humboldt appends to *Welt*), all relate back to the one, same thing—for example, again, a table; moreover, for the Husserl of *Ideas I*, the table as a perceptual object itself is nothing but the totality or system of such givens, nothing but what is accessed as the same *across* all these lived aspects and their sightings, and this feature, perhaps above all, Gadamer wishes to map on to world.[52]

For Gadamer, correspondingly, multiple worldviews indeed relate to one and the same world, just as multiple sightings of the perceptual object relate to it, precisely because the world in itself is not something that stands beyond them, but is always given through them. "Views of the world are not relative in the sense that one could oppose them to the 'world in itself,'" Gadamer writes, "as if the right view from some possible position outside the human, linguistic world could discover it [the world] in its being-in-itself."[53]

Yet, while this is doubtless a powerful account, in the present context, even as an argument strategy something unsatisfying hovers around Gadamer's treatment, especially in light of McDowell's employment of it. The possibility that McDowell turns to Gadamer to buttress, after all, is that of something given *in perception* being

---

[51] TM 444–5; Gadamer, *Wahrheit*, 451(translation altered).

[52] See Edmund Husserl, *Ideas Pertaining to a Pure Phenomenology and A Phenomenological Philosophy: First Book*, trans. F. Kirsten (Dordrecht: Kluwer, 1983), 86–9. I am following Gadamer's Husserl interpretation, which attends only to Husserl's remarks in the early going of *Ideas* I, specifically in section forty-one. Gadamer does not take up Husserl's more extended remarks on the object, as given to reason, in the last section of Husserl's volume.

[53] TM 444.

immediately intelligible. Gadamer here, however, to make his broader point, turns to the very same problem, the problem of perception, yet now *presumed as already resolved* by Husserl. If Husserl's vantage point is truly cogent, however, there is no need, of course, for McDowell's, nor to this extent, Gadamer's. McDowell turns to Gadamer's hermeneutics and its account of world and worldviews to account for how perceptions come already conceptualized; yet Gadamer's treatment presupposes Husserl's successful treatment of the same subject, such that the whole maneuver, at least as enacted by McDowell, appears circular.

A still graver problem, however, confronts Gadamer's proposal at this moment, one that, because wholly internal to it, throws a steadier and more far reaching light on what Gadamer suggests: namely, that there are multiple languages and language views, yielding multiple worldviews, all giving access to one and the same world. In the Husserlian case, such adumbrations and perspectives do indeed give access to the perceptual thing that is intended through them; the thing stands at once beyond but also within these shadings' own momentary givenness. Yet such perspectives, in Husserl's analysis, are themselves given within, and indeed appear in conformity to, *already-known schema*. If, for example, I walk around a table, I expect the changing perspectives on its color, shape, and volume to be given to me in a fashion I can *anticipate* such that the same entities—colors, surfaces, shapes, textures, and eventually the table—are constituted *as* individuals of this sort.[54] If my shadings or my perspectives somehow suddenly gave way to entirely different ones—those pertaining to the table to rabbits or newspapers, or a curved surface suddenly appeared gapped by nothing else—I would be at a loss and would no longer think I confronted an object, a thing, of any sort. In the case of perception, such schema, or "essences" in Husserl's technical and non-Platonic sense, enable anticipations of future apprehensions and the integration of past ones in any given instance. Things given through *perception*, accordingly, can be *both one and many*, not only because at each moment a thing standing beyond them is intended and implied in flesh and blood but also because *the range* of different perspectives on this one thing is pre-given in advance, not necessarily consciously, as comprising a whole, in which these perspectives and shadings all participate.[55] The entire affair is mediated by such essential frameworks, thanks to which a single selfsame object not identifiable with any of its embodiments appears precisely through them as at once given and announced.

Nothing of this order, no such forms of integration, is available, however, in the case of *world*, in the instance in question in Gadamer's account, nor, moreover, *can* it be. To put it perhaps overly concretely, a world just is not something walked around, not a thing that can be sighted from different sides, like a table. No such preexisting templates are available for how different *world-perspectives housed in different languages* can be related to one another, such that they can be taken up again and referred to the

---

[54] This will be true, in a certain fashion, even in the case of mistakes, where a different, yet still continuous schema, perhaps of a painting or a model, will retroactively be recognized as the appropriate one. It belongs to the phenomenological essence of the perceived thing, on this analysis, that its perspectives are all integratable, and, within bounds, known to be such in advance.
[55] Cf. Husserl, *Ideas*, 87, where Husserl asserts that "each determination" of what is given in person "has its system of adumbrations" that permits them and the physical thing to be there as "the Same."

same world. No anticipatable forms of continuity pertaining to *world* as the correlate of distinct linguistic traditions indeed are ever at hand. Without them, however, as in Husserl's own case, it is impossible to speak about anything one and the same, including a world, immanently giving itself through views on it, to talk at all of the *same* thing, here, *a world*, appearing perspectively.[56]

Indeed, not only do such schema not exist, they cannot even be *imagined* to exist in the case of multiple *worldviews*. Just such integratability and the relevant schemata *must* be *absent* in this singular instance. If there were such frameworks, after all, no genuine multiplicity of *worlds* could be at issue to begin with; the world as one and the same instead would have *already* been given. Were there schema of integration, the different perspectives on the world would immediately function as parts within a single greater whole, that *of* the one, same world. Without such schema, however, nothing warrants believing that genuinely multiple worldviews correspond to the appearance of simply a single one. With schema, many worlds are impossible; yet without them, the claim that in every possible case the same world is always given through distinct worldviews lacks any genuine motivation. Accordingly, neither multiple world-perspectives nor one and the same world at which they aim can truly be envisioned on Gadamer's model.[57]

What this line of inquiry, finally, yields, then, as far as the present perspective is concerned, is that multiple *worldviews*, related to each language tradition may not be spoken of, but nor then may one constant *selfsame world* be affirmed, though something like world doubtless is *the horizon* within which any instance of discourse takes place. Neither multiple worldviews giving one world, nor even in any deep (or transcendental) sense a single world enters into discourse as here conceived. Consequently, a belief or viewpoint *could* be encountered that was genuinely unintelligible—for instance, the literal belief in bodily resurrection that Wittgenstein once took as an example of such. Discourse occurring *in the world*, rather than the world in discourse, this sort of eventuality by no means can be ruled out in any given case. At the same time, for the same reasons, such an encounter would not

---

[56] Gadamer himself marks something like this difference, which he also says pertains to a specific kind of "continuity" (TM 445; Gadamer, *Wahrheit*, 452) To my mind, however, he does not take the problem fully on board, but instead, focusing on the temporality involved in thing-perception as opposed to apprehensions of world, he simply treats the issue as resolved, seemingly by definition. "But there remains a characteristic difference: every 'shading' of the object of perception is exclusively distinct from every other, and each helps co-constitute the 'thing-in-itself' as the continuum of these nuances—whereas, in the case of the shadings of verbal worldviews, each one potentially contains every other one within it—i.e., each worldview can be extended into every other. It can understand and comprehend, from within itself, the 'view' of the world presented in another language" (TM 445; Gadamer, *Wahrheit*, 452).

[57] Of course, one might be tempted to venture, that what Gadamer calls the fusion of horizons, the coming together of different perspectives in the dialogic understanding of an alien or foreign text (emanating from the past or another culture) *enacts* such a synthesis and to this extent discovers or discloses the relevant schema. Something like this may well be what Gadamer has in mind. That response, however, appears question-begging, because it makes assumptions about what is given *prior to that fusion or synthesis*: namely, different starting points in *different worlds*, owing to different languages and times. Fusion of horizons can enact a fusion of *worlds*, only if multiple *worlds* can already be spoken of meaningfully in the first place. Yet not only does talk of multiple worlds seem not possible but such fusions also bring into question that a difference *between worlds as such* ever did exist.

necessitate that the holder of this view inhabits *a different world* from our own, albeit Wittgenstein, I believe, suggests this. It would not tell us anything about a world as such, nor even necessarily the totality of the other beliefs of the individual in question, ultimately because world is something of which neither the one nor the other of us has at our disposal in the first place.

These labyrinthine paths into which Gadamer enters when attempting to affirm his stance, then, ultimately exhibit why, if discourse is to do the work with which it is credited of engaging with actual things, genuine existents, it must be conceived solely on its own, not in tandem with language of any stripe nor any established linguistic or historical world. Discourse permits grasping what is apart from, and thus prior to, any such considerations concerning language and (historical) worlds. It gears into existents and subject matters at that singular level at which alone they genuinely come to light, never consolidating itself as a medium in its own right, in part thanks to maintaining its dependence on what is other than itself for its own intelligibility. Discourse "quantifies over" neither language nor world, as the logicians say. As a consequence, only discourse can achieve that new, unprecedented "realism" (beyond the opposition to idealism, and apart from all skepticism) that McDowell, Gadamer, Davidson, and Heidegger, as well as perhaps Wittgenstein (as read by Diamond, though perhaps not Cavell) in their own way affirm.

Similarly, discourse, for these same reasons, is not compatible, then, with any history that answers to epochs and worldviews, of either the Heideggerean or Gadamerean stripe. Not only does it undermine the "synchronic" demands McDowell places on it—not because things do not show themselves, but because they do not do so in one way, nor through concepts as classically understood—but it also defeats those more "diachronic" ambitions that assemble around world, since these impasses in Gadamer's presentation indeed yield *neither* untranslatable worlds and world-perspectives *nor* their ultimate translatability. Languages individuated by time and place (including things like "the language of art" in the Renaissance) do not correlate with any actual perspectives (*Ansichten*) on what is, any understanding of some genuine subject matter. Accordingly, the entire orientation to the present problem that von Humboldt initially supplied on the current score comes into doubt. The intelligibility of all our discourse, both in our everyday existence and in the humanities being at root the same, as Gadamer himself acknowledges, understanding of any sort is incompatible with talk of historical world and worlds, as well as language and languages. Given the sophistication of Gadamer's attempt, no other account of these matters, however, is likely to fill the bill, and thus all that remains for understanding to grapple with are concrete stretches of discourse and those equally concrete existents that appear with and in them.

8

Discourse (The Early Martin Heidegger)

Two rather different questions are now seemingly on the table, which it will be the work of the final two chapters to investigate and resolve. The first, bequeathed by Michaels, concerns how texts may be conceived as the same and different over time. The second pertains to what the text or indeed any discourse is about: the standing of those subject matters to which discourse relates and refers. The two problems converge, since, as has been underscored, talk!'s existence and its own identity as discourse must include what talk! is about, reference in a broad and novel sense. Yet if in every case discourse's topics and referents already have an historical or temporal element, then, at its root, any discourse, in respect to what it talks about, would be no different from that found in texts or in literature. Every context would be in time and recur to something like a history, or, better, to historicity. Such temporal embeddedness, in turn, would enable whatever sameness accrues to seemingly more everyday examples and to texts alike.

Gadamer's philosophical hermeneutics, it became clear, ultimately is unable to reconcile the purported givenness of what discourse is about with language's differentiation into languages.[1] Its reckoning of language and languages among the things that exist clashed with his philosophy's claim that discourse genuinely accesses things in the world. By contrast, Heidegger's early writings furnish an ideal site for pursuing the possibility of the interlacing of things and discourse. In *Being and Time* (hereafter BT), Heidegger explicitly gives discourse priority over language precisely because in discourse contact with worlded subject matters is achieved. Hence, in the course of treating all understanding's relation to the world, Heidegger introduces discourse in the early going of BT.[2]

---

[1] Thaning identifies a version of the problem brought out in the foregoing, and here being summarized, in terms of a tension between the hermeneutic and transcendental features of Gadamer's endeavor; he discusses this divergence at length by way of a treatment of Viattimo on Heidegger (Thaning, 14ff).

[2] Use of the term "world" at this point and in what follows may seem to conflict with chapter seven's conclusion where it was deemed impossible to speak of world in terms of world-perspectives, *Weltansichten*. The two contexts are importantly different, however, since world as such and a whole is not in question in the present and similar formulations, as it is in Gadamer's discussion, but effectively only existing things, parts of (some) world. Moreover, later, when Heidegger's usage in BT is employed, it will be only as a "formalized" concept, as Heidegger himself perhaps misleadingly sometimes puts this. In the notion that his concepts recur to "formal indications," I understand Heidegger precisely to intend that world (and related notions) are outlined in respect to their functioning in Dasein's understanding with regard to their roles in discourse and truth, and so on, without having any specific or substantive contents attached to them—once again in contrast to *Welt* in *Weltansicht*. (Heidegger indicates the formal character of his concepts in BT when discussing

Nevertheless, discourse's status in BT itself is somewhat vexed. For one, it occupies an unusually modest site for a theme that Heidegger apparently deems central. Heidegger brings forward discourse (*Rede*) last among the factors (or "existentiale") comprising Dasein's "Being-in" (the various registers of its worlded existence), while claiming discourse has already been at work among these *existentiale* and discourse's standing is thus nevertheless "equiprimordial" with theirs. Similarly, later, summarizing Dasein's being as rooted in ecstatic temporality, Heidegger again seemingly diminishes discourse's role, omitting it from the list of those features (*existentiale*) contributing to temporality's description and there substitutes fallenness for discourse.[3]

Moreover, in his subsequent writings, Heidegger seems to assume a different perspective, at least, on *language*, if not on discourse. Language (*die Sprache*) now ceases to be viewed as subordinate to discourse or talk! (*Rede*). That development, though obviously influencing Gadamer's perspective on language and talk!, from the present vantage, is primarily wedded to Heidegger's ongoing unfolding of *Sein* (Being) in its difference from both beings and from the Being of beings. Considerations pertaining to Being play no positive role in the present study, however, since *Sein*'s conception cannot be separated from Heidegger's own talk of epochs, from his concrete views of history, world, and world epochs, which, at the end of the last chapter, came into doubt, even when as novelly conceived as by Heidegger.[4]

---

the character of phenomenology's phenomenon in his second introduction and they are implicit in his descriptions of Dasein's mode of being in contrast to both ready- and present-at-hand things.) A large literature has recently sprouted around the notion of "formal indication," which includes Theodore Kisiel's, Daniel Dahlstrom's, and Ryan Streeter's earlier treatments, and, more recently, essays by Dreyfus, R. Matthew Shockey, and S. J. McGrath. The latter declares that "*formale Anzeige* (formal indication) has emerged as the most important methodological principle in Heidegger's early work" ("Formal Indication, Irony, and the Risk of Saying Nothing," *A Companion to Heidegger's Phenomenology of Religious Life* [Amsterdam: Rodopi, 2010], 179–205; 179]). For a rather different account, including of the transformation this notion undergoes when it appears in BT, see Burt C. Hopkins' "Deformalization and Phenomenon in Husserl and Heidegger," in *Heidegger, Translation, and the Task of Thinking: Essays in Honor of Parvis Emad*, ed. Frank Schalow [Dordrecht: Springer, 2011], 49–69) (17 ff.).

[3] Lafont educes this omission as symptomatic of Heidegger's inability to successfully conceive discourse in BT, a breakdown ultimately indicative of a larger impasse in his thinking. Without denying that there may be something a bit wobbly about Heidegger's treatment of this topic, on the specific point pertaining to its later omission, as she herself concedes, Heidegger does explicitly account for it, though apparently Lafont finds Heidegger's reasons unconvincing (cf. BT 400). (Cristina Lafont, *Heidegger, Language, and World-Disclosure*. trans. Graham Harmon [Cambridge: Cambridge University Press, 2000], 82–4.)

[4] Mark Wrathall, in his *Heidegger and Unconcealment: Truth, Language, and History* (Cambridge: Cambridge University Press, 2011), provides a splendid chart of Heidegger's shifting usages in respect to both *Rede* and *Sprache*, in the service of arguing for a basic continuity in his approach, thus contesting aspects of Lafont's viewpoint (Wrathall, *Unconcealment*, 128–9). The present study, taking a finer-grained focus, emphasizes the visible break; it also proceeds thus for the reason just noted: namely, that the larger problematic involving both discourse and language is inseparable from Heidegger's unfolding of the *Seinsfrage* and his unique rethinking history. The removal, or simple ignoring, of these questions from this larger context presents a problem generally in the commentary (see my discussion later in this chapter), and is especially an issue for Lafont's undertaking. Lafont does not ignore the connection of the linguistic themes to the *Seinsfrage*, but instead views ontological difference solely in linguistic terms, simply as Heidegger's way of approaching meaning, the realm of the semantic (20 n. 16). That conception is palpably too flat, and renders her larger interpretation of Heidegger ultimately unpersuasive, despite her exemplarily powerful and provocative grappling with many of Heidegger's key texts.

Finally, within BT itself, other difficulties arise in grasping discourse that bear directly on the central issue: discourse's relation to the subject matters to which it refers. Previously, an aim at a realism of a new and unprecedented sort was credited to many of the thinkers here discussed, though whether all succeed at arriving at such a standpoint was also doubted. Not only does Heidegger's thinking harbor such an aim, but his work, as here interpreted, radically reconceives realism; Heidegger's thinking does away with all concerns pertaining to "idealism," while indeed neither warding off nor retaining the skeptic's concern.[5] Realism, and related notions such as insight and truth, or meaning and reference, in BT's first half, all undergo reinterpretation; accordingly, what precisely Heidegger thinks about any and all of them requires considerable labor to grasp. This fact, combined with discourse's oddly oblique or withdrawn position in his text, entails, that to nail down Heidegger's take on discourse, such considerations (again, of meaning, reference, etc.) in which discourse's subject matters are enmeshed must be sorted through, ultimately along with Heidegger's new realism. Grasping discourse's force requires surveying the difficulties attendant on how Heidegger at the deepest level models discourse's relation to what is and pursuing a line through the debates concerning his presentation of this topic and its consequences in the first half of BT. As a result, the questions pertaining to the text and textuality the previous chapters bequeathed will only explicitly return on the far side of the present discussion. Text, discourse generally, including literature as previously set out, on the current view, entail a working relation to what is, to truth and to insight, and hence also participate in that "realism" undergoing transformation at Heidegger's hands. Accordingly, only after coming to grips with this entire matrix of problems will the second set of issues concerning the text's sameness and identity be addressed, in Chapter 9, ultimately on the added ground supplied by some of Davidson's thinking.

8.1 Interpreting Discourse (*Rede*) in BT

To take a step back, interpretations of BT's first half run a gamut. At one extreme stand readers that see it as engaging in essentially a variant of Husserl's program; they take Heidegger's early thinking to be a type of transcendental phenomenology. At the other extreme, the primary force of Heidegger's thought is believed to consist

---

[5] William Blattner and David Cerbone have respectively pursued Heidegger's early thinking as idealist (Blattner—especially, when it comes to time) and realist (Cerbone—who specifies Heidegger's distance from these problems and has a nice feel for Heidegger's larger concerns at these moments in his text) (William D. Blattner, *Heidegger's Temporal Idealism* [Cambridge: Cambridge University Press, 1999]; David R. Cerbone "Realism and Truth," in *A Companion to Heidegger*, ed. Hubert L. Dreyfus and Mark A. Wrathall [Oxford: Blackwell, 2005], 248–64). Herman Philipse, in his "Heidegger's 'Scandal of Philosophy': The Problem of the '*Ding an Sich*' in *Being and Time*," *Transcendental Heidegger*, ed. Steven Galt Crowell and Jeff Malpas (Stanford: Stanford University Press, 2007), 168–98, has more recently canvassed both positions and the entire argument, finding Heidegger "a transcendental idealist about being, but a transcendental realist about entities," the last not unrelated to the position here eventually taken, though it could not be put that way in the present context (194–6). Though all three authors provide insight into Heidegger's texts, for reasons that become clearer later, how they pursue their questions, if not the answers they find, from the present perspective, limits full access to the singularity and force of Heidegger's analyses, sometimes crucially.

in the *detranscendentalization* of all philosophy; Heidegger, correspondingly, on the latter view, in BT's first half, is sometimes conceived as making a form of the linguistic turn *avant la lettre*.[6] Though otherwise opposed, these extremes tend to view the role of discourse in BT as either relatively minor (the first) or mistaken (the second). Discourse is deemed by both camps to be subordinate to other possibilities identified in Heidegger's analysis, ones stemming from sense and understanding more generally (on the one side), and facticity and language (on the other).

Two other positions emerge between these two. Both give greater weight to discourse in its own right; unlike the previous ones, both indeed foreground discourse and understand it to hinge on meaning (*Bedeutung*, or "signification"), not sense (*Sinn*), a distinction about to be further clarified. For both of these intermediate positions, discourse, *Rede*, is ultimately pivotal for reestablishing the possibility of the truth of *assertions*, albeit each viewpoint sees this reestablishment occurring in a different way. The first position claims to find in BT an intersection between history and essence, ultimately an historically constituted essentialism, rooted in the world of work, that places its stamp on discourse through meanings (*Bedeutungen*). For the second, discourse adds a new normative weight to BT's specifically hermeneutic, not transcendental-phenomenological, outlook; through such hermeneutic normativity, a renewed possibility for affirming assertoric truth is carved out.

The four positions can be summarized as follows.

Heidegger's aim and focus in BT:

Transcendental Normativity	Historical Essentialism	Hermeneutic Normativity	Detranscendentalizing (Linguistic Turn)
Sense	Discourse/Meaning	Discourse/Meaning	Sense

To be clear, this panoply of takeaways, despite their being opposed to one another, by no means is unmotivated by BT itself, nor is the focus found in all four on assertoric or propositional truth accidental. This last matter is soon to be further addressed, since the elaboration of such truth clearly allows some measure to be taken of the new style of realism that it is here maintained Heidegger sets forth.

More broadly, Heidegger's magnum opus, BT, indeed can be said to formulate new responses to philosophy's traditional problems (such as that concerning the assertion's capacity for truth), while also shifting philosophy and its reference points on to otherwise novel ground. BT's ability to give new, more compelling answers to traditional philosophical conundrums is intended to motivate the affirmation of the new style of philosophical (or postphilosophical) questioning there advanced. At the same time, while this tactic is clearly one Heidegger repeatedly employs, such intraphilosophical corrections, in respect to problems and solutions also depend on more complex hermeneutic considerations, calling this relatively straightforward picture of BT's work at least in part into question.[7]

---

[6] As becomes clearer in a moment, the preeminent representatives of these positions for the present study are Steven Crowell and Lafont respectively.

[7] Heidegger identifies a shift from phenomenology to hermeneutics as taking place in BT in his work's second introduction. "The phenomenology of Dasein is a hermeneutic in the primordial

The present endeavor, for its part, spans the entirety of the analyses presented in the foregoing chart. It affirms both the vector toward detranscendentalization found in various forms in the last three, while recognizing, like the initial trio, that this does not wholly account for Heidegger's aims. Ultimately, these positions, when taken together, themselves flag what in the present context is the *core question* crucial for understanding discourse's place in Heidegger's thinking at this stage. In the closing sections of BT's first half, Heidegger seemingly does embrace, within limits, a phenomenological and/or philosophical empiricism that includes the building blocks of logic and their operation, one emerging from Aristotle's logic, and Husserl's early work on this topic in his *Logical Investigations*.[8] At the same time, that affirmation comes forward *on the basis* of what *Heidegger himself* earlier presents as detranscendentalizing considerations, inherently contestatory of philosophy.[9] A phase, deemed by him more fundamental, precedes, and, in various respects, comprehends these latter findings; yet this earlier development, when it initially appears, seems to draw the latter's authority into doubt. This change is visible in the status of the assertion, of the logos as such. Heidegger proclaims it "derivative" (*abkünftiger*) in section thirty-three; yet the assertion provides the centerpiece of his analysis of truth and disclosure in section forty-four.[10]

While the extreme positions occupied on the chart given earlier tend toward one or the other side of this dilemma, the middle two thinkers, with which the present project most overlaps, attempt to resolve it.[11] For them, BT's first half ultimately arrives

signification of this word, where it designates this business of interpreting," he states (BT 62). Heidegger, furthermore, explicitly casts his inquiry as an *interpretation* at the beginning of Division II, when he projects Dasein's being toward death. He there speaks of the need to carry out "a positive Interpretation of death and its character as an end" (BT 290). What Heidegger in BT calls the "analytic" of Dasein, accordingly, initially travels under the heading of phenomenology (albeit with this notion already reinterpreted); phenomenology so understood, however, in turn, eventually reveals that all access to the phenomena, and especially the ones it addresses, must be interpretative or hermeneutic. Many have questioned whether this first phase of Heidegger's thought has the genuine philosophical status that Heidegger claims for it, without which the rest of what he accomplishes will not go through. (See especially Burt C. Hopkins, "Heidegger's Hermeneutical Critique," in *Variations on Truth: Approaches to Contemporary Phenomenology*, ed. Pol Vandevelde and Kevin Hermberg [London: Continuum, 2011], 79–93.) Yet if it is persuasive and insightful *as an interpretation*, than at least at present, until some better, that is, more true account of philosophy's practice and its truth can be found, Heidegger's interpretative view of philosophy, to which phenomenology is subordinate, seemingly suffices.

[8] See especially BT VI section 44 "Dasein, Disclosedness, and Truth" (BT 256–73). This section receives extended discussion later in the present chapter.
[9] See especially BT V section 33 "Assertion as a Derivative Mode of Interpretation" (BT 195–202). This section also is about to receive extended discussion.
[10] BT 195; Martin Heidegger, *Sein und Zeit* (Tubingen: Niemeyer, 1993), 154. "*Abkünftiger,* " coming from "*Abkünft,*" does not carry the pejorative sense that "derivative" often now has in English; it merely indicates being descended or derived from something else. This temporal distancing of assertion from what precedes it turns out to be essential to the account of Heidegger's later appraisal of it offered here. For, later, in section forty-four, Heidegger, looking to understand the agreement that correspondence theories of truth evoke, indeed turns to the assertion (*Aussage*): "Let us suppose that some with his back turned to the wall makes the true assertion" (BT 260; Heidegger, *Sein*, 217).
[11] To be clear, neither Lafont nor Crowell, of course, limit themselves to one or the other set of findings, those of section thirty-three or of section forty-four. Yet for Crowell, who first approached this problem in the context of Emil Lask's alethiology, transcendental phenomenology is never brought into question by Heidegger's undertaking nor then are the logical achievements founded on it (See his *Husserl, Heidegger, and the Space of Meaning: Paths Toward Transcendental Phenomenology*

at a novel account of the assertion's and of truth's status that also recognizes what might otherwise call the assertion's primacy into question. For the current approach, however, Heidegger does not arrive at any genuine resolution of this apparent conflict between the two points of view—between his new setting forth of assertoric truth and the phase that renders its priority doubtful. What results is thus not, properly speaking, a *philosophical* solution at all, but instead a kind of limit-problem, which itself resists the resolutions, solutions, and answers that some of his best commentators identify.

For the moment, it suffices to affirm that it is unclear how the detranscendentalizing side of Heidegger's project, his insistence on contesting philosophy, relates to Heidegger's re-intersection with philosophy's more standard concerns toward the end of BT's first half. The crux of the investigations of BT Division I for the present inquiry lies precisely in the apparent tension between these two poles, between Heidegger affirmations of a species of apophantic truth in chapter six of BT and his hermeneutic rerouting of the premises of all previous philosophy in his earlier excurses. Following out this tension eventually allows a new more capacious understanding of discourse and of that aim at truth inseparable from discourse's operation to emerge—a notion of truth that can play a role in all texts and discourse, including literary instances.

8.1.1 The Assertion's Derivativeness and Its Reaffirmation in BT Division I

As it currently exists, the first division of BT finds its center of gravity in its middle sections where discourse is framed. These portions cap BT's prior developments, where Dasein's type of Being, ex-istence, undergoes its first description; there, Da-sein's entanglement with work, equipment, and things is charted. When discourse explicitly makes its appearance in chapter five of BT, Heidegger, accordingly, arguably stands furthest from traditional philosophy's concerns.

Heidegger, at this juncture, apparently in opposition to the final chapter of Part I, explicitly announces the assertion's merely secondary status, and, correspondingly, he argues against the sort of fundamentality philosophy traditionally claims both for the logos and itself. Though the broad outline of this demonstration may be well-known to some readers, it is nevertheless worth rehearsing preparatory to a more fine-grained analysis, since that overview makes more visible the interpretative issues already raised, as well as providing the context for their later discussion. Subsequently, adding in a provisional glance at Heidegger's considerations pertaining to the assertion and truth in chapter six of BT, an overview will be gleaned of Heidegger's itinerary in BT Division I and the hermeneutic problem this trajectory raises.

In section thirty-two, two sections before discourse's explicit introduction, Heidegger identifies a tripartite interpretative structure comprised of forehaving, foresight, and foreconception, along with a second reference point, the hermeneutic "as," the revealing of something *as* something. In section thirty-three of BT, Heidegger

[Evanston: Northwestern University Press, 2002], 23–114.) For Lafont, by contrast the appeal to discourse and language are inherently detranscendentalizing, albeit at various moments, she finds this vector in conflict with Heidegger's own transcendental aspirations.

gives an account of "assertion as a derivative mode" and also of its relation to the foregoing "structures of interpretation." In section thirty-four, Heidegger introduces discourse and explicitly indicates that it is presupposed in the preceding two sections, and also, it turns out, in the entirety of his earlier analysis. Thirty-four's title is "Being-there (*Da-sein*) and Discourse. Language" ("*Da-Sein und Rede. Die Sprache*").[12]

By placing the most comprehensive topic last, Heidegger's order of presentation is unusual from the point of view of traditional philosophy. Discourse's situation is not an oversight, however, nor a function of the haste we know to be attendant upon BT's composition. Rather, because Heidegger's standpoint is through and through hermeneutic, his descriptions and "phenomenology" turn out to be everywhere inseparable from decidedly *local* interpretative inflections; specifically, his standpoint's articulation in part depends on contesting stances and starting points different than Heidegger's own, particularly ones of long-standing provenance in the philosophical tradition. Discourse's presentation on this occasion thus appears in a seemingly belated fashion owing to the line Heidegger hews across the logos' previous philosophical treatments in the two preceding sections; on other occasions, with other contestations in the foreground, Heidegger's subject matter—discourse or *Rede*—may appear differently, albeit its contours presumably would remain broadly the same. This is also the manner in which the present text works in respect to its more narrowly conceived traditions and topics.

Owing to its placement in this sequence, discourse thus arrives with a contestatory force. Discourse follows on the demotion of the assertion and participates in Heidegger's questioning of philosophy's privileging of statements. The demotion of the logos in turn depends on the treatment of understanding (*Verstehen*) generally, focused on interpretation (*Auslegung*), that Heidegger broaches before the logos and before discourse. Understanding, Heidegger tells us, may always undergo interpretation (laying out, *Auslegung*), even as every such interpretation, it turns out, assumes discourse is already in some fashion at work.[13]

Turning to this last topic, then, according to Heidegger in section thirty-two, interpretation, proceeds thanks to a threefold "forestructure," the first moment of which he calls forehaving. Forehaving implies the existence of a background, in which already included is *the thing or subject being interpreted*, albeit no prior notice of it has been taken nor expression pertaining to it actually offered. Forehaving makes available to all species of understanding, including that which takes shape in discourse, the topics these interpretations concern, what they are about.

On any given occasion, more specifically, such a background can be approached and in effect activated owing to a specific orientation or interest. Heidegger calls this orienting moment foresight (*Vorsicht*). Foresight takes the "first cut," as Heidegger

---

[12] BT 203; Heidegger, *Sein*, 160.
[13] BT 203; Heidegger, *Sein*, 160–1. Because Heidegger only introduces discourse after the preceding two sections how precisely discourse and the foregoing treatment of understanding are related is much debated in the literature, especially since understanding interpretation finally concerns and appears by way of the things, the subject matters themselves. The present view of this relationship is soon set forth .

puts it, out of the background.¹⁴ Thanks to foresight's bearing some concrete forward-looking consideration, the interpretation's subject matter is picked out from the background (a picking out, or indicating, or showing that can take a variety of forms).

Along with these interpretative parameters comes a third, pertaining to the *conception* of what emerges on this occasion (foreconception). Heidegger with this notion appears mainly to have in mind the two great categories of beings other than Dasein that inform the totality of the analysis of BT's first half: ready-at-hand (things approached *in use*) or present-at-hand, or occurrent (things stripped of these everyday significations or otherwise given simply as themselves—"in their essential unintelligibility," as Heidegger elsewhere in BT puts it).¹⁵ Foreconceptions can be variable or mistaken, and of all forestructures foreconception may be most indebted to discourse, as some commentators have suggested, albeit how deeply this debt extends, and whether it concerns what would usually be identified as individual concepts remains unclear.¹⁶

Forestructure, comprised of these three moments, is always accompanied by another formation that Heidegger introduces before it: the "as," "something as something." The relation between the two sets of structures, the two themes (forestructure and as), is by no means transparent, however. Interpretation makes available, shows, or expresses, some thing *as* something, on the basis of these frameworks that themselves do not become explicit as such. (All of the forestructure, including its futural moment, in the first instance, operate *unthematically* in any single event of understanding, though it is possible to reflect on features of that event and make the relevant facet—the foreconception or foresight—explicit.) On such an occasion, when understanding interpretation of this as yet unthematized sort takes place, what emerges, then, is not first and foremost *the interpreting* or even *an interpretation* at all, but instead a thing or subject matter, *Sache*—a specific tool or material, a matter of fact, a disposition or a mood. Though interpretation and its forestructure operate in every revelation of something *as* something, the "as," Heidegger insists, *belongs to the thing*, and appears *from out of it*. (Gadamer's standpoint here, then, may resonate.) Both the hammer *as a hammer* and its being too heavy for a certain job emanate or show themselves from the item "encountered" or "met up with," as Heidegger puts it—in this case, from *the hammer*—despite the fact that hammers, not to mention their being too heavy, seemingly could not exist apart from the interpretative dimension.¹⁷

---

14   BT 191; Heidegger, *Sein*, 150.
15   BT 194; Heidegger, *Sein*, 153. Because Heidegger's notion of *Vorhanden*, present-at-hand, unlike that of *Zuhanden*, ready-to-hand, makes use of a term already found in everyday German, some have suggested translating it as "occurrent" to capture its usual inflection as "at hand," "available," or simply existing.
16   Taylor Carman claims only foreconception is truly specific to interpretation, but this arguably is too narrow (Taylor Carman, *Heidegger's Analytic Interpretation, Discourse, and Authenticity in Being and Time* [Cambridge: Cambridge University Press, 2003], 212–14). Beyond the two great categories of Being just discussed, foreconception seemingly does include what Husserl would have called regional determinations, natural things as natural, historical as historical, which determinations for Heidegger have both a history and a historicity.
17   Heidegger uses the German verb *begegnen*; the entities or things "encounter" or "meet." MacQuarrie and Robinson find this "active intransitive sense" too "harsh" and as a rule use either a "passive construction . . . or an active transitive construction" (BT 70 n.2) As will become clearer as

The assertion or statement (claims like "the hammer," or "hammer-shaped object" "has weight" or "is heavy") are branded "derivative," by Heidegger, on the basis of interpretation and the "as" so glossed. The subject matter of an assertion becomes accessible to the assertion only thanks to an operation, interpretation so conceived, that the assertion and what it claims to show essentially *conceal*. Not only does the assertion present worlded things as present at hand, and thus as putatively uninterpreted—accordingly, at one remove from their most radical or fundamental availability—but the assertion, itself a mode of interpretation, similarly, appears as a present-at-hand entity. The assertion gives itself out as a stand-alone report, capable of operating in its own right, facing off against occurrent things deemed similarly free of context (BT 200-1). Accordingly, though both what is talked about and such talk itself are possibilities owed to the forestructures and the work of the hermeneutic "as," the "nature" of the statement is to cover over this terrain in regard to its own operation and its "objects."

Grammar and logic, as disciplines, moreover, arise from and participate in such concealment, according to Heidegger. The logos, from the time of its conception in Plato and Aristotle, is taken as something present-at-hand, thereby obscuring the contours and work of understanding, the structures of interpretation, and the kind of worldedness upon which these rest. Heidegger indeed brands assertion "a derivative mode of interpretation," owing to its reliance on possibilities of understanding that it systematically excludes. Thanks to the assertion's begetting a fascination with one type of subject matter (the present-at-hand) and itself being viewed on these same terms, the larger worlded context on which interpretation draws, as well as interpretation itself drop from view, while the assertion steps to the foreground.

8.1.2 The Trajectory of BT Division I

The foregoing thread of Heidegger's argument, none of which is simply incorrect, nevertheless falls short of a comprehensive view of Heidegger's treatment of the

> discussion continues, the present interpretation of the "as" and its relation to the forestructures of the understanding has been spurred in part thanks to contesting Steven Crowell's powerful work, especially his early work, that views Heidegger as a new kind of transcendental idealist, with things, including those ready-at-hand, operating in the space of meaning or as "logos immanent" (*Space* 84–5). Just the opposite, however, *the logos as immanent to things* is what it seems to me the first sections of BT especially reveal. Carman, it may be noted, also pushes back against Crowell's assimilation of understanding to consciousness and its operation (*Analytic* 210), but he saves the appearances, as it were, by appealing to norms built into discourse, as providing "an existential condition of semantic meaning and intentional content as the tradition prior to Heidegger conceived it" in order to "make sense of the contents of our understanding as systematically distinct from the objects they describe," which seems to me not to respond to Crowell's concerns, and also not finally the issue this development raises (*Analytic* 215). Crowell, in a later work, *Normativity and Phenomenology in Husserl and Heidegger* (Cambridge: Cambridge University Press, 2013), attempting to maintain the transcendental idealist framework against Taylor's criticism, discusses Husserl's claim of consciousness surviving the annihilation of the world and suggests that, with it, Husserl has in mind the possibility of a consciousness without intentions. Whether that is right, what Husserl and Crowell really need, however, to support any version of the transcendental, as Crowell himself concedes, is the opposite: not consciousness without intentions, but intentions without consciousness. Only thus could Crowell defend importing into the perceptual noema first-person implication and commitments analogous to those Robert Brandom finds in his third-person-pragmatist accounts of discourse (*Normativity* 117–18).

assertion and the present-at-hand in BT's first half. It indeed fails to take into account what was anticipatorily set out earlier: the view of the assertion and its truth to which Heidegger in his very next chapter comes. Granting the revelation of the logos' essential secondariness, thereby debunking or interrogating certain presuppositions informing grammar's and logic's treatment, the logos, the assertion or statement, nevertheless, a little later in BT, will be credited with its own specificity and power.

This is perhaps the nut of the paradox or problem informing BT Division I: the most primordial relation to things, Heidegger tells us, arises in and among the world of work and the ready-at-hand; these kinds of things and their interpretations dwell nearest to all understanding and to discourse itself. At the same time, what is taken to preeminently appear through such interpretations, is not the ready-at-hand, but the present-at-hand, things shorn of this sort of intelligibility. To the latter, however, the assertion relates and at Division I's close Heidegger frames an understanding of its truth, wherein the assertion's revelatory power and its access to the real seem now to be affirmed.

To be sure, at this later juncture, the truth specific to the assertion is also deemed derivative.[18] That truth redounds to a more radical instance: Dasein's, or ours, or the person's, being-in-the-world, and its own being "in the truth."[19] The assertion's truth, understood in terms of "correspondence," according to Heidegger, conceals its deeper footing in the disclosedness of Dasein, Dasein's standing in truth, just as earlier the assertion itself concealed the essentially interpretative structure of Dasein's understanding.

Nevertheless, just as discourse, being introduced *after* the assertion's derivativeness, built on the detranscendentalizing force of Heidegger's earlier considerations, so, now, because Dasein's being-in-the-truth is presented as *leading up to* the assertion's seemingly successful operation, that operation now receives a *positive* inflection. Dasein's being-in-the-truth may, yes, be more primordial and even covered over by the assertion and its truth but, so set forth, it nevertheless *underwrites* the assertion's claim to show how things are. The specific power of the assertion thus no longer is seemingly solely contested by Heidegger, but instead ratified, at least in part. *Hermeneuein* may trump *apophansis*; but *apophansis* and its truth are now viewed as legitimately emerging from the former and thereby presented in a different, more positive light.

From this development stems the temptation, then, rife in the more recent literature on Heidegger, to find in the first part of BT as a whole a newer, better, yet still philosophical account of the logos and its truth. Heidegger's thought, on this view, would indeed take on those conditions and circumstances that otherwise seem to bring the logos' functioning into doubt (as set out in BT's earlier portions), ultimately in the service of a new understanding of the logos itself. The detranscendentalizing thrust of Heidegger's work in chapter six of BT is transformed into a new, yet essentially

---

[18] See chapter six, section forty-four, "*The Primordial Phenomenon of Truth and the Derivative (Abkünftigkeit* [Derivativeness]) *Character of the Traditional Conception of Truth* (BT 262; *Sein* 219).

[19] "In so far as Dasein is its disclosedness essentially, and as disclosed, it discloses and uncovers, to this extent it is essentially 'true.' Dasein is 'in the truth.'" (BT 263; *Sein* 221; translation altered).

positive philosophical force. Some version of this project has occupied many of the best Heidegger scholars in recent years.

Accordingly, whatever else is the case, a torqued through line, winding around both discussions of the assertion, stretches across part one of BT, with discourse at its center. Discourse is implicated at once in the assertion's contestation *and* its affirmation, as much of the commentary on BT also recognizes. Arriving at Heidegger's own take on discourse, consequently, necessitates grasping more fully both termini of this twisting strand: the beginning point in what removes the logos from the throne on which philosophy has traditionally placed it, and the status discourse has when Heidegger restores the assertion's standing on its basis. Only then may discourse, talk! come clearly into view, overcoming its own opacity and relative backgrounding in Heidegger's text, and only then, with its relation to truth established, can the final phase of the present project, the account of textuality that in part depends on some new reckoning with truth, emerge.

8.2 *Sinn* and *Bedeutung* in BT

The coordinates of this unique torque or turn, setting the stage for the contestation of the assertion, but also, later, the new opening on to it Heidegger in some fashion embraces, are rightfully assigned to the section of BT begun to be discussed earlier— section thirty-two—to a portion of this section that has not, however, yet been treated. Section thirty-two, as noted, opens a sequence leading to discourse's explicit thematization. Heidegger's exposition, unusually, but characteristically, builds up to discourse, through thirty-two and then thanks to setting forth the assertion's derivative character (thirty-three), albeit the assertion is a subset of discourse, and, discourse itself, Heidegger tells us, is already at work in all of the preceding topics and analyses.[20]

Recourse to the earlier chart lets some of the key questions pertaining to this specific development in section thirty-two emerge. The contribution of interpretation and of the "as" to discourse, and thus to the assertion, in the broadest possible terms may be conceived in two ways, as attested by the commentators' treatments that have previously been set out. In one case, as the chart indicated, Heidegger's earlier holistic analyses ultimately yield *senses* (*Sinne*). Senses stand behind the "as" something, with which things appear, making the apprehension of these things' *existence* possible.

For a second approach, Heidegger's analyses, by contrast, above all, yield *reference*. They show how *access* to the beings that discourse or talk! is *about* becomes available, including in the case of the assertion. Reference in this case has not its technical logical meaning of secured, repeated identification of the same entity over time, but rather

---

[20] Joseph P. Fell, in his "The Familiar and the Strange: On the Limits of Praxis in the Early Heidegger" (in *Heidegger: A Critical Reader*, Hubert L. Dreyfus and Harrison Hall eds. [Oxford: Blackwell, 1992]: 65–80) also notes the variability of Heidegger's order of presentation, drawing some consequences from it similar to those advanced here ("Familiar" 66).

simply denotes the ability of discourse, the assertion, or other forms of communication, to supervene on something other than itself.[21]

To be sure, neither approach wholly excludes the other. Those who take Heidegger's preceding analytic and interpretation to yield senses insist that such senses make available the items discourse discusses; for these interpreters, sense begets reference. Such commentators, accordingly, also tend toward some form of idealism or constructivism. In turn, readings giving reference primacy do not simply exclude the role played by sense, or more specifically, as is about to become clearer, what Heidegger calls meaning (*Bedeutung*). Nevertheless, what ultimately goes through, and consistently remains in play for the latter is reference.

The positions *at the extremes* of the aforementioned chart, one allying Heidegger with transcendental phenomenology, the other with the linguistic turn, interestingly, *both* fall into the first camp; they both understand Heidegger's presentation of understanding to turn on sense, *Sinn*. By pursuing this coincidence, consequently, why this option, that of sense, ultimately will not be subscribed to here can be made more plain.

Indeed, these two commentators, with outlooks on Heidegger otherwise so starkly opposed, both view Heidegger's initial limning of the ready-at-hand as providing senses (or meaning in its usual acceptation), thanks to which what is given becomes accessible in its being. Transcendental intentional perspectives *and* linguistic detranscendentalizing ones both focus on sense, while understanding sense itself in diametrically opposed fashions. In the linguistic case, sense redounds to (ultimately factical) languages, and thus proves "detranscendentalizing"; in the prior case, it implies a species of intentional performance, thereby opening on to a transcendental perspective. Yet for both, sense provides whatever access there may be to what exists.[22]

In fact, two of the most prominent proponents of each view, Steven Crowell (transcendental idealism) and Christina Lafont (linguisticism), seize on the same sentence of BT in which sense is mentioned, in support of their claims, respectively, that Heidegger is a "transcendental idealist" (Crowell) or that he there makes a version of the "linguistic turn" (Lafont).[23] Both cite the same sentence from section thirty-two to establish the role of sense (*Sinn*), as they understand it. "Sense (*Sinn*)," Heidegger

---

[21] Heidegger's analysis gives a footing to both interpretations, since for him just that space where meanings and understandings, stemming from *work and practice*, thus where ones artificial or "anthropocentric," interpenetrate things, is also where access to beings is originally located.

[22] Jacques Derrida's early thought, it may be noted, would not be possible without an overlap of linguisticism and transcendentalism, also made possible by the privileging of sense (including in Husserl, its subset *Bedeutung* (meaning), differently understood and treated than by Heidegger). Derrida's work pursues both tacks simultaneously, originally as this intersection appears in the case of (written) *language* and transcendental *intentional* productions, in the final phase of Husserl's thought, where Husserl explores transcendental and intentional history. As set out in Chapter 3 of my *Essential History*, I have long believed this development is the decisive one for grasping and evaluating the early Derrida's work as a whole.

[23] *Space of Reasons* 90; *Language and World-Disclosure* 62–3. Lafont, to be clear, believes this embrace of sense is indeed Heidegger's strategy, albeit a failing one, because reference can be construed independently of sense. Crowell in his later work, specifically engaging with Taylor Carman, denies that the conceptual framework raised by externalism, which pins understanding to a referent outside or external to thinking, applies to either Husserl or Heidegger.

himself there asserts, "is that wherein the understandability of something maintains itself. What is articulable in understanding disclosure, we call sense."[24]

"Sense," for both Crowell and Lafont, accordingly, establishes "the understandability" of things, as Heidegger indeed puts it here. On this view, both entities and their existence are subordinated to meaning, *Sinn*, so understood. A pool or reservoir of meaningfulness allows beings to be given; a specifically semantic, or intentional (noetic-noematic), register founds the grasp of all beings that show themselves in understanding and in discourse or talk!

Problem arise for both interpretations, however, when Heidegger's extended presentation of sense in this stretch of BT is examined more closely. For one, *Sinn* is indeed here opposed by Heidegger, to another term, *Bedeutung*, sometimes also translated as "meaning," as well as by "reference" (especially in English translations of Frege), and by significance or signification (by MacQuarrie and Robinson in their translation of BT). (Hereafter, "meaning" will be used for *Bedeutung*, as the German lacks the relation to the sign, *Zeichen*, that *sign*ificance suggests in English.) *Bedeutung* (meaning), not *Sinn* (sense), as will become plain, for Heidegger actually forges the link between interpretation, the "as," and the beings these concern.[25]

What Heidegger says about sense comprises some of the more difficult and enigmatic declarations to be found in BT's already difficult pages. Neither Lafont nor Crowell, who in my view explicates Heidegger more faithfully on this point, finally take these characterizations fully into account; at the same time, their more straightforward, customary, interpretations of sense help point up the singularity and unusualness of Heidegger's employment of this notion.

8.2.1 *Sinn*

Heidegger's remarks on sense, then, must need be further tracked down. Right after the citation just given, the singularity of Heidegger's pronouncements on this topic emerge.[26] Most notably, Heidegger's usage deviates from the usual one, in that, according to him, sense cannot be spoken of in respect *to worldly things* at all, effectively foreclosing both of the interpretative strategies just laid out. Heidegger insists that "sense is not a property attaching to entities, lying behind them, or floating somewhere as an intermediate domain," but instead that it is "an existentiale of Dasein," and that "*only* Dasein can be senseful (*sinnvoll*) or senseless."[27]

Sense and senses, for Heidegger, do not pertain to entities other than Dasein; accordingly, they cannot be that through which other beings and their understanding are given, in a fashion bordering on the Husserlian noema that Crowell favors, nor

---

[24] BT 193; *Sein* 151 (translation altered).
[25] Sense (*Sinn*) is, of course, critical for Heidegger's greatest ambitions in SZ, a matter that will here only be touched on tangentially. Heidegger aims to find or renew a *sense* for the Being-question (a *Sinn* for the *Seinsfrage*), in part eventuated by some sense of Being, some *Sinn* of *Sein*, according to him, always already at work in everyday understanding (BT 25; *Sein* 5).
[26] Introducing this notion, Heidegger himself notes somewhat balefully that sense (*Sinn*) is a "phenomenon," of which, "copious use is made in philosophical problematics" without being clarified (BT 192).
[27] BT 193; *Sein* 151 (my emphasis).

in the linguistic one, advanced by Lafont, somewhat akin to Gadamer's speculative *Wort*. In whatever manner Heidegger may be conceiving of sense, it neither accrues to linguistic meanings nor comes to pass in an intentionality responsible for the thing's apparition, since it does not for Heidegger pertain to things at all.[28]

Put more positively, sense functions something along the lines of the world (or my world) at any given moment *making sense*, a holistic notion oriented toward a larger pool of *possibility* pertaining to my own existence. Heidegger thus speaks of the ability of Dasein's world to be filled in, to prove satisfiable or fulfillable, "*erfullbar*," through discoverable being, and that world thereby having or lacking sense.[29] Sense, to use Heidegger's terminology, transpires as the "*whereupon (Woraufhin)*" of what Heidegger calls "a projection"—projection pertaining to Dasein's own manner of existing. The understanding I have of something in the world (when I stake out a project, which necessarily always involves both myself and things) ultimately redounds to my own vantage point, endowing my own being-in-the-world with "sense."[30] Thus, in this same paragraph, Heidegger can continue to stipulate that sense itself "is not *what is understood*, but *the entity*."[31]

By contrast, meaning, *Bedeutung*, *is* actively engaged whenever such understanding of beings other than Dasein takes place. *Bedeutung*, meaning, comes to light, when beings are understood, but does so as *emanating from them*, thereby deviating from our usual understanding of meaning or of sense. Meanings, *Bedeutungen*, can neither be the function of an operative intentionality (since they are registered directly from things) nor be the function of a constituting language and its words, in this case, again, because they come from the things, not us, but also because such meanings indeed precede *language and words*, but *not discourse*, according to Heidegger's own explicit statements.[32]

How meaning functions, and its difference from sense becomes clearer when Heidegger for the first time explicitly introduces discourse in section thirty-four. In what is perhaps the single most important passage for determining meaning's relation to sense (*Bedeutung*'s relation to *Sinn*) and the status of both, he declares:

> The articul*able* (*Artikulier*bare) in interpretation, and in discourse more originally still, we name Sense, *Sinn*. The articulat*ed* (*Gegliederte*) in talk!-based articulation (*in der redenden Artikulation*) as such we name the meaning-totality (*Bedeutungsganze*). This can become dissolved into meanings (*Bedeutungen*)....

---

[28] To be sure, sense might be viewed in some general fashion as a possibility belonging to Dasein, and thus a transcendental or quasi-transcendental condition, which eventually becomes extended to things. Not only, however, does this run contrary to Heidegger's insistence that things show their meaningfulness from themselves, but it also fails to jibe with what Heidegger at this moment goes on to declare. After stating that "only Dasein has sense," he elaborates that sense accrues to Dasein, "when its own disclosedness" is able to "be filled in (*erfullbar*) through discoverable being." When other sorts of being have been uncovered or discovered, Dasein has sense (or lacks it), sense being a feature, not of their, but of Dasein's existence (BT 193; *Sein* 151).

[29] See previous note.

[30] BT 193; *Sein* 151 (translation altered).

[31] BT 192–3 (my emphasis).

[32] See BT 204; BT 266. The former passage is about to receive further discussion.

> The meaning-totality (*Bedeutungsganze*) of Understandability comes to word. To the meanings (*Bedeutungen*), words accrue. But wordthings do not get supplied with meanings (*Bedeutungen*).[33]

Sense, on its side, is indeed a notion of possibility as possibility, underlying interpretation, the *Artikulier*bare, which is never itself *actualized*, as Heidegger takes pains to make clear, since the articul*ated*, in talk-based articulation, recurs first to meaning-totalities and then to meanings, not sense—meanings, not sense, then, in turn, being that to which words finally accrue. Sense is thus, again, a notion oriented toward Dasein's own existence: the articulability made available to the threefold act of interpretation insofar as my own being and its possibilities as possibilities subtend any given act of understanding as such. In turn, meanings are what operate between understanding and things; yet even they do so differently than ordinarily envisioned, since meanings appear as *already inhering in things*, in the meaning-totalities (more about which soon), such that *the things in question*, not the meanings, turn out to be what is understood. *Bedeutung*, meaning, in this fashion, participates in the concrete commerce with beings found in discourse, in which things themselves are accessed and show *themselves*, in a fashion here set out earlier and emphasized.

Meanings thus differ from sense and senses in at least three ways: by being intertwined primarily with beings other than Dasein insofar as beings are ready-, not present-at-hand; by being articulated with those beings in discourse; and finally as operating prior to language and words, while eventually furnishing the latter, words, with *meanings*.

In turn, meanings themselves, Heidegger tells us, flow from meaning-totalities (*Bedeutungsganze*): such totalities become *articulated* (*gegliederte*) in discourse, thereby yielding meanings (*Bedeutungen*). Through the sections and joinings of these totalities, simultaneously stand forth the entities, the beings in question. Such meaning-totalities, in turn, have already been at work in the previous stage of Dasein's involvement with ready-at-hand things. Being enmeshed with and belonging to things ready-at-hand in their everyday functioning and organization, the meanings assembled in these totalities are *intrinsic to such things* (albeit tacitly). Meanings as such, accordingly, arrive in discourse as articulated from out of a previous whole embracing both them *and* the beings they concern; this permits the meanings to be parceled out along with those beings at the moment beings are articulated in discourse.[34]

Meanings themselves thus surface in discourse, not language. Meanings arrive and become articulated in discourse. Though implicit in discourse's existence and persons' prior acquaintance with it, meanings are themselves only identifiable as such at the moment they are explicitly articulated *along with the things* in which they inhere.

---

[33] BT 204; *Sein* 161 (translation altered).

[34] Meanings as already one with things and letting them appear as such thus do the work with which Crowell and others credit the *noema*, and which Crowell rightfully suggests McDowell needs to round out his account (*Space* 14ff). Crowell in some of his later work, again runs up against this issue, in that he wants to argue that something like a previous history of encounters with the object and thus its inferential relations on a perceptual level inform our understanding and apprehension of it. But even he admits that he cannot account at the relevant level of particular things in their givenness for the first-person normativity that he claims must be at work there, *Normativity* 120.

Meaning ultimately redounds to discourse as an *existentiale*, as part of Dasein's own everyday being-in-the-world.

Heidegger, in turn, on this account, indeed can insist that discourse is *prior* to both language and words. After having stated, as cited earlier, that "to meanings, words accrue. But word-things do not get supplied with meanings," Heidegger further explicates the relation of meanings, discourse, and language, and exhibits their connection as tethered to a shift from the ready-at-hand to the present-at-hand. Language, as an entity in its own right, conceived as composed of word-things only appears in terms of the present-at-hand.[35] Placing discourse and meaning (*Bedeutung*) in this way prior to language and words, Heidegger thereby emphasizes that only in such pre-engagement with worldly things, and as emerging from them, can there eventually be anything like words, linguistic meanings, or language at all, all of which at this moment indeed prove secondary. To meanings and discourse, operative within the ready-at-hand, not to sense, words, but not "word-things" originarily accrue.[36]

Sinn for its part, then, primarily answers to world in its intersection with Dasein, to Dasein's having a world at all, and to the force of that disclosure for Dasein—not, as it is so often taken, to world in its intersection with other beings. *Sinn* (about which Heidegger never in this section speaks in the plural) redounds to Dasein, while what is understood, answers, as Heidegger himself says, "to beings, or Being."[37]

Yet the two phenomena in question—sense as it pertains to Dasein, meaning as it pertains to worldly things—as began to be suggested a moment ago, in truth do comprise a single phenomenon or whole, while remaining *ontologically distinct*. What is understood, the beings, becomes articulated through *Bedeutungen*, meanings (themselves "sense-laden," "*sinnhaft*" not *sinnvoll*, senseful, as Heidegger puts it at one juncture), while this whole operation recurs to Dasein's projective understanding and Dasein's "being-in." Heidegger indeed ultimately contemplates a kind of crisscross: the entities, with their *meanings and meaningfulness*, fill in Dasein, whose world thus does or does not have *sense* for it. In turn, Dasein, making sense of, and for itself, its world,

---

[35] "The way in which discourse gets expressed (*Die Hinausgesprochenheit der Rede*) is language (*ist die Sprache*). This word-totality in which discourse has a its own 'worldly' Being, becomes something which, as in-the-world being, may be found as ready-to-hand. Language (*Die Sprache*) can be broken up into present-at-hand word-Things," ultimately in accord with Dasein's own kind of being as "a Being which has been thrown and submitted to the world" (BT 204; *Sein* 161 [translation altered]).

[36] Lafont, understandably, puts pressure on Heidegger's claim that meaningfulness functions in this manner: that it is both already at work prior to any occasion of discourse in the ready-at-hand, but that discourse itself is also to be taken as equiprimordial with this same sphere, and thus in some sense, on the foregoing basis, language and words (*Language* 77). Yet there is finally not a problem, as long as discourse is taken, as here, to be preceded by other instances of discourse, and language as so conceived ruled out of the picture, with the result that these ready-at-hand formations on every occasion function with their own integrity and a meaningfulness belonging to them, even as prior instances of discourse and its possibility have always been operating alongside, with, and in them. The angle taken on the ready-at-hand by Heidegger's analysis, as will be further evident, by no means answers to any of the standard forms of philosophical argument, in the manner Lafont seems to think. It does not trace anything back to unequivocally primary principles or formations (such as language); it is instead resolutely hermeneutic and consequently always operates in *media res*. BT articulates itself through preexisting discursive contexts, the presuppositions of which it also questions.

[37] BT 193; *Sein* 151.

or failing to, by way of what Heidegger calls projection, in this fashion, remains the standing *possibility* of things other than Dasein appearing as *meaningful*.

Thus, even though what emerge and show themselves are existing things, they do so in a context radically informed by Dasein's being. This is so, not only because projection, the entirety of the forestructure, and with it the possibility of Dasein's having sense, accompanies all understanding, but also because the meanings, *Bedeutungen*, though they belong to things when they arrive in discourse, already contain a moment inflected by Dasein's interest and possibilities. Meaning in Heidegger's technical sense, as about to become clearer, is indeed a phenomenon rooted in Dasein's interaction with things insofar as they fall within what Heidegger calls the ready-at-hand; it thus involves things, existents other than Dasein, as met up with *in the context of Dasein's own ends, needs, and practices*. In the ready-at-hand, things appear as already informed—one could say turned or troped—by circumstances that recur to Dasein (whose sense, along with that of things, including those present at hand, and of Dasein itself, for Heidegger, ultimately redounds to *Sein* and to its difference from beings). Dasein, however, as is also about to become clearer, only registers its own possibilities and interests by way of these same things; these or some other worlded matters are thus always what Dasein's understanding is of and its discourse is about.

At the core of the possibility of all beings other than Dasein *showing themselves from themselves in understanding*, then, stands *Bedeutung*, meaning. Meanings in discourse appear as intrinsic to beings, such meanings and things being understood *together*. Meaning, however, in its specificity indeed emerges at an earlier stage of Heidegger's analysis, in his discussion of Dasein's everyday involvement with things, where it will eventually turn out that discourse was already implicitly at work. Examining this prior presentation of meaning, accordingly, lets be seen how in discourse worldly beings come to be accessed and lets the *referential dimension* of discourse come to light—the register of sense, by contrast, now known to be distinct from anything that concerns either beings other than Dasein or anything tributary to meaning. The difference between what could be deemed Heidegger's early discourse-inflected realism and Gadamer's more idealist/realist characterization of meaning and language—including the "semantic" preference of the latter over against the "referential" bent of the former—ultimately rests, then, on Heidegger's presentation of meaning in the earlier sections of BT Division I.

8.2.2 *Bedeutung*

In meaning, *Bedeutung*, the reversal insisted on here so often starts to find its explanation; *Bedeutung* is the moment when Dasein's contribution to what is understood, the ineffaceable admixture its concerns make to things and their intelligibility, emerges, along with how *this contribution dovetails with that of things and why it redounds to them and not to Dasein*. *Bedeutung* presents a matrix shot through with Dasein's own ends, goals, and purposes—it is indeed housed within the world of work and pertains to the ready-at-hand (which Heidegger deems prior to any mere seeing, any less engaged registering of things). *Bedeutung*, meaning, and this matrix, everywhere inflected by Dasein's own ends, at the same time, *genuinely* gives *access* to things and to everything that may be said to be other than Dasein.

How this can be possible—*veritable access* to what is, at the same time broached through the world of *work and concern*—initially rests on the two-sidedness of meaning. Meaning implies an interimplication of Dasein and things ready-at-hand, determinative both for things and for the relevant facets of Dasein's existence. Meaning indeed redounds to a register that would not exist without Dasein: the work world, the ready-at-hand, world itself, as initially understood by Heidegger. This entire register, however, at this stage, simultaneously finds its center of gravity in the *things*, in a space where Dasein's own Being is inseparable *from entities other than itself*.

Bedeutungen (meanings) and *Bedeutsamkeit* (meaningfulness), specifically, recur to what Heidegger calls *Bewandtnisse*, translated as involvements.[38] Things ready-at-hand are involved—Dasein lets them be involved, as Heidegger puts it, and this prior to any conscious thematization—necessarily in larger matrices, greater wholes, in which they appear essentially among other things, thus in a collection or totality, in which each is also serviceable for some task, some particular form of work, some specific job, and has already been so registered. Implicit in each tool's involvement, along with serviceability and what Heidegger calls its "useability" is a second set of relations, however, that ultimately bear not on the thing, but on Dasein: the "for-sake-of which" and the "in-order-to."[39] To take Heidegger's example: the hammer is *serviceable* for pounding shingle nails, and it, with much else, comprises the roofer's toolkit; in addition, however, to the claw-hammer being so usable and serviceable, the shingles to be pounded and thus the hammer are *in order to* keep rain out of the house, which in turn is *for the sake of* sheltering Dasein.[40]

Meaning (*be-deuten*, the infinitive), in the first instance, then, indicates these *relationships* and Dasein's acquaintance with them, taken as functioning as *a single seamless whole*. Heidegger initially lists all of these aspects, both those involving Dasein and the ready-at-hand-things—the in-order to, for-the-sake-of-which, serviceability, and so on—and insists that they are not cobbled together; they are instead "relationships bound up with one another as a primordial totality." Together, they are "this being-meaningful (*be-deuten*)," he continues, "in which Dasein gives its Being-in-the-world beforehand to itself as something to be understood."[41]

Hence, meaning, to mean, *be-deuten* fundamentally designates a matrix of connections in which things ready-at-hand are bound together in advance with aspects

---

[38] In his first book, Crowell makes an interesting connection between talk of *Bewandtnisse* in a logical context, as found in Lask and in Heidegger's *Habilitationsschrift*, to Heidegger's usage of this term in BT. He argues that involvement makes possible in Heidegger what is missing in Lask: a materiality in which the logical forms of validity are themselves given, ultimately for a reflecting transcendental consciousness (*Space* 86–88, and 90 esp. 87n12). Nevertheless, Crowell also claims that Heidegger implicitly retains Husserl's notion of logical ideality even in BT (*Space* 91). Not only does everything here so far said about discourse in Heidegger, it seems to me, draw that identification into question. Moreover, Crowell concludes that Heidegger would also affirm Husserl's understanding of the eternal present, of ideality as omnitemporality, which seems to me a bridge too far, decisively so, for any and all of all of the matters at issue here (*Space* 92).

[39] Heidegger discusses involvement and the other topics here treated in section eighteen of BT, "Involvement and Meaningfulness (*Bewandtnis und Bedeutsamkeit*); the Worldhood of the World" (BT 114; *Sein* 83; translation altered).

[40] BT 116.

[41] BT 120; *Sein* 87 (translation altered). The colloquial use of "signify," said of something understandable, would be an apt translation of "*be-deuten*" as Heidegger here uses it.

of Dasein's own existence. The reference points informing meaning, accordingly, stretch beyond the things (which are fundamentally or "primordially" embedded in their involvements), both individually and collectively, while meaning (*bedeuten*) in respect to them and to Dasein functions as a *single* whole, albeit one indeed possessing a *double* character.[42] Entities ready-at-hand, for their part, do not appear in isolation but as *already* organized into groups or manifolds—totalities configured by way of their involvements, their relation to other tools, and oriented by the for-sake-of-which and the in-order-to that pertains to Dasein. Simultaneously, Dasein's own ends and purposes only take on their identities in terms of *things* so organized, only in terms of entities other than Dasein that appear in these arrangements. Things themselves emerge as inflected by Dasein's existence, while what pertains to that existence itself comes into view only as framed by these ready-at-hand, holistically, and purposefully organized totalities.[43] In a single ensemble, accordingly, both what is understood (the ready-at-hand things) and that for the sake of which understanding is for (Dasein) come to light in their *interdependence*.[44]

Meaning, then, emerges at this level—a level prior to any identifiable semantic order as would belong to assertions, statements, language, and words. On this account, it embodies both of those holistic relationships earlier identified in Gadamer's discussion, albeit in a different fashion than in Gadamer's case. Meaning so conceived indeed entails a "word/word," or better a "meaning/meaning" holism, since no meanings (or things) at this level can appear (or even exist) apart from other ones. A single meaning, or one tool, according to Heidegger, is strictly inconceivable.

The ready-at-hand's meaning/meaning holism also, however, clearly entails a radical word/world (or meaning/world) holism. At every point, the entities themselves, the ready-at-hand things, albeit not recognizable as individual subjects, are the bearers of such meanings; without these things, in which they inhere, the meanings and meaning-totalities themselves would not exist, nor could they be recognized or otherwise identified. Meanings appear with things given in their practical transparency and usefulness; they appear as the meaningfulness *of such things*; the whole of Dasein's existence and its understanding thus has been handed over to worlded formations, in terms of which the world and Dasein's own existence ultimately come to light.

A primordial holism, with meaning/meaning ultimately submitted to meaning/world, thus characterizes meaning within the ready-at-hand. Heidegger, in fact, not only speaks of this general being-meaningful, by way of which Dasein has already

---

[42] As becomes clearer in a moment, it remains important that within this interdependence the difference between Dasein and other worldly things is also maintained. This feature is the one I fear Graham Harman in his numerous discussions of the ready-at-hand consistently omits.

[43] Of course, authenticity, only introduced later, will in some fashion transform or vary this fact; yet this being given over to the world and things in it pertains to authenticity as well, which is why it has and can have no specific content or even really contours of its own.

[44] Heidegger insists that two kinds of Being, and two distinct orders of givenness are implicit in a totality of involvements, one to which discoveredness ("*Entdeckheit*") pertains (the ready-at-hand) and a second to which an understanding of its own being as disclosure or disclosedness ("*Erschleissen*") comes (Dasein) (*Sein* 85; 86). The "disclosure" of itself as "the whereupon of innerworldly encountering things already freed" is thus nothing other than "the understanding of the world," according to Heidegger (BT 118; *Sein* 86 translation altered).

understood its world, but also describes meaning's (*bedeuten*'s) concrete operation, thereby exhibiting the functioning of those meaning-totalities (*Bedeutungsganze*), and then those specific meanings (*Bedeutungen*) that he claims appear articulated in discourse and that eventually undergird language and words.

Along with things ready-at-hand in their possible involvements, including other things with their serviceability in these contexts, an actual thing or tool becomes actively involved in an "assignment" or ("reference"), *Verweisen*, as Heidegger puts it.[45] Individual ready-at-hand things—this hammer—with its usefulness (hammering), indeed slot into actual projects and larger wholes (a job in the carpenter's workshop), that again imply purposes (building tables on which to eat and so on), to which each thing itself is ultimately "referred" or "assigned."

Dasein, or "persons," however, also slot into these same wholes, along with such things ready-at-hand. Heidegger uses a term cognate with *Verweisen*, *Anweisen*, with a reflexive (*sich anweisen*) to speak of Dasein being so engaged, presumably to emphasize the closeness or mutuality of the two conditions.[46] Single thing's involvement in such totalities and Dasein's own insertion into them entail assignment and self-assignment respectively—Heidegger eventually talking of Dasein's *Angewiesenheit* in this regard, its "having being assigned onto," its dependence, or indeed "its *submission* to" the world.[47]

World itself, then, the "phenomenon of the world," accordingly, technically defined, in turn, consists in Dasein's own possibilities coinciding with those of things. World as phenomenon indicates strictly speaking that the space of Dasein's self-assignment and the locus of the concrete emergence of beings other than it, are one, that the two inherently function together.[48]

Meanings as such, then, emerge when these previously skeletal relations encompassed by *be-deuten* (meaning) become active in Dasein's navigation of its own being and of ready-at-hand things on the basis of its self-assigning. Meaningfulness (*Bedeutsamkeit*), the primordial totality of these relations, becomes drawn on and articulated, when for example a workperson, beginning to dig a hole for a shrub, says or thinks "not too deep," while choosing the appropriate spade, or, glancing at the pitch of a roof, declares "too much shade," moving the spot for digging elsewhere.[49]

"In meaningfulness (*Bedeutensamkeit*)," accordingly, Heidegger claims, "lurks the ontological condition which makes it possible ... to disclose such things as meanings," and "upon these in turn," he now further states, "is founded the Being of words and

---

[45] As Macquarrie and Robinson note, Heidegger's usage of "*verweisen*" and its related forms is somewhat unidiomatic or neologistic (BT 97n2).
[46] *Anweisen* may also mean to refer or assign; Macquarie and Robinson at times use "assign" for both terms, though it is actually more rare in the case they usually translate assignment, *Verweisen*.
[47] BT 120; *Sein* 87.
[48] Heidegger states: "Wherein Dasein understands itself in advance in the mode of assigning itself, that is the whereupon of the letting be encountered of Beings. The wherein of self-assigning understanding as the whereupon of the letting be encountered of Beings in the Beingmodus of involvement is the phenomenon of the world" (BT 119; *Sein* 86 [translation altered]).
[49] *Sein* 87. Heidegger here focuses on significance or meaningfulness (*Bedeutsamkeit*) rather than the *Bedeutungsganze* of the later section previously discussed, as he is presently approaching this phenomenon from the point of view of Dasein's acquaintance with such meaningfulness, which nevertheless, to be clear, resides neither in a conscious awareness of it nor an intending of it.

language."⁵⁰ Acquaintance with meaning, meaningfulness (*Bedeutensamkeit*) makes meanings (*Bedeutungen*) possible, and on this basis, eventually, words and language as well.

Accordingly, at this moment, meaning's functioning in respect to discourse may be better grasped, and its relation to other discourse than that coeval with the ready-at-hand clarified. What comes forward in discourse, founding of words and of language as such, are indeed meanings, Heidegger insists. Meaning is a discursive phenomenon, the contours of which Dasein is always already familiar with in ready-at-hand contexts, with language and words arising on that basis. Things ready-at-hand are organized by dint of relations familiar to Dasein, as Dasein's world's meaningfulness, in which discourse already participates. There, things and Dasein's concerns are always blended together, the latter, the concerns appearing only by way of the former, the things. Only owing to such blending, thanks to which Dasein's concerns are embedded in things, can there finally be meanings of the sort words take on, while things themselves, not verbal meanings, always remain what show themselves in any instance of discourse.

Discourse at the practical level, then, takes place on the basis of such familiarity with the meaningfulness comprising Dasein's world.⁵¹ At the same time, discourse as such, ongoing traditions of discourse, have *always already been at work* in this same register, tacitly operating, even when no actual talk occurs, though no coalescence or formalization of these capacities in a language (or words) yet explicitly takes hold.⁵² To be clear, such situating of words and language and discourse in respect to

---

⁵⁰ BT 121; *Sein* 87. This is why Heidegger can later substitute "falling" for discourse or talk! (*Rede*) when enumerating Dasein's existentiale. Dasein's working world, its environment, is articulated through such meaningfulness in which Dasein is handed over to things—thus fallen away from its own being, which fallenness is its primary and original condition.

⁵¹ John Haugeland, Hubert Dreyfus, and others, who Carman dubs pragmatists, also affirm discourse at this level, but take it simply as coextensive with our negotiating the world at all, and thus as at work in all practical distinguishing—in hammering with a hammer, not a saw, and so on. Yet, as Carman insists, this understanding appears at once too broad and too weak given discourse's specificity and its relation both to meaningfulness and to meanings (cf. *Analytic* 228-9). Discourse as such tacitly already makes a contribution at this level, even as meaning as embedded in things and their organization permits discourse's own functioning higher up the chain, when interpretation of some kind ("slab," or "too heavy"), still in a practical way, occurs. Taylor, however, arguably goes too far in the other direction. While allowing for genuine discourse in practical life, he insists that *norms* specific to discourse, as understood by H. P. Grice and others, are at work in any act of understanding and thus there operate as well. Accordingly, he speaks of a kind of "practical apophansis" taking place in the ready-at-hand (*Analytic* 220). Normativity of this type, explicitly registering the difference of the thing from its understanding, is absent from this level, however, and must be, including when discourse, is in play, as Heidegger repeatedly underscores. When asked why not grab the bolt with pliers rather than an allen wrench, the boss's response, after all, may be and often is to simply call for the wrench again.

⁵² This, again, is the issue raised by Lafont. It may now be clearer how Heidegger can both insist on discourse *factically* always accompanying the ready-at-hand, and thus contributing to meaning and meaningfulness, while also maintaining formally that the ready-at-hand supplies the precondition for meanings appearing in discourse on any given occasion. At the same time, Heidegger's way of proceeding, it should be emphasized, does not correspond to that of most philosophy. All analysis, as here should be obvious, for him takes place from a vantage in *media res*; there are no arguments from first principles. These opening pages thus already are and only can be interpretations, ones that speak to phenomena that occlude themselves and thus also demand Heidegger's unique style of hermeneutic phenomenology. That does not make them impervious to discussion, improvement, or even disqualification; the most obvious way to do so would be to discover genuine first principles

meaning so understood does not entail, as Heidegger himself later underscored, that all instances of discourse are of the type found, for example, in the language games with which Wittgenstein's *Investigations* begins.[53] The fate of discourse's more general capacities remains to be determined. At a minimum, however, because the ready-at-hand entails the radical interimplication of Dasein and beings other than Dasein as found in meaning, all discourse, Heidegger suggests, in some fashion, recurs to this initial condition in which things and their understanding are already one, which gives meanings and later words. All expression, minimally, is parasitic on the possibility that meaning in Heidegger's sense exhibits, wherein inner-worldly beings and what pertains to Dasein simultaneously operate as a single, seamless formation, without their difference for all that ever being effaced. Discourse as a making explicit of things coordinate with and oriented by their own self is indebted to this possibility, albeit discourse more generally may ultimately be more diversified than it here at first appears.[54]

Accordingly, if the question of the possibilities inherent in discourse at other levels must provisionally be suspended, the same is not true of those issues concerning *reference* in a wider sense. At this juncture, Heidegger has in fact just insisted that such familiarity with meaning renders *things discoverable* (*entdeckbar*). Dasein's familiarity with "meaningfulness," Heidegger indicates, constitutes "the ontical condition of possibility of discovering things"—first and foremost those things that "are met up with or encountered in a world with involvement (ready-at-hand), as their kind of being, and which can thus make themselves known (or 'manifest,' *bekunden sich*) as they are in their in itself."[55]

Access to individual things, to entities as such, indeed "in their in itself," according to Heidegger, arises in the inherently practical space in which they and Dasein's own mode of being have already been tied together. Whatever considerations a further unfolding of meanings and discourse may yield, then, Heidegger's presentation in the early going of BT emphasizes that contact or access to any thing, any subject matter, redounds to discourse and meaning at this level. Throughout the present portion of BT,

---

of some kind. Barring that, one must proceed from an interpretative evaluation at once immanent, yet not simply confined to the terms in question.

[53] See Fell's "Familiar," p. 66, for Heidegger's disparagement of this sort of interpretation at the Le Thor seminar. Fell, as noted, is aware of the difficulties posed by Heidegger's presentation, and he ultimately opts for a number of different ways of tracing referential and semantic priority ("Familiar" 72). He further suggests, and Philipse follows him here, that anxiety gives an alternative access to occurrent, or present-at-hand beings (beings-in-themselves) (Fell 68; Philippse194 n91). The subsection following the present offers a different construal of that being-in-itself.

[54] This is also why Heidegger's analysis of the sign and its functioning at this stage does not stand in for discourse's operation (BT Section 17 "Reference—*Verweisung*, Assignment—and Signs). The sign shows instead how everything at work in the ready-at-hand is itself already meaningful; as a tool, it is exemplary for making visible that meaningfulness, in the sense here identified, pertaining to all the ready-at-hand. Peter E. Gordon in his "The Empire of Signs: Heidegger's Critique of Idealism in Being and Time" (*The Cambridge Companion to Heidegger's Being and Time* [New York: Cambridge, 2013] 223–238) if I follow him, concurs with this conclusion, though he, later, wishes on its basis to convict Heidegger of "an idealism of human practices" (229; 235). The following section offers a suggestion that militates against Gordon's conclusion; raising this suggestion, Gordon, in the present idiom, seems not to have wholly grasped Heidegger's "word/world" holism.

[55] BT 120; *Sein* 87 (translation altered).

Heidegger insists that discourse's ability to refer originates at, and is unthinkable apart from meaning, meaningfulness, and meaning-totalities so understood. At the end of this section, he thus declares: "only if entities in the world can be encountered at all (in this way), is it possible, in the field of such entities, to make accessible what is just present-at-hand and no more."[56]

What is "present-at-hand" or "occurrent" (*vorhanden*), Heidegger's term for things as presented in statements or assertions, including those of perception, depends on entities ready-at-hand, organized in the aforementioned fashion, being already discovered, whatever subsequent variations or transformations of understanding it may bring.[57] Moreover, in this same passage, Heidegger speaks of a familiarity with meaning as the ontical condition of the discovery of things, as a discovery of them "in their in itself." Heidegger's employment of the "in itself" indicates that meaning as just glossed provides the primary access to everything that is.

Heidegger's usage at this moment, of course, is aimed polemically at the philosophical tradition and its understanding. On the latter construal, ready-at-hand things could never be in themselves, since entities, like tools, only become manifest and exist in contexts oriented by Dasein's own purposes. To the contrary, Heidegger maintains, in the ready-at hand the "in itself" alone is to be found.

How exactly things ready-at-hand are to be conceived as in themselves, Heidegger had already set out at some length in a preceding section of BT Division I. Thus, to grasp better how Heidegger conceives of the notion of the "in itself" as applying, seemingly counter-intuitively, to the ready-at-hand, and, with that, how access to things generally functions for him across the board, thereby returning us to that theme of realism, which is our terminus, Heidegger's prior treatment of this topic must be examined. This discussion, in turn, sets the stage for investigating the fate of discourse in other settings, specifically, in the case of the assertion and its *apophansis,* of things deemed present-at-hand and the truth and reality claimed to accompany their expression in statements. The latter, finally, opens the door to grasping the truth and insight that pertains to literature and other non-assertoric types of discourse—none finally being essentially distinct from any other—as taken up and more fully accounted for in Chapter 9.

8.2.3 The Ready-at-Hand and the in Itself

Heidegger begins to reconcile the obvious paradox of attributing to things subjected to Dasein's ends and uses being "in itself," by locating this presumably fundamental condition, the "in itself," in Dasein's dealing with things when *they do not appear as such*—things in this way proving withdrawn, and thus literally, "*in* themselves."[58] So doing, Heidegger believes that he is not only offering a genealogy of the "in itself," an exhibition of whence this otherwise perhaps misplaced philosophical notion derives,

---

[56] BT 122.
[57] Again, in recent Heidegger scholarship, "*vorhanden*" tends to be translated as "occurrent" in order to mark its different status than *zuhanden* (ready-at-hand); the latter is a coinage, a neologism, while the former is a somewhat common German term.
[58] BT 105.

but also accounting in a different fashion for what this same conception aims at: the givenness of something *as genuinely being or existing.*

Heidegger's "in itself" pertains to things ready-at-hand in the world of work, *prior* to any disclosure or making explicit of themselves or their individual assignments and involvements. For Heidegger, such inobtrusiveness and inconspicuousness of things, in which they are *in* themselves, is the correlate of Dasein's "absorption" in them, an absorption Heidegger deems an intrinsically *positive* phenomenon.[59]

The import of absorption and the "in itself" emerge by way of countervailing cases, where items such as a missing tool or one not otherwise useful for the job arise. Remarking on how in such instance the referential assignments become disturbed and thus practically registered—such that the "the ready-to-hand shows itself as still ready-to-hand in its unswerving presence-at-hand"—Heidegger insists that *the absence* of such reckoning, on a given tool or its assignment, is the more usual situation. Under those circumstances, ready-at-hand things exist "in themselves," he insists.[60] Things, their totalities, their involvements, and meaningfulness, all prove essentially *non-apparent* when work is successfully taking place; they remain "as holding themselves in" (*Ansichhalten*), in-drawn, and, accordingly, in themselves.[61]

Heidegger's talk of the "in itself" emerges in this way, and he indeed deems it the basis of any contact with things other than Dasein (of reference in the present broad sense) and the only viable version of the "in itself." Heidegger's suggestion, more specifically, seems to be that the condition of being held back, as found in absorption, provides a genuine in itself, because anything that subsequently appears individually, on this basis, gives itself *as already having been there* and to this extent *as already* existing *independently* of this encounter. The item in question arrives as a genuine being, owing to *having been already* there before its emergence in a given situation, and thus appears within that situation as genuinely being. Things having been registered, albeit entirely implicitly and holistically in absorption, *when* contact with a single one is explicitly made, that prior holistic givenness lets them be taken up as existing, a determination of being in which all subsequent gleanings participate. Each individual registration of being recurs to such an "already having been" as found in absorption, and its fundamental, holistic, withdrawal, it's not stepping out of itself ("*Nichtheraustren[s]*")—more or less in line with that backgrounding of discourse here previously set out.[62]

The "in itself," then, pertains to a moment when no single thing is actually given, this characterization only being applied retroactively—the thing (in its apparentness)

---

[59] BT 102; *Sein* 72–73. The German word Macquarrie and Robinson translate by absorption (and related cognates in both cases) is "*auffallen*," with obvious relation to the notion of falling discussed previously.

[60] BT 104; BT 105.

[61] BT 106; *Sein* 75. In his previous paragraph Heidegger states: "If, in our everyday concern with the 'environment,' it is to be possible for equipment ready-to-hand to be encountered in its 'Being-in-itself' [*in seinem "An-sich-sein"*], then those assignments and referential totalities in which our circumspection 'is absorbed' cannot become a theme for that circumspection."

[62] *Sein* 75. This construal of the "in itself," obviously at once, replaces and debunks the traditional notion: namely, the "in itself" as the present-at-hand thing, shorn of all involvements. That "in itself" depends on the one Heidegger sets forth, though how the present-at-hand thing and its *apophansis* as set out in the statement and this in itself are related is about to receive further investigation.

and in its "in itself" never coinciding. So conceived, Heidegger's characterization of the "in itself," nevertheless, achieves a certain genuine, albeit novel securing of being and eventually reference—leading to the new kind of realism here previously discussed. That this is the case, along with the possible limits of this conception, becomes still clearer when a notion allied to the "in itself," also set out here by Heidegger, is taken into account.

Entailed by the "in itself," along with absorption, and inconspicuousness and unobtrusiveness, as well as, finally facticity and world, turns out to be what Heidegger refers to as the having been freed or the "freegivenness" (*freigegeben* or *Freigabe*) of *everything* that Dasein may encounter and to which it may refer.[63] Everything, without limits, that may be treated or discussed recurs to the "in itself" of the ready-at-hand, according to Heidegger, since the latter also includes in such freegivenness what is *not* specifically ready-at-hand, indeed what does not derive its own character from assignments and involvements.

Speaking of the *ontological* "freeing" of things within the ready-at-hand, Heidegger indeed insists that in this case even "an entity of precisely such a sort that it ontically is not involved thereby" will also have already been freed.[64] By this Heidegger means that not only tools broadly speaking but also things like forests, stone, wind, and sun, which in their own way enter that space, are "freed" within the ready-at-hand's context and its corresponding in itself.[65]

The ready-at-hand when taken as a whole, the "in itself" in which concern is absorbed and from which all things emerge that subsequently are encountered and spoken about, thus includes in advance everything that *can* be said to be, including what properly does not belong to this sphere at all. The world, the one and sole world ontologically, albeit formally, speaking, and with it, the "in itself" found in concernful Dasein, are themselves, as it were, cross-cut in advance by all that is, including what is not wholly or simply exhausted by this first most fundamental configuration.

Thereby, as conceived by Heidegger, the "in itself" proves a passageway through which everything that comes on the scene may appear as being or existing, *even as the circumstances specific to this sphere do not necessarily apply to every item that may*

---

[63] "What we have encountered in the world," writes Heidegger, "has in its very being been freed, *freigegeben* for our concernful circumspection" (BT 114; *Sein* 83). Heidegger uses *Freigabe* later, stressing that its retains the perfect tense (*Sein* 85).("*Freigeben*" and "*Freigabe*" are not coinages of Heidegger's; they often are used in the sense of "release" or "letting loose.") The "in itself" as rooted in having already been thus ultimately dovetails with what Heidegger calls facticity, an existentiale of Dasein. Facticity describes how every Dasein confronts the conditions of own existence as handed over to it, and thus as a kind of radical fact that it must negotiate. The various structures here reviewed, meaning and the "in itself," display the thingly dimension through which this recognition finds its force (BT 174.)

[64] BT 117.

[65] On account of this development, the correlation, made some by commentators, of the occurrent or things present-at-hand with their unintelligibility as given in anxiety, though a powerful suggestion, here comes into doubt. Even if such an experience led to their unveiling as such, that possibility would be predicated on the freegiving identified here. Moreover, this notion, as traced back to anxiety, does not seem to comport well with the present-at-hand's treatment later on in BT's first part, when Aristotle and the tradition are discussed. As Philipse himself notes, the former analysis presents things in their unintelligibility; the latter, however, seemingly assigns present-at-hand things an understandability and intelligibility of their own ("Heidegger's 'Scandal'" 195 n96).

have transited across this threshold. Talking about this pretty stone, for example, I need not recall things like gravel pits or walls in which similar ones might be found, albeit without something like these circumstances already being in play, this stone's own existence also could not have been registered. Reference, understood broadly, as access to what is, remains ramified in the moment of the "in itself"; by contrast, what answers to meaning or sense, in their common acceptations, falls out as distinctly more open-ended.

The capacity of the in itself to transmit existence, while leaving the contours of what may exist underdetermined or open-ended, along with its various senses or meanings, thus appears in this notion of freegiving, specifically in its scope as extending beyond the ready-at-hand. The manner in which reference, or contact with what is, is secured, even as what is being made contact with remains unsecured, more specifically, corresponds to a certain irony or ambiguity harbored by Heidegger's choice of the term "freegiving." "Freegiving" connotes how all that is, as something that is, has been freed in advance (in the perfect, Heidegger stresses) into the in itself, thereby becoming available to subsequent appropriations—including not only the use or deployment of such material but also its further appropriation in understanding, whether that of practical circumspection, apophantics, theories of some stripe, and so on.[66] This space of freeing, the ready-at-hand, is also, however, of course, at once the space of necessity, the site of Dasein's radical *submission* to the world and worldly things. Access or reference to what is, accordingly, arises in a conjunction where Dasein and its existence are *causally* connected to things, ultimately by dint of its own needs and bodily existence, even as these things have already been integrated into ends and purposes flowing from Dasein as a condition of these things' existence being registered. Heidegger, with these provocative characterizations of the "in itself" and the "having been freed" ("*freigegeben*"), thus indicates a condition where the freedom so often assigned to Dasein (among his commentators, most recently in the guise of normativity), and the unfreedom of things are wholly implicated in one another, indeed to the point of being *reversed*: the things, not Dasein, are "free," or have been freed, with Dasein being submitted to them—in an entanglement impossible to separate or further determine in any other fashion.[67]

Heidegger's twist on the causality sometimes deemed a part of reference thus allows that causality to enter the picture in a holistic fashion, without being determined or localized in any given term or entity.[68] This is all the more the case in that the perfect of freegiving, thanks to this very coinage, gestures toward a still deeper, yet

---

[66] BT 117.
[67] Crowell, in his more recent work, Carman, and Philipse, all view important aspects of BT in terms of some version of normativity, and the list could be still further filled in. A key text for many, though not the first two, as it happens, is Heidegger's 1930 "On the Essence of Truth," which seemingly declares that truth's essence is freedom (in *Pathmarks* [Cambridge: Cambridge University Press, 1998]: 136–54). Additional comment on it is to be found a little later.
[68] More on such causality later. Obviously, the present interpretation is not, however, that of the later Dreyfus, which assimilates Heidegger's holism to Kripke's referential semantics. See Dreyfus "How Heidegger Defends the Possibility of a Correspondence Theory of Truth with respect to the Entities of Natural Science" in *Heidegger Reexamined* vol.4, eds. Hubert L. Dreyfus and Mark A. Wrathall (London: Taylor and Francis, 2002): 219–49.

structurally irretrievable past (one preceding such freeing: the *pluperfect* moment of *once having had been unfree*), wherein, as well, Dasein's presumed freedom also has been submerged. All actual things, interaction with them, and understanding of them, thus traverses this moment at once of freedom and necessity, without constraining what may follow upon it. Indeed, owing to such freegiving (of things) and submission (of Dasein), in which everything has already been withheld in itself and dissolved in the unfreedom and freedom of Dasein and of things, all subsequent capacities of picking out, manipulating, explicating, questioning, affirming, embracing, hymning, and mourning anything emerge, each in their own way bearing contact with or access to what is—without these beings' sense or these ways of talking about it there ever having been outlined or stabilized.

8.3 Assertions, Presence-at-hand, and Truth: Heidegger's Neither/Nor

Heidegger's discussion of the "in itself," in the final analysis, indicates both that all reference proves a successor to the sphere of the ready-at-hand, even as every instance of discourse by no means is tied to the specific intelligibility found in this realm. Because existence reaches beyond the world of work, in part by dint of including what is not so confined as also having been freed into that world, reference in a general, holistic fashion precedes, and subsequently can accompany any single registration of what exists. Access to what is becomes channeled holistically through the meaningfulness and meanings that reside at this level, without being restricted to them.

What remains to be ascertained, then, is the status of these and the other meanings that transpire along with things' appearances, and the events in which the latter are grasped. Granting the appearing in some fashion of actual existents other than Dasein, as well as the ability to refer to what thus appears—indicate it, trade on it, and so on—what do these capacities entail specifically for the meaningfulness (in the non-technical sense) that always accompanies such showing—especially in those privileged instances, where things are said no longer to appear from the perspective of Dasein's concern (in the world of work), but as they are "in themselves" in a more usual sense, as occurrent or present-at-hand, to use Heidegger's nomenclature? Heidegger, as noted, questions the primacy of this category and of the statement or assertion (*Aussage*), the form of discourse preeminently devoted to the exposition of the present-at-hand. According to Heidegger, the assertion necessarily loses contact with the genuine in itself, with such freegiving, and with all that it takes in and accompanies it: namely, the holistic organization of ready-at-hand things, the skeletal meaningfulness that inform these organizations, the meaning-totalities, and ultimately meaning (*be-deuten*), as well as discourse as such. In the course of Division I of BT, however, Heidegger's path indeed in some fashion twists, leading him to affirm, albeit within limits, the showing of the present-at-hand from itself and the assertion's capacity to report on it. The fate of the present-at-hand and of sense or meaning as usually understood thus lie in the details of this development.

8.3.1 Truth and Correspondence

The assertion's and the present-at-hand's seeming rehabilitation occurs when Heidegger takes up the topic of truth in the sixth chapter of *Being and Time*. Truth's treatment by Heidegger at this moment essentially falls into two phases. Heidegger first examines the truth of the assertion in its traditional understanding, as correspondence (*adequatio ad rem*), sketching this conception as held by a wide range of earlier thinkers, including Kant.[69] On this basis, Heidegger next unveils what he dubs a more primary understanding of truth than correspondence: Dasein's disclosedness, allied to those structures of world and understanding already brought forward. Dasein's own being-in-the truth—its fundamental being with, and access to things, interwoven with its own aims and existence, including confronting its own being as an issue—Heidegger insists, underpins correspondence's operation. Heidegger thus traces the latter, the truth of correspondence back to this more fundamental being-in-the-truth: the previous discoveredness of things made possible by world and Dasein's own disclosedness.

Heidegger, then, assuredly, maintains that truth, taken on its customary terms, understood as correspondence, is ontologically deficient. Heidegger in fact advances the "derivative" character of the traditional interpretation of truth, just as he earlier did the derivative character of the assertion.[70] At the same time, on this occasion, the truth of the assertion also *gives access* to Dasein's being-in-the-truth, and this feature of Heidegger's presentation reopens the question of the assertion's and its truth's understanding, rendering unclear what Heidegger finally makes of this possibility in its specificity. Previously, in section thirty-three, by contrast, the assertion's declared *derivativeness* introduced discourse. Discourse emerged on the back of doubts about the logos' primacy, thereby giving discourse priority and calling the logos and its style of showing into question.[71] In these later sections, Heidegger, contrariwise, ties the treatment of truth and Dasein that follows to the logos, to this same logos, and to what it brings forward (things occurrent or present-at-hand). The logos (and correspondence) may not give us the whole "skinny," then, when it comes to truth and Dasein's being in it; they apparently do now allow, however, for a *genuine glimpse* of the latter.

Heidegger's presentation, accordingly, is marked by an ambiguity, one that informs much of the debate pursued in the commentaries. As this ambiguity concerns the assertion in its specificity, it lets the status of the semantic and proto-semantic features of discourse as understood here be clarified; for the same reason, it eventually permits graphing a re-intersection of Heidegger's thought with those alternatives set out earlier and soon to be discussed again, especially that proposed by Davidson, since for the latter, as for the analytic tradition generally, the assertion, or statement, and its truth, serve as discourse's preeminent instances, a stance with which Gadamer at moments may concur, though arguably not Heidegger himself.[72]

---

[69] See Section 44 a): "The Traditional Conception of Truth and Its Ontological Character" (BT 257–61).

[70] BT 262ff.

[71] Carman gives a detailed account of discourse that makes some of these comparisons in the fifth chapter of his *Heidegger's Analytic*, albeit he again tilts things in the direction of a normativity in the present discussion deemed questionable (231–50).

[72] See again, Gadamer's talk of language's *Sachlichkeit* (factualness) discussed earlier. See also Thaning, *The Problem of Objectivity* 38.

The two aspect of Heidegger's account of truth just noted—that even as it questions the classic account of truth, truth taken in a more limited and traditional sense, the truth of the logos is also foregrounded in it—is in fact pivotal to perhaps the best-known discussion of this portion of BT, that of the German philosopher Ernst Tugendhat, Heidegger's erstwhile student.[73] Tugendhat's account focuses almost exclusively on the assertion and on correspondence in Heidegger's presentation, his focus intentionally answering to analytic philosophy's interests broadly speaking.[74]

Tugendhat, to be clear, of course, also recognizes Heidegger's broader notion of truth, as Dasein's disclosedness; in part, he even sympathizes with it.[75] At the same time, Tugendhat insists that truth in the narrower sense, as exhibited by the assertion and found in correspondence, remains fundamentally unexplained by Heidegger, a criticism only possible, it should be noted, insofar as Heidegger assigns the assertion's operation some privilege at this moment in his text.[76] Tugendhat maintains that though Heidegger may be right about Dasein's temporal field and practical life serving as backdrop and giving an opening on to things, his stance in BT gives no account of the being true and false of assertions themselves.[77] Accordingly, Heidegger's discussion falls short of genuinely recognizing that preeminently critical self-consciousness made uniquely available by assertions, on Tugendhat's view.[78]

Tugendhat's criticism, above all, focuses on the assertion's capacity for being non-insightful, false, which he denies Heidegger's account of truth as unconcealedness can properly credit. This version of Tugendhat's criticism of Heidegger arguably turns out to be his weakest, however. Heidegger's description of correspondence, as Tugendhat himself recognizes, and as Heidegger also indicates, draws on Husserl's notion of fulfillment in the sixth of his *Logical Investigations*. On Husserl's account, the false functions just as does the true, however, and both can equally be seen to depend on what Heidegger calls unconcealedness, or the truth of Dasein, as will be further discussed shortly.[79]

---

[73] Ernst Tugendhat, "Heidegger's Idea of Truth," in Brice Wachterhauser, ed. *Hermeneutics and Truth* [Evanston, Ill: Northwestern University Press, 1994]: 83–97).

[74] Daniel Dahlstrom in his "Transcendental Truth and the Truth that Prevails" (in *Transcendental Heidegger*, ed. Crowell and Malpas) contests Karl-Otto Apel's claim, subsequently strongly advanced by Lafont, that Heidegger in fact recanted his view of truth in the light of Tugendhat's criticism (72–3). This issue is not finally of prime importance here. Dahlstrom, largely drawing on the *Beitrage*, also gives an overview of Heidegger's changing view of truth specifically in relation to his changing notion of *Sein*, Being, which Dahlstrom dates to 1930. Dahlstrom, it seems to me, has an especially nice grasp on this last point.

[75] "Heidegger's Idea" 96.

[76] Tugendhat declares that "when we inquire into a pregiven assertion, we are trying to verify it," and that "the truth of an elementary assertion is decidable," in contrast to "untrue meaning" and its "clarification" (Ibid., 94). Heidegger's framework, according to Tugendhat, only allows for the latter.

[77] Ibid., 94–5.

[78] In his concluding remarks, Tugendhat attempts to rethink the possibility of "critical consciousness," tied to the assertion, on the basis of the disclosedness that Heidegger makes available, which Tugendhat himself does not regard as a form of truth strictly speaking (Ibid., 96).

[79] In L.VI. 6, truth is modeled as a coincidence between what Husserl calls signitively expressed intentions—that is, *statements* such as "the grass is green"—and what is presented, as Husserl likes to say, "in flesh and blood," first and foremost, things in perception, which can be categorially formed (here the grass being green) (*Logical Investigations* vol. 2, trans. J. N. Findlay [New Jersey: Humanities Press, 1970]: 674–706). Yet on this account, the false, the non-disclosing assertion, to show itself *as false*, must also refer back to something given in "flesh and blood," something

Tugendhat, nevertheless, at this moment does put his finger on a deeper and broader question, one of great importance here. How can the mode of showing specific to the assertion as such, *whether true or false*, and, with that, how what it reveals *either as being or not being the case*, be identified in its own right and returned to again with the same referents and understanding, thus offering an object for further criticism and judgment, as Tugendhat ultimately wishes?

Heidegger's view of discourse, like the present one, it should by now be clear, entails a very tight connection between the things or subject matters that come to light in it and the discourse that presents them. Whatever the ultimate background or genealogy of such events, on any given occasion, Heidegger insists, things show themselves as and what they are *from themselves*, which is why *in all of the different registers of discourse*, truth or insight of some kind must be in question. To be sure, an understanding, an interpretation or *Auslegung*, of the appropriate kind accompanies such showing. Nevertheless, the "as" does *not* simply recur to the interpreting. (Heidegger's is *not* Nietzsche's mobile army of metaphors.) Things' appearances are not the correlates of any specifically linguistic or verbal capacities, as in Nietzsche, or even in Gadamer's or McDowell's quite different accounts—since for Heidegger in BT discourse, not language, precedes them all—nor are such appearances the correlates of any kind of identifiable meaning-endowing acts, as in Husserl.

Put most simply, interpreting understanding lets things be seen as something, but what is seen, and *as* what *it is* seen, again, recurs *to the something*, not to the interpretation. The hammer, having been taken apart from its involvements, including its serviceability, comes into view *as a hammer*, and, at this moment, these involvements and meanings are seen and understood *as intrinsic to it*, as being "in" the hammer, as Heidegger likes to say. Though, as earlier noted, one could not "see" a "hammer" at all without involvement's contribution, the hammer shows itself as a hammer *from itself*, rather than recurring to Dasein's intentionality or any other factor. The "as" emanates from *what* is talked about, and, in tandem with this, both it and discourse's subject matter appear as already having been there, though only at this moment emerging as such.[80]

In the present instance, ultimately on the table, then, will be at once the intelligibility of the articulations found in discourse, but also that of the showings of the things themselves, the two here coinciding at least to some degree. The occurrent or present-a-hand, however, is indeed *the* candidate for such stability on the part of things; in

---

itself able to be discovered in Dasein's more fundamental "disclosedness," granting for the moment Heidegger's inflection of Husserl's presentation, such as, in this case, the grass being brown. The claim that "the statement 'the picture is on the wall' is false," the picture being Heidegger's example, relies on the same showing (seeing for example that the picture is really on the table or not in the room) that allows for the truth of it to be registered in the cases where it holds (BT 260). The false and the true, accordingly, come to pass in the same way in respect to the more fundamental truth that Heidegger assigns to Dasein.

[80] Again, the preceding discussion shows how this can occur without assigning any occult properties to things, thinghood, or objects. On Heidegger's account, entities show themselves meaningfully from themselves owing to emerging from a background, in which they and their meaningfulness already have been jointly submerged. I can see a hammer as a hammer, because it already has been a hammer, in its in itself, prior to any awareness of it as such, and thus it can appear to me as one. This schema demystifies much of what appears as magical in so-called object-oriented ontology.

question with its status, accordingly, is ultimately both articulateness on the thing side of the present-at-hand and its intelligibility on the discourse side, though, at the present juncture, owing to Tugendhat's way of posing the problem, the issue pertaining to discourse is foregrounded.

To stay with this phase, then, how the intelligibility found in the assertion (say in the statement "that hammer is made of metal and wood") can really be a shared acquisition, as Husserl would put it—something able to be repeatedly understood and evaluated—on Heidegger's account, and the present one, remains far from clear. If understanding, in the case now of things present-at-hand, answers to an act of understanding, allowing the showing of the things from themselves, as Heidegger insists, how can the articulations specific to the assertion as such, the logically articulated claim, be identified and maintained, along with its attribution to the relevant things in question, across numerous apparitions and subsequent evaluations in the way that statements and critical consciousness seem to demand, given that the individual things may no longer necessarily be there and thus may not be *able* to show themselves in subsequent iterations? At the epoch of BT, discourse indeed stands prior to language, and, in these instances, language does not yet probatively operate. Moreover, again, Heidegger, unlike Husserl, does not have an independent or autonomous intentionality or ideality to fall back on, nor does he have any sort of first-person normativity to account for the assertion's particular logical and semantic labor, at least as here glossed.[81] Consequently, if the "as something" is in the thing, and both it and what is said are tied to an *event* of understanding, the assertion and its sense risk losing all specificity and the entire possibility of any semantics broadly speaking, as well as talk of things showing themselves, definitively comes into doubt. Not only may the thing's own being as present-at-hand cease to be distinguishable from other recourses to it that occur in everyday life, as captured by merely occasional utterances or exclamations like "allen wrench," or "too shady," but similarly, the assertion, may also lack the ability to retain its style of insight or understanding and sustain the sort of repeated evaluation and critical consciousness that Tugendhat identifies. In a nutshell, neither what the assertion says nor what it talks about would be capable of yielding truth as usually understood, if Tugendhat's doubts are valid; yet discourse in Heidegger and as here conceived seems not to function without some such possibility.[82]

Tugendhat's question finds its genuine force, then, just where Heidegger's own thinking proves most radical, in the holistic viewpoint just sketched, affirmed as

---

[81] To be clear, in his later writings, Husserl himself identifies a version of this problem and identifies it with what he calls sedimentation: the buried senses of assertions found specifically in scientific traditions and that of their founding intuitions. (See among other places, his fragment "The Origin of Geometry" in *The Crisis of European Sciences and Transcendental Phenomenology*, trans. David Carr [Evanston: Northwestern University Press, 1970]: 353–78.) Heidegger, lacking Husserl's transcendental subject, not to mention deeming modern scientific knowledge a form of errancy, cannot presume, as Husserl does, that original senses and experiences are retrievable.

[82] To be clear, problems, relating to indexicality and demonstrativity, attend to accounts of assertions that grant to them a logical or linguistic or normative independence of the sort Tugendhat envisions. Though how assertions on such construals can retain their presumed meanings is clearer, how they can register the singular beings they talk about, even after decades of inquiry and debate, remains a question in analytic discussions. (See my "Pragmatism and Semantics: Husserl and Derrida" for further treatment of this problem.)

lying at the basis of all showing, of all contact with things, and in claiming that an understanding and showing emanating from the things in question, including that corresponding to present-at-hand statements and their truth, results from it. It now turns out that this radical conception, allowing for affirming in totality the existence of what discourse speaks about may prove incompatible with any truth about these things and any repeated understanding of discourse's own expressions, at least of a theoretical and factual sort.

Fortunately, within certain bounds, Heidegger does have a response to Tugendhat's query, one that clarifies the status of the semantic and the proto-semantic in his own thought in respect to both statements and to things. Tugendhat may not have known of this potential rejoinder, however, since it arrives, not in BT itself, but in lectures that Heidegger delivers in 1925–6 just before the former's composition, which were unpublished at the time Tugendhat's essay appeared.[83] There, the topic Tugendhat wrongly identifies as crucial, falsehood, Heidegger himself uses as the guiding thread for his discussion, already suggesting that in these lectures Tugendhat's specific concerns may be met.

8.3.2 Neither/Nor: Truth and Logic

In *Logic*, by way of a still provocative account of Aristotle's treatment of the logos, Heidegger indeed locates the assertion's form, its ongoing truth-presenting powers, in the only fashion his own vantage point permits: not in intentionality, nor in some other species of normativity, as so many of even his best commentators suggest, but in a configuration ultimately found in the things themselves, in those present-at-hand things assertions speak about. Heidegger, that is, following Aristotle, opts for the second hypothesis brought out earlier: not that discourse and its meanings (and their attendant intentions and understanding) would stabilize things, but rather that things and their character stabilize discourse and its intelligibility. "Aristotle," Heidegger writes, "showed how a condition of the possibility of falsehood lies *within beings themselves and the possible ways they can be*"—thereby underscoring beings' primacy in respect to truth and explicitly to falsehood, which is here indeed Heidegger's guiding theme.[84]

The possibility of an assertion's being true or false thus lies in the things, "not in something subjective," Heidegger goes on to further clarify. This is the case, both because *things* show how they are or are not and because the *logical form* of the statement ultimately proves rooted in these same things, on Heidegger's reading of Aristotle.[85]

---

[83] *Logic: The Question of Truth*, trans. Thomas Sheehan (Bloomington, IN: Indiana University Press, 2010).
[84] *Logic* 140; my emphasis.
[85] The fuller citation runs: "Aristotle showed how a condition of the possibility of falsehood lies within beings themselves and the possible ways they can be. This is a discovery that later fell into absolute oblivion (where it remains today), because the problem of truth was no longer understood. We think that error and deception are something subjective and have their origin in one's thinking when it violates its own laws and the like" (Ibid., 140).

More specifically, Aristotle suggests that two operations, those of *diaresis* (separation or distinguishing) and *sunthesis* (taking or setting together), characterize the logos or the statement. The logos takes apart and takes together simultaneously. Statements focus on a given thing (thus taking it *apart from* its background), and they do so in a specific way (taking it *together with* some specific feature of itself or its situation). The assertion's work in this regard thus depends on those same forestructures of the understanding set out earlier. These broader, specifically hermeneutic possibilities pertaining to all discourse enter into apophantic utterances as well, and necessarily so, given that beings inform all discourse, including in this instance.[86]

In turn, *sunthesis* and *diaresis* as specifically *logical designations* correspond to, and ultimately depend on, a structure *found in present-at-hand things themselves*—specifically, in a certain class of things, composite things. Composite things, the subjects of assertions, can lie together with and lie apart from other "things"—for example, this cup with cold (or being cold) or heat (being hot), Heidegger states. An assertion, accordingly, is true when *what* an assertion affirms or denies *as* together (or *as* separated) in the thing *is found* together or apart in *it* (this cup is, stands with cold, or stands apart from cold); when not, it is false. In this fashion, the *sunthesis* and *diaresis* characteristic of the assertion, according to Heidegger, stem from *the things assertions speak about* and the possibilities inherent in *them*.

Things present-at-hand account for the assertion's way of showing, its formatting of what is, thereby allowing this formal feature to be repeated and remain the same. Moreover, things do similar work for the intelligibility of the statement's *contents*—thereby together accounting for the assertion's overall "semantics." What might actually lie together or lie apart in specific composite things is not unlimited, Heidegger points out. Such possibilities for composition instead exist within a range. (The noise I hear in the Black Forest could never lie together with or apart from the square root of sixty-four, or, to take Heidegger's example, with "the Shah of Iran."). This range of possibilities, in turn, redounds to the thing. In this case, ultimately in question, however, are not further composites, but simples, of the kind that Aristotle calls *ousiai*, or essences. Things present-at-hand are implicated in such essences in various ways, thereby providing the statement's *contents* with an intelligibility beyond any single occasion of utterance, interpretation, or disclosure. Things and thingly determinations (*ousiai*), accordingly, undergird both the assertion's *structure*, or format, as well as its *contents*, allowing both to be repeated and understood.

Consequently, how Tugendhat's concerns might possibly be met on Heidegger's terms comes into view. If Aristotle is correct, features inhering in things present-at-hand permit a relative stabilization of the assertion's structure and its semantics. In both cases, a possibility that things may show themselves as together and as apart from other things (or subject matters)—possibilities already being given in certain ways, ultimately thanks to the forestructures of all discourse—in turn permit statements to

---

[86] Heidegger insists that the thing when it enters certain kinds of interpretation, as present-at-hand, is cut off from the totality of involvements, but also (BT 202) that in *every* interpretation that totality recedes to the background (cf. BT 201, 202). I take this to be the difference between talk of something "hammer-shaped, made of wood and iron" and talk of "a hammer," in the two cases, respectively.

be meaningful, and to show themselves and what they say to be either true or false in the fashion that Tugendhat wishes.

Nevertheless, though up to this point in the *Logic* Heidegger's presentation closely tracks Aristotle's, it next proceeds to an even more extended treatment of the forestructure and the "as," which, in BT, at least, called into question the logos' primacy. Accordingly, what Heidegger himself makes of these findings in BT and in the *Logic*, to what extent he ultimately endorses them, at the present stage of the inquiry has not been fully ascertained. Above all, the role played by *ousia* or essence for Heidegger is critical and must be further determined, since on this issue obviously depends the "semantics" of things present-at-hand and the discourse about them as just set out.[87]

Logic also points toward an answer to the question of *ousia*'s status. To preview that conclusion, what emerges from this problem's consideration is ultimately an *agnosticism* on Heidegger's part when it comes to the ultimate validity of the assertion and the truth of the present-at-hand. Accordingly, whether such intelligibility is indeed continuously available and critical consciousness is entirely assured in the way Tugendhat wishes ultimately remains *suspended* for Heidegger, neither simply affirmed nor simply denied. Beyond recognizing that statements, corresponding to the revelation of things present-at-hand, do claim to do such work, to show things as they are, whether this form of discourse that Heidegger himself deems "unavoidable" does or does not have the priority with which the philosophical tradition almost always credits it, remains unresolved, as does the standing of *what* it discloses, of the present-at-hand itself.[88]

After all, no isomorphism *can* connect that freeing that everything undergoes in the ready-at-hand to the showings found in the present-at-hand and in statements concerning it; a divergence, or *decalage* remains between such access to things as holistically determined and the semantic and proto-semantic features at once common to statements and what they talk about. As a result, the assertion's grasp of what is cannot, as in Husserl's *Ideas I* (or in McDowell's work), prove once and for all the preeminent instance of discourse generally; neither, however, are it, and what it brings forward, simply disqualified or exiled from accessing truth. The assertion and what it shows, at this moment, instead are affirmed by Heidegger as *inherently situated in time*; they appear in a tradition, or related traditions of talk, with their own branchings and further transmutations, including local controversies that may be examined and traced in their own right, among them the variations contemporary scientific discourse presents. The *ultimate validity* of these findings, or of their various avatars, however, as opposed to this implication in time, such temporal dependence, was *never* Heidegger's concern in *Logic*. Logical considerations' own temporal embeddedness

---

[87] Hubert Dreyfus, while recognizing a version of the holism of BT's setting out limned earlier, attempted to account for the assertion's functioning on this basis by bringing in essences conceived in proximity to their construal in Kripke's pathbreaking work, thus as involving causal connections with the things in question by way of rigid designators. Wrathall offers an alternative strategy that affirms essences on other terms, while also drawing on *Logic*, one arguably more faithful to Heidegger's text. (For Dreyfus, see "How Heidegger defends the possibility of a correspondence theory"; for Wrathall, see chapter one of *Unconcealedness*.)

[88] Heidegger calls the truth of statements "unavoidable" in "On the Essence of Truth" (103).

and consequent possibility of variance was. Hence, Heidegger's presentation can and, really in the end, must be agnostic about these outcomes, concerning the statement and the present-at-hand's truth.

To be sure, some of Heidegger's best commentators have taken him to be endorsing or at least adapting Aristotle's notion of essence, in order to renew Aristotle's logical approach (albeit as simultaneously inflected by Heidegger's appropriation of Husserl's *Logical Investigations*). The second category of commentary previously discussed views Heidegger as reviving a notion of essence, either adjacent to Kripke's or of an historical kind (consisting in how things of a certain sort are sighted relative to a given age).[89] Thereby, these commentators quite ingeniously view the assertion as assured on philosophical terms, and its ability to speak the same over time and so access selfsame present-at-hand beings as secured.

These approaches, however, overlook the theme that Heidegger himself foregrounds at this moment, and thus the resolutely *hermeneutic* manner with which here and everywhere, I believe, he approaches logical issues. In BT, most clearly, but in *Logic* as well, Heidegger does not aim either to *defend or condemn* the logos, nor even those *ousiai* on which they depend, but indeed to *interpret them* and their operation, and, with them, philosophy as a whole. Heidegger, more concretely, approaches this type of understanding from the first as *a tradition* of discourse, in a manner that departs from the attempt to clear up a philosophical problem on the terms almost all of his commentators appear to take for granted. His actual standpoint instead amounts to a "neither/nor" (as does that of the present endeavor on this same point); he finds neither a new ground for the assertion's functioning *nor* ones for disqualifying it once and for all.

That Heidegger's interest is a hermeneutic one, focused on the temporality, historicity, and traditionality of apophantic utterance, rather than on their ultimate validity *or lack thereof* in *Logic* becomes most plain in that the two sets of reference points for its treatment noted earlier—*ousia*, along with the entire logical structure of composite things, and the hermeneutically and situationally oriented holistic contact with things in themselves—come together for Heidegger, unlike Aristotle, solely on the plane of *time*. Heidegger in the *Lectures* indeed isolates in Aristotle's account a temporal dimension that Aristotle himself ignores. The composite's operation, assertions being *false* in the way just sketched, Heidegger tells us, depends on taking together or as separate what is not *now* such (or the reverse in the case of the statement's being true, what *now* is such) in the "moment in which I now live," according to Heidegger. Falsehood and truth, while mapping on to the capacity of things present-at-hand as set out earlier, thus require a temporal dimension and reference that is wholly *unaccounted for by*

---

[89] In particular, Wrathall, in part following the lead of Dreyfus, but also taking the latter's (Kripkean) account of essences in a different direction, has suggested that the foregoing considerations allow combining the radical holism of Heidegger's account of the ready-at-hand with the authoritativeness, normativity, and finality usually associated with the assertion and its truth, with what Wrathall earlier on calls "propositional truth" (20). Consonant with such holism, the essentialism that has come forward in Aristotle, ultimately of an historical kind for Wrathall, consisting in how things of a certain sort are to be sighted relative to a given age, permits a stabilization of the meaning of assertions and what they talk about, firming up the possibility of propositional truth on the otherwise novel philosophical terrain Wrathall and I agree that Heidegger lays bare.

Aristotle, and one that, not accidently, possesses an indexical character. Compounding this feature, Heidegger insists, is an equally profound temporal factor at work in the determination of Aristotle's *simples*: in the being, the "*ον*" in which what is together and apart are found, as well as in *ousia*, in essence as such. Their framing as being and as essence recur to temporality, now, however, understood as *timeless presence*. Aristotle's treatment of assertions and composites thus rests on a present and making present (*Gegenwart*), accompanied by a "present presence [*anwesende Anwesenheit*]" posited by Aristotle as inherently timeless. Thereby, an "unfathomable problematic" of being and time, of which "the Greeks had no suspicion" invests Aristotle's treatment of the logos, according to Heidegger, albeit this treatment is the one that Heidegger himself nevertheless deems most advanced.[90]

Heidegger's own focus in *Logic*, accordingly, is not on the re-validation of logic or the logos as such, nor its skeptical questioning, but on *temporality*, as ultimately furnishing the horizon for the logos and its accompanying presentation of beings and of their Being. This theme remains undiscussed by any of those who endorse this account, or, for that matter, who dismiss it. Neither Aristotle nor the rest of the tradition, of course, are explicitly aware of this matrix, which embodies a perspective that also departs, then, from most of Heidegger's commentators. Heidegger himself, however, clearly views the logos as residing within an interpretative and hermeneutic horizon different than any that the philosophical tradition recognizes. Recurring to the problem of the logos, at the dawn of logic's invention in the so-called West, Heidegger, specifically, wants to show how it rests on an *interpretation of being and time* that for Heidegger is to serve as a stepping stone for introducing his own new different *interpretations* of Being, time, and their relations. Heidegger's primary interest in the phenomena of logic and of meaning is, then, hermeneutic, ultimately aimed at the *Seinsfrage and at a hermeneutic of Being*—the same mission that BT also announces, while leaving the phenomena themselves otherwise untouched, except for laying bare their fundamental contours in Aristotle and traditional philosophy.

Accordingly, though for Heidegger the possibility represented by the assertion remains intact, it does so now only as a possibility lodged in *the tradition that he is interpreting* (and ultimately in the broader working of *Sein*, and eventually its sending), without, however, being otherwise embraced *or* rejected. The present-at-hand and statements concerning it are indeed never accounted for in any final way in either BT or the Lectures; nor, however, again, are these phenomenon denied all pertinence.[91] It could be said that the assertion, and what appears over and against it, remain *one*

---

[90] *Logic* 163; *Logik: Die Frage nach der Wahrheit* (*Gesamtausgabe 21*), ed. Walter Biemel Frankfurt am Main: Vittorio Klostermann, 1976), 193.

[91] Wrathall's account in its details attests to this lack of closure, it seems to me, since Heidegger's talk of the "truth of essence" (that Wrathall invokes to explain his own historical essences) not only is not propositional, as Wrathall points out, but also does not concern things present-at-hand that propositions eventually treat in the way Wrathall suggests. Though Wrathall notes at points the connection to *Sein* and its truth, he in fact redirects Heidegger's treatment of *ousia* as concerns these matters back to the traditional logical issues and questions. Yet the citation from "On the Essence of Ground" that Wrathall cites is not addressed at all to things, but to their *Being*; the latter, ultimately captured in notions like "history" or "nature," according to Heidegger, explicitly *lacks*, he tells us, both essence and concept (104–05).

possible fate of what exists and of discourse, at which Heidegger himself *never ceases to wonder.* Yet beyond such wonder, Heidegger indeed does not give this problem a resolution capable of being taken up within standard philosophical discourse, whether in its contemporary guise or some other.

Heidegger thus does not embrace a reductionism that simply cancels the logos' force, burying these possibilities in "a blob of holism," as might have seemed likely earlier, but instead takes them as phenomena to be interpreted, inroads into an interpretation of the tradition, thanks to the latter already trading on time and hence already unknowingly standing within its movement.[92] Where, then, does that leave the present inquiry in respect to these questions, given its own lack of interest in pursuing Heidegger's new hermeneutic path, at least insofar as the *Seinsfrage* is concerned? For Heidegger, discourse's emergence in practical contexts, as well as that of the things it talks about, outstrips the intelligibility found in the present-at-hand, without for all that simply ruling out the latter's sort of understanding and truth. The present project, in turns, thanks to this opening, treads a perhaps still more capacious path. It affirms the aletheiological equivalence of all sorts of discourse, even as it acknowledges that discourse's different instances, finally its different individual instances, also have their own historicity and thus distinct ways of showing what is. Every instance of discourse possesses a power of disclosure and is in its own way aimed at truth, on the present account, such that the borders between thinking, knowing, poetizing, and so on, while not unrecognizable, are also not aletheiologically fundamental.[93]

Yet for the present endeavor, thus arguably standing at a still further distance from the modeling of discourse found in the logos, itself entirely removed from any notion of *ousia* (even as founded in and given by philosophical traditionality), the question of how truth functions within this conception must be examined further; how all discourse, not just that making assertions about the present-at-hand, can be conceived as answering to truth, and, specifically, how these disclosures and discoveries operate in those repetitions foregrounded by literature and the textual (where "the moment I am now" that Heidegger himself fixes on, seems not to function as it does in Aristotle) remains not fully clear. Though some progress has been made in understanding how the things talked about may stabilize discourse—at least to the extent of clearing

---

[92] The phrase comes from Stephen Käufer's "Logic" (in *A Companion to Heidegger* eds. Hubert L. Dreyfus and Mark Wrathall [Oxford: Blackwell, 2005: 144–55; 151). Käufer offers interpretations at moments close to that here, when it comes to the "as" and interpretation, insisting that "entities are normative for assertions about them " (152). He further insists, however, that "entities do not produce the norms. Dasein's understanding of being produces norms in such a way that the entities govern the adequacy" (153). In the following section, an alternative to the second claim is offered, which also recurs to understanding (and discourse) without recourse to a normativity that any speakers or hearers know or command.

[93] For Heidegger, doubtless, all discourse in some fashion discloses and to this degree participates in the truth in the fashion embraced here. At the same time, Heidegger seems to give less weight than the present text, or for that matter Gadamer's, to the specific truth of the different sorts of discourse found in the humanities: law, history, literary studies and so on. Instead he emphasizes how history, and poetry, and philosophy or thinking, aim at something other than, or in addition to, truth, something that founds (or later "waits") beyond revealing or disclosing some facet of existence and its understanding in their own right. This founding/waiting/inviting historical-epochal thinking is what the present project cuts itself off from, at least in Heidegger's form.

up the latter's dependence on entities' showing and how such showing is possible—nevertheless, the fashion in which instances of individuated and specifically "textual" or literary discourse, along with any other, function as shared acquisitions, and the status of the truth they claim to disclose needs to be set forth more perspicuously. The assertion may isolate and coalesce in its own fashion the being taken together and apart of all discourse; yet aside from its own self-understanding as a tradition, how finally its own or any other speaking and what it may disclose can be accessed still remains to be determined, since the assertion finally in Heidegger's own treatment has proved to be comprehended by discourse and its more global operation.

To accomplish this task, one more thinker and program, accordingly, must be brought to bear. Davidson's account of truth and discourse, supplemented by Heidegger's, allows for the sort of individuation that discourse here undergoes to be further brought on board and its consequences for these issues to be more precisely gauged. Davidson's thinking, like Heidegger's, penetrates all the way to discourse's roots in individual events.[94] At the same time, though their projects are often viewed as proximate, their differences when it comes to logic, the assertion, and the appearing of things potentially draw that proximity into question. Accordingly, to take this different orientation into account, and to eventually allow Heidegger's stance toward truth and the semantic to be brought into conversation with Davidson's, the previous situating of Heidegger's views on the assertion and perception in respect to a range of thinkers on these matters, including McDowell and Gadamer, must be further canvassed. After reviewing this broader panoply of positions on assertion and perceptions, a closer look at truth's operation (including at once the understandability of things and of the discourse about them) may then be had by way of reference to Davidson as well as to Heidegger, finally permitting literature's and the text's status to emerge.

---

[94] I am, of course, aware that some recent treatments of Davidson reject this claim about his proximity to discourse; starting from his earliest essays in the philosophy of language, they see him engaged in framing a truth-theoretical semantics, capable of formalizing natural language. I myself disagree with this as an interpretation of Davidson's thinking. These commentaries and their consequences will be addressed in Chapter 9.

9

Discourse and Text (Davidson and Heidegger)

To eventually tease out what discourse and truth may be across the distinct traditions represented by Heidegger and Davidson, it is indeed worthwhile to take a step back and survey a group of related thinkers in respect to how they stand toward perception, toward statements about perception, and the insights such statements may deliver. As has been seen, McDowell borrows from Gadamer, while being in explicit conversation with Davidson, so his vantage point on these questions, along with Gadamer's own, should be included. In turn, Gadamer's perspective obviously connects with Heidegger's, whose own view, as often, usefully compares with that of his teacher Husserl. Accordingly, beginning from Husserl who establishes a baseline, the remainder of these thinkers may be surveyed, culminating with Heidegger himself. The more specific differences between Heidegger and Davidson, and their respective holisms, thanks to the foregoing, can then be brought to light.

9.1 Perceptions and Statements in Husserl, McDowell, Gadamer, Davidson, and Heidegger

On the table initially are the same questions Heidegger addresses in his *Logic*: How is what is given in perception to be understood and how gloss statements or assertions concerning what is so given? Husserl's treatment of these questions in *Ideas I* provides a measure for approaching this problem, against which the other responses may be gauged, since only Husserl grants to perceptions senses in their own right, operating without any recourse to discourse or language.

Husserl calls these senses noema (intendeds), and, more generally, in Husserl they are correlated with intendings (*noeses*)—here, ones specific to the level of perception. Within perception, the noetic-noematic correlation gives us things, attributes, properties, and so on—to which, according to Husserl, discourse and the logically articulated meanings at work in assertions (his *Bedeutungen*) may or may not come to be added. Though logical meanings ultimately are in part founded on specifically perceptual senses (*Sinne*), they are deemed by Husserl to be of a different order than perceptual ones, with capacities, and an autonomy, of their own. Husserl's analyses of these specifically perceptual matrices, in turn, show how a color or a tune, a chair, or the sun makes itself known to those confronting them, bringing out the essential, or "eidetic" guidelines belonging to percepts of these and other sorts.[1]

As framed by Husserl, what is given in perception is immediately understandable or meaningful, and this accounts for the objects so given being able to be recurred to both as they are and as identical with themselves. At the same time, Husserl's analyses confront certain problems. Laying claim to pre-predicative and nondiscursive senses operating *on the side of the perceived*, the question arises of their character as *senses* and what relation they have to the objects, things, and subject matters presented through them—are these senses the same or different from such things, or how otherwise may the sense and the things, or objects, be related?[2] Similarly, since they are senses finally thanks to being the intendeds of some intention, this intending itself, the noetic factor, the moment of *the perceiving*, also elicits questions. Ultimately the gathering and imparting of sense at the perceptual level for Husserl recurs to his version of a transcendental subject, the relation of which to the so-called mundane world and the beings in it has long been a subject of controversy in the literature. Thus, to rigorously parse and describe at this level both the intendings and the intended, as well as the presuppositions each entails, remains a labor, at the very least, still not fully performed, despite Husserl's own significant endeavors.[3]

McDowell's approach, in the present setting, can be said to fill the breach left by Husserl's. McDowell arguably improves on the foregoing insofar as for him there is no level of perception standing apart from discourse. McDowell's account bypasses the moment of perceptual *Sinn* in its specificity. Though the perceive*d* genuinely gives itself meaningfully, according to McDowell, it does so as already *conceptualized*; what is perceived comes already informed by those ideations found in discourse and language. An inherent intelligibility, and thus accountability, pertaining to all our reports on the world, especially our perceptual reports, operates, ultimately making possible the standpoint of the modern sciences and other sorts of knowledge—essentially, that same critical consciousness that Tugendhat wants to preserve.[4]

Yet McDowell's advantage over Husserl arguably also indicates his stance's signal weakness. Husserl's concerns haunt McDowell in that McDowell nowhere accounts for language's concrete operation when lending concepts to what he sometimes calls

---

[1] See *Ideas I* 213 ff. for Husserl's discussion of and distinction between the perceptual sense and its expression.

[2] Such problems, of course, stand at the heart of the now famous *noema* debate, initiated by Hubert Dreyfus in his "The Perceptual Noema: Gurwitsch's Critical Contribution," (in Aron Gurwitsch & Lester E. Embree eds., *Life-World and Consciousness* [Evanston, Ill., Northwestern University Press, 1972]: 135-9). John Drummond's *Husserlian Intentionality and Non-Foundational Realism: Noema and Object* (Dordrecht: Springer, 1990) is the most sustained treatment of this issue in the phenomenological tradition, while also presenting a new interpretation of Husserl's thinking as a whole.

[3] Dan Zahavi over the last few decades, in part drawing on indications to be found in the early writings of Maurice Merleau-Ponty, as well as a number of treatments found in Husserl's own *Nachlass*, has offered a wide-ranging and also ambitious re-reading of Husserl's project that offers a new view of Husserl's account of subjectivity, including as it pertains to the present problem. (See, among others, *Self-Awareness and Alterity* [Evanston, Ill: Northwestern University Press, 1999].)

[4] See *Mind and Nature* 66-7 where McDowell unfolds in summary why "we must conceive experiences as states or occurrences in which capacities that belong to spontaneity are in play in actualizations of receptivity" (66).

"perception's deliverances." Given that McDowell, like Gadamer, views language and discourse in combination, a tension resides in the difference between the concept's and word's presumed generality and the singularity of perceived things. Moreover, it is impossible for McDowell to give any account of the specific operation of language and words in *molding* perceptions, lest all the classical problems concerning unsynthesized sensuous substrates found in Kant, and perhaps some versions of Husserl, return; accordingly, the notion that the conceptualizations in our discourse immediately inform the perceived things remains at best a desideratum in McDowell's *Mind and Nature*.[5]

Of course, it is to answer this question in a different fashion that McDowell turns to Gadamer, ultimately to a kind of nexus between Gadamer and Wittgenstein, that also resonates with Hegel. Gadamer's account of language as tradition should fill in the acquisition and functioning of that second nature, whereby perceived things come already informed by concepts without further ado or discussion. As noted earlier, Gadamer, too, privileges the capacity of language for perceptual and factual reports of all sorts; he distinguishes this faculty by speaking of what he calls language's facticalness or factualness—its "*Sachlichkeit*."[6]

As already reviewed, however, factualness and its accomplishments redound to Gadamer's own understanding of language. Hence, its affirmation raises all the questions that here earlier emerged about Gadamer's construal of language and discourse. More specifically, Gadamer's recourse to the *Husserlian* model of the thing in perception in order to explain how to conceive that vector toward one single language that all languages purportedly harbor, arguably is a *petitio principii*, on grounds now perhaps even more striking than those earlier set out. In the present context, it is clear, were Husserl's account of perception viable in the first place, there indeed would be no need to adopt McDowell's position, or for McDowell to recur to Gadamer, since the question of perception's workings would already be resolved. Hence, appealing to that model in order to explain language's relation to world, on this account and for the reasons previously given, finally falls short of the explication at which Gadamer aims, drawing into question the ability of Gadamer's thought to perform the work in respect to perception that McDowell and Gadamer himself desire.

Davidson stands still further from the position found in Husserl wherein the perceived is granted its own sort of sense. For Davidson, perceptions are not endowed with *perceptual* senses; moreover, their deliverances also do not bear *linguistic or discourse-based meanings or concepts*. To this degree, Davidson, albeit by omission, "remedies" the difficulties posed by the functioning of language and words in

---

[5] In the introduction to his first book, as already noted, Crowell raises a version of this criticism of McDowell—in the service, however, of arguing that a more genuine transcendental analysis along Husserlian lines is needed to fill this same gap (*Space* 17).

[6] As noted earlier, facts of the sort that interest him and McDowell can be registered thanks to the factualness (*Sachlichkeit*) inherent in language, which seems at once to designate language's own predilection for the statement-form as well as its own factual existence. Language's factualness accounts for our access to matters of fact (*Sachverhalte*), Gadamer insists, apparently offering a substitute on the level of language for Heidegger's notion of a facticity (*Faktizität*) specific to Dasein (TM442-43; *Wahrheit* 421).

McDowell's and Gadamer's account, which themselves would in turn remediate the opacity of Husserl's specifically perceptual senses.[7]

In regard to perceptions as such, Davidson claims, more specifically, that while a perception, in the sense of perceiving something, may well cause someone to hold a belief—seeing the green tree can be why I believe that this tree is green—only *beliefs* are grounds for other beliefs and not any supposed contribution made by the perceived itself. *The statement* concerning what is perceived, ultimately in its relation to other statements, thus is the appropriate site for understanding the truth of such reports. On Davidson's account, furthermore, such statements and what is genuinely given in perception are only *causally* related to one another; hence, there is no requirement to say how the perceived as perceived enters language, no less how it functions within a purely perceptual intentional matrix, since the perception (or the perceived) itself remains stalwartly nonlinguistic and nondiscursive. One may still make statements of perception, of course, as well as those claims that follow from them—Davidson attends to both constantly.[8] Yet perception's "deliverances" at the level of "receptivity" no longer answer for these assertions' truth, as in McDowell. Instead, even at this, their narrowest point of contact, discourse and its understanding implicitly face the world as a whole. In a moment, Davidson's holism, about statements, including those of perception will be further unpacked. In the meantime, the following chart may be provisionally set out.

Thus we have:

Husserl	*McDowell*	*Gadamer*	*Davidson*
Nondiscursive Intentional Sense Perceived/Perceiving	Discourse and Perceived/Perceiving	Linguistically Informed Perceived/Perceiving	Statements of Perception and Truth untethered from perceptual contents

Before returning to Davidson, the extraordinary position the early Heidegger occupies, set in stark relief by this overview, should also be laid out. Heidegger's vantage point stands at once closest to *and* furthest from the final column occupied by Davidson.[9] Heidegger, as we have seen, affirms things showing themselves as themselves from

---

[7] As becomes clearer a little later in this chapter, the intersection of Heidegger's and Davidson's approaches here charted in part corrects for the worries that McDowell expresses, essentially that perceptions on Davidson's account are a sort of black box. Heidegger's insistence that things show themselves from themselves can and does respond to McDowell's worry, though its embrace requires a demotion and/or agnosticism about propositional knowledge and reason's "space" that McDowell himself presumably would resist.

[8] These considerations are set out most extensively in Davidson's essays "A Coherence Theory of Truth" and "Empirical Knowledge," (in *Truth and Interpretation: Perspectives on the Philosophy of Donald Davidson*, ed. Ernest Lepore [Oxford: Blackwell, 1986]: 307–19; 320–32). McDowell in "Davidson in Context," an Appendix to *Mind and World*, attempts to refute Davidson's view (129–61); Davidson has replied to him ("Reply to John McDowell," in L. E. Hahn, ed., *The Philosophy of Donald Davidson* [Chicago and LaSalle: Open Court, 1999]: 105–8), after an essay by McDowell, which raises the same issues as his appendix, and McDowell, then, answered Davidson, subsequently somewhat modifying his own stance in "Avoiding the Myth of the Given," [*Having the World in View: Essays on Kant, Hegel, and Sellars* [Cambridge, MA: Harvard University Press, 2009]: 256–72).

[9] Many commentators have made a connection between Heidegger and Davidson, as is in the course of being done here. The present endeavor perhaps most differs from the bulk of these at once in

themselves, including on the perceptual level, thereby siding with Husserl—perhaps even going him one better, since Heidegger explains how particular entities and states of affairs can so appear without the direct contribution of any conscious intentionality.[10] Heidegger's approach and this exhibition, at the same time, hang suspended from a thoroughgoing holism, in the fashion just sketched in Chapter 8. Heidegger's stance is most akin to Davidson's in this second respect, of all those here canvassed.

Heidegger and Davidson are thus proximate, albeit delicately so, when it comes to what is here somewhat misleadingly being called discourse's semantics, the articulations of things and features of the world that discourse brings to understanding. Though such showing of things from themselves indeed remains in play in Heidegger's account, unlike in Davidson's, the "semantics" or "protosemantics" of the showing found in perception, as well as that of the discourse pertaining to it—the two being intrinsically bound up with one another, as we have seen—for Heidegger, too, remains mobile and in flux. Though all correlations of insight and understanding emerge within traditions, and though the thing and the discourse about it buttress one another in any given instance, the holistic circumstances that allow contact with what is render no appropriations of things in discourse timelessly stable, or ultimately authoritative, without for all that disqualifying any actual understandings, insights, or perceptions.

Davidson, in turn, like Heidegger, envisions contact with the real on the basis of a kind of holism; so, too, his holism leaves open the semantics of what exists.[11] Davidson's thinking, accordingly, harbors its own distinct version of that divergence found in Heidegger's account between the saying specific to assertions ("semantics") and their contact with what is ("reference" here broadly understood), as attested by the title of one of his essays, "Reality without Reference."[12] Davidson indeed denies discourse reference, in the technical sense of a one-to-one relation between terms and individual existents, while nevertheless affirming its contact with the real. His stance, accordingly, includes a gap between accessing reality and what comes to be said about it, parallel, though not identical, to that found in Heidegger's treatment.

In that they overlap, Davidson's and Heidegger's holistic perspectives, then, can together help map the workings of truth as set out in Tugendhat's problem: they can illuminate how what discourse has to say and its traditions and occasions relate to what discourse is about, the force of which concern is brought home by the *aporiai* just reached in respect to perception. This issue indeed remains unresolved: How does the perceived come to be taken up and expressed in discourse? No presently existing

---

regard to *which* overlaps and differences it emphasizes, as well as in the emphasis it places on the two thinkers' *differences*, as well as their similarity.

[10] Wrathall also recognizes this feature of Heidegger's thought as significantly different from Davidson's (*Unconcealment* 52).

[11] Davidson, in an early essay, comments that "a feature of the present discussion that is apt to shock old hands" is "my freewheeling use of the word 'meaning,' for what I call a theory of meaning has after all turned out to make no use of meanings, whether of sentences or of words" ("Truth and Meaning" 24).

[12] Davidson himself thus earlier endorsed "correspondence," albeit "without confrontation," as he put it, thereby further buttressing the present point; cited by Wrathall (*Unconcealment* 43). For the aforementioned essay, see D. Davidson, *Inquiries into Truth and Interpretation* (Oxford: Oxford UP, 1984), pp. 215–25.

philosophical accounts on their own terms seem able to cash out such access on which truth, including Tugendhat's version, depends. Accordingly, negotiating between Heidegger's holism, which allows for the things concerned to show themselves, albeit in a variety of modes, and Davidson's, that confines such appearances to one single mode (the statement or assertion), may permit both discourse's relations here, and understanding's generally, to be sketched.

Yet, for this to take place, and for such contact with what is to be clarified, the differences between these two thinkers must also be registered and accounted for. Not only does Davidson not have any truck with the practical—more about which is discussed soon—but even the problem of discourse's semantics in Davidson differs decisively from its status in Heidegger, ultimately owing to the privilege Davidson grants to assertions. Davidson gives an extraordinary prominence to the statement-form, and its accompanying standpoint toward what is—objectivity, or things present-at-hand, as Heidegger would say—thereby departing from Heidegger, including from Heidegger's own agnosticism in regard to the finality of the latter's authority.[13] Davidson's conception of truth, insofar as it trades on reality as a whole, consists in a holism at the level of *statements*, in contrast to Heidegger's, where contact with worldly beings crucially emerges at the level of practical concern, and of meaning (*bedeuten*) and involvements. Yet, since Davidson relates any single utterance to other possible ones, implying a multiplicity of instances at work on any one occasion, thereby in his own fashion implying a past beyond his speaker's ken as the source of this multiplicity, Davidson's holism can indeed participate in modeling discourse's more wide-ranging modes of speaking (literary, legal, and so on) as conceived here, despite his and Heidegger's thought harboring quite distinct, holistic vantage points.[14]

In question in the present context, after all, finally, is neither simply Heidegger's practical holism nor Davidson's theoretical one, to employ an otherwise apt distinction first framed by Dreyfus, though Heidegger's practical outlook is indeed here given priority as far as contact with the real is concerned.[15] The current understanding draws no bright lines, however, between practical, theoretical, and other sorts of talk, instead affirming diverse capacities for insight and truth across an open-ended array of

---

[13] This privilege is of course part and parcel of Davidson's adaptation of Tarski's semantics. It is also readily evident in Davidson's later work, in his treatment of the "concept of truth." For example, Davidson insists on the necessity of there being "propositional contents," in addition to the "primitive triangle" comprised by speaker, interlocutor, and world for truth and his semantics to function ("Seeing Through Language" in *Truth, Language and History* [Oxford: Clarendon Press, 2005]: 127–42;141).

[14] On this point, the present study differs from many commentators who have attempted to connect Davidson and Heidegger, including Wrathall (but not Dreyfus). Wrathall and Cerbone relate these thinkers in regard to their analyses of truth, in a way that includes the statement and its correspondence to what is (Wrathall 47 ff.). While recognizing how this is at least in part possible, and also not initially focusing on this difference, the present study ultimately retains Heidegger's and Davidson's differing stance toward the statement and finds it significant for its own account.

[15] See Dreyfus "Holism and Hermeneutics" (*Review of Metaphysics* 34.1 [September 1980]: 3–23; 7). See also "How Heidegger Defends the Possibility of a Correspondence Theory of Truth with respect to the Entities of Natural Science" (1995); there, however, he credits both Davidson and Heidegger with a practical holism (2).

instances.¹⁶ Davidson's stance can, then, be adapted, in order to explain how discourse's relation to truth and understanding may be modeled in the present project, thereby arriving at how texts, or literature broadly understood, function. A more perspicuous view of Davidson's relation to Heidegger in respect to the statement's status, as well as of their differing, yet perhaps ultimately complementary holisms, and their respective understandings of what is and what is said, thus must be gleaned, in order that a resolution of the problem of the text's sameness and difference over time may emerge, thanks to drawing on both perspectives.

9.2 Truth Semantics in Davidson

To start by recurring to the initial issue: again, Davidson is not denying either that folks do make statements of perception ("I see a green tree") or that statements like "the tree is green" can be true. These two possibilities for him, however, differ in important respects. Making a report about oneself, including about a putative perception, and making a potentially true claim about the world, within Davidson's logical holism, are not entirely the same. The adoption of his thinking by the present project ultimately lies in the differences between these two orders of statements (ones that contain the vantage points of persons along with their claims, and ones that make claims directly), but also *the overlap* that at some point for him must need exist between the two types of reports.¹⁷

To start with the claim itself, not only can "the tree is green" be true in Davidson's account but this sentence for Davidson also only says anything at all (or commerces with "meaning" in the broad sense in question here) within a framework informed by truth. Davidson, as is well known, in the first phases of his work in philosophy of language, *reverses* a schema originally found in the writings of the logician Alfred Tarski, in order to fashion an account of the meaningfulness of a given language or idiolect as used on a given occasion, with an eye to the relation of that language as a whole to *truth*. Truth, what may be the case as registered in statements, for Davidson

---

[16] There may not be any screwdrivers without the standpoint of persons, yet this screwdriver's being too long nevertheless can still be true. To be clear, this is not to deny the importance of the ready-at-hand or the lifeworld to Heidegger's account, nor to the one here. Ultimately, the status of its specific differences recur, however, to that of the collective as set out in Chapter 5: they remain withdrawn as such while making their force felt—*Being and Time*'s signal accomplishment being to have registered both that force and that withdrawal. Moreover, that the setting of the ready-at-hand, as presented in the previous chapter, ultimately involves causal relationships will be important, as these, again, are what statements of perception depend on for Davidson.

[17] As is made clearer in a moment, ultimately Davidson assimilates direct statements to beliefs ("the tree is green" and "I believe the tree is green") as well as to other cognitive and evaluative attitudes ("I see the tree is green" and "I hope that the tree is green next spring.") For him there cannot be "propositional content" without attitudes. Yet, there also could not be attitudes without propositional contents. To this extent, Davidson ultimately understands even so-called attitudes on propositional terms, as a matter of wishing or desiring or so on that some set of contents turns out to be true on some occasion. Accordingly, though "thinking," "the mental" for Davidson goes far beyond straightforward assertion, its character is attuned to sentences of the assertoric sort, the sole ones that classically may be true or false. (See, among others, "Mental Events" in *Actions and Events* [Oxford: Oxford University Press, 1980]: 207–24.) This remains a decisive difference from Heidegger's approach and the one taken here.

makes what all discourse *says* (or its "meaning") possible—truth at once in the sense of some putative grasp of what is, but also as assigned holistically to assertions, themselves deemed capable of being true or false individually.

Tarski's theory, the one that Davidson reverses, to be clear, is a theory not about the articulateness of statements, but *about truth* in the case of *an artificial or formal language*, one where what statements say is presumed to be already available. Tarski's theory turns on what is now called "disquotational truth": the expression arrived at when the quotation marks around a given statement are removed. The sentence "the tree is green," for example, when found within quotation marks names a *sentence* used to make an assertion. Without quotation marks, this sentence *states* something about the world, about what is the case, a putative truth (namely, that the tree *is* green). The logical correlation between the two, the sentence itself, found within quotes, and the statement of the *truth* it expresses—both taken together, and joined by a biconditional (the logical operator "if and only if")—is called by Tarski a *T-sentence*. On the basis of such sentences, Tarski derived a *definition of truth* for a given formal language, L. Truth in L was defined, in a yet higher order language, by *listing all of L's T-sentences*, all the sentences correlating the names of sentences and their disquotational truths; together, they determined what is called truth's scope: all the instances falling under "truth" in L, thereby *defining truth in L*. Being a definition of truth for L, Tarksi's, to be clear, is an entirely *formal* definition of truth, solely covering *sentences* in some already given *formal* language taken to derive their meanings algorithmically.[18]

Davidson, by contrast, runs Tarski's scheme the other way. He uses it to account for the "meaning" or better meaningfulness of statements (including those of perception), thus reversing the order of Tarski's own argument.[19] Rather than define *truth* (for an artificial language), Davidson defines what is *said* in (some natural) language, its "semantics" loosely understood, on the basis of truth, as it arises across various hypothetical instances of that language's use, truth here otherwise not being defined and instead taken as a given. Thanks to this framing pertaining to an entirely implicit language, the semantics of any one given term, or so-called subsentential part, can begin to be

---

[18] In what sense "language" is in question for Davidson himself is about to be explained; its function, being both hypothetical and occasional, it does not seem to me to conflict with his commitment to discourse, understood in the radical fashion also here affirmed. Ernie Lepore and Kirk Ludwig in the first chapters of their *Donald Davidson: Meaning, Truth, Language, and Reality* (Oxford: Oxford University Press, 2005) make a strong case against the present way of reading Davidson. Nevertheless, they themselves concede that their identification of Davidson's endeavor as giving an actual theory of meaning for a language by way of truth, what they dub "truth-theoretical semantics" is not consistently born out in much of Davidson's own writings. In respect to the issue of whether Davidson affirms meaning as semantics would understand it, they write: "this passage [from Davidson] also suggests that we are not to think of ourselves as operating with an independent conception of meaning, and aiming to show that placing constraints on a truth theory can help us achieve our goal of specifying meanings in that sense for all sentences in an infinitary language," a description that answers to their own version of Davidson's project. "We feel here the frustration many readers have felt with Davidson's papers," they continue, "and we confess that it is just not obvious to us that Davidson had clearly in mind the connection between a truth theory and a meaning theory we have identified" (96n86).

[19] Davidson's own canonical setting out of the present argument can be found in his "Truth and Meaning," already cited. A useful introduction is Bjorn Ramberg's *Donald Davidson's Philosophy of Language: An Introduction* (Oxford: Blackwell, 1991).

sorted out, through the grid provided by this potential set of instances, including other possible presumed occasions when the term may appear. (Thus, for example, if I speak of the item upon which my computer stands as "wood"—if I say "what is underneath the computer is wood"—and you think what I here mean by "is wood" is what you would express as "is a table," when I subsequently use the same phrase in respect to a wooden footstool, but never in respect to a table made out of Formica, you might begin to grasp what "is wood" means for me, albeit you might never fully know or master all the ways I use this phrase.) Language as used, discourse's "sense," for Davidson, is thus reckoned by way of truth, through its capacity for bringing forward aspects of the world, rather than truth being defined for a language with already meaningful statements, as in Tarski.[20] "Sense" here, moreover, necessarily stands in quotes, since virtually the whole point of this exercise is that there are indeed not any *senses*, strictly speaking, but understanding *what is said* arrives by way of the world, by considerations pertaining to what makes sentences true, in the fashion just described.[21]

For Davidson, such "theories" about another's language, these considerations of what would make its utterances on a given occasion true, are intrinsic to understanding discourse. So proceeding, Davidson's account, moreover, requires *holistic considerations* when it comes to the truth of what is being said, thus bringing his standpoint in this respect close to Heidegger's. Specifically, the drafting of a truth-based semantics for a given speaker's "language" at a given moment, according to Davidson, entails what he calls the principle of "charity": the assumption that most of what a speaker says *is* in fact true.[22] Since the language of the other is being gotten at by grasping what they

---

[20] The delicate status of "language" in Davidson can indeed be gleaned from what has just been set out. Something like a language, a consistent use of phrases and terms, a fixed vocabulary in this sense is hypothesized on any given occasion of discourse; that hypothesis contributes to understanding that discourse. Beyond its framing on a given occasion, which may project or recover other relevant instances, no actual language, is genuinely in question; all is and remains at the level of discourse. This at least is the lesson I believe should be gleaned from Davidson's now famous "A Nice Derangement of Epitaphs" (in *Truth and Interpretation* [ed. Ernest Lepore] 432–46), where he denies language any role in understanding, under the double stipulation that language is understood (a) as a system of conventions and (b) as something given prior to the occasion of its use (436).

[21] Davidson at moments does speak of the semantics of terms, while also insisting that his truth-theoretical account does not refer to that semantics; it supposes them as given and then registers their force by way of truth and the relations among sentences. Lepore and Ludwig, clearly, begin from these sorts of claims, but whether they can overcome the resolutely occasional nature of use in Davidson's account, to put forward their own, is questionable. Ultimately the difference turns on the status of radical interpretation in Davidson, which they view merely as a tool for ascertaining meanings to arrive at empirical truth theories for some language (Lepore and Ludwig, *Donald Davidson* 97–8).

[22] Apparently a notion adapted from Paul Grice's pragmatic maxims, Davidson speaks about the principle on a number of different occasions in somewhat different ways. The present reference can be found in his "On the Very Idea of A Conceptual Scheme" (in *Truth and Interpretation*, 197) where "charity" is also declared "not a non-option," thus in this aspect already differing somewhat from Grice's more normative notion. Jeff Malpas, a trailblazer for all who have considered Davidson's work in relation to Gadamer's and/or Heidegger's offers a very nice treatment of the principle of charity and its ramifications across Davidson's work in his "What Is Common to All: Davidson on Agreement and Understanding" in *Dialogues with Davidson: Acting, Interpreting, Understanding*, edited by *Jeff Malpas* (Cambridge, Ma: MIT Press, 2011): 259–80; esp. 262. Malpas, who views Davidson in greater proximity to Gadamer than the present account, eventually offers a different interpretation of the notion of community and the communal, and thus language, than that found here (265–70).

would hold as true, it is necessary to assume that most of what they say is true; that their discourse maps the world rightly more or less en masse—and this prior to actually understanding or knowing what is being said on any given occasion or establishing any particular truth.

Davidson's holism, accordingly, implies something along the lines of Heidegger's being-in-the-truth, albeit, again, their respective holisms ultimately emerge at different levels and stand on different grounds in each thinker. Davidson, with the principle of charity, nevertheless, in the terms here used, supplements what is in a part a word/word (or a sentence/sentence) holism with a word/world one. Because the principle of charity grants being-in-the-truth as background to any utterance, because it takes what may be talked about on this occasion and more generally as largely true, a word/world holism comprehends that "word/word" holism found in Davidson's reversal of Tarski—namely, the necessity for the subsentential parts of any given sentence to be coordinated with other instances in which they may appear.[23]

On the foregoing basis, finally, it can be gleaned why for Davidson language as usually understood, as a conventional system, including individual words and their meanings, turns out to be uninvolved with *actual understanding*. Because trading on truth in this way, understanding what a speaker says always involves what the speaker or writer *talks about*, language when used *and* its subject matters are always at issue *together* in the moment of communication.[24] Accordingly, the sound or sign that happens to be used at the time, at least in principle, can be, and indeed to some extent always *must be*, construed *anew*, reenacted or recalibrated at once as a conduit of understanding (meaning) and disclosure (truth). Other sounds, or other signs, on any given occasion, may be used, since apart from this reckoning, at once of things and meanings in this broad sense, nothing else discursive or linguistic matters in the final analysis.[25]

Discourse, for Davidson, like the early Heidegger, indeed operates at a level more fundamental than language, and in Davidson's case, a parallel, yet different, holism subtends its activity, a holism wherein word/word also is subordinated to world/word. Despite this proximity, no talk *about language* might seem more removed from

---

[23] It is important to note that though in Davidson's account each word or subsentential part as used on a given occasion is in question and to this extent his semantics are compositional, ultimately there is no direct one-to-one mapping of expressions on to individual existents in Davidson's scheme, and thus no final fixed "meaning" for these terms ever comes to pass. This interpretation, moreover, contrasts with the later Richard Rorty's, which claims to glean from Davidson the necessity of subsentential parts having their functions fixed within some given domain of discourse (chemistry, philosophy, etc.) without which no question of truth, according to Rorty, can arise. Robert Brandom, it seems to me, adopts the core of Rorty's contention, while elaborating its inherent third-person normativity about subsentential usage into a marvelous and wonderfully complex theoretical edifice. Staying with Rorty, I have never found the virtually regulative lines among sorts of discourse he draws convincing, nor his erection of two great genres of them: those so regulated and others (like literature or history or ethics) not. The first seems to me ultimately not Davidsonian; the second, as applied to his own writing, leaves no room for his own work's substantive consideration, since, on his own terms, his endeavor must necessarily lack any relation to truth. (See chapter one of my *Essential History* for a fuller version of the second argument.)

[24] In his later writing's Davidson speaks about this in terms of what he calls triangulation; cf. n. 13 given earlier.

[25] See "A Nice Derangement of Epitaphs," especially Davidson's description of what he calls "passing theory," for a fuller account (101).

Heidegger's own than Davidson's (particularly from that era when Heidegger himself made language [*die Sprache*] an explicit theme). "Tarski, formal languages, radio, Sputnik," one can imagine Heidegger commenting—indeed, we all know the drill.

What concretely answers to such suspicion in the context of the early Heidegger, however, what divides him from Davidson even there, is at once the status of the assertion as such, and with it, the issue originally raised of what is given in perception (or the matters otherwise being talked about). Davidson privileges statements; only to some version of them does his account of discourse apply. Davidson, furthermore, as already indicated, rejects the notion that assertions correspond to an event in which things show themselves—give themselves "as" something, as Heidegger would say.

This latter difference, however, at least *in part*, has already been shown to be merely apparent. Heidegger, rightfully, in my view, insists on such access, in a variety of registers, including that of "mere" perceptions. Yet such showings for him also ultimately find whatever stability they have in circumstances close to Davidson's, in which things and talk! about them emerge against a holistic background—in Heidegger's case, a specifically practical one. Heidegger affirms both discourse *and* the thing's or subject matter's distinct appearing, unlike Davidson, but for Heidegger, such appearing is also tied to a holism of its own, where it depends on things and discourse in some fashion always already having been interwoven and accessed. Accordingly, though Davidson's denial of worldly entities' ability to show themselves meaningfully in their own right carries weight, and will be returned to later, the affirmation of the statement and its work as sui generis is arguably what most decisively divides the two thinkers.

On the latter score, however, though Davidson indeed distinguishes statements from all other sorts of discourse, Davidson also must and does allow, as mentioned, for the effects of attitudes: reports, parts of which record the view, condition, or vantage point of the one making them—statements such as "*I believe* the tree is green," or "*I hate* that the cat is on the mat." The latter are indeed unavoidable for any theory of *discourse*, of sentences *as used on occasions*, and Davidson thus must include the perspectives of those who use and interpret statements—not just the statements themselves, but speakers' corresponding beliefs and ultimately their other dispositions and intentions.[26]

In the present account, in fact, what Davidson's thinking most brings to the table is attitudes and the role they play in discourse and its understandings. Not yet focused on extensively, attitudes inform all discourse in the case of speakers and interpreters alike.[27] Hence, this phase of Davidson's thought, in tandem with Heidegger's hermeneutic account of subject matter's appearing, eventually lets be gleaned how literature and other texts, with the particular problems they pose, may be understood.

---

[26] Attitudes, insofar as they pertain to beliefs, are necessarily implicitly included in Davidson's "principle of charity."

[27] To be clear, attitudes are of course included from the opening of BT on, as the "for-sake-of" and "the in-order-to," not to mention the entire practical setting and eventually mood (*Stimmung*), attest. Moreover, attitudes are arguably more radically plumbed by Heidegger than by Davidson, the reason they elude statements in BT being evident—specifically owing to their being inseparable from the tacit totalities already at work in the ready-at-hand as sketched in Chapter 8. Nevertheless, for what might be called the formal indications pertaining to this feature, especially as it operates in the context of textual interpretation, Davidson's account is helpful.

Indeed, in the acknowledgment of the role of attitudes, of speakers' and interpreters' perspectives, a crack begins to open in Davidson's apparent privileging of statements, through which may be glimpsed his schema's application to the wider range of discourse and of truth that Heidegger's thinking as interpreted at the end of the previous chapter discloses.[28] Davidson's thinking, moreover, invites such an appropriation, since, for him, speaker's and hearer's attitudes in the case of statements, their contextualizing beliefs and other standpoints both toward discourse and what is, recur to a *history*, to the previous histories of the speaker/writer and auditor/reader in respect both to what exists and to what discourse is about.

On occasions when things and meanings emerge and understanding takes place, the individual speaker's *and* her interlocutor's concrete histories turn out to be decisive, for Davidson.[29] In any given situation, inherently individuated understandings and histories are in play, recurring to *prior* interactions with world (other things, facts, beliefs, and so on) and to discourse (other individuated, singular occasions of use), such that for Davidson, like Heidegger, but also in a different way, understanding is always the understanding that each one of us is (or affords). Only at this concrete level, for both thinkers, does what exists become capable of being articulated—these articulations and what is articulated both emerging from out of such individuated histories.[30]

Davidson's relation to such history must, then, be further pressed, as it supplies another, albeit still complex, link between him and Heidegger. Their differences and overlaps in respect to such individual histories, in turn, will prove decisive in bringing to a close the navigation here underway in respect to the text's status.

---

[28] Davidson, to be clear, believed he had a way of dealing with attitudes that treats both them and their contents as statements. Moreover, in his early writings on action, as noted earlier, he offered an account of action, intention, and motive, that charted agent's behavior as rationally available, in part drawing on the work of G. E. M. Anscombe on intention. Whether propositional attitudes—fearing, believing, hoping, intending, and so on—may ultimately be captured by statements, as well as the related question of Davidson's approach to actions and their understanding, are both issues that have again recently begun again to receive more attention in the literature, as has Anscombe's own work. (See, among others, Robert Myers "Holism in Action," in Claudine Verheggen ed., *Wittgenstein and Davidson on Language, Thought, and Action* [Cambridge: Cambridge University Press, 2017]: 8–27 and Frederick Stoudtland, "Introduction," in Anton Ford, Jennifer Hornsby & Frederick Stoutland eds., *Essays on Anscombe's Intention* [Cambridge, Ma: Harvard University Press 2011]: 1–22; on Davidson's handling of the reports found in attitudes, claims made in what are called oblique contexts, the classic treatment, at once explanatory and critical, is Tyler Burge "On Davidson's Saying That" [in Lepore, *Perspectives*]: 190–208.)

[29] In this respect, Davidson's standpoint offers a correction of McDowell's and Gadamer's. It allows for a history, not of language, nor even language as Ur-tradition, but of discourse. For anything to be grasped at the level of its singular existence an equally singular individual or person with her history is necessary, something implicit in Heidegger and also true of the present stance, albeit the collective as such further figures in my viewpoint and in Heidegger's in the ways that have begun to be sketched.

[30] To be sure, again, for Heidegger, unlike Davidson, the explicitly *collective* dimension of the past, tethered to the ready-at-hand, is also prominent; the history of discourse reaches back into this collective dimension, the force of which is vertical, one of depth, while Davidson's history is transverse, running serially along discourse's surface. For Heidegger, too, however, the former ultimately finds its force in the space of the individual.

9.3 Externalist Texts

Reference to an individual's history in Davidson explicitly emerges in his discussion of what is called externalism. Externalism pertains to the broader relation of meaning to individual speakers: specifically whether meanings are or are not "in the head," as it was now famously put by Hilary Putnam.[31] Are speakers the masters of the meanings and the references found in their utterances—should meaning in this broad sense be credited *to them*, by dint of a speaker's intending to say something about a given object, perhaps along the lines that Husserl classically set out when discussing logical meanings (his *Bedeutungen*) in his first *Logical Investigation*?

Speaker-dependence of this sort was *denied* by Putnam and others, and that for two sorts of reasons: either because some *necessary relation* holds between the terms speakers use and things in the world, of which the speakers are not themselves always aware (such as "gold" referring to an element having a certain atomic weight)—deemed "physical externalism"—or because some *collective* understanding of what words mean and designate, often channeled through *experts* (who know, for example, the difference between a beech and an aspen), operates in our talk, again resulting in the possible ignorance of what they are actually meaning on the part of those using certain words or terms—deemed "social externalism." For externalism, meaning (and reference) arrives by way of some physical necessity or some social authority or both.

Now, in Davidson's case, his account distinguishes itself from the proceeding in that it can make no use of that collective dimension upon which social externalism, obviously, and physical externalism, implicitly, draws. Hence Davidson, taking up the externalism of Putnam and others, insists that his externalism is compatible with what he calls "first-person authority."[32] Externalism, for Davidson, can operate, even as the speaker *also* retains what is ultimately a *novel kind* of privileged status in regard to her own utterances. Whatever authority the first person has for Davidson, it is thus *not* an epistemological one (as first found in Descartes), nor does it entail a greater self-transparency of her meaning for the speaker herself; first-person authority, after all, for Davidson, is genuinely compatible with *externalism*.

Grasping Davidson's version of externalism aids in accounting for how truth and understanding operate in the different discourses found in the humanities, the distinctions among which Heidegger's schema, rather than Davidson's own, makes available. For Davidson, an externalist dimension ultimately is at work in *both* positions ("I" and "other"); the speaker, or author, possesses a novel style of authority, yet that authority ultimately redounds to the interpreter, to the one understanding.[33] Davidson's

---

[31] Hilary Putnam, "The Meaning of Meaning," *Minnesota Studies in the Philosophy of Science* 7 (1975): 131–93; 131.

[32] Davidson first recognizes something like externalism, without using this term, in his "First Person Authority" (*Subjective, Intersubjective, Objective* [Oxford: Oxford UP, 2001]: 3–14). He revisits this topic, now explicitly addressing the externalism debate, in "Knowing One's Own Mind" (*Subjective, Intersubjective, Objective*): 15–38.

[33] Ernie Lepore and Kirk Ludwig claim to find a contradiction, or at least "tension" between what they call Davidson's "synchronic externalism" in the case of radical interpretation, dependent upon *the interpreter*, and the diachronic externalism they claim evident in Davidson's famous swampman example, about to be discussed, which focuses *on the author and speaker*; they thus restrict present

recasting of the author, accordingly, allows for her utterance's or text's harboring a vector *toward the same*, toward some style of self-identity (ultimately owed to the author's—externalist—history), while that identity or sameness remains radically located in time, open to a change across its repetitions, and thus informed by difference, ultimately thanks to the *interpreter's* contribution and her situation.[34]

Davidson's externalism not only involves author and interpreter but also, indeed, rests on the role played by a speaker's or an author's and interpreter's *previous history* in respect at once to things and to discourse. In the second of the two essays he wrote on this topic, "Knowing One's Own Mind," Davidson declares: "What words mean depends in the most basic cases on the kinds of objects and events that have caused the person to hold the words to be applicable; similarly for what the person's thoughts are about."[35] A history, at once with words and things, informs a speaker or author's meanings. Thus, I now call this thing a shofar—I say "this shofar is hard to blow," for example—because I have encountered *items* I take to be like it in the past and because I have also previously run up against "shofar," or what I take to be such, used in roughly this manner.

Davidson himself stresses the necessity of there being such prior encounters with the *subject matters* that enter discourse, and such an active priority or past, what I call historicity, allows for his approach to externalism to intersect with Heidegger's practically oriented account of discourse. The previous encounters that Davidson's version of discourse require resonate with, and at some level ultimately require, Heidegger's account in which everything that discourse can be about was *freed* for its subsequent appropriations by way of a passage across the world of work, meaning (*bedeuten*), and discourse. In Heidegger's treatment, Dasein and things are also *causally* bound together, in that reversal where one (Dasein) underwent submission, and the other (things) turned out to have been freed. For Davidson's version of externalism in question is again a *causal* relation: most proximally, whatever contact "*caused* the person to hold the words to be applicable." In both cases, a connection with what is is thus ultimately established causally beyond any semantic parameters, while making the latter or some version of it possible. For both thinkers, in the final analysis,

---

usage's recurring to past instances (diachronic externalism) solely to *language-learning* (*Donald Davidson* 338). Since, however, even in radical interpretation, the speaker's usage, his own beliefs and "attitudes," as Davidson himself says, as well as parts of the world are both in question, and since the usage obviously, and the attitudes implicitly, recur to the past, I would maintain that the diachronic and synchronic cannot ultimately be separated.

[34] To be clear, the present account still leaves room for interpretative disputes, and for saying what a text says in its difference from its reader's orientation, ultimately owing to the text's inherently open texture, an openness that recurs to its having an entirely temporal character. Hence, the case is really not like that Michaels offered earlier where two interpreters of James offered two contradictory accounts of his text. Nor does authorship, then, as in AT somehow provide a fixed quantum of intention of which interpretations, like mental rulers, are to take the measure. The author's history instead resides within the horizon of a text's interpretation, and appears as implied by its own mode of being, such that while for certain sorts of interpretations authorial history may turn out to be disqualifying (say if someone claims Ptolemy's observations were obviously wrong because he never mentions Pluto), nevertheless, for the most part, the subject matters being spoken about and the interest that opens their interpretation remain broad enough that new interpretations—for example, pertaining to the question of environmentalism or its absence in the Hebrew bible—of many sorts may turn out to be genuinely consequent, though by no means all.

[35] "Knowing" 37.

discourse's *current access* to things rests on a previous causal contact that permits, while outstripping, the meaningfulness that now accompanies it.[36]

The parallelism between Davidson and Heidegger when it comes to an externalist point of contact is all the more powerful, moreover, since, though, again, Davidson does not acknowledge the dimension of the ready-at-hand, he assigns an unprecedented type of privilege to the author's standpoint. The past contact, that history, allowing for the speaker's or author's talk to meaningfully access what is, is by no means one of which the author herself is aware. The author is not privileged owing to her knowing or being conscious of her own externalist history with things or with words. Indeed, more nearly the opposite is true. Davidson stipulates that "the agent herself . . . is not in a position to wonder whether she is generally using her own words to apply to the right objects and events, since whatever she regularly does apply them to gives her words the meaning they have and her thoughts the contents they have."[37]

Authority accedes to the author's perspective, then, only insofar as that authority is built *into the speech situation and into the act of interpretation itself*. The individual's speaking, writing, and thinking, according to Davidson, are shaped by encounters in her own past—none of which she thinks about or is conscious of at the moment of utterance or inscription. The speaker or author does not ask about their words and their objects, and the history of their being encountered, all of which are submerged in forgetfulness, while the interpreter does at least at times so inquire. This is why the author's or speaker's history with things just *is* the *externalist* factor in Davidson's account; a functional identity, tied to such history, invests speakers' and writers' sayings, playing a parallel role to the other more standard externalist instances cited earlier.

Authorial externalist history, accordingly, operates implicitly; at the same time, what is being said and its understanding always emerge within the *interpreter's* or hearer's own horizon. The externalist history of author or speaker really exists and has relevance only for *the one interpreting*, who alone is aware, or able to become aware of that history, even as something similar, of course, operates in their own case, the interpreter, too, being subject to a parallel externalism, including on the occasion when she interprets. In part on the basis of her own past, but also the future and present in which she engages, the interpreter parses the other's meanings and references, to some extent by referring back to the other's sayings and their history.

"An interpreter of another's words and thoughts must depend on scattered information, fortunate training, and imaginative surmise, in coming to understand the other," as Davidson puts this.[38] Externalism, finally, then, grips both *speakers and hearers*, while their respective positions within it simultaneously diverge. The author's meanings and references, owed to their externalist pre-history, are primary, but these,

---

[36] Heidegger's deep background and its implied history in which things and Dasein have reversed roles, owing to *its causal* character can be conceived as subtending the individual history that Davidson here sketches; the latter history is a transverse, serial historicity, while Heidegger's, as has previously been indicated, is a vertical and virtual one functioning in transverse history's depths.

[37] "Knowing" 37.

[38] "Knowing" 37. Davidson, at this moment mainly wishes to distinguish what goes into the interpreter's understanding of another's talk from what that other herself brings to the table. Nevertheless, cues, training, imaginative surmise, and so on, all finally relate to the interpreter's own history with discourse and with its worldly subject matters.

and that primacy, only hold sway or take shape from the interpreter's perspective, within a setting that the interpreter provides.[39]

An example or limit case Davidson offers illuminates the complexity and radicality of his externalism, as does the controversy surrounding this example in the literature. In his second essay on this topic, "Knowing One's Own Mind," Davidson invites readers to imagine a "swampman"—a person who spontaneously emerges full grown (from a swamp, hence the name) and immediately begins to talk about all the things that Davidson, or, in this case, the reader might normally talk about: their parents, the breakfast they ate that morning, the most recent presidential election, and so on. Davidson interrogates what, under such circumstances, the swamperson's discourse actually *says*; what meaningful contents and references does it bear, absent all *previous history* with things, events, and discourse on the part of this same swamperson. The swamperson's apparent utterances, Davidson concludes, say *nothing at all*, under such circumstances; they are completely void of reference and entirely meaningless. Davidson indeed denies that such a "swampman's" talk! *is* talk! at all.

Nothing shows better than this example, then, how for Davidson, too, finally, as for Heidegger, and the present work, any instance of discourse presupposes a historicity: prior encounters with other instances of discourse and with the worldly things that discourse needs to function. Lacking such a pre-history, in which the linkage of talk and the world active on any given occasion already unknowingly has begun to be forged, the nub of Davidson's externalism, no meanings or references of any sort can be imputed to any stretch of discourse, even in cases where any mark of that history is not actually discernible, as in the swamperson's case.

Indeed—and this turns out to have been Davidson's commentators' expressed concern—in the swamperson example, *nothing* has apparently changed for the interpreter, within whose own history and horizon that meaningfulness backstopped by the speaker's history appears. Yet the commentators' rebuttal of Davidson, which would have everything proceed apace, envisioning a kind of algorithm at work between the interpreter's understanding and the externalist cues offered by the speaker (one entirely based on the interpreter's own prior training), underestimates the extent to

---

[39] Lepore and Ludwig, and Nathaniel Goldberg, in his "Swampman, Response-Dependence, and Meaning," (in *Donald Davidson on Truth, Meaning, and the Mental*, ed. Gerhard Preyer [Oxford: Oxford University Press, 2012]: 148–64) all recognize this last fact; Goldberg even goes so far as to simply identify what a speaker means by some assertion with what the proper sort of interpreter would understand by it (7). Goldberg, who sees the tension Ludwig and Lepore recognize between synchronic and diachronic accounts as running much more deeply, and as tied respectively to radical interpretation (RI, synchronic) and language learning (LL, diachronic) believes one must, against Davidson, choose one or another, and opts for RI, albeit this yields in the case of swampman, about to be discussed, what Goldberg calls an "epistemic zombie" (a speaker who does not know her own meaning) (21–2). I, however, opt for LL (which Goldberg himself considers, thus making plain that the present reading in its broad strokes is defensible), while, again, also doubting that the difference between diachronic and synchronic ultimately can be maintained as he and Lepore and Ludwig wish. I believe all three give too little credit to the necessity of the speaker knowing what communication is and being actually engaged in talk, even in the case of simple assertions, a necessity tied to that propositionality and objectivity that Davidson says precedes any single interpretation. By contrast, Goldberg explicitly, and Ludwig and Lepore implicitly, would allow the speaker to "mean nothing" and still be speaking, as Goldberg puts it (16). (For Lepore and Ludwig see *Donald Davidson* 338; cf., however, 341n263.)

which discourse is indeed a genuine event for Davidson, as it also is for Heidegger. For both Heidegger and Davidson, discourse has *always already* opened onto a world and made contact with what it is about; that opening, for both, shapes itself holistically and encompasses speakers as well as interpreters in a way that, among other things, bars any algorithm or one-to-one correspondences of cues and meanings from taking hold. "Epistemic zombies," *meaning* nothing and still *say*ing something, are thus impossible in either account, since it is always the other's saying *as other* that the interpreter must understand and this cannot be fashioned without that broader opening on to what is, and without that being-in-time of discourse, distinct for each, yet always already given beforehand, and common to both.[40] There are indeed no things, subject matters, for talk to be about, barring this opening, which in Davidson's terms requires that a triangulation among *persons*, discourse, and the world is always already at work. To be sure, in Heidegger's and in the present instance that opening does not, as it does for Davidson, assemble itself as focused on statements and a certain sort of *objectivity*; it instead emerges from the world of necessity and labor. Yet for both Heidegger and for Davidson, discourse must have already traversed the threshold of the world and must arrive immersed in the thickness of time for discourse to be understandable on any occasion of use.

Davidson's commentators' objections, despite themselves, thus make visible the complex, folded structure of all interpretation, all understanding, an arrangement especially visible *not* in everyday instances, but in textual, or "literary," discourse in the broad sense here in question. Davidson's account of externalist interpretation indeed effectively maps on to Gadamer's question and answer and fusion of horizons, something of which Davidson himself was aware.[41] Davidson's account, however, illuminates in a fashion that Gadamer's ultimately does not, both how *open-ended* this exchange is and upon what it specifically turns, since for Davidson no history of words, no basic tradition, or language, to any degree subtends it—only a prior opening and a history of past contacts unregistered as such by the speaker or author, and the interpreter in their own case. Davidson's treatment exhibits how discourse's subject matters, the things discourse is about, along with possible insights into them, become available entirely and solely on the level of discourse itself. The complex movement of interpretation that Gadamer envisions so well occurs in the context of such radically individuated histories, ones in which contact with things, as well as with prior instances of discourse concretely register, along the lines of the externalist history just sketched, a development in which words and language in any broad or universal sense, including Gadamer's, play no role.

Recognizing discourse's specificity for hermeneutics, the intersection of Davidson's thinking with Heidegger's here contemplated, moreover, fecundates. The holistic insertion into what is that Heidegger sketches must indeed be compounded with Davidson's correction of Gadamer and his sketch of interpretation as conducted

---

[40] For this commonness and the collectivity it implies, again, see Chapter 5.
[41] See Davidson's "Gadamer and Plato's *Philebus*" in *Truth, Language and History* (Oxford: Clarendon Press, 2005): 261–75; esp. 275, where Davidson remarks on his difference from Gadamer consisting in his rejection of "a common language."

entirely in discourse. Only Heidegger's investigations in the beginning of BT exhibit how it is possible for all sorts of *subject matters*, in a variety of fashions, to have *already* made their way into discourse. Heidegger alone provides the pre-history of that historicity of understanding that Davidson's account implies. BT discloses in a unique fashion how the real can appear under different guises in the various historicities and traditions of discourse of which different speakers already dispose (among them those attitudes and beliefs more generally for which Davidson I believe finally cannot wholly satisfactorily account)—historicities that are themselves still ongoing, entailing differences in vantage point that continue to play themselves out.

Davidson's limitation of discourse and its truth to propositional contents and a corresponding objectivity, indeed, cannot be fully sustained, both if things of all sorts are to genuinely appear and also because talk containing attitudes finally cannot be conceived as reducible to statements, albeit Davidson apparently hoped to find workarounds to minimize this difficulty. The world's making contact with the author or speaker in various ways—practically, aesthetically, ethically, and politically, as well as theoretically, and so on—has indeed always already occurred; given discourse's background as Heidegger alone presents it, none of these configurations and their specific instantiations, then, can be excluded, nor could any theory of discourse really be deemed adequate in which they cannot receive an account. Previous contacts with multiple styles of discourse with their distinct perspectives inflect externalist understanding, granting to the authors and speakers and interpreters the ability to manifest what exists in different ways, to realize different styles of insight about different sorts of beings and matters of concern, albeit such sorts or kinds cannot be sorted out in advance, or always expressed finally in statements, nor otherwise mastered, including by genre.[42] Such diverse gateways on entities and existence have already entered (each individual's discursive) history, and all of these different kinds of expressions, it should now be clear, stand on the same footing, each in their own way making some bid for truth or insight, often at times on unprecedented terms.[43]

Heidegger's more radical holistic backgrounding, accordingly, exhibits how a partially shared externalism ultimately informs every instance of discourse, with all discourse, and its understanding retaining a vector toward truths of different stripes, within parameters broader than Davidson allows. So doing, the question aimed at all along in the present discussion thus finds its fullest response: namely, how a text at once the same and different, literature in a new broader sense, in a more or less unprecedented range of cases, may be conceived as existing and be understood. As

---

[42] To grasp more concretely why this is the case, see my discussion of Cavell's "Learning a Word," at the end of Chapter 3.2 in Part One of the present volume.

[43] As previously explored, the distinction between the assertion and other types of speech is finally not itself fundamental. Ultimately, this is due to the sentence not being the basic unit of discourse in any case (as I further explain in my forthcoming "The Silence of the Concepts (in *After Finitude and Gottlob Frege*)"). Hence, none of these metadescriptions are fundamental and the divide between speech involving actions (and intentions) and other sorts also is not. Yet this erasure does not take shape in favor of statements' and intentions' own rationality as in Davidson, nor by some speech being wholly removed from truth or insight as in Altieri. From a sentential perspective, the mixed genre ("the couch is in the other room," in answer to the question of what piece of furniture "I want moved") is the closest working paradigm.

began to come forward, an interpreter indeed attempts to understand what is said in light of what is being talked about, with an eye to some interest in truth in the broadest sense, employing appropriately modified versions of Davidson's principle of charity and making references back to the author's or text's history and precursors, as became roughly apparent in the discussion of Brooks' work earlier in Chapter 4. At the same time, this whole endeavor falls within the interpreters' own history and horizon. The speaker or author and her history retain their authority solely on externalist grounds, and they account for the text's *identity* and thus for its *difference* from, or foreignness for, *the interpreter*. The *reader or interpreter*, in the meanwhile, brings to bear her own history, including, in this case, those questions and issues she wants to resolve, problems and subject matters that the text in question in some fashion also pursues. Owing to the hermeneutic situation of the interpreter, intimations that these texts and utterances bear on her concerns are always already in place, albeit other concerns, as well as texts, may be discovered while the reader advances from her starting points. The auditor's or reader's vantage and the interpreter's own, thus, together account for the text's identity and difference, yielding an inherently open-ended range of readings and confrontations with authors, texts, genres, discourses, or whatever else is to be interpreted (Brooks' balloon), which never, however, simply belong to the reader, or mouth her understanding, nor function apart from some consideration of truth. The double immersion in history (of both author and interpreter) that Davidson's externalism lets be envisioned underpins a repeated resurgence of different cuts into the text, as Heidegger might put it, all of which are at least potentially cuts into *the text* and unfoldings of what *it* says, the historicity and history in question (related to the author) nevertheless ruling out nothing in advance concerning these events themselves.

Moreover, as all of the authors in question—Davidson, Gadamer, and Heidegger—in their own way conclude, these moments of sameness and of difference are never in competition, nor in fact can they register as such in any actual single instance of interpretation. The *longue durée* of any single text's comings and goings is indeed always comprised of seemingly unitary events, at once involving text, author/speaker, reader/hearer, and the things/truths they are about. At that moment, neither the difference of the text nor of course its sameness is apparent—again yielding a certain neither/nor. Texts are themselves ultimately neither identical nor different; since they come to light in a single, albeit complex, occurrence in which alone they appear *as texts*.

Such a conclusion is only fitting, since texts, assertions, like all discourse, operate within time, in an inherently open-ended temporality; they are indeed events, and thus could never assume any final fixed shapes. Assertions and their truth, as has been indicated, cannot be credited with the stability analytic philosophers, seemingly by definition, assign to them, without their force and understandability in situ being canceled. Texts and their interpretation similarly do not attain fixity, since they know no forms, beget no literariness, nor conceal an unspeakable iterability (even if the latter, too, would undo such identity) when they appear and offer themselves to understanding and insight. Hence, in the end, all that remains to do is what really we have all always been doing all along, since it is all criticism can achieve: namely to interpret, to understand, and to talk!

Selected Bibliography

Affeldt, Steven. "The Ground of Mutuality: Criteria, Judgment, and Intelligibility in Stephen Mulhall and Stanley Cavell." *European Journal of Philosophy* 6.1 (1998): 1–31.
Altieri, Charles. *Reckoning with the Imagination: Wittgenstein and the Aesthetics of Literary Experience*. Ithaca, NY: Cornell University Press, 2015.
Andrews, Bruce and Bernstein, Charles, eds. *L=A=N=G=U=A=G=E Book*. Carbondale, IL: Southern Illinois University Press, 1984.
Attridge, Derek. *The Singularity of Literature*. London: Routledge, 2004.
Benardete, Seth. "Sophocles' *Oedipus Tyrannus*." In *The Argument of the Action: Essays on Greek Poetry and Philosophy*. Chicago: Chicago University Press, 2000, 71–83.
Bennett, Tony. "Sociology, Aesthetics, Expertise." *New Literary History* 41.2 (Spring 2010): 253–76.
Bernstein, Charles. *Content's Dream: Essays 1975–1984*. Los Angeles: Sun and Moon Press, 1986.
Bernstein, Charles. *With Strings*. Chicago: The University of Chicago Press, 2001.
Black, Max. "Metaphor." *Proceedings of the Aristotelian Society*, New Series, 55 (1954–1955): 273–94.
Brandom, Robert. *Tales of the Mighty Dead: Historical Essays in the Metaphysics of Intentionality*. Cambridge, MA: Harvard University Press, 2002.
Bronzo, Silvio. "The Resolute Reading and Its Critics an Introduction to the Literature." *Wittgenstein-Studien* v.3 (2012): 45–80.
Brooks, Cleanth. "Irony as a Principle of Poetic Structure," orig. in Morton Zabel (ed.), *Literary Opinion in America*. New York: Harper and Row, 1951; reprinted in David Richter (ed.), *The Critical Tradition*, 2nd ed. Boston: St. Martin's Press, 2006, 758–65.
Brooks, Cleanth. "Metaphor, Paradox, and Stereotype." *British Journal of Aesthetics* (1965): 315–28.
Brook, Cleanth. *The Well-Wrought Urn: Studies in the Structure of Poetry*. London: Dennis Dodson Ltd., 1947.
Bruns, Gerald. *Hermeneutics Ancient and Modern*. New Haven, CT: Yale University Press, 1995.
Carman, Taylor. *Heidegger's Analytic: Interpretation, Discourse, and Authenticity in Being and Time*. Cambridge: Cambridge University Press, 2003.
Cavell, Stanley. *A World Viewed: Reflections on the Ontology of Film*. Enlarged ed. Cambridge, MA: Harvard University Press, 1979.
Cavell, Stanley. *Disowning Knowledge: In Seven Plays of Shakespeare*. Cambridge: Cambridge University Press, 2003.
Cavell, Stanley. "Existential and Analytic Philosophy." *Daedalus* 93 (Summer 1964): 946–74.
Cavell, Stanley. *In Quest of the Ordinary: Lines of Skepticism and Romanticism*. Chicago: University of Chicago Press, 1994.
Cavell, Stanley. *Little Did I Know: Excerpts from Memory*. Stanford, CA: Stanford University Press, 2010.

Cavell, Stanley. *Must We Mean What We Say?: A Book of Essays*. Cambridge: Cambridge University Press, 2002 (orig. 1969).
Cavell, Stanley. "On the Opening of the *Investigations*." In Hans Sluga and David G. Stern (eds.), *Cambridge Companion to Wittgenstein*. Cambridge: Cambridge University Press, 1996, 261–95.
Cavell, Stanley. "The Aesthetic Problems of Modern Philosophy." In *Must We Mean What We Say?: A Book of Essays*. Cambridge: Cambridge University Press, 2002 (orig. 1969), 44–96.
Cavell, Stanley. *The Claim of Reason*. Oxford: Oxford University Press, 1999 (orig. 1979).
Cavell, Stanley. *The Senses of Walden*. Chicago: University of Chicago Press, 1992 (expanded edition; orig. 1972).
Conant, James. "Wittgenstein on Meaning and Use." *Philosophical Investigations* 21.3 (July 1998): 222–50.
Crary, Alice. *Wittgenstein and the Moral Life: Essays in Honor of Cora Diamond*. Cambridge, MA: MIT Press, 2007.
Crary, Alice and Read, Rupert, eds. *The New Wittgenstein*. New York: Routledge, 2000.
Crowell, Steven Galt. *Husserl, Heidegger, and the Space of Meaning: Paths toward Transcendental Phenomenology*. Evanston, IL: Northwestern University Press, 2002.
Crowell, Steven. *Normativity and Phenomenology in Husserl and Heidegger*. Cambridge: Cambridge University Press, 2013.
Crowell, Steven and Malpas, Jeff, eds. *Transcendental Heidegger*. Stanford, CA: Stanford University Press, 2007.
Dahlstrom, Daniel. "Transcendental Truth and the Truth that Prevails." In S. Crowell and J. Malpas (eds.), *Transcendental Heidegger*. Stanford, CA: Stanford University Press, 2007: 63–73.
Davey, Nicholas. "Hermeneutics, Structuralism, and Poststructuralism." In Jeff Malpas and Hans-Helmuth Gander (eds.), *The Routledge Companion to Hermeneutics*. New York: Routledge, 2015, 660–73.
Davidson, Donald. *Truth, Language and History*. Oxford: Clarendon Press, 2005.
Davidson, Donald. *Subjective, Intersubjective, Objective*. Oxford: Oxford University Press, 2001.
Davidson, Donald. *Inquiries into Truth and Interpretation*. Oxford: Clarendon Press, 1984.
Davidson, Donald. "What Metaphors Mean." In Sheldon Sacks (ed.), *On Metaphor*. Chicago: University of Chicago Press, 1978, 29–46.
Davis, Colin. *Critical Excess: Overreading in Derrida, Deleuze, Levinas, Žižek, and Cavell*. Stanford, CA: Stanford University Press, 2010.
de Man, Paul. *Blindness and Insight: Essays in the Rhetoric of Contemporary Criticism*, 2nd rev. ed. Minneapolis: University of Minnesota Press, 1983.
Diamond, Cora. "Does Bismarck Have a Beetle in His Box." In Alice Crary and Rupert Read (eds.), *The New Wittgenstein*. New York: Routledge, 2000, 262–92.
Diamond, Cora. "Having a Rough Story about What Moral Philosophy Is." *New Literary History* 15.1 (Autumn 1983): 155–69.
Diamond, Cora. "Henry James, Moral Philosophers, Moralism." In Todd F. Davis and Kenneth Womack (eds.), *Mapping the Ethical Turn: A Reader in Ethics, Culture, and Literary Theory*. Charlottesville, VA: University of Virginia Press, 2001, 252–70.
Diamond, Cora. "Throwing Away the Ladder." *Philosophy* 63.243 (January 1988): 5–27.
Diamond, Cora. "What Nonsense Might Be." *Philosophy* 56.215 (January 1981): 5–22.

Diamond, Cora. "Wittgenstein, Mathematics, and Ethics: Resisting the Attractions of Realism." In Hans Sluga and David G. Stern (eds.), *The Cambridge Companion to Wittgenstein*. Cambridge: Cambridge University Press, 1996, 226–60.
Dreyfus, Hubert L. "Holism and Hermeneutics." *Review of Metaphysics* 34.1 (September 1980): 3–23.
Dreyfus, Hubert L. "How Heidegger Defends the Possibility of a Correspondence Theory of Truth with Respect to the Entities of Natural Science." In Hubert L. Dreyfus and Mark A. Wrathall (eds.), *Heidegger Reexamined*, vol. 4. London: Taylor and Francis, 2002, 219–49.
Dreyfus, Hubert L. "The Perceptual Noema: Gurwitsch's Critical Contribution." In Aron Gurwitsch and Lester E. Embree (eds.), *Life-World and Consciousness*. Evanston, IL: Northwestern University Press, 1972, 135–9.
Dreyfus, Hubert L. and Wrathall, Mark, eds. *A Companion to Heidegger*. Oxford: Blackwell, 2005.
Dreyfus, Hubert L. and Hall, Harrison, eds. *Heidegger: A Critical Reader*. Oxford: Blackwell, 1992.
Eldridge, Richard and Rhie, Bernard. "Introduction." In Richard Eldridge and Bernard Rhie (eds.), *Stanley Cavell and Literary Studies: Consequences of Skepticism*. London: Continuum, 2011, 1–13.
Elkin, Stanley. *Boswell: A Modern Comedy*. Normal, IL: Illinois State University (Dalkey Archive), 1999 (orig. 1964).
Elkin, Stanley. *Criers and Kibitzers, Kibitzers and Criers*. New York: Plume Books, 1973.
Elkin, Stanley. *George Mills*. New York: E. P. Dutton, 1982.
Elkin, Stanley. *The Franchiser*. Boston: Nonpareil Books, 1980.
Elkin, Stanley. "The Making of Ashenden." In *Searches and Seizures*. New York: Random House, 1973, 129–88.
Eliot, T. S. *Selected Prose of T. S. Eliot*. New York: Harcourt, 1975.
Fell, Joseph P. "The Familiar and the Strange: On the Limits of Praxis in the Early Heidegger." In Hubert L. Dreyfus and Harrison Hall (eds.), *Heidegger: A Critical Reader*. Oxford: Blackwell, 1992, 65–80.
Fried, Michael. "Art and Objecthood." In Philip Auslander (ed.), *Performance: pt. 1. Identity and the Self*. London: Taylor and Francis, 2003 (orig. 1967), 165–87.
Gadamer, Hans-Georg. *Truth and Method*, 2nd rev. ed., trans. Joel Weinsheimer and Donald G. Marshall. London: Continuum, 2004.
Gadamer, Hans-Georg. *Wahreit und Methode: Grundzüge einer philosophischen Hermeneutik; Gesammelte Werke Band* 1. Tubingen: J. C. B. Mohr, 1986.
Gang, Joshua. "Behaviorism and the Beginnings of Close Reading." *ELH* 78.1 (Spring 2011): 1–25.
Gordon, Peter E. "The Empire of Signs: Heidegger's Critique of Idealism in Being and Time." In Mark Wrathall (ed.), *The Cambridge Companion to Heidegger's Being and Time*. New York: Cambridge, 2013, 223–38.
Grice, H. P. "Utterer's Meaning and Intentions." In *Studies in the Ways of Words*. Cambridge, MA: Harvard University Press, 1989, 86–116.
Grondin, Jean. *Sources of Hermeneutics*. Albany, NY: SUNY University Press, 1995.
Heidegger, Martin. *Being and Time*, trans. John Macquarrie and Edward S. Robinson. New York: Harper and Row, 1962.
Heidegger, Martin. "Foreword" to *Heidegger: Through Phenomenology to Thought*. William J. Richardson, S. J. The Hague: Martinus Nijhoff, 1963.

Heidegger, Martin. *Logic: The Question of Truth*, trans. Thomas Sheehan. Bloomington, IN: Indiana University Press, 2010.

Heidegger, Martin. *Logik: Die Frage nach der Wahrheit. Gesamtausgabe 21*. Walter Biemel (ed.). Frankfurt am Main: Vittorio Klostermann, 1976.

Heidegger, Martin. "On the Essence of Ground." In William O'Neill (ed.), *Pathmarks*. Cambridge: Cambridge University Press, 1998, 97–135.

Heidegger, Martin. "On the Essence of Truth." In William O'Neill (ed.), *Pathmarks*. Cambridge: Cambridge University Press, 1998, 136–54.

Heidegger, Martin. *Sein und Zeit*. 17 Durchges. Aufl. mit den Randbemerkungen aus dem Handex. des Autors im Anh. Tubingen: Niemeyer, 1993.

Hopkins, Burt C. "Deformalization and Phenomenon in Husserl and Heidegger." In Frank Schalow (ed.), *Heidegger, Translation, and the Task of Thinking: Essays in Honor of Parvis Emad*. Dordrecht: Springer, 2011, 49–69.

Husserl, Edmund. *Ideas Pertaining to a Pure Phenomenology and A Phenomenological Philosophy: First Book*, trans. F. Kirsten. Dordrecht: Kluwer, 1983.

Kates, Joshua. "Against the Period." *Differences: A Journal of Feminist Cultural Studies* 23.2 (Summer 2012): 136–64.

Kates, Joshua. "Document and Time." *History and Theory* 53.2 (May 2014): 155–74.

Kates, Joshua. *Essential History: Jacques Derrida and The Development of Deconstruction*. Evanston, IL: Northwestern University Press, 2005.

Kates, Joshua. *Fielding Derrida: Philosophy, Literary Criticism, History and the Work of Deconstruction*. New York: Fordham University Press, 2008.

Kates, Joshua. "Neither a God nor ANT Can Save Us: Latour, Heidegger, Historicity, and Holism." *Paragraph* 40.2 (July 2017): 153–73.

Kates, Joshua. "Phenomenology's Intersection with Literary Criticism." In S. Overgaard and S. Luft (eds.), *The Routledge Companion to Phenomenology*. New York: Routledge, 2011, 644–54.

Kates, Joshua. "Semantics and Pragmatics and Husserl and Derrida." *Philosophy Compass* 10.12 (December 2015): 828–40.

Kates, Joshua. "'Signature Event Context'... in, Well, *Context*: Revisiting a Linguistic Turn." *Journal of the Philosophy of History* 12.1 (2018): 117–41.

Kates, Joshua. "The Silence of the Concepts (in *After Finitude* and Frege)." In Michel Chaouli (ed.), *Poetic Critique*. Berlin: Walter de Gruyter, forthcoming.

Käufer, Stephen. "Logic." In Hubert L. Dreyfus and Mark Wrathall (eds.), *A Companion to Heidegger*. Oxford: Blackwell, 2005, 144–55.

Kertscher, Jens. "Gadamer's Ontology of Language Reconsidered." In Jeff Malpas, Ulrich Arnswald, and Jens Kertscher (eds.), *Gadamer's Century: Essays in Honor of Hans-Georg Gadamer*. Cambridge, MA: MIT Press, 2002, 135–56.

Knapp, Steven and Michaels, Walter Benn. "Against Theory." In W. J. T. Mitchell (ed.), *Against Theory: Literary Studies and the New Pragmatism*. Chicago: University of Chicago Press, 1985, 11–30.

Knapp, Steven and Michaels, Walter Benn. "Against Theory 2: Hermeneutics and Deconstruction." *Critical Inquiry* 14.1 (Autumn 1987): 49–68.

Knapp, Steven and Michaels, Walter Benn. *Against Theory 2 : Sentence meaning, Hermeneutics: Protocol of the Fifty-second Colloquy, 8 December 1985*. Berkeley, CA: Center for Hermeneutics Studies on Hellenistic and Modern Culture, 1986.

Lafont, Cristina. *Heidegger, Language, and World-Disclosure*, trans. Graham Harmon. Cambridge: Cambridge University Press, 2000.

Lepore, Ernest, ed. *Truth and Interpretation: Perspectives on the Philosophy of Donald Davidson*. Oxford: Oxford: Basil Blackwell, 1986.
Lepore, Ernie and Ludwig, Kirk. *Donald Davidson: Meaning, Truth, Language, and Reality*. Oxford: Oxford University Press, 2005.
Malpas, Jeff, Arnswald, Ulrich, and Kertscher, Jens, eds. *Gadamer's Century: Essays in Honor of Hans-Georg Gadamer*. Cambridge, MA: MIT Press, 2002.
Malpas, Jeff and Gander, Hans-Helmuth, eds. *The Routledge Companion to Hermeneutics*. New York: Routledge, 2015.
Malpas, Jeff. "What Is Common to All: Davidson on Agreement and Understanding." In Jeff Malpas (ed.), *Dialogues with Davidson: Acting, Interpreting, Understanding*. Cambridge, MA: MIT Press, 2011, 259–80.
Mankin, Robert. "An Introduction to *The Claim of Reason*." *Salmagundi* n.67 (Summer 1985): 66–89.
Mao, Douglas. "The New Critics and The Text-Object." *ELH* 63.1 (Spring 1996): 227–54.
Marrati, Paola. "The Fragility of Words, the Vulnerability of Life." *MLN* 130.5 (December 2015; Comparative Literature Issue): 1055–66.
McDowell, John. "Gadamer and Davidson on Understanding and Relativism." In Jeff Malpas, Ulrich Arnswald, and Jens Kertscher (eds.), *Gadamer's Century: Essays in Honor of Hans-Georg Gadamer*. Cambridge, MA: MIT Press, 2002, 173–94.
McDowell, John. *Mind and World*, with a new introduction by the author. Cambridge, MA: Harvard University Press, 2002.
Michaels, Walter. *Our America: Nativism, Modernism, and Pluralism*. Durham, NC: Duke University Press, 1995.
Michaels, Walter. "Saving the Text: Reference and Belief." *MLN* 93.5 (Comparative Literature; December 1978): 771–93.
Michaels, Walter. *The Beauty of A Social Problem: Photography, Autonomy, Economy*. Chicago: University of Chicago Press, 2015.
Michaels, Walter. *The Gold Standard and the Logic of Naturalism*. Berkeley, CA: University of California Press, 1987.
Michaels, Walter. *The Shape of the Signifier: 1967 to the End of History*. Princeton, NJ: Princeton University Press, 2004.
Moi, Toril. *Revolution of the Ordinary: Literary Studies after Wittgenstein, Austin, and Cavell*. Chicago: Chicago University Press, 2017.
Moran, Richard. "Seeing and Believing: Metaphor, Image, and Force." *Critical Inquiry* 16.1 (Autumn 1989): 87–112.
Mulhall, Stephen. *On Being in the World: Wittgenstein and Heidegger on Seeing Aspects*. London: Routledge, 1990.
Nussbaum, Martha. "Flawed Crystals: James's *The Golden Bowl* and Literature as Moral Philosophy." *New Literary History* 15.1 (Autumn 1983): 25–50.
Philipse, Herman. "Heidegger's 'Scandal of Philosophy': The Problem of the '*Ding an Sich*' in *Being and Time*." In Steven Galt Crowell and Jeff Malpas (eds.), *Transcendental Heidegger*. Stanford, CA: Stanford University Press, 2007, 168–98.
Poovey, Mary. *Genres of the Credit Economy: Mediating Value in Eighteenth- and Nineteenth-Century Britain*. Chicago: Chicago University Press, 2008.
Pratt, Mary Louise. *Toward a Speech Act Theory of Literary Discourse*. Bloomington, IN: Indiana University Press, 1977.
Schutz, Alfred. "Husserl and Transcendental Intersubjectivity." In *Edmund Husserl: Critical Assessments of Leading Philosophers V.5*. New York: Routledge, 2005, 90–116.

Sluga, Hans and Stern, David G., eds. *Cambridge Companion to Wittgenstein*. Cambridge: Cambridge University Press, 1996.
Staten, Henry. *Wittgenstein and Derrida*. Lincoln: University of Nebraska Press, 1986.
Staten, Henry. *Techne Theory: A New Language for Art*. London: Bloomsbury Academic, 2019.
Thaning, Morton. *The Problem of Objectivity in Gadamer's Hermeneutics in Light of McDowell's Empiricism*. The Hague: Springer, 2005.
Tugendhat, Ernst. "Heidegger's Idea of Truth." In Brice Wachterhauser (ed.), *Hermeneutics and Truth*. Evanston, IL: Northwestern University Press, 1994, 83–97.
Winters, Yvor. "The Experimental School in Modern Poetry." In *In Defense of Reason*. New York: New Directions, 1947, 30–74.
Wittgenstein, Ludwig. *The Blue and Brown Books*. New York: Harper, 1960 (2nd ed).
Wittgenstein, Ludwig. *Philosophical Investigations*, trans. G. E. M. Anscombe. Oxford: Basil Blackwell, 1986.
Wittgenstein, Ludwig. *Tractatus Logico-Philosophicus*. London: Kegan Paul, 1922.
Wrathall, Mark. *Heidegger and Unconcealment: Truth, Language, and History*. Cambridge: Cambridge University Press, 2011.
Wrathall, Mark, ed. *The Cambridge Companion to Heidegger's Being and Time*. New York: Cambridge, 2013.

Index

Abrams, M. H.   101
absolute idealism   159
Adorno, Theodor   4
"The Adventure of Reading"
    (Moi)   65 n.51
"Aesthetic Problems of Modern
    Philosophy" (Cavell)   43–9, 51,
    53–5, 64, 72–4, 77, 86, 95
aesthetics   40
    art   43, 46–7, 48 n.12, 87, 95–6
    aesthetic judgments   45 (*see also*
        Kant, I.)
    literature and literary studies (*see*
        literature and literary studies)
Affeldt, Steven   50 n.15
After Strange Gods (Eliot)   96 n.47
"Against Theory" (Michaels and
    Knapp)   xxi, 133–43, 147 n.35,
    148, 221 n.34
"Against Theory 2: Hermeneutics and
    Deconstruction" (Michaels and
    Knapp)   xxii, 133, 143
*Against Theory 2: Sentence meaning,
    Hermeneutics* (Michaels and
    Knapp)   136–8
"Against the Period" (Kates)   97 n.48
Althusser, Louis   4, 112 n.22
    Reading Capital   112 n.22
Altieri, Charles   4, 38, 39, 108 n.14,
    225 n.43
    artwork   25 n.34
    confessions   25–6
    discourse (*see* discourse)
    literature   21–6 (*see also* literature and
        literary studies)
    Reckoning with the Imagination   21,
        22, 22 nn.27–9, 23, 23 n.30, 24,
        25, 25 n.34
    and resolute reading of
        Wittgenstein   24 n.33
    truth (*see* truth)
analytic–continental divide   xiii

analytic philosophy   xiii, 5
Anscombe, G. E. M.   56 n.31, 57 n.35,
    219 n.28
anthropocentrism   xvi n.13
AP. *See* "Aesthetic Problems of Modern
    Philosophy" (Cavell)
Apel, Karl-Otto   198 n.74
"The Argument of the Ordinary"
    (Cavell)   64 n.49
Aristotle   11, 74, 105, 174, 178, 194 n.65,
    201–2, 202 n.85, 202, 203, 204,
    205, 206
    metaphor in *Poetics*   74–5 n.3
Armstrong, Nancy   111–12
    *How Novels Think: The Limits of
        Individualism from 1719–
        1900*   111–12
art   43, 46–7, 48 n.12, 87, 95–6
"as". *See* Heidegger, Martin, hermeneutic "as"
Ashbery, John   22 n.29, 23
    "Instruction Manual"   23
assertion
    derivativeness   175–9
    statements/propositions (*see*
        statements/propositions)
    subject matter of   178
    truth   196–207
assertion as a derivative mode   176
AT. *See* "Against Theory" (Michaels and
    Knapp)
attitudes   92, 92 n.37, 93
Attridge, Derek   4, 5, 6, 8, 9, 13–15
    The Singularity of Literature   13–15
"Attunement and Ordinary Language"
    (Putnam)   58 n.36
Austen, Jane (as discussed by
    Poovey)   17–21
    Emma   86
Austin, J. L.   7, 17–21, 38, 39, 43, 44 n.7,
    116 n.29
"The Avoidance of Love: A Reading of
    King Lear" (Cavell)   73 n.1

avowals   22, 22 n.28

Badiou, Alain   112 n.22
Bailey, Peter J.   105 n.7, 106 n.9
   Reading Stanley Elkin   105 n.7
Bakhtin, Mikhail   xi
Balibar, Etienne   112 n.22
   Reading Capital   112 n.22
Beardsley, Monroe   76 n.4, 88 n.28
The Beauty of a Social Problem
   (Michaels)   95–6 n.43
Beckett, Samuel   40, 109 n.18
   Endgame   40, 109 n.18
bedeuten/be-deuten   188, 189, 213, 221
Bedeutsamkeit (meaningfulness)   187
Bedeutung (meaning). *See Being and Time*
   (Heidegger)
"Behaviorism and the Beginnings of Close
   Reading" (Gang)   81 n.16
Being and Time (Heidegger)   xv, xxiii,
   170–82. *See also Sein und Zeit*
   Bedeutung   173, 181 n.22, 182, 183–4,
     185, 186–92
   Bewandtnisse   187
   freeing/freegiving (*Freigegeben* or
     Freigabe)   194–6, 203–4
   "in itself"   192–6
   interpretations of   172–80, 173
     (chart)
   Sinn   180–6
   truth   196–201
"Being Odd, Getting Even"
   (Cavell)   31 n.9, 57 n.33,
   63 n.48, 65–71, 71–2 n.62
belief
   Davidson   154 n.7, 211, 214, 218, 221,
     225
   Michaels   141–6, 148
Benardete, Seth   125, 125 n.47, 129,
   130 n.58, 130
Benjamin, Walter   x n.1, 156 n.15,
   163 n.43
Bennett, Tony   xiii, xiii n.6
Benoist, Jocelyn   xiii n.4
Benveniste, Emile   xi
Bergson, Henri   98
Bernstein, Charles   xviii–xix, 10, 29 n.6,
   30–7, 82

"Stray Straws and Strawmen"   35
With Strings   31, 33, 34 n.15
Best, Stephen   3, 3 n.1
biopolitics   124
Black, Max   xx, 76, 76 n.5, 77, 78–9
Blanchot, Maurice   134
Blanton, Dan   4
Blattner, William   172 n.5
Blindness and Insight (de Man)   147 n.35
Boswell (Elkin)   109, 120–1 n.40
Bourdieu, Pierre   16
Brandom, Robert   xvi n.12, 97 n.49,
   178 n.17, 217 n.23
   Tales of the Mighty Dead: Historical
     Essays in the Metaphysics of
     Intentionality   97 n.49
Bromwich, David   105 n.5
Bronzo, Silvio   50 n.16
Brooks, Cleanth   xix, xx, 53, 54, 70, 72,
   73, 75, 76 n.6, 81, 81 n.16, 82,
   86–95, 96, 99, 144, 226
   argument with Winters   53–5, 88–9
   "free ballon" (*see* discourse, as "free
     balloon")
   irony   89–90
   "Irony as a Principle of Poetic
     Structure"   89, 89 n.29
   literary form   54, 81 nn.14, 16, 87
   metaphor   88–9
   "Metaphor, Paradox, and
     Stereotype"   88 n.28
   paradox (*see* irony)
   statements/propositions   90–2
   The Well-Wrought Urn   81 nn.15, 16,
     86 n.24, 89, 90
Browning, Robert   88
Bruns, Gerald   71 n.60
BT. *See Being and Time* (Heidegger)
The Burdens of Perfection
   (Miller)   65 n.51, 104 n.3
Burge, Tyler   219 n.28
Burke, Edmund   105 n.5

Cage, John   35
Carman, Taylor   177 n.16, 178 n.17,
   181 n.23, 190 n.51, 195 n.67,
   197 n.71
Carnap, Rudolf   91, 91 n.35, 92 n.36

Caro, Anthony 95–6 n.43
Cartesian Meditations (Husserl) 118
Castañeda, Héctor-Neri 34 n.14
catachresis 83, 84
Cavell, Stanley xiv, 4–5, 6, 8, 9, 10, 16,
 30, 38–70, 106, 109 n.18, 129,
 151, 152, 153, 159
 "Aesthetic Problems of Modern
  Philosophy" 43–9, 48 n.12, 51,
  53–5, 64, 72–4, 77, 86, 95
 "The Argument of the
  Ordinary" 64 n.49
 art 43, 46–7, 48 n.12, 87, 95–6
 "The Avoidance of Love: A Reading of
  King Lear" 73 n.1
 "Being Odd, Getting Even" 31 n.9,
  57 n.33, 63 n.48, 65–71, 71–2
  n.62
 on Brooks 86–7
 The Claim of Reason xix, 39, 40,
  42 n.3, 43 n.4, 50 n.15, 53–63,
  58 n.36, 71, 103, 115, 115 n.28,
  116 n.29
 *Conditions Handsome and
  Unhandsome* 64 n.49, 65 n.51,
  69 n.58
 "Declining Decline" 63 n.48
 *Disowning Knowledge: In Seven Plays of
  Shakespeare* 125 n.46
 early work on Wittgenstein 24 n.32
 "Existential and Analytic
  Philosophy" 40 n.2, 43,
  49 n.14, 57 n.34, 69 n.58
 forms of life (*Lebensformen*) 46 n.8,
  52 n.21, 57–8, 60–4
 *In Quest of the Ordinary:
  Lines of Skepticism and
  Romanticism* 54 n.26, 65–9,
  65 n.52, 68 n.54, 69 n.58
 Little Do I Know 40
 "A Matter of Meaning It" 40,
  95 nn.41–2
 metaphors xix–xx, 54–5, 57, 72, 75,
  77, 79–80
 on modernist work/literature 95–6
 Must We Mean What We Say? 39, 40
 and Ordinary Language Philosophy
  (*see* Ordinary Language
  Philosophy)
 others (*see* otherness)
 person/personhood for 43–53,
  104–5, 115–19, 125
 revolution (in art and philosophy) 95
 The Senses of Walden 43 n.4, 55 n.27,
  57 n.33
 skepticism (*see* skepticism)
 traditionality and 95–6
 Unbecoming 70
 words 53–72, 81–2, 84 n.19, 85
 The World Viewed 40, 95 n.42
Cerbone, David 172 n.5, 213 n.14
charity (principle of) 216–17, 216 n.22,
 226
chart
 catachresis, metaphor, synonym 83
 form's role in literary studies 9
 history's and language's role in literary
  studies 5, 6, 38
 imaginary and textual, interactions
  of 11
 individual and collective in
  literature 112
 interpretations of *Being and
  Time* 173
 modern construals of metaphor 75
 person's role in literary studies 9, 38
 Rede and *Sprache* in Heidegger
  (Wrathall) 171 n.4
 statements relation to
  perceptions 211
 structure of "Aesthetic
  Problems" 48 n.12
 of tradition 100
 versions of discourse 8
Chomsky, Noam 43
The Claim of Reason (Cavell) xix, 39, 40,
 42 n.3, 43 n.4, 50 n.15, 53–63,
 58 n.36, 71, 103, 115, 115 n.28,
 116 n.29
Clarke, Thompson 116 n.29
cogito (Descartes) 66, 67, 70
 Emerson's rewriting 65–6
collective xx–xxi, 23, 104–5, 110–30
 and individual in literature, chart 112
collectivity 104–5, 113–30
common sense empiricism 154
compositionality/composition
 principle 84 n.19

Conant, James   24 n.32, 52 n.21, 60 n.42
Conditions Handsome and Unhandsome (Cavell)   64 n.49, 65 n.51, 69 n.58
confessions/confessional discourse   25–6
context   xx, 32–4, 36, 51, 60, 100, 139, 194
　in Altieri   23
　in Attridge   14
　in Brooks   88–90
　Dasein   186
　in externalism   224–6
　and metaphor   76–9
　in Poovey   16–17
　principle (Frege)   52 n.21
　　vs. composition principle   84 n.19
　semantics dependence on   137 n.10
　and text   146–7
　worlded   178 (*see also* worlded matters)
Course of General Linguistics (Saussure)   12 n.12
CR. See *The Claim of Reason* (Cavell)
Crary, Alice   4, 105
creative writing   27
Critique of Judgement (Kant)   45, 96 n.44
Crowell, Steven Galt   173 n.6, 174 n.11, 177–8 n.17, 181–2, 184 n.34, 187 n.38, 195 n.67, 210 n.5
　Husserl, Heidegger, and the Space of Meaning: Paths Toward Transcendental Phenomenology   174–5 n.11, 177–8 n.17, 181 n.23, 184 n.34, 187 n.38, 210 n.5
　Normativity and Phenomenology in Husserl and Heidegger   178 n.17
Culler, Jonathan   135, 135 n.5
Cultural Capital (Guillory)   16
cultural studies   6
Culture and Government (Hunter)   16
Culture and Society (Williams)   97 n.48

Dahlstrom, Daniel   170–1 n.2, 198 n.74
The Dance of the Intellect (Perloff)   29 n.5
Danto, Arthur   100 n.54
Davey, Nicholas   155 n.11, 157 n.17

"Hermeneutics, Structuralism, and Poststructuralism"   155 n.11, 157 n.17
Davidson, Donald   xiii, xv, xx, xxiii, xxiii, 8, 8 n.7, 41, 75, 76–80, 82, 84 n.19, 92 n.37, 104, 135, 136, 153, 154, 154 n.7, 160, 161–2, 164 n.46, 165 n.49, 169, 172, 197, 207, 207 n.94, 208, 210–26
　belief   154 n.7, 211, 214, 218, 219, 225
　externalism   92 n.37, 220 n.32, 220–3
　"First Person Authority"   220 n.32
　"Gadamer and Plato's *Philebus*"   224 n.41
　holism (*see* holism)
　Inquiries into Truth and Interpretation   84 n.19, 161 n.35, 164 n.46, 212 n.12
　"Knowing One's Own Mind"   221–3
　metaphor   76, 78
　"A Nice Derangement of Epitaphs"   8 n.7, 84 n.19, 216 n.20, 217 n.25
　"On the Very Idea of a Conceptual Scheme"   164 n.46, 216 n.22
　"Reality without Reference"   161 n.35, 212, 212 n.12
　"Seeing Through Language"   213 n.13
　semantics and language   216–18 (*see also* statements)
　statements/propositions   211, 213, 214–16, 218–19, 224–5
　swampman   223 n.39, 223–4
　"Theories of Meaning and Learnable Languages"   84 n.19
　on truth   214–19
　Truth, Language and History   8 n.7, 224 n.41
　Truth and Interpretation (ed. Lepore)   211 n.8, 216 n.20
　"Truth and Meaning"   76 n.7, 212 n.11, 215 n.19
　"What Metaphors Mean"   76 n.7, 76 ff.
Davis, Colin   71–2 n.62
"Declining Decline" (Cavell)   63 n.48
Deleuze, G.   xvi nn.12–13
de Man, Paul   133, 134 n.3, 146–51, 147 n.35

Blindness and Insight 147 n.35
"Form and Intent in the American New Criticism" 148–50
"Heidegger's Interpretation of Hölderlin" 150 n.44
"The Purloined Ribbon" 146–7
"The Rhetoric of Blindness" 147 n.35
"The Rhetoric of Temporality" 147 n.35
demonstratives 7, 33–4, 34 n.14
depsychologizing of psychology 44
Derrida, Jacques x, xvi n.13, 12 n.12, 30, 33 n.12, 44 n.7, 65, 67, 68, 72 n.62, 133, 134 n.3, 148 n.35, 181 n.22
Voice and Phenomenon 44 n.7
Descartes, René 41
cogito 66–70
Meditations on First Philosophy 66
detranscendentalizing 173, 174, 175, 179, 180, 181
diachronic externalism 220 n.33, 223 n.39. *See also* synchronic externalism
Diamond, Cora xx–xxi, 4, 24 n.32, 50 n.16, 52 nn.21–2, 53 n.23, 55 n.29, 57 n.35, 105, 106–11, 115, 119 n.34, 122, 129, 169
"Does Bismarck Have a Beetle in His Box?" 52 n.21
"Rough Story" 107 n.13
"Throwing Away the Ladder" 50 n.16
"What Nonsense Might Be" 52 n.22
"Wittgenstein, Mathematics, and Ethics" 107 n.13
Dick Gibson Show (Elkin) 106 n.9
disassociation of sensibility 98
disciplinary functions 17
discourse xi–xii, 3–7
distinguished from "discourse theory" xii–xiii, 7–8
as event (*see* event)
as "free balloon" 86–94, 101, 142, 226
language (*see* language)
literary form and xiii, xix, 7–10, 35–7
in Altieri 22–4
in Attridge 14
in Poovey 17
literary studies (*see* literature and literary studies)

and "my dog" 112 n.23, 120 n.39
text and (*see* text)
traditionality and 94–101
versions of, chart 8
Disowning Knowledge: In Seven Plays of Shakespeare (Cavell) 125 n.46
displays 22–3, 22 n.29
models of various modes of 24–5
disquotational truth 215
Disraeli, Benjamin 76 n.6, 79 n.13
"Document and Time" (Kates) 100 n.54
"Does Bismarck Have a Beetle in His Box?" (Diamond) 52 n.21
Doležel, Lubomír xii n.3, 11 n.10
Donne, John 98, 101
Dosse, Francois 12
History of Structuralism v.1 12 n.12
Dougherty, David C. 106 n.9
Shouting Down the Silence: A Biography of Stanley Elkin 106 n.9
Dreyfus, Hubert L. xiii n.4, 60 n.43, 170–1 n.2, 190 n.51, 195 n.68, 203 n.87, 204 n.89, 209 n.2, 213
Drummond, John 209 n.2
Husserlian Intentionality and Non-Foundational Realism: Noema and Object 209 n.2
Dryden, John 98, 101

EAP. *See* "Existential and Analytic Philosophy" (Cavell)
Eliot, T. S. xx, 17, 43, 44, 47, 96–101
After Strange Gods 96 n.47
The Idea of a Christian Society 96 n.47
The Love Song of J. Alfred Prufrock 43, 44, 47
"The Metaphysical Poets" (Eliot) 98–101
"Tradition and the Individual Talent" 96–8
traditionality (*see* tradition/traditionality)
Elkin, Stanley xvi n.13, xvii, xx–xxi, 105–6, 108–9, 111, 113–15, 117, 118–30
allegory 114, 120–2, 129
audience, problem of 106
Boswell 109, 120–1 n.40

collective in (*see* collective; collectivity)
Dick Gibson Show 106 n.9
The Franchiser 108, 108 n.15
"I Look Out for Ed Wolfe" 113–14, 120–1
interviews 105 n.7
"The Making of Ashenden" 122–4, 126–8
"A Poetics for Bullies" 105 n.7
and politics (*see* politics)
Emerson, Ralph Waldo 54 n.26, 65–8, 68 n.54, 70, 69 n.58
"Self-Reliance" 65–6
Emersonian perfectionism 103
"Emerson's gag" 68 n.55
Emma (Austen) 86
Empson, William 74
Endgame (Beckett) 40, 109 n.18
English, James 4 n.2
epistemic zombies 224
Essential History (Kates) 12 n.12, 134 n.3, 181 n.22, 217 n.23
Esty, Jed 97 n.48
A Shrinking Island 97 n.48
ethics 24, 104, 105
event (discourse as) xi, xiv, xvi, xxiv, 13–15, 19–20, 33, 38, 79, 82, 115, 135, 140–1, 145–6, 153, 161–3, 168, 177, 196, 197, 200, 207, 214 n.17, 218, 221–6
"Existential and Analytic Philosophy" (Cavell) 40 n.2, 43, 49 n.14, 57 n.34, 69 n.58
externalism 92 n.37
in Davidson 220–3
defined 220
in Heidegger 225–6
and Husserl 181 n.23

factualness. *See Sachlichkeit* (Gadamer)
Faulkner, William 100 n.54, 127
"The Bear" 100 n.54, 127
Fell, Joseph P. 180 n.20, 191 n.53
Felski, Rita 3
fiction xii, 17, 105–6. *See also* literature and literary studies; novels
in Armstrong, Nancy... 111–12
Elkin 106–8, 113
legibility in discourse xvi, 36 n.18

in Poovey, Mary 19–20
realist 106
Fielding, Henry 18
Fielding Derrida (Kates) 5 n.5, 147 n.32
figures/figural language 36, 53–4
catachresis 83, 84
metaphor (*see* metaphor)
Finnegan's Wake (Joyce) 93
"First Person Authority" (Davidson) 220 n.32
Fish, Stanley 144
Fitzgerald, F. Scott 93
flat ontology xiii, xiii n.6, 8
Floyd, Juliet 51 n.20
Fodor, Jerry 43 n.46, 45
"Foreword" to *Heidegger: Through Phenomenology to Thought* (Heidegger) 153 n.2
"Form and Intent in the American New Criticism" (de Man) 148–50
Foucault, Michel x, xi, xvi n.13, 7–8
The Franchiser (Elkin) 108, 108 n.15
"free ballon". *See* "free balloon", discourse
freeing/freegiving (*Freigegeben* or *Freigabe* in Heidegger) 194, 194 n.63, 195, 203–4
Frege, Gottlob 44, 52 n.21, 84 n.19, 101 n.55
Fried, Michael 95–6 nn.43–4
Friedman, Michael 91 n.35, 154 n.8
fusion of horizons xxii, 168 n.57, 224

Gadamer, Hans-Georg x, xiv, xxii, 135, 136, 143, 143 n.25, 146, 148, 149, 150–1, 152–69, 170, 171, 183, 188, 197, 199, 206 n.93, 207, 208, 210–11, 216 n.22, 219 n.29, 224–5, 226
Being (*Sein*) as language 159–60
fusion of horizons xxii, 168 n.57, 224
and Husserl's model of perception 166–8, 168 n.56, 210
language as discourse and tradition 153–8
"Language as the Medium of Hermeneutic Experience" 155
multiple worldviews and one world 163–9

Sachlichkeit (factualness) of
   language   158 n.24, 197 n.72,
   210, 210 n.6
speculative word   159–60
statements/propositions   160 n.33,
   161
text (*see* text, temporal)
translation as interpretation   155–6
Truth and Method   143, 152–69
Wahrheit und Methode (*see Wahreit und Methode* (Gadamer))
word/word and word/world
   holism   159–63
"Gadamer and Plato's *Philebus*"
   (Davidson)   224 n.41
Gang, Joshua   4, 81 n.16
   "Behaviorism and the Beginnings of
   Close Reading"   81 n.16
Gass, William   106 n.9
GCE. *See Genres of the Credit Economy*
   (Poovey)
Genres of the Credit Economy
   (Poovey)   15–21
George, Rolf A.   91 n.35
Goddard, Harold   144 n.28
Goldberg, Nathaniel   223 n.39
The Golden Bowl (James)   106, 107
*The Gold Standard and the Logic of
   Naturalism* (Michaels)   135–6
   n.6, 139 n.16, 147 n.33
Gordon, Peter E.   191 n.54
*Greek Mathematics and The Origins of
   Algebra* (Klein)   70 n.59
Grice, H. P.   xiii, xiii n.5, 8, 41, 104,
   137 nn.9–11, 190, 190 n.51,
   216 n.22
   Studies in the Ways of Words   8 n.7,
   137 nn.9–11
Grondin, Jean   155 n.10
   Sources of Hermeneutics   155 n.10
Guillory, John   3, 4 n.2, 16, 16 n.21,
   81 n.16

Habilitationsschrift (Heidegger)   187 n.38
Hacking, Ian   94 n.39
   *The Social Construction of
   What?*   94 n.39
Hamacher, Werner   4
Harmon, Graham   153 n.3

Harvard Society of Fellows   39
Haugeland, John   190 n.51
Hebrew bible   221 n.34
Hegel, G. W. F.   23 n.30, 125, 125 n.47,
   159, 160, 161, 161 n.37, 210
   *The Phenomenology of
   Spirit*   125 n.47, 161 n.37
   Philosophy of World History   125 n.47
*Heidegger, Language, and World-
   Disclosure* (Lafont)   153 n.3,
   171 n.3
Heidegger, Martin   x, xv, xv n.11,
   xxii–xxiii, 8, 41, 42, 59,
   60 n.43, 69, 69 n.58, 84 n.19,
   104, 115, 135, 136, 149, 150,
   152–3, 153 nn.2–3, 154, 157,
   160, 160 n.33, 161–2, 162 n.41,
   164, 165, 169, 170–207,
   208, 211–14, 216, 217–19,
   219 nn.29–30, 220, 221, 222,
   223–6
   Being and Time (*see Being and Time*
   (Heidegger))
   "Foreword" to *Heidegger: Through
   Phenomenology to Thought*
   (Heidegger)   153 n.2
   freeing/freegiving (*Freigegeben* or
   Freigabe)   94 n.63, 194–6,
   203–4
   Habilitationsschrift   187 n.38
   hermeneutic "as"   xxiii, 154, 174 n.7,
   176, 178
   holism (*see* holism)
   intersection with Davidson   224–6
   Letter on Humanism   153 n.2
   Logic: The Question of Truth   201–5,
   201 n.83, 208
   meaning (*Bedeutung*) as preceding
   words   185, 189–90 (*see
   also bedeuten; Bedeutung;
   Bedeutsamkeit*)
   neither/nor (on logos)   204
   "On the Essence of Ground"   205 n.91
   "On the Essence of Truth"   195 n.67,
   203 n.88
   Sein and *Seinsfrage* (Being and
   Question of Being)   171, 182,
   186, 198 n.74, 205–6
   Sein und Zeit (*see Sein und Zeit*)

Sense (*Sinn*) as pertaining to
  Dasein 182–4 (*see also Sinn*)
 statements/propositions 176, 188,
  192, 198, 202–3, 205
 on truth 197–207
 word/word and word/world
  holism 188
*Heidegger and Unconcealment: Truth,
  Language, and History*
  (Wrathall) 171 n.4
"Heidegger's Interpretation of Hölderlin"
  (de Man) 150 n.44
*Heidegger: Through Phenomenology to
  Thought* (Richardson) 153 n.2
Heilman, Robert 144 n.28
"Henry James, Moral
  Philosophers, Moralism"
  (Diamond) 109 n.14
hermeneutic "as" (*see* Heidegger, Martin)
hermeneutic normativity 173
hermeneutics xi, 42–3, 64, 67, 69, 70,
  71 n.60, 71, 82–3, 103, 104 n.2,
  138–9, 141, 143, 145–6, 148–9,
  150, 151, 152, 156, 157, 159,
  163, 166, 170, 204–6, 218–19
"Hermeneutics, Structuralism,
  and Poststructuralism"
  (Davey) 155 n.11,
  157 n.17
Herrnstein-Smith, Barbara 16
Hintikka, Jaako 66
historicity/history x, xv, xvii, xx, 4–5, 6,
  34, 71, 80, 94, 96, 98, 129, 130,
  135, 137 n.10, 156, 157, 204,
  206, 221, 223, 225, 241
 event and (*see* event)
 temporality and (*see* temporality)
 tradition/traditionality and (*see*
  tradition/traditionality)
History of Structuralism v.1
  (Dosse) 12 n.12
Hobbes, Thomas 93
holism 60 nn.41–3, 151, 160–3, 211–13
 "blob of" (in Heidegger) 206
 in Davidson 219, 219 n.28
 forms of life (*see* forms of life, Cavell)
 in Heidegger and Davidson 208,
  211–13, 214
 and history (in Heidegger) 204 n.89
 practical 21, 60 n.43, 160 n.33,
  213–14
 theoretical xxiii, 213
 word/word and world/world 160,
  161
  in Davidson 161, 217
  in Gadamer 160–2
  in Heidegger 161, 188, 191 n.54,
   195 n.68, 203 n.87
Hopkins, Burt C. 170–1 n.2, 174 n.7
*How Novels Think: The Limits of
  Individualism from 1719–1900*
  (Armstrong) 111–12
Hoy, David Couzens 136 n.7
Hunter, Ian 3, 4 n.2, 16
 Culture and Government 16
Husserl, Edmund x, 44, 49 n.13, 51 n.17,
  70 n.59, 81, 83, 118, 119 n.36,
  165–7, 167 n.55, 172, 174,
  178 n.17, 181 n.22, 187 n.38,
  198–200, 200 n.81, 203, 204,
  208–11, 212, 220
 Cartesian Meditations 118
 *Crisis of European Sciences
  and Transcendental
  Phenomenology* 200 n.81
 Logical Investigations 174, 198, 204
 Phenomenological Psychology 44 n.7
*Husserl, Heidegger, and the Space of
  Meaning: Paths Toward
  Transcendental Phenomenology*
  (Crowell) 174–5 n.11,
  177–8 n.17, 181 n.23, 184 n.34,
  187 n.38, 210 n.5
*Husserlian Intentionality and Non-
  Foundational Realism:
  Noema and Object*
  (Drummond) 209 n.2
hypothetical realism (in de Man) 147

Ideas I (Husserl) 166, 166 n.52, 203, 208
The Idea of a Christian Society
  (Eliot) 96 n.47
idiocultures 13
illocutionary rules 7
"I Look Out for Ed Wolfe" (Elkin) 113–
  14, 120–2
imaginary literature. *See* literature,
  imaginary and textual

"In a Station of the Metro" (Pound)   31, 53
information theory   33 n.13
Ingarden, Roman   xii n.3, 15 n.16, 81, 81 n.15
"in itself"   192–6
In Quest of the Ordinary: Lines of Skepticism and Romanticism (Cavell)   54 n.26, 65–9, 65 n.52, 68 n.54, 69 n.58
Inquiries into Truth and Interpretation (Davidson)   84 n.19, 161 n.38, 169 n.36
"Instruction Manual" (Ashbery)   23
intentionally   31, 32, 35
intentions   xxii, 69, 69 n.58, 134, 135–43, 146–9, 178 n.17, 181–2, 201, 209, 219 n.28, 225 n.43
Inuit   61
IQO. *See In Quest of the Ordinary: Lines of Skepticism and Romanticism* (Cavell)
"Irony as a Principle of Poetic Structure" (Brooks)   89 n.29
Izenberg, Oren   4

Jakobson, Roman   xi, 15 n.16
James, Henry   xx–xxi, 106–7, 108, 109–10, 142 n.21, 144, 145
  The Golden Bowl   106, 107
  Turn of the Screw   142 n.21, 144
Jamesian realism   113
Jameson, Fredric   139 n.16
Jocasta   129–30
Joyce, James   93
  Finnegan's Wake   93
  "Two Gallants"   122
Juhl, P. D.   133 n.2
Jupiter   149

Kant, Immanuel   40, 44–7, 49, 52 n.22, 69 n.58, 96 n.44, 100, 147 n.33, 197, 210, 211 n.8
  Critique of Judgement   45, 96 n.44
Kates, Joshua   137 n.11
  "Against the Period"   97 n.48
  "Document and Time"   100 n.54
  Essential History: Jacques Derrida and the Development of

  Deconstruction   12 n.12, 134 n.3, 181 n.22, 217 n.23
  Fielding Derrida   5 n.5, 147 n.32
  "Neither a God nor ANT Can Save Us: Latour, Heidegger, Historicity, and Holism"   129 n.56
  "Phenomenology's Intersection with Literary Criticism"   81 n.15
  "Semantics and Pragmatics and Husserl and Derrida"   137 n.11
  "'Signature Event Context'… in, Well, Context"   7 n.6, 33 n.12
  "Silence of the Concepts (in *After Finitude* and Gottlob Frege)")   xvi n.9, 101 n.55, 225 n.43
Katz, Jerry   43 n.6, 45
Käufer, Stephen   206 n.92
Keats, J.   86
  Ode on a Grecian Urn   86
Kertscher, Jens   152 n.1
King Lear (Shakespeare)   40, 73 n.1, 103
Kishik, David   60 n.40
  Wittgenstein's Form of Life   60 n.40
Kisiel, Theodore   170–1 n.2
Klein, Jacob   70 n.59
  Greek Mathematics and The Origins of Algebra   70 n.59
Knapp, Steven   xxi–xxii, 4, 133–40, 143, 150, 152
  "Against Theory"   xxi, 133–43, 147 n.33, 148, 221 n.34
  "Against Theory 2: Hermeneutics and Deconstruction"   xxii, 133, 143
  Against Theory 2: Sentence meaning, Hermeneutics   136–8
"Knowing One's Own Mind" (Davidson)   221–3
Korsgaard, Christine   xvi n.12
Kripke, Saul   64 n.49, 65 n.51, 70 n.59, 195 n.68, 203 n.87, 204, 204 n.89

Lacan, Jacques   xi, 65, 133, 134 n.3
Lafont, Christina   153 n.3, 162 n.41, 171 nn.3, 4, 173 n.6, 175–4 n.11, 181–2, 182 n.23, 183, 185 n.36, 190 n.52, 198 n.74
  Heidegger, Language, and World-Disclosure   153 n.3, 171 n.3

language 5, 152–69
  absence of xi–xii, xii n.2, xxiii
  in Davidson xv, 216 n.20 (*see also* Davidson, Donald, semantics and language)
  in early Heidegger xvi, xxii, 152–3, 171 (*see also Bedeutung*)
  figural (*see* figures)
  imaginary (*see* literature and literary studies, imaginary and textual)
  in information theory 33 n.13
  in L=A=N=G=U=A=G=E poetry xviii
  in Michaels and Knapp xxii, 133ff.
  not needed for catachresis, synonymy, and metaphor 111
  as problem in Cavell and Gadamer xiv, 152
  signifiers 33
  space of (in literary criticism) 13, 15, 19–20, 24
  text and (*see* text)
  words (*see* words)
  written (*see* literature and literary studies, imaginary and textual)
"Language as the Medium of Hermeneutic Experience" (Gadamer) 155
language-game 52 n.21, 191. See also forms of life
L=A=N=G=U=A=G=E poetry xviii–xix, 29–32, 34
Lask, Emil 174 n.11, 187 n.38
Latour, Bruno xvi nn.12–13, 3, 3 n.1, 129
LeMahieu, Michael 4
Lepore, Ernie 215 n.18, 216 n.21, 220 n.33, 223 n.39
Letter on Humanism (Heidegger) 153 n.2
Levinas, Emmanuel x
lifeworld 119 n.36, 214 n.16
linguistic turn 163
literariness xiii, xviii, 9, 13–15, 23, 28, 67, 68, 81, 89–90, 226
literary criticism x, xi, xiii, xvi, 8, 10, 22, 27, 40, 88, 89
literature and literary studies xi–xxi, 3–26
  Altieri's account of 21–6
  Bernstein's account of 27–37
  exceptionality of 6
  and history and language, chart 6, 9, 38
  as imaginary and textual
    Altieri's account of 21–6
    Attridge's account of 4, 11, 13–15, 38
    interaction of imaginary and textual, chart 11
    Poovey's account of 15–21
  literariness (*see* literariness)
  metaphors (*see* metaphors)
  novels (*see* novels)
  person/personhood (*see* person/personhood)
  Poovey's account of 15–21
  self-understanding of 3
  singularity of 4, 11, 13–14, 38
Little Do I Know (Cavell) 40
Logic: The Question of Truth (Heidegger) 201–5, 201 n.88, 208
Logical Investigations (Husserl) 174, 198, 204
logic and truth 201–7
logos 75, 174, 175, 176, 178, 178 n.17, 179–80, 197–8, 201–7
Locke, John 129
Longenbach, James 96 n.45
  Modernist Poetics of History 96 n.45
Love, Heather 4
The Love Song of J. Alfred Prufrock (Eliot) 43, 44, 47
Ludwig, Kirk 215 n.18, 216 n.21, 220 n.33, 223 n.39
Lyotard, François x

McCaffrey, Larry 105 n.7
McCaffrey, Steve 29, 29 n.6
McDowell, John 154, 159, 164, 165, 166, 169, 184 n.34, 199, 203, 207, 208, 209–11, 219 n.29
  Mind and World 153
McGrath, S. J. 170–1 n.2
McGurl, Mark 3
Macquarrie, John 153 n.2, 177 n.17, 182, 189 n.45, 193 n.59
"The Making of Ashenden" (Elkin) 122–4, 126–8

Malpas, Jeff 216 n.22
  "What Is Common to All: Davidson on Agreement and Understanding" 216 n.22
Mankin, Robert 54 n.26
Mao, Douglas 81 n.14
Marcus, Sharon 3, 3 n.1
Marcuse, Herbert xv n.11
Marrati, Paola 61 n.46
Marvell, Andrew 98
Marx, Karl 4, 6, 139 n.16
Mates, Benson 43 n.6, 45
"A Matter of Meaning It" (Cavell) 40, 95 nn.41–2
meaning 173, 181 n.22, 182–92. *See also Bedeutung*; *Being and Time* (Heidegger)
Meditations on First Philosophy (Descartes) 66
Meillassoux, Quentin xv n.9, 28 n.2
Melia, Daniel F. 136 n.7
Merleau-Ponty, Maurice 209 n.3
"Metaphor, Paradox, and Stereotype" (Brooks) 88 n.28
metaphor xix–xx, 73–101
  in Aristotle 74–5 n.74
  in Black, Max 76
  in Brooks 88–9
  in Cavell xix–xx, 54–5, 57, 72, 75, 77, 79–80
  in Davidson 76, 78
  modern construals of, chart 75
  nothing is 64, 74, 80
  "paraphrasability" 53–5, 86–90
  time and 73–80
  words 81–6
"The Metaphysical Poets" (Eliot) 98–101
metered poetry 36 n.17
Michaels, Walter Benn xxi–xxii, 4, 8, 90 n.32, 91 n.34, 95–6 n.43, 111 n.21, 133–51, 152, 170, 221 n.34
  "Against Theory" xxi, 133–43, 147 n.33, 148, 221 n.34
  "Against Theory 2: Hermeneutics and Deconstruction" xxii, 133, 143
  Against Theory 2: Sentence meaning, Hermeneutics 136–8

The Beauty of a Social Problem 95–6 n.43
  belief (in early Michaels) 140–6, 148
  "conversions" 135, 148
  on de Man, Paul (*see* de Man, Paul)
  The Gold Standard and the Logic of Naturalism 135–6 n.6, 139 n.16, 147 n.33
  on holism (qualms) 144–5
  intention (*see* intention)
  objectifying the text 140–1
  Our America: Nativism, Modernism, and Pluralism 111 n.21
  questions (important) 134–5, 140–1, 143
  representation 136–7, 140, 143
  resemblance of shapes to signifiers 139
  "Saving the Text" 141–4, 146, 147
  The Shape of the Signifier (Michaels) 134 n.4, 138 n.15, 147 n.33, 148
Miller, Andrew 65 n.51, 104 n.3
  The Burdens of Perfection 65 n.51, 104 n.3
Milton, John 98, 101
Mind and World (McDowell) 153
Modernist Poetics of History (Longenbach) 96 n.45
modernist poetry 53, 54
modernist writers 96
Moi, Toril 5 n.5, 51, 65 n.51
  "The Adventure of Reading" 65 n.51
  Revolution of the Ordinary 5 n.5
Monk, Ray 92 n.36
Montague, Richard 41
Moore, G. E. 116 n.29
moral imagination 105 n.5
Moran, Richard 76–7 n.9
  "Seeing and Believing: Metaphor, Image, and Force" 76–7 n.9
Morrison, Toni 93, 111 n.21
Mulhall, Stephen 50 n.15, 52 n.22, 55–6 n.30, 56 n.33, 59 n.39, 65 n.52, 104 n.3
  Stanley Cavell: Philosophy's Recounting of the Ordinary 65 n.51
Murdoch, Iris 57 n.35, 105–7

Must We Mean What We Say?
(Cavell) 39, 40, 57 n.34
Myers, Robert 219 n.28

"Neither a God nor ANT Can Save Us: Latour, Heidegger, Historicity, and Holism" (Kates) 130 n.56
neither/nor 204, 226
Nietzsche, Friedrich 15, 199
New Criticism 9, 16, 28, 40, 69, 73
New Formalism 4
Ngai, Sianne xv n.10
"A Nice Derangement of Epitaphs" (Davidson) 8 n.7, 84 n.19, 216 n.20, 217 n.25
Normativity and Phenomenology in Husserl and Heidegger (Crowell) 178 n.17
North, Michael 97 n.48, 99
novels xii, 17–20, 105–7, 109–11, 120 n.40. See also fiction
Nussbaum, Martha xx–xxi, 105–12, 115, 122, 129
  "Flawed Crystals: James's *The Golden Bowl* and Literature as Moral Philosophy" 106
observation statements 91–2

Ode on a Grecian Urn (Keats) 86
Oedipus 19 n.23, 117, 119, 124 n.26, 125, 129–30
Oedipus Turannos (Sophocles) 124–6, 128–9
OLP. See Ordinary Language Philosophy
"On the Essence of Ground" (Heidegger) 205 n.91
"On the Essence of Truth" (Heidegger) 195 n.67, 203 n.88
On Deconstruction (Culler) 135
On Metaphor, ed. Sheldon Sacks 76 n.7
"On the Very Idea of a Conceptual Scheme" (Davidson) 164 n.46, 216 n.22
ontology/ontological 12, 21, 28, 37, 134, 137, 138, 149, 171 n.4, 185, 189, 194, 197, 199 n.80. See also *Sein* and *Seinsfrage* (Being and Question of Being)

Ordinary Language Philosophy (OLP) xvi, xix, xx, 4, 48, 53, 105, 112, 155
  and collectivity 118
  use of "we" 45–6, 49–50
otherness 5, 13, 27, 71, 124
  in Attridge 13–15
  of persons (other minds) 73 n.1, 109 n.18, 115–17 (in Cavell), 117–18 (in Schutz)
  or foreignness of texts 56, 71, 82, 86, 137 n.10, 161 n.57, 226
outcasts 116–17

paraphrase/paraphrasing 40, 53–4, 74, 77, 86–90
Partch, Harry 35
perceptions 208–14
  and statements (Husserl to Davidson) chart 211
  visual perception (*see* visual perception)
perfectionism 65
Perloff, Marjorie 4, 29 nn.5–6
  The Dance of the Intellect 29 n.5
  Poetic License 29 n.5
Perry, John 34 n.14
person/personhood 43–53, 103–30
  chart 38
  collectivity and 104–5, 113–30
  as a conception 120 n.39
  other minds (*see* otherness, of persons (other mind))
  realism 105–13
  skepticism (*see* skepticism)
Phenomenological Psychology (Husserl) 44 n.7
The Phenomenology of Spirit (Hegel) 125 n.47, 161 n.37
"Phenomenology's Intersection with Literary Criticism" (Kates) 81 n.15
Philipse, Herman 172 n.5, 191 n.53, 194 n.65, 195 n.67
Philosophical Investigations (Wittgenstein) 24, 46, 50, 52 n.21, 56, 57 n.35, 58, 58 nn.36, 37, 59 n.39, 60

Philosophy of World History
    (Hegel) 125 n.47
PI. *See Philosophical Investigations*
    (Wittgenstein)
Pippin, Robert xiii n.4
Plato 49 n.13, 155
Pluto 221 n.34
Poe, Edgar Allan 54 n.26, 65, 65 n.52,
    68 n.54
Poetic License (Perloff) 29 n.5
"A Poetics for Bullies" (Elkin) 105 n.7
Pole, David 43 n.46
    A Treatment of Wittgenstein's Later
        Philosophy 43 n.46
Politics. *See* politics, talk!
Poovey, Mary xviii, 3–6, 8, 9, 15–21, 26,
    28, 38, 94, 104, 110, 111
    Genres of the Credit Economy 15–21
poststructuralism xv, xvi n.13, 29, 69,
    134
Pound, Ezra 31, 35, 53, 96
    "In a Station of the Metro" 31, 53
practical holism 21, 60 n.43, 160 n.33,
    213–14. *See also* holism;
    theoretical holism
pragmatics 41, 137 n.11. *See also* charity;
    Grice, H. P.
Pratt, Mary Louise xxi n.14, 27 n.1
The Problem of Objectivity in Gadamer's
    Hermeneutics in Light of
    McDowell's Empiricism
    (Thaning) 163 n.42
Ptolemy 221 n.34
Puckett, Kent 4
"The Purloined Ribbon" (de Man) 146–7
Putnam, Hilary 58 n.36, 220, 220 n.3
    "Attunement and Ordinary
        Language" 58 n.36

Quine, W. V. O. 154 n.9, 164 n.46
Quine–Duhem thesis 91

Ramberg, Bjorn 215 n.19
Ramsey, Andrew 107 n.13
Ranciére, Jacques 112 n.22
Reading Capital (Althusser and
    Balibar) 112 n.22
Reading Stanley Elkin (Bailey) 105 n.7

realism (in fiction). *See* realism, persons/
    personhood
"Reality without Reference"
    (Davidson) 161 n.35, 212,
    212 n.12
Reckoning with the Imagination
    (Altieri) 21, 22, 22 nn.27–9,
    23, 23 n.30, 24, 25, 25 n.34
Rede xv, xxiii, 8, 153, 171–80
Reinfeld, Laura 29 n.5
representation 135–40
resolute reading 24 n.33, 50 n.16,
    51 n.20
Revolution of the Ordinary (Moi) 5 n.5
"The Rhetoric of Blindness" (de Man)
    148 n.35
"The Rhetoric of Temporality" (de Man)
    147 n.35
RI. *See Reckoning with the Imagination*
    (Altieri)
Richards, I. A. 74, 75, 76, 81 n.16, 141–4
Richardson, William 153 n.2
    Heidegger: Through Phenomenology to
        Thought 153 n.2
Ricoeur, Paul x
Robbe-Grillet, Alain 93
Robinson, Edward S. 153 n.2, 177 n.17,
    182, 189 n.45, 193 n.59
Ronen, Ruth 91 n.10
Rooney, Ellen 4
Rorty, Richard xiii n.4, 217 n.23
"Rough Story" (Diamond) 107 n.13
Rousseau, Henri 127
Rousseau, Jean-Jacques 18
Rudrum, David 65 n.51
    Stanley Cavell and the Claim of
        Literature 65 n.51
Russell, Bertrand 141, 144

Sachlichkeit (Gadamer) 158 n.24,
    197 n.72, 210, 210 n.6
Sale, Richard B. 108 n.17
Sapir, Edward 61
Saussure, Ferdinand de 12 n.12, 62, 160
    Course of General Linguistics 12 n.12
"Saving the Text" (Michaels) 141–4, 146,
    147
Schmitt, Carl 129

Schutz, Alfred   118–19, 119 nn.36–7, 120 n.38
scientific discourse   90–3
Searle, John   xi, 7, 8, 41
Second World War   41, 112 n.22
Sedgwick, Eve   104 n.3
"Seeing and Believing: Metaphor, Image, and Force" (Moran)   76–7 n.9
"Seeing Through Language" (Davidson)   213 n.13
Sein and *Seinsfrage* (Being and Question of Being)   171, 182, 186, 198 n.74, 205–6
Sein und Zeit (Heidegger)   174, 176 n.12, 177 nn.14–15, 179 nn.18–19, 182 nn.24–7, 183 n.28, 184 n.33, 185 nn.35–7, 187 nn.39–41, 188 n.44, 189 n.47, 48, 190 n.50, 191 n.55, 193 n.59, 194 nn.61–3. See also Being and Time (Heidegger)
self-authoring   66–9
self-expression
   confessional discourse   25–6
self-referential form   18
"Self-Reliance" (Emerson)   65–6
"Semantics and Pragmatics and Husserl and Derrida" (Kates)   137 n.11
The Senses of Walden (Cavell)   43 n.4, 55 n.27, 57 n.33
Shannon, Claude   33 n.13
The Shape of the Signifier (Michaels)   134 n.4, 138 n.15, 147 n.33, 148
Sheehan, Thomas   201 n.83
Shell, Marc   19 n.23, 125, 125 nn.46–7, 129, 130 n.58
Shockey, R. Matthew   170–1 n.2
Shouting Down the Silence: A Biography of Stanley Elkin (Dougherty)   106 n.9
A Shrinking Island (Esty)   97 n.48
"'Signature Event Context'... in, Well, Context" (Kates)   7 n.6, 33 n.12
signification   33 n.13. See also language
   Bedeutung   173, 181 n.22, 182–92
   information theory   33 n.13
"Silence of the Concepts (in *After Finitude* and Gottlob Frege)"
(Kates)   xvi n.9, 101 n.55, 225 n.43
Sillimann, Ron   29 n.5, 30
The Singularity of Literature (Attridge)   13–15
Sinn (senses). See Being and Time (Heidegger)
skepticism   41–2, 42 n.3, 50 n.15, 61 n.46, 64 n.50, 109 n.18, 115–19, 169, 172, 205
   external world   116–17
   philosophical   42 n.3, 116 n.29
   other minds (see otherness, of persons (other mind))
The Sleeping Gypsy (Rousseau)   127
social–classification of object   16
The Social Construction of What? (Hacking)   94 n.39
socialized subject   24
Sonderegger, Ruth   xiii n.4, 152 n.1
Sources of Hermeneutics (Grondin)   154 n.9
speech–act theory   7–8
   Austin (see Austin, J. L.)
   Juhl, P. D.   133 n.2
   Pratt (see Pratt, Mary Louise)
   Searle (see Searle, John)
Spengler, O.   63 n.48
Sprache   xv, xxiii, 162 n.40, 162, 164, 171, 176, 185 n.35, 218. See also language
Stanley Cavell and the Claim of Literature (Rudrum)   65 n.51
Stanley Cavell: Philosophy's Recounting of the Ordinary (Mulhall)   65 n.51
statements/propositions   53 n.28, 75, 76, 86–7, 94, 144, 154
   in Brooks   90–2
   in Davidson   211, 213–16, 218–19, 224–5
   in Gadamer   160 n.33, 161
   in Heidegger   176, 188, 192, 198, 201–5
   perceptions and   208–14
   chart   211
Staten, Henry   vii, 28 n.3, 134 n.4
Stein, Gertrude   xix, 35
Sterne, Laurence   93
Stoutland, Frederick   219 n.28

"Stray Straws and Strawmen"
 (Bernstein)   35
Streeter, Ryan   170–1 n.2
structure   86, 89–90. *See also* discourse, literary form and
 literary form (Brooks)   54, 81 nn.14–16, 87
 form's role in literary studies (chart)   9
Studies in the Ways of Words (Grice)   8 n.7, 137 nn.9, 11
sunthesis   202
synchronic externalism   220 n.33, 223 n.39. *See also* diachronic externalism
synonymy   83–4

Tales of the Mighty Dead: Historical Essays in the Metaphysics of Intentionality (Brandom)   97 n.49
talk!   xi–xviii, xx–xxii, 7–10, 16–23, 24 n.33, 25–37, 59, 80, 140, 218. *See also* discourse
 as event (*see* event)
 in Cavell   39, 42, 50 n.15
 and forms of life   60–4
 in Heidegger (*see Rede*)
 overview   31–7
 and politics   113, 130
 in "series" (*see* traditionality, as series)
 swampman's   223
 and texts   56, 59
Tarski, Alfred   213 n.13, 214–18
Taylor, Charles   xiii n.4
temporality   xx, 42, 69–72, 120 n.38, 147, 150, 168 n.56, 171, 204, 205, 226. *See also* tradition/traditionality
 event (*see* event)
 metaphor and   73–80
 text   145–7, 149–51
Terada, Rei   4
text   134–51
 as event (*see* event)
 deobjectifying   141, 152, 155
 externalist   220–6 (*see also* literature and literary study, imaginary and textual as)

representation   135–40
 saving   140–6
 temporal text   145–6, 147, 149, 150–1
Thaning, Morton   163 n.42, 170 n.1, 197 n.91
The Problem of Objectivity in Gadamer's Hermeneutics in Light of McDowell's Empiricism   163 n.42
theoretical holism   xxiii, 213. *See also* holism; practical holism
"Theories of Meaning and Learnable Languages" (Davidson)   84 n.19
theory, literary   x–xi
"Throwing Away the Ladder" (Diamond)   50 n.16
time. *See* temporality
TLP. *See Tractatus Logico-Philosophicus* (Wittgenstein)
TM. *See Truth and Method* (Gadamer)
Tractatus Logico-Philosophicus (Wittgenstein)   24, 24 nn.32–3, 52 n.21, 57 n.35, 92
"Tradition and the Individual Talent" (Eliot)   96–8
tradition/traditionality   94–101
 Cavell and   95–6
 chart of   100
 Eliot's conception   96–101
 event (*see* event)
 historicity/history (*see* historicity/history)
 language as   153–8
 as a sequence of past instances   99–101
 as series   xvii, 71, 87, 95, 99
 and truth   100
translation   155–6
A Treatment of Wittgenstein's Later Philosophy (Pole)   43 n.46
truth   xv, xviii, xxii, 172, 214–19, 225–6
 in Altieri   22, 25
 apophantic (in Heidegger)   179, 202, 204
 beliefs *vs.* (in Michaels)   143–6
 coherence theory   144, 145
 confessional discourse   25–6
 correspondence theory   144

Heidegger on 197–207
of literature 92–4
logic and 201–7
necessity for discourse xiv, xviii, 140, 145, 172, 206, 217
and paraphrase 86
of philosophy 48, 173–4 n.7
and tradition 100
  in Gadamer 151
and Tarski and Davidson 214–18
Tugendhat's problem 197–201, 212
unique to statements (claimed) 87, 90–2, 173, 213
Truth, Language and History (Davidson) 8 n.7, 224 n.41
Truth and Interpretation (ed. Lepore) 211 n.8, 216 n.22
"Truth and Meaning" (Davidson) 76 n.7, 212 n.11, 215 n.19
Truth and Method (Gadamer) 143, 152–69
Tugendhat, Ernst 198–201, 203, 209, 212–13
Turn of the Screw (James) 142 n.21, 144
"Two Gallants" (Joyce) 122
Tzara, Tristan xix, 35

Unbecoming 70
United States x, 122
Urtradition 155, 219 n.29

Vandevelde, Pol 174 n.7
Vendler, Helen 106 n.9
Verstehen 157, 158, 176. *See also* hermeneutic "as"
  foreconception 177
  forehaving 176–7
  foresight 177
  forestructure 176–8
visual perception 166. *See also* statement, perceptions and chart 211
  in Husserl 166–7, 208–9
  in McDowell 209–11
Voice and Phenomenon (Derrida) 44 n.7
von Humboldt, Wilhelm 155, 164–6, 169
Vorhanden 177 n.15

Wahrheit und Methode (Gadamer) 149, 155 n.12, 157 nn.18–20, 159 nn.27–30, 160 nn.31–3, 161 nn.36–7, 164 nn.44–5, 165 nn.47–50, 166 n.51, 168 n.56
Walton, Kendall xii n.3, 11, 11 n.9
Warminski, Andrzej 4
Watt, Ian 111
Weaver, Warren 33 n.13
Weber, Max 120 n.38
Weber, Samuel x n.1
Wellek, Rene 81
The Well-Wrought Urn (Brooks) 81 nn.15, 16, 86 n.24, 89, 90
Welty, Eudora 93
"What Metaphors Mean" (Davidson) 76 n.7
"What Nonsense Might Be" (Diamond) 52 n.22
Whorf, Benjamin 61
Williams, Bernard 66
Williams, Raymond 97 n.48
  Culture and Society 97 n.48
Winch, Peter 16, 16 n.20
Winters, Yvor 53, 53 n.24, 54, 88–9
  In Defense of Reason 53 n.24
Wisdom, John 39
With Strings (Bernstein) 31, 33, 34 n.15
Wittgenstein, Ludwig xiv, xviii, 4, 5, 8, 16, 21–5, 30, 38–9, 43–60, 63 n.47, 63 n.48, 71, 74, 91, 92, 95, 105, 107, 153, 160, 168, 169, 191, 210
  Philosophical Investigations 24, 46, 50, 52 n.21, 56, 57 n.35, 58, 58 n.36, 59 n.37, 59 n.39, 60
  Tractatus Logico-Philosophicus 24, 24 nn.32–3, 52 n.21, 57 n.35, 92
"Wittgenstein, Mathematics, and Ethics" (Diamond) 107 n.13
Wittgenstein's Form of Life (Kishik) 60 n.40
Wollheim, Richard 136–7, 137 n.11
Woolf, Virginia 12, 93, 107 n.13
words 53–72
  catachresis 83, 84
  in Cavell 53–72, 81–2, 84 n.19, 85

in discourse (*see* discourse)
  forms of life and   57–64
  in Gadamer   159–63
  internal logic   59
  in interpretation and reading
      64–72
  metaphors and   53–5, 73–86
  "ontology" (as example)   85
  primary *vs.* secondary meanings
      55–7
  projections   54, 58
  seem but aren't required, chart   83
  synonymy   83–4
Wordsworth, William   138, 139, 142
word/word and word/world holism   159–
    63, 188, 217
  holism (*see* holism)
  worlded matters (*see* worlded matters)
worlded matters   100–1, 136, 151, 154,
    170, 193
  holism (*see* holism)

  word/word and word/world holism
      (*see* word/word and word/world
      holism)
worldview (*Weltansicht*)   162–4, 170 n.2
The World Viewed (Cavell)   40, 95 n.42
Wrathall, Mark A.   171 n.4, 203 n.87,
    204 n.89, 205 n.91, 206 n.92,
    212 n.10, 213 n.14
  *Heidegger and Unconcealment:
    Truth, Language, and
    History*   171 n.4
Wyatt, Thomas   95

Yale School   101
Yeats, W. B.   35
Yorck, Count   157

Zabel, Morton   89 n.29
Zahavi, Dan   209 n.3
Zbigniew, Herbert   53 n.23
Zuhanden   177 n.15

www.ingramcontent.com/pod-product-compliance
Lightning Source LLC
Chambersburg PA
CBHW072132290426
44111CB00012B/1863